INTRODUCTION TO CASINO MANAGEMENT

Anthony F. Lucas

Jim Kilby

For information related to our other gaming materials and software, please visit our
website at **www.IntroductionToCasinoManagement.com** or contact us via email at
jimkilby@usa.net.

ISBN: 978-0-9817399-1-5
ISBN: 0-9817399-1-1

Table of Contents

Preface

As gaming proliferates across the globe, many people have become interested in the casino industry. With so few quality materials for educators, it is very difficult to teach people about this unique and complex business. This book represents an opportunity for any interested parties to gain a detailed understanding of a fascinating industry.

The gaming industry certainly has a language all its own. While this is part of its intrigue, it can also be something of a hurdle for outsiders who want to understand the business. This text was written for someone with little or no exposure to the gaming industry. Therefore, much of the jargon common to topics covered in each chapter is defined prior to deeper discussions of the material. With further regard for sequence, we recommend that the chapters are read in the order that they appear in the book.

This text was designed to expose readers to a wide range of topics critical to casino management, including an introduction to casino marketing. While casino management and casino marketing are inextricably linked, the latter is thoroughly covered in our text entitled, *Principles of Casino Marketing*, which can be found at *principlesofcasino marketing.com*.

We have put forth our best effort to make this book error free. In fact, this text and all of its supporting materials have been used in the classroom prior to publication. These supporting materials include all homework and exam questions, as well as all PowerPoint presentations. In spite of this vetting process, it is likely that some errors are still present. Should you find errors, please report them by sending an email to jimkilby@usa.net. Corrections will be posted on *introductiontocasinomanagement.com*. Also, please feel free to send us any suggestions that you think would improve the book. Suggestions should also be emailed to jimkilby@usa.net

Acknowledgements

Anthony Lucas would like to thank his daughter, Sarah Lucas, and his parents, Frederic and Dana Lucas for their love, encouragement, and support.

The authors would like to sincerely thank all those who contributed to this text. Without their contributions and assistance, this book could not have been written. We were consistently amazed by the willingness of casino operators to answer our never-ending stream of questions. We greatly appreciate the time of those who were there for us.

Peggy Jacobs and Andrew Montgomery must be recognized for their invaluable contributions. Peggy co-authored the chapter on currency and suspicious activity reporting and extensively counseled us on the drop and count processes described in

Chapter 6. Peggy's knowledge of currency reporting requirements is nothing short of impressive. She also directed us to many other executives with expertise in various fields. Had Peggy not generously donated her time, influence, and considerable knowledge of the industry, this book would have been a lot shorter and less accurate. Andrew Montgomery co-authored the chapter on Nevada gaming regulation, serving as the majority content contributor. Formerly a Senior Agent in the Investigations Division of the NGCB, Andrew's level of expertise and depth of knowledge are evident in Chapter 5. Andrew also contributed homework and exam materials for Chapter 5. Given the detailed nature of gaming regulation, his contributions to this book were no less than critical. We are most grateful for Andrew's willingness to share his extensive knowledge. By the way, he is a great writer!

We would also like to thank Melody Bittinger, Brandee Wade, and JoAnn Harrison for their time and insight related to cage operations and the drop and count processes. Jon Ibarguen made significant contributions to the discussion of these topics as well. We learned a lot from Jon. All four of these contributors were more than happy to donate their personal time to our cause. Thank you all for making yourselves available to us.

We would be remiss if we did not mention the education we received from Eric Pearson, regarding slot operations. Thank you, Eric, for your time and insight. You made this a better book.

The following gaming executives also made very important contributions to this text in the area(s) following their names:

> Janice Fitzpatrick, Macau casino operations
> Phil Hickman, financial reporting
> Alex Berejnoi, casino marketing and operations analysis
> Greg Hilton, cage operations
> Josh Dunn, slot tracking systems
> Albert Jang, slot tracking systems
> Paul Garcia, Jr., casino operations and poker
> Ray Womer, poker
> Maria Jose Gatti, the guest experience
> Matthew Mohler, mechanics of the slot machine
> Keith Emord, slot operations
> Francisco Torres, drop, count, and cage operations
> Rob Terry, race and sports book operations and off-shore gaming operations
> Brad Goldberg, marketing
> Yvette Harris, financial reporting
> Jackie Murphy, nongaming operations
> Will Dunn, slot operations and slot analytics

The following individuals were most helpful in the production of this text:

> Maria Jose Gatti, editing/proofreading and project/research facilitation
> Dr. Eunju Suh, editing/proofreading

Anthony Lucas would like to thank the following individuals for their great ideas and enduring support for gaming publications and research: Dr. Bo Bernhard, Dr. A.K. Singh, Jim Kilby, Janice Fitzpatrick, Brad Goldberg, Yvette Harris, Michael Harrison, Danny Munk, Anthony Sobb, Dr. Kate Spilde, Eric Pearson, Jackie Murphy, and Will Dunn.

Jim Kilby would like to express his gratitude for the love and support of his mother, Minnie Kilby. He would also like to thank the following individuals for their contributions to this text:

Weldon Russell, Station Casinos
Andrew MacDonald, Executive Vice President, Marina Bay Sands Casino
William F. Bonar
Claudio Ferrari, Gaming Manager, Grand Casino Luzern
David Packer, former Operations Director at Casino Iguazu in Argentina, and current Director of Poker at London's Hippodrome Casino
Billy Ray of Paris, France, veteran casino executive and one of the few remaining experts on Chemin de Fer
Roger Snow, Executive Vice President, Shuffle Master
John Strickland, Director of Marketing, Shuffle Master
Stephanie Gutierrez, Senior Graphic Designer, Shuffle Master
Dan Mandarino, Director of Planning Operations, Caesars Entertainment
Bart Pestrichello, casino industry executive
Michael Harrison, gaming consultant
David R. Longhurst, President & CEO, Loncol International, Inc.
Tyrus Mulkey, casino historian
Tom Newman, casino executive
Marc Weiswasser, Managing Member, CasinoRecruiter.com
Grant Novack, life coach

INTRODUCTION TO CASINO MANAGEMENT

Chapter 1
A History of Casino Gaming

Was gambling legal in Nevada before 1931?
Was the Flamingo Bugsy Siegel's epiphany?
How would you describe the historical significance of Las Vegas' Moulin Rouge?
Which casino mogul is often linked to the need for Nevada's Corporate Gaming Act?
What events paved the way for Indian gaming in the United States?
Macau's gaming history was heavily influenced by which European nation?
Who is credited with bringing baccarat to Macau?

Scope

This chapter begins with a brief overview of gambling, prior to the passage of Nevada's Wide Open Gambling Bill in 1931. From there, the historical highlights of the next 40 years are recounted by decade. The focus then shifts to Atlantic City, Deadwood, and the historical mining towns of Colorado, as these were the next jurisdictions to offer legal land-based casino gambling. The continued expansion of U.S. gaming is tracked through the rise of riverboats and Indian casinos. The chapter closes with a geographic, historical, and operational overview of Macau and its gaming industry. This story begins with the 16th-century occupation of Macau by the Portuguese and concludes with a brief review of the factors that fueled the explosive growth of Macau's modern casino industry. The remarkable success of the Singaporean casinos is also addressed in the closing pages. Unfortunately, not all important contributions and events related to gaming history can be covered in a single chapter. Any such omission is certainly not intended to imply a lack of historical significance.

Chapter Goals

- Highlight key events preceding the legalization of gaming in Nevada
- Introduce the early gaming entrepreneurs who helped shape the modern casino industry
- Establish the roots of several current casino operating practices and design principles
- Describe the proliferation of the U.S. casino industry in the late 1980s, including the rise of riverboat and Indian gaming properties
- Provide a historical overview of Macau's rich gaming history
- Describe the critical changes that led to the success of Macau's gaming industry

1

Overview

Like fire, the wheel, and many other inventions, the precise origin of gambling is not so easy to pinpoint. Evidence suggests that gambling dates as far back as the Stone Age. These ancient civilizations are likely to have gambled on simplistic guessing games and games based on the outcome of tossed objects, similar in concept to modern dice.[1] The ancient Greeks gambled by throwing objects known as astragali, which also resembled the basic idea of modern dice.[2] The astragali were fashioned from the heel bones of sheep.

In what is now the United States of America, various forms of gambling have existed for thousands of years. For example, Native Americans adopted many games of chance as a way of life.[3] More recently, the English settlers brought their own brand of gambling to North America. In his work entitled *Gambling and the Law*, Professor I. Nelson Rose stratified American gaming into three periods.[4] The first period ranged from colonial times until the mid 1800s. The second period began at the end of the Civil War and lasted until the early 1900s. The third period started during the Great Depression and remains ongoing.

For purposes of the following discussion, early American settlers are classified into two groups: The Puritans and the remainder of the English (hereafter, English). Although English themselves, the Puritans are isolated as a subgroup because of their very different views on gambling. The Puritans saw the new world as a place to advance their religious and social agendas, and gambling was not something that fit into their way of life. The English had a much more relaxed view on gambling, as it did not run counter to the defining principles of their culture.

As a result of these divergent views, the acceptance of gambling differed greatly by colony. In some colonies, the English attitudes prevailed. In others, the Puritan beliefs took hold. Entire colonies tended to be dominated by the views of one group. For example, the Massachusetts Bay Colony, led by the Puritans, not only outlawed gambling but also the possession of any gambling paraphernalia such as cards, dice, and gaming tables.[5] For a brief period, this ban extended to private homes. For good measure, the Puritans also made dancing and singing illegal.

In the English colonies, the settlers were much more tolerant of gambling. They saw it as a form of entertainment and a harmless diversion from the considerable challenges of pioneer life. In the English settlements, gambling was accepted and quite popular.

---

[1] Jones, J. P. (1973). *Gambling: Yesterday and Today*, Newton Abbot, Great Britain: David & Charles, p. 13.
[2] Mlodinow, L. (2009). The *Drunkard's Walk: How Randomness Rules our Lives*, New York: Vintage Books, p. 27.
[3] Chafetz, H. (1990). *Play the Devil*. New York: Bonanza Books, p. 8.
[4] Rose, I.N. (1986). *Gambling and the Law*. Secaucus, N.J.: Lyle Stuart.
[5] Ibid.

Gambling was certainly no stranger to England. The first known sanctioning of a national lottery by the Crown occurred in 1569.[6] Consequently, it is no surprise that America's first flirtation with gambling was through lotteries. All 13 colonies established lotteries to raise funds for the government.[7] Lotteries were also used to help fund some of the nation's most prestigious universities, including the following: Harvard, Yale, Columbia, Dartmouth, Princeton, and William and Mary.[8] Lastly, the colonists turned to lotteries to help finance the revolutionary war.[9]

Even Thomas Jefferson, a principal author of the Declaration of Independence, had at least a recreational interest in gambling. In fact, Jefferson kept a notebook of his gambling exploits, as shown in the following excerpt.[10]

> "Lost at Backgammon, 7/6
> Won at Backgammon, 7d 1/3
> Won at Cross and Pyle, 3 3/4d
> Mrs. Jefferson, lost at cards, 1/3
> Lost at lotto, 18/."

During the 1800s, gambling centers were established in major cities, from New Orleans to New York City. The westward expansion of the population, in general, and the California gold rush, in particular, brought gambling to the West. Mining camps sprung up overnight, and with them came gambling. San Francisco became the gambling Mecca of the West. The demand for gambling there was incredible. The market for gambling space was strong enough to command an annual fee of $40,000 for nothing more than 15-by 25-foot canvas tent.[11] This fee was typically paid in advance with gold dust.

With the discovery of vast quantities of silver ore in the Nevada Territory, miners and gambling quickly migrated to what would eventually be known as the silver state. Similar to the California gold rush, mining towns and gambling venues soon followed. An early form of commercial gaming had made its way to Nevada.

The operation of commercial casinos dates back to the 1500s in Northern Italy.[12] Therefore, it could be argued that Italy is where commercial gaming began. However, it is Nevada that is recognized as the birthplace of the modern era of commercial casinos. It was the "Nevada experiment," as it was called, that advanced casino gambling into the science that it has become. Were it not for the success experienced in Nevada, casino gaming is not likely to have matured into the successful and global industry that we know today.

---

[6] Schwartz, D.G. (2006). *Roll The Bones*. New York: Gotham Books, p. 122.

[7] Clotfelter, C.T. & Cook, P.J. (1989). *Selling hope: State lotteries in America*, Cambridge, MA: Harvard University Press, p. 20.

[8] Rose, op. cit.

[9] Schwartz, op. cit., p. 146, & Chafetz, op. cit., p. 23.

[10] Chafetz, op. cit., p. 31.

[11] Rose, op. cit.

[12] Schwartz, op. cit., p. 93. "Commercial" implies that the casinos were operated on a for-profit basis.

Early History of Nevada Gaming

Long before frontiersman Jedidiah Strong Smith[13] set foot in the territory that would eventually become known as Nevada, the Paiute, Shoshone, and Washoe Indian tribes frequently engaged in gambling activities. The Indians bet on foot races and rope games. The stakes for these wagers were items such as baskets, eagle feathers, jewelry, and buckskins.

In 1859, near Virginia City, the discovery of silver known as the Comstock Lode would attract tens of thousands of people to the area. Within two years, the population of Virginia City grew from 200 to 20,000.[14] In addition to the supplies needed by the miners, the town provided entertainment in the form of saloons, women, and gambling. Soon there would be one casino for every 150 residents and one prostitute for every 35 men.[15] The casinos of this era would typically offer a roulette table, faro bank, three-card monte, and a few poker tables. Most of these early gambling establishments were located in a saloon or bordello. The one exception to this rule was Virginia City's luxurious and modern International Hotel, whose guests included U.S. President, Ulysses S. Grant. At the International, gas lights provided the illumination and a brass elevator moved the guests from floor to floor.[16]

In 1861, the Nevada Territory was created. The first territorial governor was a New Yorker by the name of James Nye, appointed by none other than U.S. President, Abraham Lincoln. Unfortunately for gamers, Nye was opposed to gambling. He convinced the first territorial legislature to enact anti-gambling laws, which carried some stiff penalties for violators. Specifically, operating a casino was a felony and placing a wager was a misdemeanor. Further, to encourage enforcement, prosecuting attorneys were offered a $100 bounty for every conviction. In spite of all the political grandstanding, these anti-gambling laws were largely ignored.

The Nevada Territory became the State of Nevada in 1864. During the first state legislature, the anti-gambling prohibition was reenacted in Nevada. Apparently, the new legislature was more tolerant toward gambling, as the penalty for operating a casino was reduced from a felony to a misdemeanor. The State's first governor, Henry Blasdel, would prove to be on par with Nye, in terms of his anti-gambling position.[17] In 1866, the first bill allowing all forms of gambling was drafted and passed by both houses. However, Governor Blasdel vetoed the bill. The legislation was defeated, as the proponents of the bill could not muster enough votes to override the governor's veto.

The gambling advocates did not to give up. In 1869, the previous bill was reintroduced, passed by both houses, and once again vetoed by Governor Blasdel. Of course, the

---

[13] The first European known to venture into the area that would eventually become the state of Nevada. Cabot, A. (Ed.), (1995), *Nevada Gaming Law, 2nd ed.*, Las Vegas: Lionel, Sawyer, & Collins, p. 3.

[14] Cabot, op. cit., p. 4.

[15] Ibid.

[16] Ibid.

[17] Blasdel was known as the "coffee and chocolate" governor, as he did not serve alcohol at state receptions and was not in favor of legalized gambling. Many of Nevada's early settlers were cut from different cloth.

outcome was no surprise. However, this time, the proponents were able to attract enough votes to override the Governor's veto. Finally, gambling was legal in Nevada, but how long would it last?

Although the bill legalized gambling, it severely curtailed the operation and marketing of casinos. The law stated that gaming could not be conducted in front rooms where it could be viewed by passers-by, and all signs and advertising were prohibited.[18] Proprietors were required to obtain a license and pay a fee for the right to operate the casino. Although legal, it would be decades before gambling would be accepted as a legitimate business.

During the early years of legal gambling, like today, problem gambling was an issue. As the citizenry began associating many social ills with legalized gambling, public sentiment forced lawmakers to enact many anti-gambling laws. In 1877, a law to protect families from excessive gambling was enacted.[19] The law stated, "The family man has no right to squander any portion of money necessary to maintain the family." This law also allowed family members to notify saloonkeepers that the husband (or father) was gambling excessively. After notification, the gambling operator was to prohibit the "problem" gambler from placing wagers in his establishment. If the operator failed to enforce the ban, he was charged with a misdemeanor. The same act also declared that gambling could no longer be conducted on the bottom floor of a dwelling (i.e., at street level). It was now forced to the second story of buildings. While gambling was clearly legal, it was also clear that some challenged the suitability of the law.

In the late 1800s, Nevada's population was concentrated in its northern region. Mining towns like Goldfield, Tonopah, and Stingaree Gulch offered all the trappings of big city life, including gambling and prostitution. Some of the most famous casinos were the Northern Clubs, operated by George Lewis "Tex" Rickard. Rickard was primarily a boxing promoter. In one of his most notable efforts, he staged the "fight of the century" between Jack Johnson, the first black heavyweight champion, and Jim Jeffries. Jeffries was a retired white heavyweight champion from Kansas and was lured out of retirement to fight Johnson. Given the considerable racial tension surrounding the fight, Jefferies was billed as "the great white hope." However, in Reno, Nevada, on July 4, 1910, Johnson knocked out Jeffries in the 15th round. It was the first time Jeffries had been knocked down in his professional boxing career. In any case, Nevada has been hosting premier prize fights for over 100 years.

Rickard would eventually own Northern Clubs in Goldfield, Tonopah, and, of course, Stingaree Gulch.[20] One of Rickard's partners in both the Goldfield and Tonopah clubs was none other than famous lawman Wyatt Earp, who also worked in the two casinos as a pit boss.[21] The Goldfield club was known as "the Monte Carlo of the desert"[22] and

---

[18] Even today, operators in the Australian club market must abide by similar restrictions.
[19] Cabot, op. cit., p. 7.
[20] Cabot, op. cit., p. 8.
[21] Ibid., p. 8. Wyatt Earp is best known for his participation in the 1881 gunfight at the O.K. Corral, in Tombstone, Arizona.

Stingaree Gulch was reportedly the only true rival to San Francisco's Barbary Coast. Pioneered in late 1907, Stingaree Gulch was said to have had "five or six hundred girls on the line - all nations, all colors!"[23] It is important to note here that most of Nevada's early gambling operators were far more interested in the business of prostitution. Gambling was something of a supplemental activity.

Nevada's population distribution was soon to change with the opening of the railroad between the Pacific Ocean and the Great Salt Lake. This railroad travelled through an area that would eventually be known as Las Vegas. The steam engine locomotives required watering stops, and Las Vegas was known for its abundant underground springs.

The railroad was owned by William Clark, a U.S. Senator from Montana. Clark was certain that the watering stop would grow into a community. Seizing the opportunity, he purchased 1,800 acres of prime real estate for $55,000.[24] Clark then divided the land into 1,140 town lots, sold the lots, and pocketed a $195,000 profit. As anticipated, downtown Las Vegas would eventually be built on this land. The county was named Clark County, after the owner of the railroad that passed through it.

Because of the railroad construction, Nevada now had population centers in both the north and the south. With this growth in population, came an influx of easterners who were opposed to gambling. Their opposition would result in the passage of a law in 1909 prohibiting all forms of gambling in Nevada. This ended a 41-year run of legal gambling. Interestingly enough, the law allowed gambling proprietors 20 months to cease operations, after which time, the local sheriffs were ordered to seize and destroy all gambling equipment.[25] Rather than shutting down, gambling operators used this 20-month window to move their casinos "underground." While the law banning gambling surely looked righteous on the books, it was rarely enforced.

As of 1910, every state in the U.S. had outlawed casino gambling. In 1911, Nevada's lawmakers amended the 1909 prohibition by legalizing social games such as poker, provided that the deal rotated and the house took no fee for the game. Two years later, in 1913, the Nevada legislature once again voted to prohibit all forms of gambling, including social games. However, the 1913 legislators convened a second time to declare social gambling games once again legal, with certain caveats. Additionally, they voted to legalize nickel slot machines, provided these games paid winners in cigars or drinks.

1930s

The events of 1929 and 1930 would forever change the United States and the history of gambling. Specifically, these events were the stock market crash of 1929, the ensuing

---

[22] Coyle, C.W. (1911). The desert rat. *The Overland Monthly, Vol. LVII*, Second Series, January-June, San Francisco: The Overland Monthly Co. Publishers, p. 70.

[23] Evans, M. (2002). *Madam Millie: Bordellos from Silver City to Ketchikan*, Albuquerque: University of New Mexico Press, p. xi.

[24] Burbank, J. (2009). San Pedro, Los Angeles and Salt Lake Railroad. *Online Nevada Encyclopedia*. Retrieved on April 30, 2011, from http://onlinenevada.org/san_pedro,_los_angeles_and_salt_lake_railroad.

[25] Ibid., p. 9.

depression, and the federal funding of the Hoover Dam project.[26] Together, these events created a set of conditions that would eventually bring us to Nevada's modern gaming industry. Like every other state, Nevada was severely affected by the depression. Nevada legislators were eagerly looking for ways to stimulate the State's ailing economy. The second year of the depression, 1931, proved to be one of the worst. No state could afford to lose jobs, nor could any state government afford to diminish its ability to provide basic services to its inhabitants.

The Hoover Dam project was a ray of hope for Nevada. This project would stimulate the economy by bringing thousands of employed workers to Southern Nevada. However, prior to the construction of the Hoover Dam, illegal gambling had established itself as a critical component of the nearby Las Vegas economy. Given the extent of the federal presence in Southern Nevada, city leaders believed that the federal government would surely force them to shut down these illegal casinos. In an effort to keep the casinos open and allow both the gaming industry and the State to prosper, the Nevada State Legislature decided to legalize gaming.

It was Phil Tobin, a 29-year-old assemblyman from tiny Winnemucca, Nevada, who introduced Assembly Bill 98, which would forever be known as the Wide Open Gambling Bill. On March 19, 1931, Governor Fred Balzar signed Assembly Bill 98 into law. This began what the national press referred to as the "Nevada experiment." However, the state legislature did not stop with the legalization of gaming.

The Divorce Industry

In 1931, Nevada, along with Mexico City and Paris, France, served as the divorce capitals of the world. Unhappy spouses came to these destinations, stayed long enough to gain residency, and then filed for a legal divorce. During the time of the residency requirement, they would spend money in the community and fuel the economy. In order to gain a leg up on the competition, the Nevada legislature lowered the residency requirement for divorce from three months to six weeks. This measure was passed during the same legislative session as AB 98, making Nevada the leading player in the "divorce" tourism industry.

Boulder City

AB 98 did not apply to Boulder City, Nevada, as it was specifically created to house workers from the Hoover Dam construction project. In this case, state legislators were concerned over the possible fallout resulting from federal employees gambling away their hard-earned salaries.[27] To this day, casinos are not permitted to operate in Boulder City.

---

[26] Originally known as Boulder Dam, the name was subsequently changed to Hoover Dam.
[27] To gamble, these workers would at least be required to make their way to nearby Las Vegas, which many of them did.

The Bull Pen Casino

In 1932, the Bull Pen casino was established in the Nevada State Prison, in which inmates were permitted to operate gambling tables. If an inmate had sufficient funds to bankroll the table, the prison administration allowed the inmate to serve as the game boss. Each game boss was required to contribute a portion of the gaming win to an inmate welfare fund. Aside from this requirement, the game boss was allowed to keep all remaining profits. At the height of the Bull Pen Casino, an inmate could play poker, blackjack, craps, chuck-a-luck, and roulette. Prisoners could also place bets on any horse race or sporting event. The Bull Pen Casino survived until 1967 when the prison administration decided that the inmates should engage in more wholesome forms of entertainment.

Early Nevada Operators

Per Nevada's AB 98, the first gaming license was issued to a woman named Mayme Stocker, for the operation of the Northern Club in downtown Las Vegas. Although Mrs. Stocker was the first licensee on record, the Northern Club was actually operated by her husband and sons, all of whom worked for the Union Pacific Railroad. These men could not be named as licensees, as the railroad frowned upon any official association with the gambling business. Consequently, it could be said that the first casino front man was actually a woman. The Northern Club was located on a site currently occupied by the La Bayou Casino. A few days after the Northern Club's debut, the Las Vegas Club opened at a location less than one block away.

In general, the legalization of gambling in Nevada provided a forum for criminals to legitimately operate their business. That is, the operators of illegal casinos, bookmakers, bootleggers, and speakeasies from all parts flocked to Nevada. After all, these were the people with operational expertise. In Reid and DeMaris' work entitled, *The Green Felt Jungle*, the authors chronicle the control that former and even practicing gangsters had over early Las Vegas casinos. Nearly all of the Las Vegas Strip's founding fathers were associated with some form of illegal or extralegal gaming activity. Several had direct involvement with the gambling ships operating off the coast of Long Beach, California. At the time, these operations were neither legal nor illegal, provided that all gambling occurred at least three miles from shore. It was not until 1955 that the State of Nevada became committed to preventing those with an unsuitable background from operating a casino.

The Meadows

One example of an early Nevada operator with a criminal background was Tony Cornero, a.k.a. Tony Stralla and Admiral Cornero. Prior to his arrival in Nevada, Cornero was a bootlegger. Unfortunately for him, he was a convicted bootlegger, which also made him a felon. After his release from prison, Tony Cornero and his brothers Frank and Louis moved to Las Vegas to build a hotel-casino. Since Tony was a felon, his two brothers applied for and held the gaming license.

On May 2, 1931, the Meadows Supper Club opened at the intersection of East Fremont and Charleston, about two miles southeast of downtown Las Vegas. On the day it opened, the following passage appeared in the Las Vegas Age newspaper:

> "Potent in its charm, mysterious in its fascination, the Meadows, America's most luxurious casino, will open its doors tonight and formally embark upon a career which all liberal minded persons in the West will watch closely."[28]

The Meadows was built at a cost of $31,000. It had 30 rooms, each with its own bath and plumbed hot water. Its floors were carpeted, in contrast to the wood and sawdust surfaces found in the downtown casinos. It was also the first casino to offer live entertainment.

The casino offered the following game mix: Two roulette tables, two craps tables, two blackjack tables, two poker tables, one English hazard game, one faro game, one Big-6 wheel, one chuck-a-luck game, and five slot machines.[29] The Meadows also featured its own landing strip to accommodate the aircraft of its wealthy customers. Two months after the hotel-casino opened, the Cornero brothers sold the hotel portion of the property to a Southern California hotel owner and builder.[30]

Overall, the property was plagued by bad luck. Fire destroyed the hotel on Labor Day 1931, after Las Vegas firemen refused to fight the fire because it was outside the city's limits. Although the casino portion of the property survived the fire, the Corneros sold it in early 1932. The subsequent owners went bankrupt in 1937.

In 1955, Tony Cornero was overseeing the construction of the Stardust, his 1,000-room hotel-casino. He had invested over $3 million of his own money in this facility and the project was near completion. Late in the evening of July 30, 1955, he decided to cross the street and shoot some craps at the Desert Inn. The next morning, July 31, after many hours at the tables, Tony clutched his chest, collapsed, and died. On the day following Cornero's death, a Las Vegas Review-Journal reporter wrote the following passage:

> "Tony died the way he had lived. He died at a gambling table. Probably, the diminutive gambler was happy as hell when he felt the surging heat whip across his chest and blot out the world. What other way was there for him to go? In a bed? Never! In a gun battle? They tried that! In an ambush? They tried that too! Tony went the way any tough gambling hombre wants to get it. Fast and painless! The pain that hit Tony Cornero Stralla lasted something less than 10 seconds and then it was all over. He had crapped out."[31]

---

[28] Balboni, A. (2010). *The First 100: Portraits of the men and women who shaped Las Vegas*. Las Vegas: Las Vegas Review-Journal. Retrieved on November 13, 2010, from http://www.1st100.com/part1/cornero.html.

[29] Burbank, J. (2010). Meadows Club. *Online Nevada Encyclopedia*. Retrieved on November 4, 2010, from http://onlinenevada.org/meadows_club.

[30] Balboni, op. cit.

[31] Ibid.

The Early Las Vegas Strip

Built in the 1930's, during prohibition, Frank Detra's Pair O'Dice nightclub was located on Highway 91, known then as the Los Angeles Highway. Frank Detra was an associate of Chicago mobster Al Capone. The club, for members only, was actually a speakeasy that offered alcohol as well as illegal gambling. When gambling was legalized, the Pair O'Dice applied for and received a gaming license on May 5, 1931. The club offered one roulette table, one craps table, and one blackjack table. But it was not the first property on the Los Angeles Highway to receive a gaming license.

Although it actually opened as a business a year after the Pair O'Dice, the Red Rooster was issued a gaming license on April 1, 1931. This was the first gaming license issued to a property located on the Los Angeles Highway, which would eventually be known as the Las Vegas Strip. The Red Rooster was permitted to operate one blackjack table and three slot machines. However, in July of that same year, the Red Rooster gained the dubious distinction of being the first Clark County casino to lose its gaming license. The license was revoked after federal agents raided the club and charged the owner with the sale of illegal liquor. In July of 1933, it met the fate of many early Nevada casinos - destruction by fire. However, it reopened in late December of the same year, enjoying popularity throughout the 1930s and World War II.

The Red Rooster was located about one mile south of the Pair O'Dice, on the land currently occupied by the Mirage. Despite the popularity of the rebuilt Red Rooster, The Pair O'Dice was the more successful of the two clubs. Besides gaming, it regularly featured live singers, dancers, and orchestras.

The Smiths

Although gaming was growing in Southern Nevada, in the 1930s, the State's population center was concentrated in the North, primarily in the Reno and Carson City areas. The 1930 U.S. census listed Nevada's population at 91,058, with 5,165 people residing in Las Vegas and 18,529 living in Reno. Judging from the census data alone, Reno must have looked like a more attractive market for business. In any case, these were the conditions of the day for Raymond "Pappy" Smith and his twenty-five year old son, Harold.

Prior to gaming, Pappy Smith worked as a pitchman on the carnival circuit. One of the most important takeaways from Smith's carnival experience was his observation that honest games made more money than crooked ones. This principle could certainly be applied to the casino business, especially in the 1930s.

Harold eventually joined his father on California's carnival circuit. However, California instituted a crackdown on carnival games, which convinced Harold that it was time to try his luck in the gaming business. In Nevada, he could pursue a career in gaming, without concern for the law or other forms of sanctions. After all, in concept, casino games were similar to carnival games in many ways.

With a loan of $500 from his father, Harold and his brother Raymond A. opened Harold's Club on Virginia Street.[32] The casino opened on Harold's twenty-fifth birthday, February 23, 1935, in a space that was 25 feet wide and 150 feet deep. However, by the 1970s, it had grown into the largest casino in Nevada. Additionally, its operators had gained international acclaim for some of their aggressive and creative promotional tactics.

It was not long after the casino's debut that Pappy joined the team, but not as an owner. Initially, he worked as the general manager, with Harold owning 2/3[rds] of the business and Raymond A. owning 1/3rd. Eventually, Pappy would acquire equity in the casino.

Harolds Club instituted several innovative casino operating practices. For example, the Smiths made the casino visible from the street. That is, the front of the property featured windows, affording a view of the casino to those passing by it. This had never been done before in gaming. Throughout Nevada's history, gambling had always been relegated to the back room or the 2nd story. The Smiths also emphasized friendliness, encouraging dealers to engage in light conversation with the players. Pappy was known to walk through the casino and double the bet of customers with the house's money. Additionally, he would occasionally commandeer the table and deal what he called a "poor bastards" hand, where he would hit until he broke and then say, "Pay the poor bastards."

While Southern Nevada had few if any women dealers, Harolds Club hired mostly women dealers, because the Smiths thought it would be good for business. In this era, women were generally not welcome in the gaming industry. In fact, the Reno City Council proposed an ordinance forbidding women dealers from being placed near windows where they could be seen from the street, arguing that such a sight was immoral. However, the Smith's were successful in defeating the proposal.[33]

Other firsts included the adoption of a uniform for its women dealers that included pants. Although this might sound trivial today, it was somewhat controversial at the time it was instituted. Harolds Club was also the first Nevada casino to adopt a theme that permeated the entire property. Albeit an old west theme, it was nonetheless the first conspicuously themed casino.

Operationally, Pappy Smith developed a reputation for his willingness to try anything. For example, his mouse roulette game gained national attention. This game featured a live mouse which was released from the center of a specially built roulette wheel. Upon release, the mouse would take refuge in one of the numbered holes on the special wheel. The number of the hole the mouse ran into determined the outcome of all wagers.

Harolds Club was probably best known for marketing to people outside Nevada through their extensive array of outdoor billboards. These billboards could be found throughout the United States and as far away as the African Congo. Many featured a rushing stagecoach with "Harolds Club or Bust" emblazoned on its side. Other billboards

---

[32] Circa 1950, "Harold's Club" lost its apostrophe and became "Harolds Club."
[33] Bledsoe, B. (2010). Meadows Club. *Online Nevada Encyclopedia*. Retrieved on November 17, 2011, from http://onlinenevada.org/harolds_ club_innovations.

featured a naked man standing inside a barrel proclaiming, "I Lost my shirt at Harolds Club." At the height of the outdoor marketing campaign, there were over 2,300 billboards located across the U.S. Of course, this billboard blitz occurred in an era when most traveling occurred by way of automobile.

Guy McAfee

In 1933, after nearly 15 years of prohibition, the Volstead Act was repealed. Passed in 1919, the Volstead Act had banned the sale of alcoholic beverages, along with several other activities related to the manufacture and transportation of intoxicating spirits. With the end of prohibition, Nevada operators were able to legally offer alcoholic drinks as well as gambling. However, during prohibition, many of Nevada's early operators did not adhere to the letter of law, especially when it came to the Volstead Act.

As a vice squad captain in Los Angeles, Guy McAfee became acquainted with the operation of brothels, nightclubs, and casinos. Based on his observations, he concluded that he could make more money in vice than he could policing it. He established himself as a successful operator of nightclubs on the Sunset Strip, where illegal alcohol was served during the prohibition era. In 1938, after a grand jury investigation, the Mayor of Los Angeles, Fletcher Bowron, promised to rid the Sunset Strip of all vice. Facing the distinct possibility of indictment, McAfee and his wife decided to move to Las Vegas.

In 1938, the Pair O'Dice was sold to McAfee for $20,000. After remodeling, he changed the name of his new property to the 91 Club. His primary target market was wealthy Southern Californians. The refurbished club offered a luxurious interior, affordable steak dinners, as well as casino gambling. McAfee would become one of the most influential gambling operators of his day.[34] He and his partners eventually purchased the Pioneer Club, the SS Rex, and the Last Frontier. They also opened the Golden Nugget in 1946.

1940s

In 1941, Marion Hicks opened the El Cortez in downtown Las Vegas along with partner J.C. Grayson. Hicks was a friend of California mobster Bugsy Siegel. He was also a Los Angeles real estate developer who had operated a gambling boat off the shore of Long Beach. Hicks migrated to Las Vegas after authorities shut down his Long Beach operation. The 59-room El Cortez opened at a cost of $245,000 and was considered the finest casino in Las Vegas.[35] In 1945, Hicks sold the El Cortez to Bugsy Siegel, whose co-investors included Moe Sedway, Gus Greenbaum, "Ice Pick" Willie Alderman, Dave and Chickie Berman, and silent partner, Meyer Lansky.[36] Although the Bermans had operated illegal casinos in Minneapolis, Sedway and Greenbaum were charged with managing the El Cortez's casino.

Siegel and company would only operate the casino for six months before selling it to William J. Moore, who operated the Last Frontier, and J. Kell Houssels Sr., who ran the

---

[34] McAfee is often credited with naming a section of Highway 91 "The Strip," after L.A.'s Sunset Strip.
[35] Chung, S. K. (2005). *Las Vegas: Then and Now*. San Diego: Thunder Bay Press, p.56.
[36] Lacey, R. (1991). *Little Man*, 1st ed., Toronto, Canada: Little, Brown & Company, p. 152.

Las Vegas Club. Houssels and Moore then sold the property to Jackie Gaughan in 1963, which leads to an interesting story. After Gaughan had purchased the property, he discovered that one of the hotel's residents had not paid his bill in 17 years. This guest/resident was known as "Fat Irish" Green, and he occupied Penthouse 1. Fat Irish had served as Bugsy Siegel's bodyguard, bagman, and companion. He had also operated the El Cortez race book during Siegel's brief control of the property.

Green was an old-school bodyguard whose philosophy could be described as "violence first – ask questions later." Loyalty and honesty were two of his more redeeming qualities. Two weeks after Siegel's death, Irish showed up at Meyer Lansky's office with a locked briefcase. Siegel had given the briefcase to Irish to hold. When Lansky popped open the case he found $300,000 in $100 bills. Lansky was taken aback by Irish's honesty and, to reward him for it, he made Irish a guest of Penthouse 1 in the El Cortez, for the remainder of his life.[37]

Not aware of the arrangement, Gaughan approached Green about paying his hotel bill. Green replied, "I never paid any rent and I don't have to pay any rent."[38] Gaughan subsequently phoned Houssels and asked if he would move Green to Houssels' new hotel, the Tropicana. Houssels replied, "Sorry, he went with the deal."[39] Gaughan knew that Green liked to eat at the Horseshoe, a few blocks west of the El Cortez, so he called the owner, Benny Binion, and asked if he would take Fat Irish. Benny replied, "I feed Irish for nothing, you got to keep him at your hotel for nothing."[40]

Thomas Hull

On April 3, 1941, Thomas Hull opened his $500,000 El Rancho Vegas on the southwest corner of the intersection of Highway 91 and the dirt road that would eventually be called Sahara Avenue. Mr. Hull first worked for his father who operated a hotel in San Francisco. Hull went on to operate seven hotels in California, including the famous Hollywood Roosevelt in Los Angeles. Later, he decided to build motels and auto courts, which featured a level of service and luxury similar to that of first class hotels. Each of his new properties would feature the name El Rancho. Hull opened the El Rancho Fresno, the El Rancho Sacramento, and the El Rancho Vegas.[41]

The El Rancho Vegas location was just outside the Las Vegas city limits, which afforded Hull many benefits. For starters, the land was cheaper, the taxes were lower, the water costs were less, and it was cheaper to build in the county. The water costs were lower because hotel developers were allowed to drill their own well, when building on county land. Surprisingly, Hull's original plans did not call for a casino. However, at the urging of his friends, he decided to build one.

---

[37] Fischer, S. (2006). *When the Mob Ran Vegas*, 1st ed. Omaha: Berkline Press Kindle Edition, p. 46-48.

[38] Green, M. (2010). El Cortez Hotel-Casino. *Online Nevada Encyclopedia*. Retrieved on November 1, 2011, from http://onlinenevada.org/el_cortez_hotel_casino.

[39] Ibid.

[40] Ibid.

[41] Hopkins, A.D. (n.d.). *The First 100: Portraits of the men and women who shaped Las Vegas*. Las Vegas Review-Journal. Retrieved on November 12, 2011, from http://www.1st100.com/part2/hull.html.

The single-story hotel featured 63 ground-level guest rooms, with guest parking in front of each room. The hotel was built in the shape of a horseshoe, with the swimming pool and casino located in the center of the horseshoe. The pool was positioned in the front of the property and visible from the highway, providing an enticing oasis. A giant windmill sat atop the casino, which became something of a landmark feature.

The El Rancho offered a chuck wagon buffet, free breakfast and coffee (between 4:15 a.m. and 6:30 a.m.), and the largest dining room in Las Vegas, featuring a capacity of 250 persons.[42] Amenities such as its beautiful swimming pool made the property popular with both locals and tourists. It was also "100% air conditioned," by way of swamp coolers.

Although it achieved instant and enduring success, the El Rancho Vegas suffered the fate of several early Las Vegas resorts. On June 17, 1960, a pre-dawn fire broke out and nearly burned the facility to the ground. Arson was suspected but never proven. The owner collected on the fire insurance and moved to Los Angeles. The El Rancho Vegas was never rebuilt. The land was subsequently purchased by Howard Hughes and remained vacant for over 40 years until it was eventually sold to the Hilton Corporation. In 2004, a 1,200-room timeshare property was built on a section of the original El Rancho site.

R.E. Griffith

In 1941, there were three casinos on Highway 91: The Red Rooster, 91 Club, and the recently constructed El Rancho Vegas. On October 30, 1942, the 107-room Last Frontier opened on the site where the 91 Club once stood. In fact, the 91 Club structure was incorporated into the design of the Last Frontier. The resort was built by R.E. Griffith and William J. Moore. Griffith was a wealthy Texan who owned a chain of movie theaters and Moore was his architect nephew.

In 1941, Griffith purchased a 35-acre plot that included the 91 Club. He was determined to outshine the El Rancho Vegas as a tourist attraction. He built a hotel and outfitted the lobby, bar, and restaurant with authentic western saddles and antique guns. He also reproduced a western pioneer town called The Last Frontier Village, complete with Old West memorabilia. Unfortunately, R.E. Griffith died less than a year after the hotel opened. It would be Moore who would take Griffiths' dream forward.

The property made some significant contributions to the industry. The Last Frontier Village was a hit as a tourist attraction, representing one of Nevada's early successes in the area of nongaming amenities. The resort housed the town's first wedding chapel, the Little Church of the West. Finally, the Last Frontier orchestrated some of Las Vegas' first gambling junkets, under Moore's direction.[43]

---

[42] The Chuck Wagon Buffet was the first buffet in Las Vegas.
[43] In short, a junket refers to the general process of recruiting/aggregating gamblers in another city and flying them to the casino. Of course, gambling and travel incentives are used to recruit players. In the 1960s and 1970s, junkets were a popular marketing tool to attract premium players.

Billy Wilkerson

Although Bugsy Siegel is often credited with creating the template for today's upscale hotel-casino resort, it was Billy Wilkerson who envisioned, planned, and began working toward the construction of Las Vegas' first luxury resort.[44] The next several pages review the background/story of both men, beginning with Billy Wilkerson.

In 1916, the 25-year-old Wilkerson was studying medicine in Philadelphia when his father died unexpectedly.[45] The death of his father, a renowned gambler, left the family facing a mountain of debt and forced Wilkerson to abandon his aspirations of becoming a doctor, in order to support himself and his mother. A few weeks later, he accepted a job managing a silent movie theater in New Jersey. This experience eventually led to a partnership in a trade newspaper devoted to the film industry.

In October of 1929, Wilkerson's friend advised him to play the stock market "at rock bottom." Heeding his friend's advice, Wilkerson sold half interest in his trade paper for $20,000 and borrowed an additional $25,000 to play the stock market. Unfortunately, he walked into the Wall Street Stock Exchange on Thursday, October 24, 1929, at 9:15 a.m. Forty-five minutes later, the market tanked and Wilkerson was broke. Billy Wilkerson became one of many victims of the day that would forever be remembered as Black Thursday.[46]

Now broke, Wilkerson, his wife, and his mother headed for Hollywood. Once established in California, he formed the Wilkerson Daily Corporation and published the first issue of The Hollywood Reporter on September 3, 1930.[47] It was a very successful business venture. His publication gained national prominence, giving him Hollywood influence on par with that of movie studio moguls.

Although extremely successful in the publishing business, Wilkerson had a yearning to become a nightclub operator and did so in a grand fashion. His clubs, Vendome, Café Trocadero, Sunset House, Ciro's, La Rue, and L'Aiglon would all become nightclub landmarks. As the names of the clubs would suggest, Wilkerson brought the sophistication and culture of Paris to Hollywood.

Wilkerson had a penchant for gambling, and 1930s Hollywood offered plenty of illegal gambling options. Unfortunately, it became evident that Wilkerson's penchant was more of an addiction. Hollywood's gambling industry was dealt a severe blow, when virtually all illegal casinos were shut down in 1938. With the closure of the casinos, Wilkerson explored a wide variety of gambling options, ranging from breeding thoroughbred horses to opening a casino in Cuba. His urge to gamble remained a driving force in his life.

---

[44] There is a paucity of literature on Billy Wilkerson's involvement in the creation of the Flamingo. The primary source of information for this chapter was the following book: Wilkerson III, W.R. (2000), *The Man Who Invented Las Vegas*, 1st ed., Bellingham, WA: Ciro's Books.

[45] Wilkerson III, W.R. (2000). *The Man Who Invented Las Vegas*, 1st ed., Bellingham, WA: Ciro's Books, p. 1.

[46] Ibid., p. 3.

[47] Wilkerson, T. & Borie, M. (1984). *The Hollywood Reporter*. New York: Coward-McCann, p 2.

In 1940, he was asked to manage the Arrowhead Springs Hotel in Lake Arrowhead, California. Located over three hours from Los Angeles, the hotel had operated at a loss for several years. Wilkerson improved the restaurants, brought in the best waiters from Hollywood, upgraded the menu, and added special events and parties. He used his Hollywood Reporter to advertise the magnificence of the venue and, within a few months, the property was producing a profit.

Soon after Wilkerson had turned the hotel around, he started hosting back-room card games. With gambling dried up in Los Angeles, word of the games traveled fast. Before long, Wilkerson was accommodating scores of Southern Californian gamblers. The heavy demand for gaming required Wilkerson to grow the hotel's casino. To satisfy the demand, he partnered with operators from the defunct Los Angeles casinos. Although not his initial aim, he had developed a very successful casino in Lake Arrowhead. In fact, his casino became too big to succeed. That is, the authorities eventually learned of Wilkerson's impressive operation. In May of 1940, U.S. marshals raided his casino, overturning tables and smashing slot machines.

Although Wilkerson's business ventures were quite profitable, nearly all of his disposable income was lost to his gambling habit. In the first six months of 1944, Wilkerson's gambling losses totaled $1,000,000.[48] It was then that a friend advised him to consider owning the casino, if he had to gamble to that extent.[49] Since Nevada was the only state where gambling was legal, it was natural for Wilkerson to turn his attention there.

In December of 1944, he leased the El Rancho Vegas operation for six months, but Billy had greater aspirations. He saw Las Vegas as a destination for die-hard gamblers like himself. The Las Vegas properties lacked the glamour and sophistication of the Beverly Hills and Monte Carlo clubs. Further, he saw the remote location of Las Vegas as an asset. It allowed the gambler to be free of distractions, providing more time to gamble.

Wilkerson's Las Vegas Vision

In the 1940s, travel from Los Angeles to Las Vegas was almost exclusively by car, and cars of this era did not have air conditioning. Wilkerson believed that only an incredible resort destination would entice a gambler to endure the arduous seven-hour journey through the often scorching heat.

Wilkerson's vision was to build a casino like no other in the world. His extraordinary resort would not only lure gamblers from Southern California, it would serve as a peaceful oasis for non-gamblers who only desired rest and relaxation. The plan included world class dining, top name entertainment, and extravagant outdoor activities. Specifically, Billy intended to offer the following amenities:

---

[48] Wilkerson, op. cit., p. 12.
[49] Ibid., p. 12.

Casino	Shopping
Showroom	Health Club
Nightclub	Swimming Pool
Bar	Tennis
Lounge	Handball
Restaurant	9-hole golf course
Parisian Café	Trap shooting range
Hotel	45-horse stable

The five-story hotel would feature 250 rooms, making it the largest hotel in Nevada. It would be designed to attract the wealthy Beverly Hills clientele. The bathrooms would be modeled after Parisian hotel baths, complete with sunken bathtubs and bidets. The health club would be on par with the magnificent spas of Baden-Baden, Germany. He planned on housing ten retail shops, featuring luxury brands such as Cartier and Chanel. The showroom would be modeled after the Moulin Rouge in Paris.

In the early 1940s, indoor cooling was provided by either electric fans or swamp coolers. However, Wilkerson planned to cool his indoor spaces with a new technology known as air conditioning. Wilkerson's project would be the first in the U.S. to utilize this new cooling system.

The plans included locating the casino in the center of the property, to force foot traffic through the gaming areas. To create the illusion of a perpetual night, the casino would have no windows and the lights would be permanently dimmed. There would be no clocks in the casino, in an effort to suspend the patron's notion of time.

As a gambler himself, Wilkerson knew the value of keeping players comfortable. To this end, he insisted that all the tables in the casino be equipped with a padded rail around their edges. In the 1940s, table games featured hard edges covered only by a thin layer of felt. This comfort-based innovation survived, as it is difficult to find a table in a modern casino without a padded rail.

Wilkerson had no concern for the casual gambler or the pedestrian tourist. His property would be designed to attract the wealthy and powerful - a playground for the rich. He would name his grand vision the Flamingo Club.

Realizing the Wilkerson Vision

To get the project rolling, Wilkerson would first need to purchase land. On a trip to Las Vegas, Wilkerson spotted a parcel of land for sale, about one mile south of the El Rancho Vegas. The 33-acre plot was owned by Margaret Folsom who was living in Hawaii and operating a successful bordello. Wilkerson dispatched his attorney to negotiate the deal, which culminated in the purchase of the land for $84,000, in February of 1945. The land was acquired in his attorney's name, as Wilkerson feared that knowledge of his involvement in the transaction would escalate the purchase price.

Although a gambler himself, he knew his limitations with respect to casino management. After all, he could not afford to make a mistake in the area of his chief profit center – the casino. Consequently, he recruited the expertise of two established Las Vegas casino operators, Gus Greenbaum and Moe Sedway. In exchange for their counsel, Wilkerson offered them a percentage of the future profits (i.e., a piece of the business).

Construction of the Flamingo Club commenced in November of 1945. Consistent with his vision, Billy wanted glittering chandeliers, the finest woods, polished mirrors, and costly marble surfaces throughout the property. As the construction advanced, so too did the project's budget. Wilkerson estimated that he would need $1.2 million to complete the resort, per the current plan. Due to his gambling addiction, he did not have sufficient funding, so he turned to the Bank of America for a loan. Bank officials were well aware of Mr. Wilkerson's gambling habit, but they were also aware of his successful business record. After weighing the potential risks and rewards, Bank of America agreed to lend Wilkerson $600,000, provided he agreed to pledge his successful Los Angeles businesses as collateral. However, he was still $600,000 short. He then turned to his friend, Howard Hughes, who agreed to prepay $200,000 for advertising in the Hollywood Reporter. This left Wilkerson $400,000 short. Wilkerson decided to take $200,000 to the tables, to make up the shortfall. He lost it all and found himself short $600,000, once again.

Wilkerson's Demise

Due to the funding shortfall, the project was scaled back to include only a casino, restaurant, and café. Shortly after Wilkerson downsized the project, he came to the realization that he could not control his gambling addiction. He decided that his association with the project would only aggravate his habit. Wilkerson feared that he would lose everything he had accumulated, if he stayed in Las Vegas.

Moe Sedway knew of Wilkerson's gambling addiction and, believing in the project, agreed to cover Wilkerson's gambling debts in return for a greater ownership percentage. This type of transaction occurred more than once. In a matter of months, Wilkerson gambled away his remaining ownership in the hotel-casino. Soon after, Wilkerson signed over 100% ownership of his land to Sedway. He bowed out of the project and swore never to return to Las Vegas.

It looked like Wilkerson's grand plan would never come to fruition. However, Billy had a friend named Joe Schenck, President of 20th Century Fox, and one of the most influential and powerful people in the film industry. Schenck believed in the project and begged his friend to reconsider his decision to give up on his dream. A persuaded Wilkerson raised enough money to buy back the land from Sedway and the project was on again. However, it was a scaled-down version of the original plan.

Back in the game again, Wilkerson faced a new dilemma. Although the war was over and labor was plentiful, building materials were not. When materials could be found, the cost far exceeded his budget. After investing $300,000 of his own money, he needed another $400,000 to complete the Flamingo Club. Once again, he turned to the tables for the answer to his funding problems. He went to the casino with $150,000 of his remaining

$200,000 in cash. Once again, he lost it all. In January of 1946, he settled all project-related debts and shut down the project.

Wilkerson's Rescue?

In the throes of Wilkerson's demise, Moe Sedway brought the project to the attention of his boss, the notorious Meyer Lansky. Like Sedway, Lansky saw the potential of Wilkerson's plan. However, enticing Billy to re-start the project would not be easy. Someone would have to make him an offer he could not refuse. For this job, Lansky sent Harry Rothberg, whom Wilkerson did not know.

Rothberg approached Wilkerson and his builder while they were inspecting the shuttered construction site. He said he represented a New York firm that wanted to invest in the Flamingo Club. Rothberg told Wilkerson that the interested investors knew he was broke and wanted to supply him with sufficient funds to complete the project. In return for this investment, the firm wanted 2/3rds ownership of the property. Wilkerson was assured he would maintain creative control. Further, when the club opened, it was promised that he would be the sole operator. Rothberg then asked Wilkerson how much he needed to complete the original concept. Without hesitation, Wilkerson answered, "One million dollars." It was also agreed that Wilkerson would retain 100% ownership of the land.

Lansky directed Rothberg to assemble a group of investors to buy 2/3rds of the project. On February 26, 1946, the contract between Wilkerson and Rothberg was signed and the sum of one million dollars was transferred to Wilkerson Enterprises. Wilkerson renamed his project the Flamingo Hotel.

Wilkerson told Rothberg he needed one year to complete the project. Less than one month after inking the agreement, Moe Sedway, Gus Greenbaum, and Bugsy Siegel visited Wilkerson at the building site. Siegel presented himself to Wilkerson as his new partner. Wilkerson was no stranger to organized crime, but he was not a gangster. In any case, he could not have foreseen the events that would unfold.

Bugsy Siegel

For Benjamin "Bugsy" Siegel, it was his death that made him a household name in the U.S. On June 20, 1947, he was murdered at the Beverly Hills home of his girlfriend, Virginia Hill.[50] The story of the gruesome murder made national headlines and shocked America. In particular, it was the grim photographs of his lifeless body that made the violence of the act such a stunning reality.

Born in Brooklyn in 1905, Bugsy wasted little time choosing a life of crime. As a teen, he was already leading a gang with none other than Meyer Lansky. By adulthood, Siegel was "credited" with killing thirty men.[51] His teenage partner in crime, Meyer Lansky, would eventually become one of the most powerful figures in organized crime. Lansky

---

[50] Schwartz, D.G. (2006). *Roll the Bones*, Gotham Books, Kindle edition, location 7348.
[51] Denton, S. & Morris, R. (2001). *The Money and the Power,* Kindle Edition, New York: Alfred A. Knopf, p. 49.

would come to be known as the godfather of godfathers, the mafia's banker, and the chairman of the board of the national crime syndicate.

After Prohibition was repealed in 1933, Meyer Lansky sent Bugsy to Los Angeles. His assignment was to extort the movie industry, establish a bookmaking operation, and run illegal gambling operations. By 1937, he was shaking down studios for protection money, running a $500,000-a-day bookmaking operation, and operating several of the gambling ships moored off the shore of California.[52]

Siegel Hits Las Vegas

People most often associate Bugsy with the Flamingo, but he actually came to Las Vegas four years prior to his involvement with that resort. He and Moe Sedway were dispatched to Las Vegas in 1941 by Meyer Lansky, after the Nevada Legislature voted to legalize horserace betting parlors. These parlors were known as race books, and they allowed bettors to wager on races held at many of the most popular U.S. tracks. For example, bettors in Nevada could now bet on races run at tracks such as Aqueduct, Santa Anita, Del Mar, Churchill Downs, and more.

In 1941, there was no satellite television. In fact, few homes had a television of any kind. To facilitate betting, the race book had to obtain the results of the races, including critical information such as the names of the winning horses and the payoffs for various winning wagers. In those days, this was accomplished by telegraph, which was also known as a wire service. Once a race was completed, the results were sent via wire service to the hundreds of illegal race books across the U.S., and to Nevada's legal race books.

On the west coast, there was only one wire service that provided these results - Al Capone's Trans America Wire Service. Although owned by Al Capone, Bugsy operated the equivalent of a west coast franchise of Trans America. If a race book operator wanted to accept bets, he would have to do business with Bugsy. As a regional monopoly, Bugsy dictated take-it-or-leave-it terms. In fact, he owned the El Cortez race book outright and 50% of every other downtown race book. He also had a 33% stake in the race books at the El Rancho Vegas and the Last Frontier.[53]

The Siegel-Wilkerson Dynamic

As he grew older, Siegel craved legitimacy, wanting to be seen as a respectable businessman. Although his management tenure was brief, he had successfully operated the El Cortez, he was already in Las Vegas, and Lansky needed someone he could trust to oversee the mob's investment in the Flamingo. Pressured by Lansky, Siegel reluctantly agreed to the assignment. Bugsy hoped that his involvement in the high-profile Flamingo project would earn him the respectability he desired.

Siegel and Wilkerson could not have been more different. Siegel was a notorious gangster and Wilkerson was a successful and well-respected businessman. Wilkerson was

---

[52] Ibid., p. 50.
[53] Fischer, S. (2006). *When the Mob Ran Vegas*, 1st ed. Omaha: Berkline Press Kindle Edition, p. 45.

suave and debonair, while Siegel was little more than a well-dressed thug. Early on, the two men managed to work together. Siegel seemed willing to learn from Wilkerson, as Billy embodied many of the qualities Bugsy sought for himself. Initially, Siegel would prove useful in obtaining hard-to-find building materials through his underground connections. However, as Siegel became more familiar with the project and Wilkerson, he grew increasingly disrespectful of Billy.

It began simple enough: Wilkerson would issue an order and Siegel would reverse it. Soon after, Siegel began to claim that the Flamingo was his idea. He envisioned himself as the gambling czar of Las Vegas, at the helm of this magnificent hotel. The conflict came to a head when Siegel demanded a hands-on role. In an attempt to appease the gangster, Siegel was put in charge of the hotel's construction, while Wilkerson retained control of all other areas. Each would have their own crew and soon neither would have anything to do with the other – a formula for disaster.

With little experience in construction and not knowing a budget from a bidet, Siegel went through his entire construction budget within one month. Bugsy demanded more funds, but Wilkerson denied him, and Siegel became angry. Wilkerson desperately hoped that the investors would remove Siegel from the project, after learning of the damage he had done. This did not happen.

In May of 1946, Siegel decided that the whole deal was a mistake and demanded an amended agreement, giving him full control of the project. He convinced Lansky and his partners of his argument, assuring them that Wilkerson would remain on board as the creative genius. Soon after, Bugsy decided that he needed to control the creative process as well. He offered to buy out Wilkerson's creative participation with stock, as cash was in short supply. Billy was offered an additional 5% interest in the company and he accepted. At this point, Wilkerson was still a major stockholder and he owned 100% of the land, so he felt somewhat protected.

Siegel Takes Control

On June 20, 1946, Siegel formed the Nevada Project Corporation of California, declaring himself president and principal stockholder. All others, including Wilkerson, were merely stockholders, with no direct say in the development of the resort. Siegel fired everyone Wilkerson had brought on board and replaced them with his own crew. He delegated the responsibility of interior design to his movie star girlfriend, Virginia Hill. Wilkerson was promised the hotel manager position, once the project was completed.

After wresting control of the project from Wilkerson, he saw the Flamingo as an opportunity to enhance his own reputation as a businessman. He would spare no expense in completing the resort. Siegel immediately embarked on a spending spree that completely ignored Wilkerson's meticulous construction plan. With no concern for a budget, the project quickly spiraled out of control. Checks started to bounce and the mad scramble for additional funds had begun.

At this point, Wilkerson still owned the land, but Siegel would scheme to acquire that as well. In two separate transactions, Wilkerson relinquished ownership of the land to the

Nevada Project Corporation for an additional 10% equity in the company, bringing Wilkerson's total ownership to 48%. This made Wilkerson the largest single shareholder of Bugsy's company.

In November of 1946, Bugsy's mobster partners demanded a full accounting of the project. If Siegel refused to provide it, they would refuse his requests for additional funding. Siegel countered by forcing the largest shareholder, Billy Wilkerson, to sign for a large bank loan to keep the project alive. Wilkerson had little choice in the matter. He owned 48% of the stock. If he didn't sign for the loan, the company would declare bankruptcy, and his shares would be worthless. On November 29, 1946, Wilkerson signed a bank loan for $600,000. He was the sole signatory. While helpful, even the loan was not enough to stay the course. Desperate for additional funds, Siegel began selling nonexistent equity (i.e., false ownership in the Flamingo).

By November of 1946, the casino was nearly finished, but the hotel was not. Wilkerson had originally planned to open on March 1, 1947, but in dire need of cash flow, Siegel rescheduled the opening for December 26, 1946. The decision made Wilkerson furious, as the hotel would not be ready. Additionally, he felt that opening during the holidays was a terrible idea. However, Siegel would listen to no one. He had to have cash flow from operations to avert a financial catastrophe.

In early December of 1946, Wilkerson received an unexpected and alarming phone call from a friend, J. Edgar Hoover, the Director of the F.B.I. Hoover called to warn him of the distinct possibility that the Flamingo was under the mob's full control, and that his life was possibly in danger. It is difficult to imagine that such news would come as a surprise to Wilkerson.

Two weeks before the hotel's scheduled opening, Siegel called a stockholder's meeting. At this point, Wilkerson owned 48% of a $6 million project. Billy attended the meeting with his attorney. Siegel wasted no time telling Wilkerson that he would have to part with a portion of his equity in the project, with no compensation. Siegel told him that everyone would have to take a haircut, because he had sold 150% of the equity in the Flamingo. Siegel used firm and threatening language to clearly convey that Wilkerson had no choice in the matter. Wilkerson now questioned the value of his shares, not to mention the value of his life. Echoing Billy's thoughts, his attorney suggested that Wilkerson leave Las Vegas immediately.

Wilkerson caught the first flight to New York, where he boarded an ocean liner for Paris. Once in Paris, he registered in a hotel under an assumed name. Not only was Wilkerson out of the development process, he was out of the country, and left questioning the value of his stake in the project.

Siegel Opens the Flamingo

On December 26, 1946, the Flamingo opened as Siegel had planned, but without a hotel. Invited guests had to be housed in downtown hotels. The casino was jammed with locals, but the celebrities Siegel had hoped to attract were absent. Arriving guests were met with the noise of construction. Just after opening, the air conditioning system broke down, leaving the guests to swelter in the crowded casino. Suffice it to say, the grand opening fell somewhere short of successful.

After two weeks of operation, the casino had lost $275,000. Siegel ordered the Flamingo closed until the hotel was operational. In the meantime, Wilkerson's attorney urged him to sell his stake in the project, arguing that the operation was far too unstable under Siegel's control. Heeding the advice of counsel, Wilkerson offered to sell his purported 48% interest for $2 million. Siegel countered with an offer of $300,000. Wilkerson then dropped his asking price to $1 million, which prompted Siegel to make a final offer of $600,000. On March 1, 1947, the completed Flamingo opened. On March 19, 1947, the final document was signed, liquidating Wilkerson's equity position in the property.

Another of the Flamingo's investors was Lucky Luciano, who was also a notorious mobster and long-time friend of Siegel's. Luciano was also concerned about the value of his investment. After Luciano failed to invite Bugsy to something of a mafia summit meeting, Siegel grew concerned. Following several unsuccessful attempts to contact Luciano by phone, Siegel flew to Havana, Cuba, to meet with the deported gangster. As described in the *Green Felt Jungle*, their conversation quickly turned to the Flamingo.[54] Bugsy boasted of its class, and Luciano commented on the investment's poor return. Bugsy knew something was wrong, as his friend was clearly agitated. Siegel pleaded for more time, but Luciano commanded him to part with the wire service to compensate the Chicago mob for its investment in the Flamingo. A defiant Siegel refused to comply and harsh words were exchanged.

By May of 1947, the Flamingo was generating a profit, but to Bugsy's associates and investors, it was too little too late. His gangster partners had finally come to realize that he had terribly mismanaged the project. Worse yet, they believed that he and his girlfriend, Virginia Hill, had stolen money from the casino, though there was no direct evidence to corroborate their suspicions. However, it was evident that Billy Wilkerson had promised to deliver the Flamingo for $1 million, and under Bugsy's leadership the construction costs had eclipsed $6 million. On June 20, 1947, as he sat on the sofa leisurely reading the newspaper, the fatal shots rang out. Benjamin "Bugsy" Siegel was dead at the age of 41. Upon his death, it was discovered that Bugsy had actually sold 400% of the Flamingo.

Marion Hicks

One more hotel-casino was opened in the 1940s. Marion Hicks, former owner of the El Cortez, opened his 76 room, $7 million dollar Thunderbird, on the Las Vegas Strip. The Thunderbird opened on September 2, 1948. While supposedly owned by Hicks and operated by Hicks and Nevada's former Lieutenant Governor, Cliff Jones, investigative journalists soon revealed Meyer Lansky's hidden ownership position in the resort.[55]

---

[54] Reid, E. & Demaris, O., (1964), pocket edition, *The Green Felt Jungle*, Montreal: Pocket Books of Canada, p. 26-27.
[55] Bernhard, B., Green, M.S., & Lucas, A.F. (2008). From maverick to mafia to MBA. Cornell Hospitality Quarterly, 49(2), 177-190.

1950s

The first casino to open in the 1950s was Benny Binion's Horseshoe, located in downtown Las Vegas. Lester "Benny" Binion was a convicted murderer looking for a fresh start in Nevada's legal gaming industry.[56] He was born in Texas and moved to Dallas in his early twenties where he set up shop as a bootlegger. He learned the gambling trade by working for Warren Diamond, who operated a famous no-limit craps game in Dallas' St. George Hotel. In 1926, at the age of 22, Binion went into competition with his mentor when he opened a rival game at the Southland Hotel.[57] After establishing the craps game, Binion expanded his gambling operation to include loan sharking and the numbers racket. By the early 1940s, there were 27 illegal casinos in Dallas. In 1946, a gang war broke out in Dallas, forcing Benny to relocate. If you were a felon and an illegal casino operator looking for work in 1946, Las Vegas was perfect for you. To no one's surprise, Binion, his wife, and five kids headed for Las Vegas in a chauffeur driven Cadillac, hauling several suitcases stuffed with cash.[58]

Once in Las Vegas, he invested in a casino owned by J.K. Houssels, and by January 1, 1947, he was part owner of the Las Vegas Club. Over the course of the next four years, Binion would own and then sell interest in two other downtown casinos. In 1951, he purchased a lease on a property owned by Meyer Lansky's organization and opened Benny Binion's Horseshoe.

The Horseshoe became known throughout the gambling world for its high wagering limits. At the Horseshoe, the dollar-amount of a gambler's first bet determined his maximum wagering limit. Benny Binion also gained attention for accepting a $1 million don't pass bet on a craps game. In November of 1984, William Lee Bergstrom deposited $1 million dollars in the Horseshoe's cage. Benny's son, Ted, then followed Bergstrom to a craps game, where Bergstrom put his finger on the *don't pass line* and said, "$1 million on the don't pass."[59] The next toss was a come-out throw. The shooter threw a seven, causing Bergstrom to lose $1 million on a single toss of the dice. Although Bergstrom had won several big bets at the Horseshoe in the years preceding his greatest wager, he committed suicide three months after losing the $1 million bet.[60]

The Moulin Rouge

The Moulin Rouge was short-lived but historically significant. Located in West Las Vegas, it opened on May 24, 1955, as the city's first racially integrated hotel-casino resort. Prior to the Moulin Rouge, the only blacks permitted in Las Vegas casinos were laborers and entertainers. At an estimated cost of $3 million, the Moulin Rouge offered 110 rooms, a gorgeous showroom, a swimming pool, two restaurants, and a bar. It was the only property of its day to employ blacks in positions such as dealer and cocktail

---

[56] Ibid., p. 155.
[57] The Southland Hotel was owned by Sam Maceo, a future associate of Meyer Lansky.
[58] Denton & Morris, op. cit., p. 30-32.
[59] Hopkins, A.D. (n.d.). *The First 100: Portraits of the men and women who shaped Las Vegas*, Las Vegas Review-Journal. Retrieved on November 1, 2011, from http://www.1st100.com/part2/binion.html.
[60] Ibid.

waitress. Former heavyweight boxing champion Joe Louis was a host at the Moulin Rouge, in return for a 2% stake in the property.

On May 30, 2003, the Las Vegas Review-Journal reflected on this historic hotel:[61]

> While the likes of the Platters, Gregory and Maurice Hines, and jazz pianist Ahmad Jamal worked the stage or lounges, the stars in the audience -- Pearl Bailey, Sammy Davis, Jr., Harry Belafonte -- attracted just as much attention. "It was the place to meet," says Anna Bailey who danced in the show and goes on to say entertainers such as Frank Sinatra, Cary Grant and Edward G. Robinson could entertain their black show-business friends there. "The crowds would follow them."

In the 1950s, top black entertainers such as Sammy Davis, Jr., Nat King Cole, Pearl Bailey, and Louis Armstrong would perform in the showrooms on the Strip, but they were not permitted to stay or gamble at the Strip resorts. While in town, these entertainers would not only patronize the Moulin Rouge, they would perform there as well.

The Moulin Rouge became instantly popular for both blacks and whites. Given the tense racial climate of the 1950s, the hotel made the cover of the June 20, 1955-issue of Life Magazine. The same issue reported that business was suffering in the Strip casinos, resulting from too much supply and too little demand.[62] Much to the dismay of the casino operators from the five major Strip resorts, the Moulin Rouge was stealing their business.

The Moulin Rouge's 1:30 a.m. breakfast show was attracting many of the entertainers contracted by the Strip resorts. Once the late shows were over on the Strip (around midnight), the entertainers and their crews went to the Moulin Rouge. On a typical night, the showroom audience would include the likes of Sammy Davis, Jr., George Burns, Gracie Allen, Nat King Cole, Jack Benny, Frank Sinatra, and Harry Belafonte. Simply put, where celebrities congregate so too does the public.

The investors who built the Moulin Rouge stated that it was "designed and planned to attract the Negro gambling crowd."[63] But the Moulin Rouge would prove to have a much broader appeal. Opening night was packed, followed by an impressive string of sold-out midnight and breakfast shows. When the Moulin Rouge first opened, the owners of the *big five* assumed the casino would only attract blacks.[64] After all, that was the stated intent of the property's developers. To their surprise, this was not the case.

---

[61] Weatherford, M. (May 30, 2003). Casino's short life belies storied history, *Las Vegas Review-Journal*. Retrieved on October 10, 2011, from http://www.reviewjournal.com/lvrj_home/2003/May-30-Fri-2003/news/21426714.html.

[62] Gambling town pushes its luck. (1995, June 20). *Life Magazine, 38*(25), p. 20-27. Retrieved on July 31, 2011, from http://books.google.com/books?id=RVYEAAAAMBAJ&printsec=frontcover#v=onepage&q&f=false.

[63] Denton & Morris, op. cit., p. 30-32.

[64] "Big five" refers to the five major Strip resorts in 1955: The Royal Nevada (later the Stardust), Frontier, Riviera, Dunes, and Flamingo.

Due to the consistent midnight exodus of Strip entertainers, the night belonged to the Moulin Rouge. After midnight, the tables at the Flamingo and the Dunes were empty, while empty seats were difficult to find at the Moulin Rouge. The owners of the big five resorted to heavy-handed tactics, in an effort to stem the tide of Moulin Rouge customers. For example, Strip operators began threatening their staff with termination, if they were seen at the Moulin Rouge. Liquor distributors were threatened with the loss of major Strip resort accounts, if they continued to sell to the Moulin Rouge. The big five, together with Benny Binion, pressured food and liquor suppliers to demand cash payment for any deliveries to the Moulin Rouge. They also leaned on two Las Vegas banks to call short-term notes issued to several key Moulin Rouge investors.

In a 2001 interview, a former stage manager at the Moulin Rouge claimed, "The money was going out the back door as fast as it was going in the front," suggesting that less than above-board business practices may have also hurt the property.[65] In any case, the Moulin Rouge's liquor license was suspended on what appeared to be a trumped up charge of price discrimination.[66] To make matters worse, in October of 1955, the Las Vegas police along with agents from the Nevada Tax Commission entered the Moulin Rouge and closed the casino.[67]

Without a casino or a liquor license, the Moulin Rouge closed its doors in November of 1955, less than six months after opening. In December of 1955, the Moulin Rouge filed for bankruptcy. Although its tenure as a hotel-casino was brief, it demonstrated the power of and demand for a racially integrated resort. Its tremendous popularity changed the business model for Las Vegas Strip resorts, making the historical significance of the Moulin Rouge undeniable.

The Lay of the Land

Thus far, we have mentioned many different early Las Vegas properties. Figure 1.1 illustrates the locations of the previously discussed properties. Notice the dotted line depicting the Las Vegas city limit, as defined by Sahara Avenue. This is an important boundary, as the construction costs were much less expensive on the Clark County side of the line.

1960s

Jay Sarno

Jay Sarno was a visionary on par with Billy Wilkerson. As the mastermind of Caesars Palace, Sarno gave Las Vegas its most enduring property to date.[68] After more than 45 years, Caesars Palace remains a must-see attraction for Las Vegas visitors.

---

[65] Weatherford, op. cit.
[66] Fischer, S. (2006), *When the Mob Ran Vegas*, 1st ed. Omaha: Berkline Press Kindle Edition, p. 107. More specifically, the license was suspended for charging blue-collar blacks greater prices for drinks than those charged to white-collar blacks, resulting in a charge of price discrimination.
[67] Ibid.
[68] Officially, "Caesars" has no apostrophe. Although there are a few stories behind the rationale for its omission, it is most likely the result of an oversight.

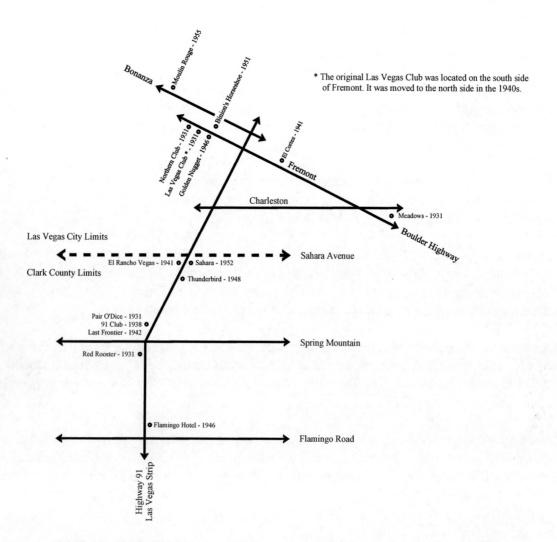

Figure 1.1. Map of Early Las Vegas Casino Locations: 1931 - 1955.

Born in Missouri in 1922, Sarno would later attend the University of Missouri where he majored in business.[69] His early business ventures included a laundry delivery service, selling corsages for campus events, cutting hair, and, of course, running an illegal craps game.

In the late 1940s, after World War II, he moved to Miami and became a tile contractor. This led to a house building stint in Atlanta, Georgia. By the late 1950s, he had built the Atlanta Cabana Motor Hotel, a concept that merged the convenience of a motel with the luxury of a traditional hotel. This project exposed Sarno to the Teamsters Union and their Central States Pension Fund, which would eventually be controlled by organized crime. As the Atlanta Cabana was a success, it was followed by the Dallas Cabana and the Palo

---

[69] Sheehan, J. E. (1997). *The Players: The Men Who Made Las Vegas*. Reno: University of Nevada Press, p. 92.

Alto Cabana in Palo Alto, California. All of these very successful projects were financed by the Central States Pension Fund.

Sarno was an avid craps player and a frequent visitor of Las Vegas. From a hotelier's perspective, he saw the Las Vegas resorts as rather uninteresting destinations. Further, he noticed the uncommitted attempts to theme the properties, with most clinging to the tired notion of a western theme. Seeing an opportunity for a different type of Las Vegas resort, he purchased a plot of land from Kirk Kerkorian and, in 1964, began construction on Caesars Palace.

Caesars exuded opulence. The Bacchanal Restaurant featured wine goddesses who massaged diners, as part of the dining experience. Another of the property's more notable features was Cleopatra's Barge, which was a floating lounge.

Sarno had experimented with this concept in his Palo Alto Cabana, which featured a hotel resembling Caesars Palace. However, nearly every facet of the Las Vegas resort incorporated the Roman theme. For example, all employee uniforms were consistent with the theme. Even the stationery resembled weathered Roman parchment.

As a student of architecture, Sarno incorporated the idea of locating the casino in the center of the resort complex. He configured the overall complex in the shape of a wheel, with the casino as the hub. On August 5, 1966, the 680-room, $25-million Caesars Palace opened to rave reviews.

Soon after the debut of Caesars Palace, Sarno began construction on his next project, a casino that incorporated a circus theme. On October 18, 1968, he opened Circus Circus, at a cost of $15 million. The casino was designed to look like a giant circus tent, featuring all the attractions one would expect to find at a circus. While gamblers played, trapeze artists would perform overhead.

Periodically, the ringmaster would announce the next act over the public address system, in a booming circuslike fashion. Then, for example, a door would open in the pit, and an acrobat would dive some 50 feet into a sponge. Nearly every act found at a circus could be found at the Circus Circus resort. Additionally, the casino housed a traditional circus midway, complete with sideshows and carnival games. Even the children were permitted to play the carnival games. On the adult side, Tanya the baby elephant would pull the handle on the oversized Big Bertha slot machine. With all this entertainment, Sarno charged an entry fee for admission to the casino, but after a couple of years, the entry fee was lifted.

As you might have guessed, Circus Circus was marketed as a family-oriented gaming destination. Although conceptually provocative, the property was not without its challenges. For example, the serious gamblers saw the performances as distractions, instead of entertainment. Additionally, the dealers were often distracted by the circus acts, providing a window for card cheats to practice their trade. Finally, many of the midway games were owned by operators who became known for cheating the customers.

In fact, the property actually lost money under Sarno's management. In 1974, he decided to sell Circus Circus to William Bennett and William Pennington. The new owners made a few modifications and turned Sarno's concept into a monumental success.

In 1969, Sarno sold Caesars Palace to Milton and Stuart Perlman, a decision he would later regret. Financially, Caesars was a very successful project, but it was also the site of much personal tragedy for the Sarno family. Two of Jay's brothers died of a heart attack at the property's craps tables.[70] On July 24, 1984, at the age of 62, Jay Sarno died of a heart attack in a Caesars Palace suite. Reportedly, he died in bed with two beauties that were less than half his age.[71]

In the years before his death, he spent most of his time gambling, golfing, and attempting to build his next resort concept – the Grandissimo. The plans for this resort featured a 6,000-room hotel, a pair of cascading waterfalls, and moving sidewalks to transport patrons to the casino. Like Wilkerson, many of Sarno's ideas would shape the design of casino resorts for years to come. In fact, many of these innovations can be found in today's casino resorts.

Howard Hughes

No other individual did more for the image of Nevada's gaming industry than industrialist and billionaire, Howard Robard Hughes, Jr. He brought much needed credibility to an industry previously dominated by those directly involved in or closely associated with organized crime. Hughes paved the way for corporate ownership of casino properties, which greatly improved the public opinion of the gaming business.

In 1905, Howard Hughes was born in Dallas, Texas. His father, Howard Sr., owned the patent on an oil well drilling bit that revolutionized the drilling process, in the early part of the 20th century. This invention, known as the Hughes rotary bit, produced a fortune for his business, the Hughes Tool Company of Houston.

In 1924, at the age of 19, Howard Jr. was an engineering student at Rice University, when his father died unexpectedly. Upon Howard Sr.'s death, most of the ownership of Hughes Tool was transferred to his 19-year-old son. However, at that time, the legal age of adulthood in Texas was 21. As a minor, Hughes could not access his inheritance. Undeterred, an ambitious Howard Jr. was able to convince a judge to declare him an adult. After purchasing the remaining shares of the company left to surviving relatives, he owned 100% of Hughes Tool.

Although Hughes Tool was a very successful business, Howard Jr.'s interests were elsewhere. His passions were flying, which he had learned as a teen, and the movie industry. Hughes moved to Los Angeles to pursue both interests.

---

[70]Evans, K.J. (n.d.). *The First 100: Portraits of the men and women who shaped Las Vegas*. Las Vegas Review-Journal. Retrieved on November 4, 2010, from http://www.1st100.com/part3/sarno.html.
[71] Sheehan, op. cit., p. 103.

Once in Hollywood, Hughes wasted little time. He produced three major films: "Hell's Angels," in 1930, "Scarface," in 1932, and "The Outlaw," in 1941. "Scarface" introduced Jean Harlow and Paul Muni to the silver screen. In "Hell's Angels," some of the stunt flying featured aircraft piloted by Hughes himself. In fact, during one of his stunt flights, he crashed his plane and suffered injuries that would plague him for the rest of his life.

While in Hollywood, Hughes was a celebrated bachelor, dating many of the most promising starlets. By the age of 25, he was a powerful figure in the motion picture industry. Hughes would later own RKO Studios.

Hughes Tool Company remained a steady source of cash, capable of financing his many investments. For example, Howard Jr. founded Hughes Aircraft Company, which was responsible for the design and construction of the Apollo 11 spacecraft and lunar landing module. In the summer of 1969, the Apollo 11 mission was accomplished by performing a crewed lunar landing and safe return to Earth.

While the Apollo spacecraft may have been the crowning achievement of the Hughes Aircraft Company, its founder was no stranger to aeronautical firsts. In 1935, he piloted the H-1 Silver Bullet, which he had designed and built, to a world-record speed of 352 mph. In 1937, in the same plane, he set a transcontinental flight-time record – coast-to-coast in 7½ hours. In 1938, Hughes set another world record, circumnavigating the globe in less than four days. This feat earned Hughes a ticker-tape parade and made him an American hero. More than one million people attended his New York City parade.

In 1939, Hughes purchased Trans World Airlines (TWA) and shortly thereafter became a major defense contractor during World War II. As a pilot, he continued to push the envelope. In 1943, Hughes crashed an amphibian plane at Lake Mead, near Las Vegas. In 1946, he almost died in yet another catastrophe, when he flew his experimental plane into a Beverly Hills home. The injuries from this crash led to an addiction to pain killing medication that would haunt Hughes for the remainder of his life. By 1950, Hughes had gone into seclusion. Very few individuals, other than his top aides, would ever see him again.

In the late 1950s, he was diagnosed with a venereal disease that affected his brain function. Once the disease set in, Hughes became irritable, delusional, and unconcerned for his personal hygiene and appearance. He developed a fear of contamination that caused him to create a germ-free zone, in which he would open and close doors with tissues.

Hughes Arrives in Las Vegas

Still in seclusion and dressed in pajamas, he arrived in Las Vegas by train on November 27, 1966. He rented the entire 9th floor of the Desert Inn and the 8th floor as well, to prevent anyone from eavesdropping on his conversations. At that time, the Desert Inn was controlled by Moe Dalitz.

When it came to casinos, Hughes was not a gambler. In fact, he never left his living quarters at the Desert Inn. His agreement with Dalitz required him to vacate the hotel by the holidays, to provide rooms for gamblers. As New Year's Eve approached, Hughes showed no sign of leaving. Dalitz asked Hughes, through his top aide Robert Maheu, to leave the property. Not wanting to leave, Hughes decided to buy the resort. Dalitz quoted him a price of $13.2 million. In spite of the inflated price, Hughes accepted, and on March 31, 1967, the Desert Inn became the first in his legendary string of casino purchases.

Hughes continued to buy Nevada casinos until he eventually bowed to pressure from the U.S. Department of Justice and the Nevada Gaming Commission, as both bodies feared his dominance in the industry was detrimental to free and fair competition. His purchases included the following properties: Sands, Castaways, New Frontier, Silver Slipper, Landmark, and Reno's Harolds Club. He had negotiated the purchase of the Stardust as well. However, at that time, he owned 20% of the available rooms on the Las Vegas Strip, causing regulators to block the Stardust deal.

Prior to Hughes, few banks would lend to casino developers, which greatly limited the industry's capacity for growth. Additionally, every individual owning stock in a company was required by Nevada law to be licensed, making it incredibly difficult for public companies to own casinos. However, once Hughes entered gaming, things began to change. The Corporate Gaming Act was passed in 1969, relaxing the requirement to license each shareholder. This act made it much easier for public companies to purchase casinos. Of course, public companies had access to far greater amounts of capital than most individuals. Increased access to greater amounts of capital allowed gaming to grow by way of corporate investment. Hughes' reputation as a legitimate businessman combined with his corporate ownership model set the stage for this critical regulatory revision.[72] In many ways, Howard Hughes, Jr. legitimized the hotel-casino industry, while simultaneously propelling it forward.

In 1976, the 6-foot plus Hughes weighed only 93 pounds when his aides found him unconscious in his Acapulco hotel room. He was rushed via chartered jet to a Houston hospital, but the 70-year-old Hughes died in flight. The aviator had died where he lived – in the sky.

Nevada Loses its Monopoly

In November of 1976, a statewide referendum was presented to the citizens of New Jersey, to legalize gambling in Atlantic City. Previous measures to legalize gambling in 1970, 1972, and 1973 were all defeated at the polls. In 1974, with the support of Governor, Bryndan Byrne, another such referendum was advanced. With this measure, the casinos would be state owned, located throughout New Jersey, and all gaming taxes

---

[72] Some question the extent of Hughes' direct influence on the crafting of the Corporate Gaming Act, as corporate ownership was clearly in step with the direction of the industry in 1969. This is not to say that Hughes did not influence the prevailing direction of the industry. Hughes himself actually opposed the act, as it allowed bigger players into an industry he wanted to control.

would go to the State's general fund. There was also a stipulation that limited the location of the casinos to Atlantic City, for the initial five-year period.

The 1974 referendum seemed certain to pass. September polls showed that 56% of the voters favored the legalization of gaming, while only 38% opposed it. Contrary to the polling results, the amendment was soundly defeated. However, casino proponents were not deterred by this unfavorable outcome.

In November of 1976, a referendum similar to the one advanced in 1974 was put before the New Jersey voters. Unlike previous attempts, the campaign to pass this measure was not met by a well-financed opposition. Some of the key stipulations were different as well. For example, the 1976 referendum stated that the casinos would be privately owned, all gaming taxes would be used to support the elderly and disabled, and all casino locations would be restricted to Atlantic City.

The 1976 measure was passed by a comfortable margin. This outcome was due at least in part to better funding. In 1974, proponents of gaming spent $17 to every $1 spent by the opposition. In 1976, this ratio was $65 to $1. Gaming proponents also employed Stanford Weiner, a successful political advisor, to orchestrate their campaign. The economic climate and general condition of Atlantic City certainly bolstered any argument for much needed improvement. In the year before the vote, a CBS news video described Atlantic City in the following terms:[73]

- One of the nation's most distressed cities;
- A city that had lost 25% of its population in the previous 15 years;
- The poorest city in New Jersey;
- A city at the top of the FBI crime statistics in seven different categories;
- The nation's 2nd oldest city, in terms of the average age of its citizens; and
- An unemployment rate of 20% during tourist season and 40% in the off-season.

On Memorial Day, 1978, Resorts International opened its doors to the public. On an investment of less than $50 million, the casino won $232 million in its first full year of operation. Of course, this performance occurred under monopolistic conditions, as Resorts International had no competitors in Atlantic City during its first year of operation. In fact, to ensure the safety of the guests, a fire marshal often stood at the entrance to prevent the casino from exceeding its occupancy capacity. With the opening of Resorts International came the end of Nevada's national monopoly on casino gambling.

Deadwood

Nevada and New Jersey remained as the only two casino gaming jurisdictions in the U.S. until 1988. It was the fall of 1988 when South Dakota voters were presented with an opportunity to legalize the operation of card games and slot machines in the city of Deadwood. After the measure had passed at the state and local level, Deadwood's first casino opened its doors to the public on November 1, 1989.

---

[73] CBS News (Producer). (1986). *The Big Gamble in Atlantic City* [VHS Tape].

Just as it was in Atlantic City, gambling was legalized in Deadwood to save a historic city. Deadwood had fallen upon on hard times. Its businesses were dying and its historic buildings were crumbling. The hope was that gaming tax revenues would provide the funds needed to restore and preserve the fallen city. The tax rate for gaming revenues was set at 9%, with 89% of the tax revenues earmarked for the historic restoration and preservation of Deadwood.

The law allowed Deadwood casinos to operate no more than a total of 30 card and/or slot games. The card games were limited to blackjack and poker, with a maximum bet of $5. In 1993, the $5 maximum bet was increased to $100. As of September 2011, Deadwood's casinos housed a total of 3,748 slots and 103 card games.[74]

Colorado

In November of 1990, Colorado voters legalized casino gambling in the historic mining towns of Cripple Creek, Black Hawk, and Central City. By October 1, 1991, the first casino was opened. Like Deadwood, the initial measure limited gambling to the following forms: Slot machines, blackjack, and live poker. Further, bets were limited to a maximum of $5. Effective July of 2009, the maximum bet limit was increased to $100, and casino operators were permitted to offer craps and roulette games.

In Colorado, the gaming tax rate is subject to annual adjustments, and is capped at 40% of gaming revenues. However, to date, gaming taxes have not exceeded 20% of gaming revenues. The majority of the gaming tax revenue is either diverted to Colorado's general fund, or eligible for uses other than the preservation of Cripple Creek, Black Hawk, and Central City.[75]

Riverboat Gambling

On July 1, 1989, riverboat gambling was legalized in Iowa, subject to approval at the county level. Ultimately, voters in 11 Iowa counties approved excursion gambling boats. On April 1, 1991, riverboats offering casino gambling began cruising within the Iowa borders.[76] Initially, Iowa regulations limited the maximum wager to $5 and imposed a maximum loss limit of $200 per customer, per trip. However, in February of 1990, Illinois became the second state to legalize riverboat gambling. The Illinois law did not impose a maximum wager limit, nor did it specify the maximum dollar-amount a customer could lose per trip. The more liberal Illinois law forced Iowa voters to approve a referendum eliminating the maximum wager and trip loss constraints. Had Iowa not relaxed these regulations its riverboat industry might have cruised to Illinois. Today, a total of six states offer riverboat gambling.[77]

---

[74] South Dakota Gaming Statistics - Monthly Summary (2011, September). Deadwood: South Dakota Commission on Gaming. Retrieved on November 5, 2011, from http://gaming.sd.gov/industrystats.aspx.

[75] Colorado Department of Revenue – Division of Gaming. Retrieved on November 15, 2011, from http://www.colorado.gov/cs/Satellite/Rev-Gaming/RGM/1213781235116.

[76] Chronology of the Iowa Gaming Racing Commission. Des Moines: Iowa Racing & Gaming Commission. Retrieved on November 2, 2011, from http://www.iowa.gov/irgc/Chronology.htm.

[77] Gambling in the United States. California State Library. Retrieved on October 3, 2011, from http://www.library.ca.gov/crb/ 97/03/Chapt1.html.

Indian Gaming

For decades, Native Americans have operated bingo games to benefit their tribes. However, beginning in the late 1970s, tribal bingo games began offering significantly greater prizes, which were perceived as a threat to other in-state gambling operations, such as lotteries. State governments began to threaten the tribes with closure of their bingo facilities. The tribes countered by filing law suits in Federal court. The rulings from two of these law suits dramatically changed the landscape of casino gaming in the United States. These landmark cases were *Seminole Tribe vs. Butterworth (1979)* and *California vs. Cabazon Band (1987)*.

In both rulings, the courts essentially held that state law could only prohibit gambling that was not otherwise legal within the state where the reservation resided. That is, if gambling was legal within the state, it was legal on any reservation within that state, and free of state control.[78] Although ostensibly about bingo operations, these federal rulings would have much broader implications. Specifically, the general nature of the court's language applied to any form of gambling, opening the door to land-based casino operations. For example, if a state permitted churches or other organizations to raise money for charity via events such as "Las Vegas Night," then tribes could offer the same games on a permanent basis. Suddenly, the breadth of games permitted on Las Vegas Night took on an exaggerated importance.

In 1988, by way of the Indian Gaming Regulatory Act (IGRA), Congress formally recognized the rights of tribes to conduct gaming operations. However, the act required tribes to negotiate with state governments, regarding key matters such as the variety of games to be offered and regulatory structures. These critical negotiations culminate in the drafting of a very important document known as a tribal-state compact. For a tribe to offer gaming such as that found in a Las Vegas casino, a tribal-state compact is required.[79]

The IGRA established the National Indian Gaming Commission (NIGC) to regulate gaming activities on Indian lands. The NIGC is a federal agency put in place to ensure that gaming is conducted fairly and honestly by both operators and players, and to ensure that Indian tribes are the primary beneficiaries of gaming revenues.[80] Overall, its regulatory powers are similar in scope to those of the Nevada Gaming Commission. The NIGC is comprised of a chairman and two commissioners. These three full-time members serve a term of three years. The Chairman is appointed by the President of the United States and must be confirmed by the U.S. Senate, while the remaining two Commissioners are appointed by the U.S. Secretary of the Interior.[81]

---

[78] History of Native American Gaming, Retrieved on October 31, 2011, from http://www. santaynezchumash.org/gaming_history.html.
[79] This level of gambling is referred to as Class III gaming.
[80] National Indian Gaming Commission, Mission and Responsibilities. Retrieved on December 6, 2011, from http://www.nigc.gov/About_Us/Mission_and_Responsibilities.aspx.
[81] Ibid.

As of this writing, there are 565 federally recognized Indian tribes, less than half of which are engaged in gaming operations. Of those engaged in gaming, only about one fourth produce enough revenue to issue per capita payments to individual tribal members. Before issuing per capita payments, profits from gaming operations are used to cover expenses such as: Tribal government services, economic and community development initiatives, and charitable contributions. While casinos have certainly provided windfall profits for some tribes, most have not experienced substantial economic gains from gaming.

Macau

Historical Overview

In the 16th century, the Portuguese were permitted to settle in Macau (also Macao) in exchange for ridding the region of piracy. In 1887, by way of treaty with the Chinese, Macau became an official Portuguese territory.[82] It remained so until December 20, 1999, when Macau once again became part of China.[83] However, the terms of the handover declared Macau as a Special Administrative Region (SAR) of China. As a SAR, Macau is permitted to maintain its own police force, passports, currency, and more. Per the agreement with the People's Republic of China, Macau will have such autonomy until at least December 20, 2049.

Geography

Prior to any further discussion of Macau's history, it will be helpful to gain a basic understanding of the lay of the land. Figure 1.2 is a map of the Macau SAR.[84] When it comes to maps of Macau, the date is important. This is due to the fact that the coastline continually changes from the reclamation of land. That is, the land mass is expanded by way of dumping various land-building materials into the surrounding sea. In fact, the Sands Macau and the resorts on the Cotai Strip were built on reclaimed land. The entire Cotai region is reclaimed land, as Taipa and Coloane were previously separated by the South China Sea. Although the map shown in Figure 1.2 does not reflect it, the Macau SAR was formerly comprised of three distinct regions: The Macau Peninsula, Taipa Island, and Coloane Island.

As you can see from Figure 1.2, the Macau SAR is now comprised of four primary regions: The Peninsula, Taipa, Cotai, and Coloane. The Macau Peninsula is connected to the island of Taipa by three bridges. A fourth bridge known as the Lotus Bridge connects the reclaimed area of Cotai to Hengqin Island, which is part of mainland China. As you may have guessed from studying Figure 1.2, the Macau International Airport was also built on reclaimed land. Macau's casinos are concentrated in the Peninsula and Cotai regions.

---

[82] Gwillim Law (2011). Retrieved on October 23, 2011 from http://www.statoids.com/umo.html.

[83] Gaming Inspection and Coordination Bureau, Macao SAR (2011). Retrieved on October 3, 2011, from http://www.dicj.gov.mo/web/en/history/index.html.

[84] Adapted from a map retrieved on October 25, 2011, from http://www.lib.utexas.edu/maps/cia11/Macau _sm_2011.gif.

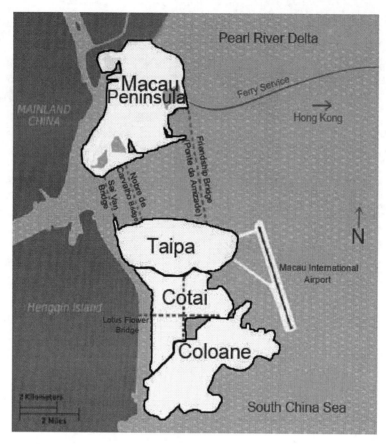

Figure 1.2. Macau SAR, as of January 2012.

Gaming Operations

In 1847, gaming was legalized by Macau's Portuguese government.[85] With gaming activity in Macau dating to the 16th century, it should come as no surprise that gaming operations were already abundant in 1847. However, legalization gave the government the right to tax the industry. The tax revenues were sorely needed, as Hong Kong had replaced Macau as the primary shipping hub of the region. This was an important development, as Macau's economy had relied heavily on maritime commerce prior to the legalization of gaming.

At the time gaming was legalized and for nearly a century afterword, fan tan was the most popular gambling game.[86] During this time, commercial gaming continued in a rather haphazard manner, as the city became littered with individually operated fan tan stalls. In 1930, Macau's gaming industry began to change, as the Portuguese government granted a monopoly gaming concession to the Hou Heng Company.[87]

---

[85] Gaming Inspection and Coordination Bureau, Macao SAR (2011). Retrieved on October 3, 2011, from http://www.dicj.gov.mo/web/en/history/index.html.
[86] The rules of fan tan are covered in a subsequent chapter.
[87] The Hou Heng Company was headed by Fok Chi Ting.

The monopoly concession of 1930 gave the Hou Heng Company the exclusive right to operate all forms of approved casino games in Macau. With its concession, Hou Heng brought many innovations to the Macau gaming market. For example, they introduced novel operating practices such as awarding players complimentary entertainment, food, and cigarettes. They also reimbursed players for the cost of their ferry tickets to Macau. Additionally, Hou Heng invested in the gaming infrastructure by refurbishing and renovating existing casino facilities. This was sorely needed.

In 1937, the monopoly gaming concession was granted to a new operator, the Tai Heng Company. It was Tai Heng that brought baccarat to Macau in that same year. The game would not reach Las Vegas for another 22 years.[88] Tai Heng retained the monopoly concession until 1961, which proved to be a watershed year for Macau gaming.

In 1961, Governor Jaime Silverio Marques designated Macau as a "permanent gaming region."[89] This act provided a favorable tax structure for gaming operators and formerly acknowledged gaming and tourism as cornerstones of the Macau economy. Also in 1961, prior to the expiration of the Tai Heng concession, Governor Marques sponsored another piece of legislation that opened the monopoly gaming concession to public bidding. While Tai Heng competed for the 1961 monopoly concession, it was awarded to a new company eventually known as Sociedade de Tursimo e Diversoes de Macao (STDM). One of the founders of STDM was none other than Stanly Ho Hon San (a.k.a. Stanley Ho).

The End of the Monopoly Concession

While opening the bidding for the monopoly concession was a step toward a more competitive means of conducting business, the Portuguese government continued to question its own operating protocol. In fact, Macau's legislative assembly passed a 1986 law which limited the maximum number of gaming concessions to *three*. Of course, this law was not consistent with the defining condition of a monopoly. However, STDM would remain as the only licensed gaming operator in Macau until the expiration of their 40-year monopoly concession in December of 2001.[90]

In 1999, just two years prior to the expiration of STDM's concession, the Portuguese government officially ceded the sovereignty of Macau to China. As noted previously, the People's Republic of China agreed to designate Macau as a Special Administrative Region (SAR). This new form of government ushered in a new form of gaming industry.

In late 2001, the Macau government received 21 applications for a gaming concession. In accordance with Law no. 10/86/M, three concessions were granted.[91] Of the three companies awarded a gaming concession, one was Sociedade de Jogos de Macau (SJM), a subsidiary of STDM. The other two concessions were awarded to Galaxy Casino, S.A.

---

[88] Renzoni, T. (1973). *Renzoni on Baccarat*. Secaucus, NJ: Lyle Stuart, 11.
[89] Gaming Inspection and Coordination Bureau, op. cit.
[90] STDM received a three month extension, officially ending its monopoly concession in the spring of 2002. The extension was caused by a delay in the assignment of the three new concessions.
[91] Ibid.

and Wynn Resorts (Macao), S.A. The government subsequently allowed each of these three concessionaires to issue a sub-concession to a gaming company that was not granted one of the original concessions. SJM issued a sub-concession to a company that is now known as MGM Grand Paradise, S.A. Galaxy and Wynn issued sub-concessions to companies now known as Venetian Macau, S.A. and Melco Crown Entertainment, Ltd., respectively.

The increased competition in Macau contributed to incredible market growth. In fact, it took less than a decade for Macau to surpass Nevada in terms of gross gaming revenues. While Macau now faces competition from very successful Singaporean casinos, it remains as the world leader in gaming revenues.

The Casino Environment

While references to Macau as the Monte Carlo of the Orient or the Las Vegas of the East were abundant prior to 2002, the Macau casino experience fell well short of the Las Vegas and Monte Carlo standards. In fact, Macau battled a serious image problem. There was too much crime, violence, and corruption in and around its gaming industry.[92] Additionally, the Macau casinos were in dire need of refurbishment, as they failed to even approach the level of luxury offered by the Las Vegas resorts.

Following the 1999 handover of Macau to China, the central government (of China) took aggressive steps toward improving the image of Macau.[93] Specifically, the presence of organized crime in Macau was greatly diminished by way of swift and purposeful action. Prior to the central government's efforts, Macau resembled Chicago in the 1920s, when public violence was not uncommon. For example, gunfights, stabbings, and murders could hardly be considered unexpected in a Macau casino. Obviously, such conditions severely limited the appeal of casino gaming to many would-be customers.

Macau was tough on dealers as well. It was not unusual for a dealer to be shot and/or stabbed by a disgruntled gambler. As jobs were in short supply, it was common practice for dealers to pay a portion of their humble salary to the person that hired them. Such payments were made for the duration of the dealer's employment.

Although violence in today's Macau casinos has declined dramatically, remnants from a more turbulent time can still be found at the entrances of the casinos. That is, all customers pass through a metal detector before they are permitted to enter the casino. Despite this and other precautions, there are still occasional deaths from unnatural causes. This violence is almost always related to disputes arising between external parties involved in VIP junket operations.

By 2002, with the support of China's central government, Macau's business environment was improving just in time for the gaming concession bidding process. While the marked

---

[92] See "Broken Tooth sent to jail." Retrieved on October 27, 2011, from http://news.bbc.co.uk/2/hi/asia-pacific/533226.stm.
[93] See "Macau – gaming capital of the world." Retrieved on October 3, 2011, from http://www.guardian.co.uk/travel/2011/may/11/macau-gambling-capital-of-world.

decrease in criminal activity was certainly a critical component of Macau's success, increased competition also played an important role. The presence of multiple casino companies from different parts of the world brought increased investment to the casinos. The standard for a new a casino in Macau was dramatically increased. The new operators also introduced an increased level of service. Upgrades to both customer service and the hotel-casino facilities had made gaming in Macau attractive to many new types of customers.

The Macau Market Factor

There is no question that improvements to safety, customer service, and the casino facilities were all required for the Macau gaming industry to achieve its current level of success. However, there is one component of Macau's success that has not been mentioned. The casinos are operating in a market with a tremendously favorable supply-demand condition. There is an incredible number of willing and nearby gamblers available to relatively few casino operators.

Singapore

While many countries around the world can lay claim to successful casino properties, few have accomplished more than the two found in Singapore. Although Singapore's Casino Regulatory Commission has not been forthcoming with gross gaming revenue figures, most estimates put it on par with the Las Vegas Strip's gross gaming win.[94] This is an incredible result, as there are 41 casinos on the Las Vegas Strip.[95] Further, these 41 properties generated an aggregate gross gaming win of nearly $6 billion, for the 12-month period ended September 30, 2011.[96] If the estimates are correct, the two Singaporean casinos were able to match this level of production, after less than two years of operation.

Questions/Exercises:

1. In Macau, casino gaming is concentrated in which two geographic areas?
2. Which monopoly gaming operator is credited with bringing baccarat to Macau?
3. Post 2001, Macau's gaming industry realized incredible market growth. What were some of the key factors that led to this success?
4. By what means did Congress formally recognize the rights of Indian tribes to conduct gaming activities?
5. What federal agency was established to regulate Indian gaming activities?
6. What event first brought Bugsy Siegel to Las Vegas?
7. What were some of the more notable casino operating and marketing innovations advanced by Raymond "Pappy" Smith and his two sons, Harold and Raymond A.?
8. In the 1980s, which State was the first to legalize riverboat gambling?

---

[94] As of December 6, 2011.

[95] Nevada Gaming Control Board (2011, September 30). *Gaming Revenue Report, Sep.*, p. 12, Carson City: Nevada: Author.

[96] Ibid.

9. With regard to Howard Hughes, Jr., why were Nevada gaming regulators and the U.S. Department of Justice concerned about the state of competition in Nevada's casino industry?

10. Who developed both Caesars Palace and Circus Circus, and what key characteristic did these two properties share?

11. Who conceptualized the blueprint for the modern luxury gaming resort?

12. In terms of historical significance, what was the most notable contribution of the Moulin Rouge to the hotel-casino business model?

13. Who is credited with naming a section of Nevada's Highway 91 "The Strip," after L.A.'s Sunset Strip?

14. In 1859, what event brought gaming to the territory that would eventually be known as Nevada?

15. Who developed the Thunderbird?

16. Who developed the Last Frontier?

17. What was undeniably unique about Nevada's Bull Pen Casino?

18. What was Thomas Hull's contribution to Las Vegas gaming?

Chapter 2
Profit Structure of Integrated Resorts

What is an integrated resort?
What is drop and how is it calculated?
What does coin-in represent?
Which departments produce the greatest revenues?
Which departments produce the greatest profits?

Scope

This chapter reviews the annual operating results of a Las Vegas Strip hotel-casino resort. This review examines the property-wide results as well as the results of key operating departments. Although this chapter provides rare insight into the performance of an actual hotel-casino, it should be noted that there are no two resorts that are alike. Readers should know that differences in gaming, hotel, and retail capacities can produce considerably different results, even among direct competitors. Differences such as the amenity mix[1] and the internal and external quality and appearance of the resort can also influence results.

Chapter Goals

- Define the key industry terms used to discuss operating results
- Familiarize readers with the profitability of integrated resorts on the Las Vegas Strip
- Demonstrate the diverse sources of revenues and profits within an integrated resort
- Identify the top-performing profit centers
- Identify the contribution of nongaming profit centers

Terminology

Before reading this chapter, you will need to know the definition of some common industry terms. The definitions of these terms are arranged by operating department. Specifically, the following paragraphs include definitions of terms used to describe the financial and operating results of selected departments. These departments are profit centers, as they contain both revenues and expenses.

---

[1] Amenity mix represents the collection of nongaming attractions offered by the resort. Examples of amenities include: Restaurants, retail outlets, showrooms, nightclubs, and spas.

Integrated Resorts

This term refers to a gaming resort that features many other nongaming amenities. For example, *integrated resorts* often feature thousands of hotel rooms, several dining establishments, shows, nightclubs, spas, golf courses, and retail shopping malls. In the more extreme cases, these resorts offer amenities such as wildlife exhibits, botanical gardens, and multi-purpose arenas capable of hosting major sporting events and concerts. This chapter demonstrates the diverse revenue and profit contributions of the departments that comprise integrated resorts.

Slot Department

The term *slot*, as in Slot Department, is often used to refer to all coin- or voucher-operated devices, including video poker, video keno, video/mechanical reels, and multi-program machines.[2] This general use of the term is common when discussing financial and operating results, as there is no Video Poker Department. In this chapter, any unqualified use of the term slot shall categorically refer to all coin- or voucher-operated devices.

Coin-in represents the dollar-amount of wagers placed in slot machines, over a specified period of time. For example, a Las Vegas Strip casino might accept $2.5 billion in coin-in, over the course of a year. Coin-in is not revenue or win. It is a business volume indicator that expresses wagering activity related to one or more coin-operated machines, over a specified period of time.

Given the advent of voucher-based systems, the terms *ticket-in* and *voucher-in* are also used to describe the dollar-amount of wagers placed. Alternatively, *handle* is sometimes used to describe the dollar-amount of wagers placed in a given period of time. This term comes from the days of the one-armed bandits. Before slot machines were equipped with spin buttons, players had to pull a handle mounted on the right side of the machine to activate the game.

Despite the variety of terms that represent wagering volume, coin-in will be used from this point forward as a proxy for the dollar-amount of wagers placed in a given period of time. That is, coin-in shall represent any form of slot machine wager, including currency, and tickets/vouchers.

In simple terms, *win/(loss)* refers to the difference between the dollar-amount of wagers placed and the dollar-amount of all payouts, over a specified period of time. For example, casino executives might discuss win/(loss) for a given day, month, or year. When the dollar-amount of payouts exceeds the dollar-amount of wagers, a loss is incurred. Payout forms include *coin-out, voucher-out, hand-paid jackpots,* and *progressive accruals.*

---

[2] Multi-program machines allow players to choose from several video programs, all on one terminal. For example, players could choose to play any of the following games: Video reel, video poker, video keno, video blackjack, etc. Players could not choose to play a mechanical reel game on multi-program terminal.

Coin-out and voucher-out refer to machine-issued payouts, while hand-paid jackpots are issued by casino personnel. Hand-paid jackpots usually occur when players win substantial top awards such as progressive jackpots. Progressive accruals represent the dollar-amount of wagers diverted to the *progressive jackpot meters*, which display the dollar-amount of the progressive jackpots. Although these accruals do not represent actual payouts, the casino must recognize these amounts as losses in the period in which they occur. Once wagers are diverted to the progressive jackpot meters, the money belongs to the betting public. So, in effect, progressive accruals decrease win just as payouts do.

Casinos do not retain all wagers (i.e., coin-in). Of course, some of these wagers are paid-out to players. The difference between the dollar-amount of wagers placed and the dollar-amount of all forms of associated payouts is referred to as win. If the payouts are greater than the amount wagered, the casino records a loss for the period. Casino win is also referred to as revenue. *Actual hold percentage* refers to the casino's slot win/(loss) divided by the dollar-amount of wagers placed (i.e., coin-in), over a specified period of time.

Table Games

Drop represents the net dollar-value of the contents of each table game's drop box. Each table game has a detachable drop box that rests under a drop slot on the surface of the table. It is detachable so that the boxes can be removed, emptied, and the contents counted. Drop boxes can contain several different items. For the purposes of this chapter, drop is most easily described by a formula. In Nevada, drop = markers issued – markers redeemed + cash + gaming cheques + foreign gaming cheques.

Markers issued represent the dollar-amount of credit issued to players by the casino. That is, the marker issue slips found in the drop box list the dollar-amount of gaming cheques advanced to table game credit players. *Markers redeemed* represent the dollar-value of payments made against outstanding marker balances, resulting from marker issues.

Cash makes its way to the drop box via customer buy-ins and losing cash wagers. For example, a customer sits down to play blackjack, presents the dealer with a $100 bill, and asks for $5 gaming cheques. The dealer will present twenty $5 cheques to the player and place the $100 bill in the drop box.

Gaming cheques are occasionally found in drop boxes. In most cases, these are high-limit cheques and poker cheques. High-limit cheques are sometimes referred to as biscuits, due to the greater circumference of the cheques. In fact, the greater size of these cheques makes them difficult to store in the standard table game tray. Because of the greater size and dollar-value of biscuits, they are often dropped. Poker cheques are dropped because they have different face values from those of standard table game cheques. That is, there is no logical place (i.e., tube) to store poker cheques in the tray of a table game. *Foreign gaming cheques* represent the dollar-value of all gaming cheques from other casinos. For example, Casino A may allow the lower denominations of Casino B's cheques to be wagered on its table games. As a result of this policy, Casino A's drop boxes may contain foreign gaming cheques from Casino B.

Hold percentage is computed by dividing win/(loss) by drop. *Win* represents the difference between the dollar-amount won by winning players and the dollar-amount lost by losing players. In the case of a casino loss, the dollar-amount won by players exceeds that lost by players. This definition is sufficient for now. The formula for computing table game win/(loss) will be covered in a subsequent chapter. Win is also referred to as revenue.

Race & Sports Books

Write represents the dollar-amount of wagers placed, serving as a measure of business volume in both the race book and the sports book. For example, let's assume that a single wager of $100 is made by a customer on a given day. Assuming no other wagers were received, the book's write for that day would be $100. As the details of individual wagers were once written on small pieces of paper (a.k.a. tickets), wagering volume in race and sports books is referred to as write.

In general, sports book *win/(loss)* is the difference between the dollar-amount of payouts on winning tickets and the dollar-amount wagered on losing tickets. In race books, pari-mutuel wagering is the norm. Under this system, the casino's *win* is essentially a constant percentage of write (e.g., 20%). That is, a race book loss is not likely to occur under the pari-mutuel system,[3] especially over a monthly reporting period. For now, these definitions of win will suffice. Subsequent chapters will address the many details associated with race book and sports book operations.

In the race book and the sports book, *hold percentage* is equal to the casino's win (or loss) divided by the write. However, in the race book, under the pari-mutuel system, a negative hold percentage is extremely unlikely, even for daily results. To the contrary, the sports book can post negative hold percentages, as losses do occur.

Poker

Rake represents the dollar-value of the casino's fee, which is collected from the pot. The *pot* is the dollar-value of all player wagers placed on a hand of poker. As poker does not pit players against the casino, there is no casino advantage. Therefore, the rake compensates the casino for supplying and staffing the game. In most cases, the rake is based on a percentage of the pot, up to a maximum dollar amount (e.g., $4).[4] Some poker rooms charge the players via an hourly fee. Although this is technically different from

---

[3] Most states now require a winning wager to pay a minimum of $2.10 ($2.20 in some). Therefore, it is theoretically possible for a track and, consequently, a casino's race book to lose money on a particular race.
[4] In Nevada, the rake on any given hand may not exceed 10% of the dollar-value of the pot. See: Regulations of the Nevada Gaming Commission and State Gaming Control Board. Regulation 23, Card Games, § 0.50, part 1.

rake, its purpose is the same. Rake (or hourly fees) could be thought of as win or revenue, but, not as a loss, as neither rake nor hourly fees could result in a negative number.

General Expense Items

Cost of sales expense represents the resort's acquisition cost of items sold to its customers. For example, a casino-operated restaurant might buy a steak for $8.00, but the steak is sold to the customer for $32.00. In this case, the cost of sales would be $8.00. Cost of sales is often expressed and managed via margin. That is, $8.00 is 25% of the $32 retail value. The income statements of gaming departments do not feature cost of sales line items.

Comp. (hereinafter, comp) is an abbreviation for complimentary. *Comp expense* represents the recorded cost of complimentary awards to the casino.[5] Typically, these awards are earned by players when they reach defined levels of gaming activity or produce a certain level of profit for the casino. In essence, comps represent a form of reinvestment in players. Alternatively, comps could be thought of as a partial refund of the casino's win. Comps are also issued by management to recover service delivery failures. Although comps are common in U.S. casinos, they are far less relied upon in Asian casinos.

In this chapter, *payroll expense* refers to the dollar-amount of all salaries, wages, taxes, and benefits bestowed upon the employees and management. Benefits include the cost of group health insurance, employee meal subsidies, vacation pay, and more. Employer-paid payroll taxes are also included in payroll expense. Payroll is often referred to as the greatest controllable expense in hotel-casinos.

Operating expenses include items such as gaming taxes, supplies, and administrative expenses. In Nevada, gaming taxes appear in the income statements of gaming departments and represent the tax liability owed to the state's gaming regulatory agency. In short, if an expense item is not classified as cost of sales or some form of payroll expense, it is most likely an operating expense.

Income Statements for an Integrated Resort

The income statements shown in this section are based on the operating results of an integrated resort on the Las Vegas Strip. The purpose of these exhibits is to demonstrate the relative contribution of the various profit centers within such resorts. Again, results will vary based on the resort's specific nongaming amenities and its gaming and nongaming customer capacities. The income statements shown in this chapter do not necessarily represent a typical Las Vegas Strip hotel-casino.

---

[5] Internally, comp expenses should always equal comp revenues. For example, when Slot Marketing comps a player's hotel room, the Hotel Department records an amount of comp revenue that is equal to the comp expense recorded in Slot Marketing. However, no money actually changes hands. The amount recorded as comp revenue and comp expense is established by the property's internal policy.

Consolidated Income Statement

Table 2.1 summarizes the operating results of the overall property, with some revenue detail at the department level. The percentage (i.e., "%") column expresses the dollar-value of each line item as a percentage of net revenue.

Table 2.1
Las Vegas Strip Hotel-Casino Resort
Consolidated Income Statement
For the 12-month Period Ended 12/31/20XX

Description	Amount	%
Revenue:		
Table Games	$214,619,359	21.44
Slots	168,082,058	16.79
All Other Games (1)	13,239,362	1.32
Hotel	246,030,551	24.58
Food & Beverage	230,872,037	23.06
Entertainment	103,291,592	10.32
Retail	30,785,125	3.08
Other	90,730,866	9.06
Total Revenue	$1,097,650,950	109.65
Less: Comp. Expense	96,617,848	9.65
Net Revenue	$1,001,033,102	100.00
Expenses:		
Cost of Sales	$65,408,352	6.53
Payroll	315,921,600	31.56
Operating Expenses	292,099,434	29.18
EBITDA	$327,603,716	32.73

Notes. (1) Includes Race & Sports and Poker revenues.

Notice the ranking of departmental revenue production, from greatest to least (Top 5 producers only):

1. Hotel ($246M)
2. Food & Beverage ($231M)
3. Table Games ($215M)
4. Slots ($168M)
5. Entertainment ($103M)

The top two ranks belong to nongaming departments. In fact, only 40% of this property's net revenue comes from gaming areas. However, it is important to remember that revenue is not profit. Within the gaming areas, the Table Game Department outperformed the Slot Department. This is not likely to occur in properties in most U.S. markets; however, the Las Vegas Strip attracts many high rollers. These premium players often prefer table games over slots. For gaming resorts in most U.S. markets, the Slot Department will outperform the Table Game Department in terms of revenue production.

Comp Expense ($97M) represents the retail value of all comp revenues. Failure to deduct Comp Expense from Total Revenue would overstate the resort's true revenue.

The expenses of this property are typical in that payroll and operating expenses comprise the majority of the cost structure. Although not shown in Table 2.1, marketing expenses, gaming taxes, and building maintenance costs represent three of the greatest contributors to Operating Expenses. The bulk of the Cost of Sales (COS) comes from the Food & Beverage Department, while the Retail Department contributes most the remaining COS expense.

EBITDA stands for earnings before interest, taxes, depreciation, and amortization. At the property level, management teams are often evaluated by their ability to produce EBITDA. This performance metric represents the cash flow produced by the assets and the management of the property. In Table 2.1, the resort posted EBITDA of $327M, which represented 32.73% of net revenue.

Operating Income/(Loss) represents a profit center's contribution to the property-wide EBITDA listed in Table 2.1. Further, it is often used to evaluate the effectiveness of the profit center's management team. Although it does not appear as a line item in Table 2.1, Operating Income/(Loss) is the bottom line of each profit center's income statement. Examples of these income statements are reviewed throughout the remainder of this chapter.

Table Game Summary

Table 2.2 is a consolidated income statement summarizing results from the Table Games, Casino Marketing, VIP Services, and Limousine Services Departments.[6] It is most meaningful to include casino marketing costs in the analysis of table game results, as these costs drive table game revenue. To omit them would paint an optimistic bottom line for the Table Game Department. No results from poker or keno are included in Table 2.2. Only the results from the following games are included in Table 2.2: Baccarat, Blackjack, Craps, Roulette, and several carnival games such as Pai Gow. The term "carnival games" is used in the industry to describe the category of niche table games.

The win ($215M) divided by the Drop ($945M) equals the Hold % (22.70%). The drop and hold figures have little meaning as performance measures, because drop does not represent wagering volume. Comps expense includes the retail (or near retail) value of room, food, and beverage awards earned by rated players.[7] There are other forms of comps, but these are the most common categories. Operating Income ($60M) represents the contribution of the departments comprising the Table Game Summary to the overall property's EBITDA. Table 2.2 portrays a very good year. That is, for a Table Game Summary, an operating income margin of 28.03% is very good. This property has

---

[6] The VIP Services and Limousine Services Departments serve the casino's high-roller segment. The cost contributions from these departments are much less than those from the Casino Marketing Department.

[7] Management attempts to estimate the value of players with observed average bets equal to or greater than a specified dollar-amount. For example, policy might dictate that management rate any player with an observed average bet of $50 or more.

produced single-digit operating income margins in other years. The operating income volatility is driven by high-roller baccarat outcomes. The outcomes produced by a few premium players can exert a tremendous influence on the bottom line of the Table Game Summary.

Table 2.2
Las Vegas Strip Hotel-Casino Resort
Income Statement: Table Game Summary
For the 12-month Period Ended 12/31/20XX

Description	Amount	%
Volume & Hold:		
Drop	$945,459,730	n/a
Hold %	22.70%	n/a
Revenue:		
Win	$214,619,359	100.00
Expenses:		
Comps	$58,159,928	27.10
Payroll	43,870,759	20.44
Operating Expenses	52,424,504	24.43
Operating Income/(Loss)	$60,164,168	28.03

Slot Summary

Table 2.3 is a consolidated income statement summarizing results from both the Slot and Slot Marketing Departments. Slot marketing expenses are included, given their contribution to slot revenue generation.

Table 2.3
Las Vegas Strip Hotel-Casino Resort
Income Statement: Slot Summary
For the 12-month Period Ended 12/31/20XX

Description	Amount	%
Volume & Hold:		
Coin-in	$2,546,697,847	n/a
Hold %	6.60%	n/a
Revenue:		
Win	$168,082,058	100.00
Expenses:		
Comps	$25,887,969	15.40
Payroll	8,187,297	4.87
Operating Expenses	22,642,622	13.47
Operating Income/(Loss)	$111,364,170	66.26

The Slot Department accepted $2.5B in wagers in 20XX, retaining $168M in revenue. Despite producing less revenue than the Table Game Department, the Slot Department's contribution to the property EBITDA is substantially greater (i.e., $111M vs. $60M). Again, the Table 2.2 results represent a good year for the Table Game Department. The annual operating income on the Table Game Summary could easily dive to $20M in subsequent years. This volatility stems from high-roller wagering in the baccarat room.[8]

The Slot Summary contains much less expense than the Table Game Summary. Notice the difference in the operating income margins, with Table Games at 28.03% and Slots at 66.26%. The comp expense margin in Table Games (27.10%) is nearly twice that of Slots (15.40%). The payroll margin in Slots (4.87%) is remarkably lower than that of Table Games (20.44%), as the slot operation is much less labor intensive. Finally, the Slot Summary's operating expense margin (13.47%) is considerably less than the same margin in the Table Game Summary (24.43%).

Race & Sports Book Summary

Table 2.4 includes the combined results of the race and sports book operation. The operating income margin is impressive, at 57.85%. However, the dollar-amount of the operating income contributed to the property appears modest, next to the contributions from the Table Game and Slot Departments. Over the course of the year, the race book retained 20.50% of every dollar wagered, while the sports book retained 6.50% of every dollar wagered. Remember, in the books, Win divided by Write equals Hold %.

Poker

Despite all of the publicity, interest, and media coverage of poker, the direct contribution to an integrated resort's EBITDA is negligible. Table 2.5 provides support for this position, as the annual operating income for this 22-table poker room was only $2.2M. The operating income margin of 32.74% is impressive. However, the poker room requires a large area of the casino floor. An annual return of $2.2M on this space may be insufficient. That is, poker may not be the highest and best use of scarce casino floor space.

---

[8] Baccarat is the preferred game of most high-rollers. Given the relative magnitude of the wagers placed by these players, the operating income reported on the Table Game Summary is largely dependent upon baccarat wagering outcomes.

Table 2.4
Las Vegas Strip Hotel-Casino Resort
Income Statement: Race & Sports Book Summary
For the 12-month Period Ended 12/31/20XX

Description	Amount	%
Volume & Hold:		
Sports Book Write	$60,874,340	83.24
Race Book Write	12,260,596	16.76
Total Write	$73,134,936	100.00
Sports Book Hold %	6.50 %	n/a
Race Book Hold %	20.50%	n/a
Revenue:		
Sports Book Win	$3,956,832	61.15
Race Book Win	2,513,422	38.85
Total Win	$6,470,254	100.00
Expenses:		
Comps	$285,725	4.42
Payroll	741,197	11.46
Operating Expenses	1,700,347	26.28
Operating Income/(Loss)	$3,742,985	57.85

Table 2.5
Las Vegas Strip Hotel-Casino Resort
Income Statement: Poker
For the 12-month Period Ended 12/31/20XX

Description	Amount	%
Revenue:		
Rake	$6,769,107	100.00
Expenses:		
Comps	$1,094,060	16.16
Payroll	2,854,124	42.16
Operating Expenses	604,510	8.93
Operating Income/(Loss)	$2,216,413	32.74

Hotel Summary

The Hotel Summary includes the aggregated results from the following departments: Housekeeping, Bell & Door Services, Concierge, Reservations, Sales, and Hotel Administration. Table 2.6 demonstrates the tremendous EBITDA contributions from the hotel departments. This particular property is home to one of the Strip's largest hotels, in terms of the number of rooms. With operating income of $158M, hotel operations contribute more EBITDA than any other area of the property. The operating income margin of 64.58% is second only to the Slot Summary's 66.26% margin. However, it is not likely that the Hotel would post such impressive results without the draw power of the casino, retail, dining, and other amenities. Further, Las Vegas Strip resorts have thousands of hotel rooms. That said, integrated resorts in Las Vegas are increasingly reliant upon hotel operations for profits.

Table 2.6
Las Vegas Strip Hotel-Casino Resort
Income Statement: Hotel Summary
For the 12-month Period Ended 12/31/20XX

Description	Amount	%
Revenue:		
Cash	$200,848,069	81.64
Comp	45,182,482	18.36
Total Revenue	$246,030,551	100.00
Expenses:		
Payroll	$58,090,586	23.61
Operating Expenses	29,057,886	11.81
Operating Income/(Loss)	$158,882,079	64.58

Food Summary

Table 2.7 summarizes the results of 22 company-owned/operated dining outlets and the departments that support these outlets. The lease income from 12 additional outlets is also included in the Other Revenue line of Table 2.7. The leased outlets are owned and operated by external restaurant companies. In total, there are 34 outlets, which is a great number of dining establishments for any hotel-casino property. Moreover, this property features some world-class restaurants and celebrity chefs. Notice the operating income ($41M) and the associated margin (23.35%). These results may be interesting to those who subscribe to the theory of operating restaurants at a loss, to spur gaming volume. Table 2.7 includes costs from each internally-operated dining outlet and the following support departments: Cashiers, Stewards, Bakery, Butcher, and Garde Manger (prep. kitchen). The cost of operating the employee dining room is not included in Table 2.7, as it is considered to be an employee benefit.

Beverage Summary

Table 2.8 contains the annual operating results of 22 beverage outlets. Although the Beverage Summary's operating income margin (33.87%) is greater than that of the Food Summary (23.35%), the EBITDA contribution ($18M) of the beverage operation is far less than that of the restaurant operation ($41M). However, it should be noted that restaurants require a greater capital investment and more operating space.

Although casinos are known for not charging gamblers for drinks, notice the percentage of beverage comps (23.85%). That is, only 23.85% of all beverage sales are complimentary. Similarly, Tables 2.6 and 2.7 list comp sales just under 20% of total sales, in both the Food and Hotel Summaries. This may be surprising to some, as casino comp policies are often thought of as generous, if not cavalier.

Table 2.7
Las Vegas Strip Hotel-Casino Resort
Income Statement: Food Summary
For the 12-month Period Ended 12/31/20XX

Description	Amount	%
Revenue:		
Food – Cash	$113,409,764	64.09
Food – Comp	25,463,646	14.39
Beverage – Cash	22,382,187	12.65
Beverage – Comp	7,561,385	4.27
Other Revenue	8,132,150	4.60
Total Revenue	$176,949,132	100.00
Expenses:		
Food – COS	$35,404,087	20.01
Beverage – COS	6,839,852	3.87
Payroll	65,964,405	37.28
Operating Expenses	27,425,463	15.50
Operating Income/(Loss)	$41,315,325	23.35

Notes: There are 22 internally-operated dining outlets and 12 leased outlets.

Table 2.8
Las Vegas Strip Hotel-Casino Resort
Income Statement: Beverage Summary
For the 12-month Period Ended 12/31/20XX

Description	Amount	%
Revenue:		
Food – Cash	$2,899,868	5.38
Food – Comp (1)	2,185	0.00
Beverage – Cash	34,688,655	64.33
Beverage – Comp	12,861,178	23.85
Other Revenue (2)	3,471,019	6.44
Total Revenue	$53,922,905	100.00
Expenses:		
Food – COS	$550,804	1.02
Beverage – COS	9,199,341	17.06
Payroll	17,682,426	32.79
Operating Expenses	8,224,492	15.25
Operating Income/(Loss)	$18,265,842	33.87

Notes: (1) Less than 0.005% of Total Revenue. (2) Primarily cover charges in nightclubs. (3) There are 22 beverage outlets.

Showroom Entertainment

Table 2.9 includes results from the operation of a major Las Vegas Strip production show. Table 2.9 does not include revenues and expenses from the property's other entertainment venues. However, profit-sharing payments to the show's co-developer are included in Operating Expenses. While the show's $21M contribution to property EBITDA would appear substantial, if not surprising, it is likely that the capital investment in the showroom and show development would be equally shocking. Typically, the return on investment for production shows in hotel-casinos is less than stellar. Many believe that extravagant shows indirectly drive the more profitable gaming business, hence the tolerance for poor returns. However, research findings suggest that these indirect contributions to gaming volumes may be minimal.[9] The relationship between show attendance and critical nongaming business volumes remains largely unexamined.

Table 2.9
Las Vegas Strip Hotel-Casino Resort
Income Statement: Showroom
For the 12-month Period Ended 12/31/20XX

Description	Amount	%
Revenue:		
Show – Cash	$71,312,917	96.17
Show – Comp	2,837,359	3.83
Total Revenue	$74,150,276	100.00
Expenses:		
Payroll	$12,565,673	16.95
Operating Expenses	40,970,215	55.25
Operating Income/(Loss)	$20,614,388	27.80

Nightclub

The results shown in Table 2.10 are also included in the Beverage Summary (Table 2.8). The nightclub recorded annual operating income of $3.9M, with an operating income margin of 33.73%. Less than 5% of the $11M in total sales were comp sales. For this property, the EBITDA contribution from this single nightclub ($3.9M) was greater than that produced by the race and sports books ($3.7M) and the 22-table poker room ($2.2M).

Spa

Table 2.11 contains the annual operating results for the Spa Department. These results include lease payments from the external operator of the salon. That is, the hotel-casino does not operate the salon, choosing to lease this outlet to an external salon company.

---

[9] Suh, E.J. &, Lucas, A.F. (2009). Estimating the impact of showroom entertainment on the gaming volumes on Las Vegas hotel-casinos. Manuscript submitted to *Journal of Hospitality & Tourism Research*.

Altogether, the Spa Department contributed $3.6M in EBITDA, while posting an operating income margin of 39.43%.

Table 2.10
Las Vegas Strip Hotel-Casino Resort
Income Statement: Nightclub
For the 12-month Period Ended 12/31/20XX

Description	Amount	%
Revenue:		
Food – Cash	$1,778,377	15.48
Food – Comp (1)	213	0.00
Beverage – Cash	6,472,165	56.33
Beverage – Comp	557,050	4.85
Other Revenue (2)	2,681,998	23.34
Total Revenue	$11,489,803	100.00
Expenses:		
Food – COS	$335,911	2.92
Beverage – COS	1,089,063	9.48
Payroll	3,125,962	27.21
Operating Expenses	3,063,265	26.66
Operating Income/(Loss)	$3,875,602	33.73

Notes: (1) Less than 0.005% of Total Revenue.
(2) Primarily cover charges.

Table 2.11
Las Vegas Strip Hotel-Casino Resort
Income Statement: Spa
For the 12-month Period Ended 12/31/20XX

Description	Amount	%
Revenue:		
Salon	$6,833,484	75.09
Spa – Cash	748,465	8.22
Spa – Comp	1,331,715	14.63
Spa – Other	186,673	2.05
Total Revenue	$9,100,337	100.00
Expenses:		
Payroll	$4,145,447	45.55
Operating Expenses	1,366,796	15.02
Operating Income/(Loss)	$3,588,094	39.43

Departmental Profit Rankings

From Table 2.1, the following list ranks the top five sources of revenue, from greatest to least.

1. Hotel ($246M)
2. Food & Beverage ($231M)
3. Table Games ($215M)
4. Slots ($168M)
5. Entertainment ($103M)

From the departmental income statements, the next list ranks the top five sources of operating income (EBITDA contributions), from greatest to least.

1. Hotel ($158.9M)
2. Slots ($111.4M)
3. Table Games ($60.2M)
4. Food & Beverage ($59.6M)
5. Entertainment – Showroom only ($20.6M)

The revenue contributions are much more evenly distributed than the profit contributions, which are heavily reliant on the Hotel and Slot Departments. The pie charts shown in Figures 2.1 & 2.2 highlight the differences between revenue and profit contributions. For example, the Hotel and Slot Departments contributed 44% of the revenues produced by the top five revenue sources and 65% of the profits generated by the top five profit sources.

Finally, both of these charts suggest that the management of this property should consider tackling the difficult task of tracking nongaming revenues. That is, instead of only offering customers a tracking card to record their gaming activity, attempts should be made to record their nongaming purchases as well. Given the profit contributions of these nongaming departments, they can no longer be thought of as amenities.

Unfortunately, there are many information technology challenges related to tracking nongaming expenditures. A strong commitment from senior management and financial resources are required to overcome these challenges. That said, industry leaders have made considerable progress tracking and recording the nongaming expenditures of individual patrons, while other companies still have a long way to go.

Moving Beyond Casinos

Given the magnitude of nongaming revenues and profits, the idea of the integrated resort has gained some political traction in emerging markets. This is especially true for markets outside the United States. That is, the notion of legalizing gaming in new jurisdictions is softened by the integrated resort's increased reliance on nongaming profit centers. This allows proponents of gaming to argue that these properties are resorts first and casinos second. Given the considerable resistance to gaming development initiatives, the integrated resort offers an improved position when debating the benefits and consequences of legalized gaming.

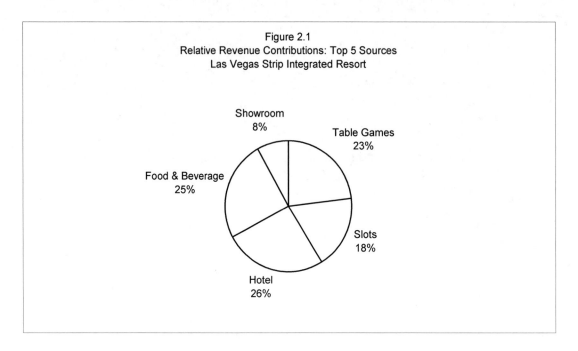

Figure 2.1
Relative Revenue Contributions: Top 5 Sources
Las Vegas Strip Integrated Resort

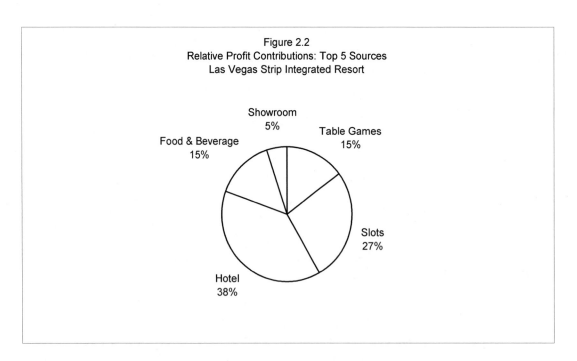

Figure 2.2
Relative Profit Contributions: Top 5 Sources
Las Vegas Strip Integrated Resort

Questions/Exercises:

1. Which term from Chapter 2 best describes a gaming property that features a wide variety of nongaming amenities?

2. Use the following data to compute the dollar-value of the foreign gaming cheques in the drop boxes.

> Markers issued: $1,000,000
> Markers redeemed: $800,000
> Cash: $90,000
> Casino cheques: $0
> Total drop for the period: $298,000

3. In Nevada, what does table game drop represent? That is, does it represent the dollar-value of customer buy-ins, where "buy-ins" represents the dollar-value of all gaming cheques purchased in a given period? Does it represent wagering volume? Explain your answers.

4. Which term best describes the difference between the dollar-amount of all wagers accepted by slot machines and the dollar-amount of all forms of slot machine payouts?

5. If a casino's slot win is $255,400 and its coin-in for the same period is $2,900,000, what is the associated hold?

6. Which profit center made the greatest contribution to property-wide EBITDA?

7. Which profit center reported an operating income margin greater than that reported on the Hotel Summary?

8. Which *gaming* profit center made the greatest property-wide contribution to EBITDA?

9. In the poker department, both win and revenue are also referred to as _____.

10. Consider the following scenario. A slot player's wagering activity earns her a dinner for four in the resort's gourmet restaurant. With respect to the Slot Summary Income Statement, in which line item would the internal cost of this dinner appear?

11. _____ is a general measure of business volume in the race book.

12. With regard to the top five sources of profit contributions (as presented in this chapter), what percentage of profit came from nongaming sources?

13. What percentage of the Net Revenue in Table 2.1 came from gaming departments? Show your work/calculations. Assume "Other" refers to nongaming revenue sources.

Chapter 3
Profit Structure of Repeater-Market Resorts

What is a repeater-market resort?
How are repeater-market resorts different from integrated resorts?
Which departments produce the greatest revenues?
Which departments produce the greatest profits?

Scope

This chapter reviews the annual operating results of a Las Vegas hotel-casino, which features a customer base characterized by frequent visitation (i.e., a *repeater clientele*). Those who rely on such a clientele are said to operate in *repeater markets*. Selected results are compared and contrasted with those produced by the Las Vegas Strip resort examined in Chapter 2. The Las Vegas Strip may represent the most pure form of a *destination market*. That is, the majority of the patrons are tourists who live outside of Nevada. This chapter will highlight the critical differences and similarities in the operating results of these two very different forms of hotel-casinos.

Chapter Goals

- Define key industry terms used to discuss types of markets and resorts as well as forms of clientele
- Demonstrate the profitability of a repeater-market hotel-casino
- Demonstrate the divergent sources of departmental revenues and profits within a repeater-market hotel-casino
- Compare and contrast the critical results of the repeater-market property with those from the integrated resort reviewed in Chapter 2.

Terminology & Conditions

The bulk of terminology critical to the discussion of a hotel-casino's income statements has been defined in Chapter 2. Any terms or conditions directly related to repeater-market operators will be defined in this chapter. All other terms will be defined as they appear in the text.

Markets & Clientele

In the U.S. and abroad, most casinos cater to a customer base characterized by frequent visitation. This type of customer base is referred to as a repeater clientele. In general, a repeater clientele is comprised of local residents and patrons residing within a short drive of the property (e.g., a one-hour drive). A repeater clientele might average three gaming trips per week, as opposed to the clientele of a property in a destination market, which might average three trips per year.

General language is used to define terms related to market types and customer bases, as no precise definition is available. Consider the Las Vegas Strip, possibly the most pure form of a destination market. Although Las Vegas Strip resorts heavily rely on a tourist clientele, local Las Vegans do patronize Strip resorts, creating a hybrid customer base. Now let's consider the case of the off-Strip hotel-casino properties in Las Vegas. This market is often referred to as the *Las Vegas locals' market*. However, according to Nevada law, these Clark County properties must build a hotel with at least 300 rooms to receive a non-restricted gaming license.[1] In order to fill the hotel rooms, these properties are forced to pursue tourists in markets outside of Nevada. Of course, this results in a hybrid customer base that features the opposite condition from that of the hybrid base found in Strip resorts. That is, off-Strip properties rely primarily on local residents, but also cater to tourists to fill the hotel rooms.

Save the extreme cases, the nature of a gaming property's clientele may be most easily described by way of a continuum. Figure 3.1 illustrates a continuum anchored by "100% Tourist Clientele" and "100% Local Resident Clientele." Although very few, if any, gaming properties would fall on these anchor points, the majority of resorts would be clearly positioned toward one end of the continuum. For example, a Las Vegas Strip property, such as the one reviewed in Chapter 2, has been positioned on the continuum along with an off-Strip property.

Figure 3.1
Hotel-Casino Resort Clientele Continuum

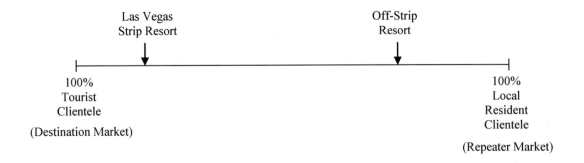

---

[1] Kilby, J., Fox. J., & Lucas, A.F. (2004). *Casino Operations Management*, 2nd ed. New York: Wiley.

Differences in Property Structure

Integrated Resorts

Integrated resorts are born out of long-standing competitive pressures common to mature markets. The Las Vegas Strip features many integrated resorts. As gaming has been legal for many years in Nevada, operators on the Strip have endeavored to differentiate themselves from the competition. Las Vegas must continually reinvent itself, as its economy relies heavily on tourism. If the city fails to provide new reasons to visit, the economy will stall. The integrated resort is the result of efforts to develop new and innovative attractions. World-class shopping and dining, incredible hotel suites, and amazing entertainment venues have all been used to attract more visitors. Specifically, they have been developed to attract the most valuable customers – the premium players, also known as high-rollers. Even the properties themselves have become must-see destinations, featuring amenities such as erupting volcanoes, dolphin habitats, pirate ship battles, and magnificent fountains and gardens.

As most of the recent innovations have been related to premium accommodations, high-end retail, and gourmet dining experiences, it is the non-gaming areas that have experienced remarkable growth. However, these amenities were funded with profits from the casino. These extravagant attractions require considerable sums of development and construction capital. Additionally, a tremendous amount of physical space is required to develop these non-gaming amenities. Given the capital and physical space requirements, most gaming companies either cannot or do not offer the type of non-gaming attractions offered in integrated resorts. Moreover, most U.S. gaming locations would not attract the high-end clientele drawn to the integrated resorts on the Las Vegas Strip.

Repeater-market Properties

The primary attraction of these resorts is usually gaming itself. In most cases, these properties are built in markets that are far less competitive than the Las Vegas Strip. In fact, competition in most U.S. gaming jurisdictions is either restrained by a limited number of licenses or the acquisition of a tribal-state compact. Further, most successful U.S. casinos are surrounded by considerable population bases. To the contrary, Las Vegas is a remote location, with the nearest major population base over 300 miles away. The remote location requires operators to develop more compelling attractions, as patrons are asked to travel a greater distance to visit the property.

In repeater markets, revenue and profit contributions are dominated by gaming departments, as there is usually insufficient market pressure to develop extensive non-gaming amenities. Also, non-gaming amenities such as gourmet restaurants and high-end retail offer considerably greater profit margins than dining and retail outlets at lower price points. Most properties in repeater markets do not have a clientele capable of supporting profitable high-end amenities, so the development of extravagant non-gaming attractions is inherently less attractive.

For the most part, Atlantic City is a repeater market, given its reliance on *drive-up business*. That is, patrons who live within a three-hour drive of Atlantic City. These customers are also referred to as *day-trippers*. Macau could also be considered a day-trip market, although the goal of the Cotai Strip is to extend the average stay of visitors. These two markets are mentioned because they both attract a considerable number of premium players, yet neither has developed the non-gaming infrastructure of the Las Vegas Strip. In both cases, the operators in these markets seem to feel little pressure to develop such attractions. In Macau, casino operators cater to a clientele primarily interested in gaming, making amenity development less of concern. The Cotai Strip resorts (in Macau) offer more non-gaming amenities in an attempt to diversify the tourism base and extend the length of time spent on the island.

Income Statements for a Repeater-market Property

The income statements shown in this section compare the results of a repeater-market resort with those from the integrated resort examined in Chapter 2.[2] The purpose of this section is twofold. First, for the repeater-market resort, the diverse operating results of the profit centers are examined. Second, these results are compared against those produced by the integrated resort. This side-by-side presentation of income statements should provide a unique perspective, regarding the differences and similarities of these two types of resorts.

Consolidated Income Statement

Table 3.1 summarizes the operating results of the overall properties, with some revenue detail at the department level. The percentage (i.e., %) column expresses the dollar-value of each line item as a percentage of Net Revenue.

It is common for the Slot Department to be the dominate revenue producer for resorts operating in repeater markets. The resort examined in Table 3.1 is certainly no exception to this rule. With $151M in revenue, the Slot Department contributed 49.33% of the net revenues. The Food & Beverage Department was the second greatest producer of revenues, with $83M, $68M less than the Slot Department's contribution.

The Table Game Department's revenue production ($29M) was remarkably low. This is not uncommon in repeater markets, as the supply of profitable table game players is much less than that of profitable slot players.

Non-gaming revenues were much less of a factor in the off-Strip resort. In fact, gaming revenues comprised 64.63% of Net Revenue, while the same three line items accounted for only 39.55% of Net Revenue in the Las Vegas Strip resort.

---

[2] The LV Strip resort did not offer bingo, so no comparable results were available for this department.

Table 3.1
Las Vegas Repeater-Market Resort v. Las Vegas Strip Resort
Consolidated Income Statement
For the 12-month Period Ended 12/31/20XX

Description	Repeater-Market Resort		Las Vegas Strip Resort	
	Amount	%	Amount	%
Revenue:				
Table Games	$28,776,387	9.43	$214,619,359	21.44
Slots	150,513,597	49.33	168,082,058	16.79
All Other Games (1)	17,894,834	5.87	13,239,362	1.32
Hotel	43,064,380	14.11	246,030,551	24.58
Food & Beverage	82,703,927	27.11	230,872,037	23.06
Entertainment	436,711	0.14	103,291,592	10.32
Retail	6,408,998	2.10	30,785,125	3.08
Other	5,819,100	1.91	90,730,866	9.06
Total Revenue	$335,617,935	110.00	$1,097,650,950	109.65
Less: Comp. Expense	30,518,638	10.00	96,617,848	9.65
Net Revenue	$305,099,296	100.00	$1,001,033,102	100.00
Expenses:				
Cost of Sales	$24,476,437	8.02	$65,408,352	6.53
Payroll	94,027,689	30.82	315,921,600	31.56
Operating Expenses	93,378,830	30.61	292,099,434	29.18
EBITDA	$93,216,340	30.55	$327,603,716	32.73

Notes. (1) Within the repeater-market resort, includes poker, race & sports book, bingo, and keno revenues. Strip resort includes poker and race & sports revenues. Keno and bingo were not offered by the Strip resort.

Notice the rankings of departmental revenue production, from greatest to least (Top 5 producers only). The revenue contributions in the Strip resort were much more balanced, while the Slot Department dominated the revenues of the off-Strip resort.

Repeater-Market Resort	Integrated Resort
1. Slots ($151M, 49.33%)	1. Hotel ($246M, 24.58%)
2. Food & Beverage ($83M, 27.11%)	2. Food & Beverage ($231M, 23.06%)
3. Hotel ($43M, 14.11%)	3. Table Games ($215M, 21.44%)
4. Table Games ($29M, 9.43%)	4. Slots ($168M, 16.79%)
5. All Other Games ($18M, 5.87%)	5. Entertainment ($103M, 10.32%)

Notice the percentage-point difference between the #1 and #3 revenue producers. In the Strip resort, Hotel led the way with 24.58% of net revenues, with the #3 producer, Table Games, contributing 21.44% of net revenues, for a difference of 3.14 percentage points. In the repeater-market resort, Slots produced 49.33% of the net revenues, with the #3 producer, Hotel, contributing 14.11% of net revenues, for a staggering difference of 35.22 percentage points.

One final note on the revenue section; the Comp Expense Margin was 10.00% for the repeater-market property. This mark was very near the 9.65% margin produced by the Strip resort. The Comp Expense line item represents the retail value of the comps awarded to customers. Because comp expenses equal comp revenues, this line item could be labeled Comp Revenue. Comps are subtracted from Total Revenues, as the property receives no money from the customers who receive these awards. To include comp revenues, would overstate the property's true revenues. In any case, the margin itself means very little. That is, management could have done a terrible job of managing individual comp decisions, while producing a 10.00% margin. To the contrary, management could have done a great job of awarding comps to players, while producing the same 10.00% margin. Meaningful analysis of comp management is something that occurs at the individual player level, as opposed to the aggregate level (as shown in Table 3.1). Reviewing a Comp Expense Margin on a consolidated income statement will not tell you whether casino executives have managed comps effectively.[3]

For the repeater-market resort, nothing in the expense section of Table 3.1 was surprising, as payroll and operating expenses were the primary cost contributors. The property EBITDA was $93M, with an impressive margin of 30.55%. In terms of expense and EBITDA margins, the two resorts posted similar results; however, the Strip resort produced much more EBITDA, in terms of dollars. The Strip resort should produce more EBITDA, as it would certainly require a greater investment to build an integrated resort on the Las Vegas Strip. In fact, the number of hotel rooms in the Strip resort was more than four times that of the off-Strip resort.

Table Games Summary

Table 3.2 is a consolidated income statement summarizing results from the Table Game Department, Casino Marketing Department, and other smaller support departments such as VIP Services. With respect to the repeater-market property, no results from the Poker, Keno, Bingo, or Race & Sports Book Departments are included in Table 3.2. Only the results from the following games are included in Table 3.2: Baccarat, Blackjack, Craps, Roulette, and several carnival games such as Let it Ride and Pai Gow Poker. The term "carnival games" is used to describe the category of niche table games.[4]

The most remarkable result is the Operating Income Margin. Only 5.13% of every dollar of win made its way to the bottom line. Single-digit profit margins (i.e., below 10%) on Table Game Summaries are not uncommon in the contemporary casino industry. In fact, the Strip resort posted a single-digit operating Income Margin in the previous fiscal year.

---

[3] For more on comp theory, see: Lucas, A.F. & Kilby, J. (2008). *Principles of Casino Marketing*. San Diego: Okie International.

[4] In the U.S., "carnival games" is used to collectively refer to all table games other than blackjack, baccarat, craps, and roulette. Several of these carnival games will be further described in a subsequent chapter.

Table 3.2
Las Vegas Repeater-Market Resort v. Las Vegas Strip Resort
Income Statement: Table Games Summary
For the 12-month Period Ended 12/31/20XX

Description	Repeater-Market Resort		Las Vegas Strip Resort	
	Amount	%	Amount	%
Volume & Hold:				
Drop	$211,417,962	n/a	$945,459,730	n/a
Hold %	13.61%	n/a	22.70%	n/a
Revenue:				
Win	$28,776,387	100.00	$214,619,359	100.00
Expenses:				
Comps	$8,355,365	29.04	$58,159,928	27.10
Payroll	11,365,580	39.50	43,870,759	20.44
Operating Expenses	7,577,865	26.33	52,424,504	24.43
Operating Income/(Loss)	$1,477,577	5.13	$60,164,168	28.03

The Payroll Margin for the off-Strip resort was nearly twice that of the Strip resort. However, the Strip resort's Payroll Margin looks to be artificially low, due to elevated win levels. That is, in a given period, high-rollers can offer tremendous contributions to casino win, with relatively small increases in labor expense. This results in favorable payroll margins. However, high-rollers can destroy income statements when they win.

When comparing results, it must be noted that the Strip resort had a very successful year, recording an Operating Income Margin of 28.03%. Further, the Strip resort won 22.70% of the drop, while the off-Strip resort held only 13.61%. Although both drop and hold percentage are questionable performance measures, a difference in the annual hold percentage of 9.09 percentage points is considerable.

Slot Summary

Table 3.3 is a consolidated income statement summarizing results from both the Slot and Slot Marketing Departments. Slot marketing expenses are included, given their contribution to slot revenue generation.

The Slot Department of the off-Strip resort accepted $2.8B in wagers in 20XX, retaining $151M in revenue. The coin-in level exceeded that produced by the Strip resort, while the win fell just short of the Strip resort's mark of $168M. In slots, the hold percentage is meaningful, as coin-in does represent the amount of money wagered by players. That said, the off-Strip resort held 5.47%, while the Strip resort held 6.60%. This is not unusual, as resorts catering to a repeat clientele usually do have lower hold percentages.

Table 3.3
Las Vegas Repeater-Market Resort v. Las Vegas Strip Resort
Income Statement: Slot Summary
For the 12-month Period Ended 12/31/20XX

Description	Repeater-Market Resort		Las Vegas Strip Resort	
	Amount	%	Amount	%
Volume & Hold:				
Coin-in	$2,752,543,172	n/a	$2,546,697,847	n/a
Hold %	5.47%	n/a	6.60%	n/a
Revenue:				
Win	$150,513,597	100.00	$168,082,058	100.00
Expenses:				
Comps	$15,897,909	10.56	$25,887,969	15.40
Payroll	5,213,567	3.46	8,187,297	4.87
Operating Expenses	30,399,078	20.20	22,642,622	13.47
Operating Income/(Loss)	$99,003,043	65.78	$111,364,170	66.26

The executives of properties in repeater markets realize that the spend-per-trip for their clientele is smaller than that of a destination resort's customer base, but the average number of trips per year is much greater. Slot players in repeater markets are thought to have a greater awareness of and sensitivity to the casino's advantage, resulting in slot machines with lower house advantages. Conversely, a tourist-based clientele is thought to be less aware of the casino advantage, resulting in games with a greater house edge.

Finally, and most importantly, the Slot Department's $99M contribution to the property's EBITDA is substantially greater than that of any other department in the off-Strip property. In fact, it is $75M greater than the second greatest EBITDA contribution. The Operating Income Margin of 65.78% is also greater than that of any department in the off-Strip resort, and very near the Strip resort's margin (66.26%).

Race & Sports Book Summary

Table 3.4 includes the combined operating results of the Race & Sports Book Department. The Operating Income Margin was impressive, at 47.85%. However, the dollar-amount of Operating Income contributed to the property appears inconsequential, next to the Slot Department's $99M contribution. Over the course of the year, the race book retained 16.91% of every dollar wagered, while the sports book won 5.49% of the dollar-amount wagered.

Although the Operating Income Margin (47.85%) was less than the Strip resort's mark of 57.85%, the race and sports books in the off-Strip resort produced $5.1M in operating income, while the Strip resort's books produced $3.7M of the same. This result was surprising. Typically, the books in a Strip resort would be expected to outperform those in off-Strip resorts.

Table 3.4
Las Vegas Repeater-Market Resort v. Las Vegas Strip Resort
Income Statement: Race & Sports Book Summary
For the 12-month Period Ended 12/31/20XX

Description	Repeater-Market Resort		Las Vegas Strip Resort	
	Amount	%	Amount	%
Volume & Hold:				
Sports Book Write	$94,369,325	74.56	$60,874,340	83.24
Race Book Write	32,204,981	25.44	12,260,596	16.76
Total Write	$126,574,306	100.00	$73,134,936	100.00
Sports Book Hold %	5.49%	n/a	6.50%	n/a
Race Book Hold %	16.91%	n/a	20.50%	n/a
Revenue:				
Sports Book Win	$5,178,493	48.74	$3,956,832	61.15
Race Book Win	5,446,513	51.26	2,513,422	38.85
Total Win	$10,625,006	100.00	$6,470,254	100.00
Expenses:				
Comps	$1,327,015	12.49	$285,725	4.42
Payroll	1,102,245	10.37	741,197	11.46
Operating Expenses	3,111,196	29.28	1,700,347	26.28
Operating Income/(Loss)	$5,084,550	47.85	$3,742,985	57.85

Poker

As mentioned in Chapter 2, the popularity of poker is far greater than its contribution to the property's EBITDA. Table 3.5 contains the annual operating results of the off-Strip property's 20-table poker room. The $3.0M of Operating Income was considerably greater than the $2.2M produced by the Strip resort's 22-table poker room. The Operating Income Margin of 51.59% was impressive and well beyond the Strip resort's mark of 32.74%. Typically, the poker room of a Strip resort would be expected to outperform a poker room located in an off-Strip resort. These two rooms had nearly the same number of tables, with the Strip resort offering two more tables than the off-Strip property.

The poker room did produce twice the Operating Income of the Table Game Department. This result is alarming, as there were over three times as many table games on the casino floor. When the physical space required to offer the games is considered, the profit per square foot in the poker room would be considerably greater than that produced by the area housing the table games.

Table 3.5
Las Vegas Repeater-Market Resort v. Las Vegas Strip Resort
Income Statement: Poker
For the 12-month Period Ended 12/31/20XX

Description	Repeater-Market Resort		Las Vegas Strip Resort	
	Amount	%	Amount	%
Revenue:				
Rake	$5,777,226	100.00	$6,769,107	100.00
Expenses:				
Comps	$777,084	13.45	$1,094,060	16.16
Payroll	1,738,012	30.08	2,854,124	42.16
Operating Expenses	281,926	4.88	604,510	8.93
Operating Income/(Loss)	$2,980,204	51.59	$2,216,413	32.74

Bingo

From Table 3.6, the off-Strip resort recorded $9.1M in write. In bingo, *take* and *sales* are alternative terms for write. Write represents the dollar-amount of bingo ticket sales. Payouts are subtracted from write to arrive at win. The win of $715,659 was equal to 7.86% of the write. Therefore, the hold percentage was 7.86%.

Table 3.6
Las Vegas Repeater-Market Resort
Income Statement: Bingo Room
For the 12-month Period Ended 12/31/20XX

Description	Amount	%
Volume:		
Write	$9,110,511	n/a
Hold %	7.86%	n/a
Revenue:		
Win	$715,659	100.00
Expenses:		
Comps	$98,776	13.80
Payroll	411,820	57.54
Operating Expenses	25,349	3.54
Operating Income/(Loss)	$179,714	25.11

The bingo room may be the most curious use of space in the entire property. That is, this was an enormous room that produced a mere $179,714 in operating income. Of all the gaming areas, the bingo room undoubtedly produced the least profit per square foot. The Strip resort did not offer bingo, so no comparable results were available.

Bingo is often credited with indirect contributions to slot revenue, hence the tolerance for the low levels of departmental operating income. The theory holds that the bingo players choose to patronize a given resort because it offers bingo, but, after playing bingo, these patrons become slot players.[5] While popular, this theory lacks empirical support for the production of meaningful incremental slot profits from bingo players.[6]

Hotel Summary

The Hotel Summary includes room sales and the aggregated expenses from the following departments: Housekeeping, Bell Desk, Valet, Concierge, Reservations, Group Sales, and Hotel Administration. With Operating Income of $24.3M, the Hotel Summary shown in Table 3.7 represents the second greatest contribution to the property's EBITDA. As previously noted, the Strip resort's hotel capacity was over four times that of the off-Strip resort, hence the considerable difference in operating income between the two properties.[7]

The Operating Income Margin of 56.44% was impressive, but less than the Strip resort's 64.58%. Perhaps the greater room capacity allowed for greater sales, which, in turn, allowed the Strip resort to offset more of its fixed operating costs. With regard to revenues, the percentages of cash and comp sales were nearly identical across the two resorts, as was the percentage of payroll expense.

Table 3.7
Las Vegas Repeater-Market Resort v. Las Vegas Strip Resort
Income Statement: Hotel Summary
For the 12-month Period Ended 12/31/20XX

Description	Repeater-Market Resort		Las Vegas Strip Resort	
	Amount	%	Amount	%
Revenue:				
Cash	$35,205,703	81.75	$200,848,069	81.64
Comp	7,858,677	18.25	45,182,482	18.36
Total Revenue	$43,064,380	100.00	$246,030,551	100.00
Expenses:				
Payroll	$10,010,556	23.25	$58,090,586	23.61
Operating Expenses	8,748,938	20.32	29,057,886	11.81
Operating Income/(Loss)	$24,304,886	56.44	$158,882,079	64.58

[5] Lucas, A.F. & Kilby, J. (2008). *Principles of Casino Marketing*. San Diego: Okie International.
[6] Lucas, A.F., Dunn, W.T., & Kharitonova, A. (2006). Estimating the indirect gaming contribution of bingo rooms. *Gaming Research & Review Journal, 10*(2), 39-54.
[7] The specific number of rooms is withheld here to protect the anonymity of the two casinos that donated the data for this chapter.

Food Summary

Table 3.8 summarizes the annual results of the off-Strip resort's 14 dining outlets, which ranged from snack bars to gourmet restaurants. Seven of these outlets were operated by the hotel-casino company. The remaining seven outlets were operated by external restaurant companies. Although this is a considerable number of dining outlets for an off-Strip resort, the number falls well short of the Strip resort's 34 dining outlets. Table 3.8 includes costs from each internally-operated dining outlet and the following support departments: Cashiers, Stewards, Bakery, Butcher, and Garde Manger (prep. kitchen). The cost of operating the employee dining room is not included in Table 3.8, as it is considered to be an employee benefit. Although Table 3.8 aggregates the results of all dining outlets, management would produce and review a monthly income statement for each individual dining outlet.

Table 3.8
Las Vegas Repeater-Market Resort v. Las Vegas Strip Resort
Income Statement: Food Summary
For the 12-month Period Ended 12/31/20XX

Description	Repeater-Market Resort		Las Vegas Strip Resort	
	Amount	%	Amount	%
Revenue:				
Food – Cash	$37,738,885	62.50	$113,409,764	64.09
Food – Comp	10,074,764	16.68	25,463,646	14.39
Beverage – Cash	6,340,133	10.50	22,382,187	12.65
Beverage – Comp	2,113,378	3.50	7,561,385	4.27
Other Revenue	4,115,057	6.82	8,132,150	4.60
Total Revenue	$60,382,216	100.00	$176,949,132	100.00
Expenses:				
Food – COS	$13,125,187	21.74	$35,404,087	20.01
Beverage – COS	3,001,509	4.97	6,839,852	3.87
Payroll	26,099,960	43.22	65,964,405	37.28
Operating Expenses	9,183,529	15.21	27,425,463	15.50
Operating Income/(Loss)	$8,972,031	14.86	$41,315,325	23.35

The EBITDA contribution from the Food & Beverage Department was $9.0M, well short of the $41.3M produced by the Strip resort. However, the Strip resort offered more than two times the number of dining outlets (i.e., 34 vs. 14). Further, the Strip property offered a greater number of gourmet/signature restaurants, which are capable of producing significant operating income contributions.

It is important to remember that Table 3.8 includes comp revenues which overstate the operating income levels of both properties. That is, the restaurants receive no cash for the comp sales, yet the outlets are credited for this business as though cash was received. The

Operating Income results shown in Table 3.8 would be noticeably less, if the effects of the comp transactions were removed. However, as there are costs associated with comp sales, such as cost of goods sold and labor costs, it is difficult for management to accurately segregate these costs. As a result, the comp sales and the associated costs are left in the Food and Beverage Income Statement, allowing executives to determine how well the dining outlets are managed. Remember, if only comp sales were removed, all the expense margins would be overstated, making it difficult for management to assess the operating efficiency of the outlets.

Beverage Summary

Table 3.9 contains the annual aggregated operating results of nine beverage outlets/bars. The revenue section was dominated by cash sales, which may be surprising to some, given the notoriety of industry practices such as the provision of free drinks to gamblers. Just under one third of the off-Strip resort's Total Revenue was comp revenue. The off-Strip resort produced Operating Income of $7.7M, with an Operating Income Margin of 34.54%. While the margin was competitive with the Strip property, the Operating Income was well below that of the Strip resort. Despite the moderate level of comp revenue, adjusting the income statement for the net effects of comp transactions would cut deeply into the Operating Income lines of both properties.

Table 3.9
Las Vegas Repeater-Market Resort v. Las Vegas Strip Resort
Income Statement: Beverage Summary
For the 12-month Period Ended 12/31/20XX

Description	Repeater-Market Resort		Las Vegas Strip Resort	
	Amount	%	Amount	%
Revenue:				
Food – Cash	$527,940	2.37	$2,899,868	5.38
Food – Comp (1)	88,168	0.39	2,185	0.00
Beverage – Cash	14,034,101	62.87	34,688,655	64.33
Beverage – Comp	7,215,046	32.32	12,861,178	23.85
Other Revenue	456,456	2.04	3,471,019	6.44
Total Revenue	$22,321,711	100.00	$53,922,905	100.00
Expenses:				
Food – COS	$349,517	1.57	$550,804	1.02
Beverage – COS	5,556,708	24.89	9,199,341	17.06
Payroll	6,832,379	30.61	17,682,426	32.79
Operating Expenses	1,872,143	8.39	8,224,492	15.25
Operating Income/(Loss)	$7,710,964	34.54	$18,265,842	33.87

Notes: (1) Less than 0.005% of the Strip resort's Total Revenue.

The Beverage Cost of Sales (COS) margin was noticeably greater in the off-Strip resort. This could be an artifact of the higher drink prices on the Las Vegas Strip. With a clientele heavily dependent on locals, the off-Strip property chose to competitively position itself as an attractive price-value option. Lower drink prices were part of this comprehensive strategy.

Nightclub

From Table 3.10, the nightclub recorded annual Operating Income of $649,329, with an Operating Income Margin of 25.84%. Only 8.08% of the $2.5M in Total Revenue was achieved via comp sales. As expected, the Strip resort's nightclub produced a considerably greater amount of Operating Income. Again, the higher drink prices on the Las Vegas Strip aid in the success of the nightclub business model. Additionally, thousands of nearby hotel rooms provide Strip nightclubs with many patrons who are not required to drink and drive. Finally, the Strip itself provides an exciting atmosphere, in line with the nightclub experience. This is not to say that nightclubs in repeater-market resorts cannot achieve success.

Table 3.10
Las Vegas Repeater-Market Resort v. Las Vegas Strip Resort
Income Statement: Nightclub
For the 12-month Period Ended 12/31/20XX

Description	Repeater-Market Resort		Las Vegas Strip Resort	
	Amount	%	Amount	%
Revenue:				
Food – Cash	n/a	n/a	$1,778,377	15.48
Food – Comp (1)	n/a	n/a	213	0.00
Beverage – Cash	$2,310,115	91.92	6,472,165	56.33
Beverage – Comp	203,074	8.08	557,050	4.85
Other Revenue (2)	n/a	n/a	2,681,998	23.34
Total Revenue	$2,513,189	100.00	$11,489,803	100.00
Expenses:				
Food – COS	n/a	n/a	$335,911	2.92
Beverage – COS	$404,262	16.09	1,089,063	9.48
Payroll	818,478	32.57	3,125,962	27.21
Operating Expenses	641,120	25.51	3,063,265	26.66
Operating Income/(Loss)	$649,329	25.84	$3,875,602	33.73

Notes: (1) Less than 0.005% of the Strip nightclub's Total Revenue.
(2) Primarily cover charges in the Strip resort's nightclub.
"n/a" indicates line items that are not applicable to the nightclub in the repeater-market resort.

Spa

From Table 3.11, the off-Strip resort produced Operating Income of $900,166, with an Operating Income Margin of 19.32%. Both of these performance measures were well below those generated by the Strip resort's spa. Again, the lower price points of the off-Strip resort were likely to have contributed to its lower operating income margin. That is, the higher price points of the Strip resort's spa produced revenue levels that exceeded the fixed operating costs to a degree that off-Strip resorts could not achieve.

Table 3.11
Las Vegas Repeater-Market Resort v. Las Vegas Strip Resort
Income Statement: Spa
For the 12-month Period Ended 12/31/20XX

Description	Repeater-Market Resort		Las Vegas Strip Resort	
	Amount	%	Amount	%
Revenue:				
Salon - Cash	$856,310	18.38	$6,833,484	75.09
Salon - Comp	115,529	2.48	n/a	n/a
Spa – Cash	3,201,584	68.71	748,465	8.22
Spa – Comp	486,174	10.43	1,331,715	14.63
Spa – Other	n/a	n/a	186,673	2.05
Total Revenue	$4,659,597	100.00	$9,100,337	100.00
Expenses:				
Cost of Sales	$141,092	3.03	n/a	n/a
Payroll	2,793,549	59.95	$4,145,447	45.55
Operating Expenses	824,790	17.70	1,366,796	15.02
Operating Income/(Loss)	$900,166	19.32	$3,588,094	39.43

Notes. "n/a" indicates line items that were not applicable to each of the spa operations. The LV Strip salon was leased to an external operator, hence the absence of cost of sales expense.

Departmental Revenue & Profit Rankings: Off-Strip Resort

From Table 3.1, the following list ranks the top five sources of revenue, from greatest to least. Next to these rankings, the top five sources of operating profits are ranked in the same manner. Tables 3.2 through 3.11 served as the sources for the profit rankings.

Revenue Rankings	Profit Rankings
1. Slots ($151M)	1. Slots ($99M)
2. Food & Beverage ($83M)	2. Hotel ($24M)
3. Hotel ($43M)	3. Food & Beverage ($17M)
4. Table Games ($29M)	4. All Other Games ($8M)
5. All Other Games ($18M)	5. Table Games ($1M)

Both the revenues and profits are dominated by the Slot Department. It is also important to remember that the non-gaming departments are credited with comp revenues, which overstate their revenue and profit contributions. The pie charts shown in Figures 3.2 & 3.3 highlight the differences between revenue and profit contributions. For example, the Table Game Department contributed 9% of the revenues produced by the top five revenue sources and 1% of the profits generated by the top five profit sources.

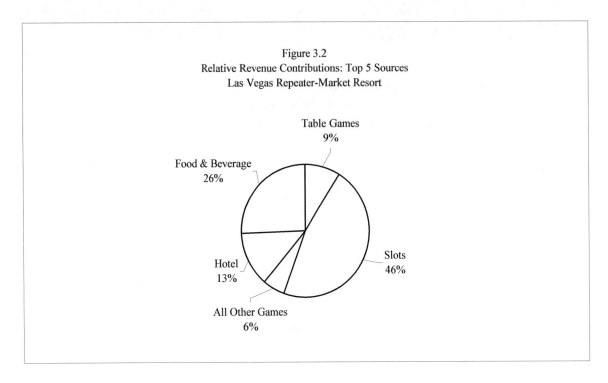

Figure 3.2
Relative Revenue Contributions: Top 5 Sources
Las Vegas Repeater-Market Resort

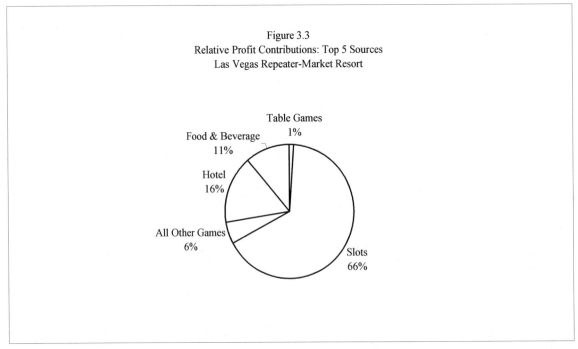

Figure 3.3
Relative Profit Contributions: Top 5 Sources
Las Vegas Repeater-Market Resort

Finally, these charts highlight the importance of the slot operation to the overall success of a repeater-market property. To the contrary, the profit contribution from table games appears trivial. Additionally, the non-gaming profit centers are far less critical to the success of the repeater-market property. This is especially true when the effects of comp transactions are removed from the results.

Questions/Exercises:

1. In a repeater-market gaming resort, which profit center is likely to be the most critical to the success of the operation? Why?
2. In terms of operating income, which two off-Strip profit centers unexpectedly outperformed their like-kind counterparts in the Las Vegas Strip resort?
3. How would you describe a profit center's operating income, as it applies to the overall property?
4. Within the repeater-market resort, did any department/profit center record more comp sales than cash sales? If so, which one(s)?
5. How do comp revenues overstate Total Revenue and Operating Income?
6. Why do you suppose the Bingo Department is permitted to post such unimpressive operating income levels?
7. How would you describe the purpose of the Consolidated Income Statement reviewed in this chapter?
8. Describe the role of non-gaming profit centers in repeater-markets. Provide support for your answer.
9. Within the repeater-market resort, which profit center posted the lowest Operating Income Margin?
10. Consider a gaming resort that is a one-hour drive from a city of two million people. This resort has 200 hotel rooms. There are two other gaming competitors within a two-hour drive of the same city. All other direct competitors are located at least 7 hours from the city (drive time). Place this property at some point on the continuum illustrated in Figure 3.1. Provide support for your placement decision.
11. Why would a Las Vegas locals' market operator build a hotel? The construction costs of hotels are great and a local clientele would have little use for hotel rooms.
12. With regard to the top five sources of profit contributions, what percentage of profit comes from gaming sources, within the repeater-market property?
13. Within the repeater-market resort, which departments comprise the revenue reporting category of All Other Games?
14. Which departments (not games) comprise the Table Game Summary Income Statement? Aside from the Slot Department, which gaming departments are not included in the Table Game Summary Income Statement?
15. Within the repeater-market resort, what percentage of the Net Revenue in Table 3.1 comes from gaming departments? Show your work/calculations. Assume "Other" refers to non-gaming revenue sources.

Chapter 4
Organizational Structure of Casino Departments

How would you describe the organizational structure of a hotel-casino resort?
What are the primary duties of each position within the casino's operating departments?
How must skill sets change as employees ascend the organizational hierarchy?
How might a good Bench Technician add value to a property?
Why do Pit Clerks report to the Manager of Cage Operations?

Scope

This chapter is designed to provide an overview of the organizational structure of a casino's critical areas of operation. Although the job duties of each position in the organizational charts are described, the scope of these descriptions is limited. That is, if the job descriptions were too detailed, an excessive amount of related terminology and process would also need to be defined. While the job descriptions described in this chapter are certainly meaningful, the intent is to provide the reader with a general idea of each position's responsibilities. Additional details related to critical operating processes are provided in subsequent chapters. Departments outside of casino operations are only briefly addressed in this chapter.

Chapter Goals

- Provide an overview of the organizational structure of a hotel-casino property
- Illustrate organizational charts of key operating departments within the casino
- Describe the primary responsibilities of each position within the listed organizational charts

Terminology

Although some jargon is used in the description of certain job duties, most of the terms are described as they appear in the text. Additionally, footnotes are used to describe several unique industry terms, policies, and processes. To the contrary, some items are only briefly described, with references to more detailed discussions in upcoming chapters. Extensive discussion of complexities such as Title 31 reporting requirements would obscure the purpose of this chapter, which is to provide basic descriptions of the jobs that are central to casino operations.

Senior Management

It is important to note that there are many forms of organizational structure within the gaming industry. The structure depicted in Figure 4.1 is more likely to be found in smaller U.S. casino properties. That is, Las Vegas Strip resorts would have additional layers of senior management comprised of positions such as Executive Vice President and Chief Financial Officer. Most importantly, Figure 4.1 provides a framework for a general discussion of senior management structure within a hotel-casino property. The positions reporting directly to the Vice President (VP) of Casino Operations are also shown in Figure 4.1, as the focus of this text is on casino operations management.

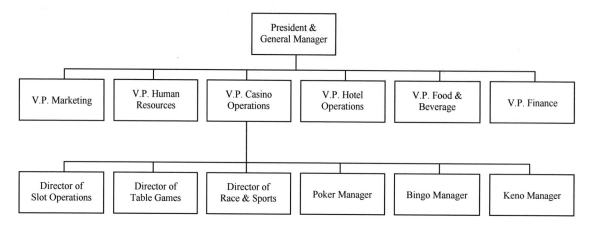

Figure 4.1. Organizational Chart: Senior Management of a Hotel-Casino Property.

President & General Manager (GM)

This position usually reports to an owner, corporate office, or in the case of Indian gaming, the tribal government. The GM is responsible for all matters relating to the operation and performance of the property. One of the greatest challenges facing this position is ensuring that all the VPs and department heads are working together to maximize property cash flows, as opposed to profits at the individual department level. Business acumen, leadership, and diplomacy skills are traits common to many successful GMs.

Although not shown in Figure 4.1, departments such as Security, Observation (or Surveillance), and Internal Audit would all appear on a more inclusive organizational chart. That is, the President would have direct contact with the department heads from these areas.

Vice Presidents

These positions report directly to the President/GM of the property. Although the names of these positions indicate the general areas of responsibility, the following section provides an abridged summary of the departments/activities that would typically fall under the responsibility of each listed VP position. Of course, the organizational structure would vary by property at this level as well.

> **Marketing:** Entertainment; Casino Marketing; Other responsibilities include involvement in public relations, advertising, promotions, and more. The degree to which public relations and advertising activities are outsourced varies by resort.
> **Human Resources:** Employee Relations; Personnel; Training
> **Casino Operations:** Slots; Table Games; Race & Sports; Poker; Bingo; Keno (with Bingo and Keno offered by far fewer casinos)
> **Hotel Operations:** Reservations; Group Sales; Valet; Bell Desk; Housekeeping; Concierge
> **Food & Beverage:** All company-operated food & beverage outlets; Cashiers; Stewards; Bakery; Butcher; Garde Manger (prep. kitchen)
> **Finance:** Accounting; Planning & Analysis; Cage Operations; Purchasing

The Director/Manager level of Figure 4.1 will be examined in detail in subsequent sections of this chapter.

Slot Operations

When discussing the organizational structure of the slot operation, some assumptions must be made. There are many structural variations of Slot Departments, most of which depend on the size of the property. Figure 4.2 represents what we believe to be a typical organizational structure for a slot operation, if such a thing exists. Notice that Figure 4.2 does not include any of the positions that would report to the Director of Slot Marketing, such as Slot Host, Players' Club Manager, Database Marketing Manager, and so forth. Figure 4.2 is limited to the organizational structure of slot operations, which does not include slot marketing.[1]

Director of Slot Operations

This position reports to the VP of Casino Operations, as shown in Figure 4.2. Larger properties would have a VP of Slot Operations; however, typically, the Director of Slot Operations would be the senior management position in most Slot Operations Departments. The duties of this position are listed next.

- Strategic planning and implementation
- Recruit, develop, discipline, evaluate, and terminate slot operations management personnel
- Represent the interests of the Slot Department at the property level
- Prepare capital and operating budgets
- Manage profit optimization efforts

---

[1] For more on slot marketing see: Lucas, A.F., & Kilby, J. (2008). *Principles of Casino Marketing*, Escondido, California: Okie International.

- Manage the service delivery process
- Evaluate performance analyses prepared by the Slot Analyst
    - Buy vs. lease decisions (for operating equipment and slot machines)
    - Negotiate game acquisitions (e.g., slot machine purchases) with game suppliers
    - Manage the slot mix[2]

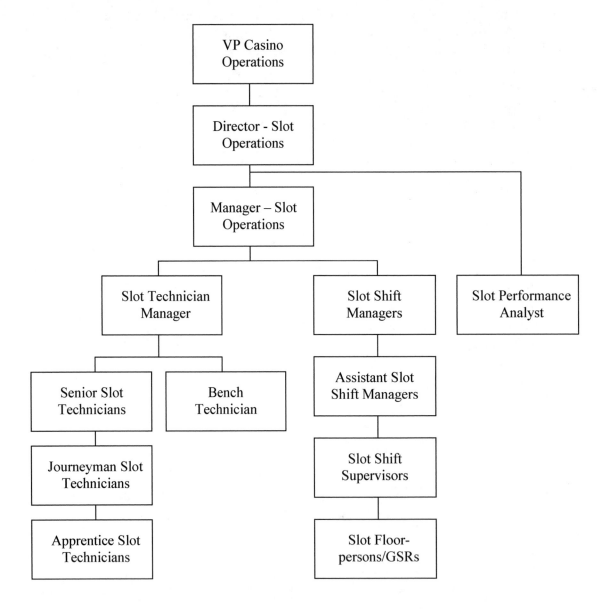

Figure 4.2. Sample Organizational Chart: Slot Operations Department.

---

[2] The slot mix could be defined in many ways. It often refers to the type (e.g., video poker or reel machines) and the denomination (i.e., minimum wagering unit) of the games offered by a casino. As noted, there are many other variables that could be considered in the complex process of mix management.

Slot Operations Manager

This is the chief tactical manager of the slot operation. That is, this person implements the strategies initiated by the Director and senior management. The following job duties are often assigned to the Slot Operations Manager.

- Oversight of all operating and technical activities occurring on the slot floor
- Recruitment, development, discipline, and termination of direct reports
- General scheduling responsibilities for each shift
- Manage and seek to improve service delivery processes
- Information source for Title 31 reporting requirements[3]
- Training and skill development of employees
    - Train employees to use new computer systems and new technology
    - Identify skill deficiencies of employees
    - Design training modules to improve deficient skills
- Authorize the payment of jackpots (above a specified dollar amount)
- Participate in performance analysis of the slot floor

Slot Shift Manager

This position could be thought of as a managerial generalist, at the shift level. The Shift Manager is the primary administrator for his or her shift. The duties of this position are listed next.

- Scheduling at the shift level
    - Match staff to expected business volumes
    - Develop and implement a process that fairly addresses employee requests for specific days off (on the weekly schedule)
    - Make determinations related to vacation requests
- Recruitment, development, discipline, and termination of direct reports
- Succession planning: Identifying management prospects among the Floor Persons
- Provide administrative support to Shift Supervisors and Floor Persons for common/recurring transactions (to be described in the next two sections)

Slot Shift Supervisor

This position supervises the Slot Floorpersons, who may also be known as Guest Service Representatives (GSRs), or Slot Ambassadors. Although the Slot Shift Supervisor does oversee the activities of the GSRs, they perform many of the same duties as the GSRs. The GSR duties will be described in the next section, but the responsibilities unique to the Slot Shift Supervisor are listed next.

---

[3] Title 31 is a complex federal currency reporting regulation which will be covered in depth in a subsequent chapter.

- Customer dispute resolution
- Verify, witness, and authorize hand-pay jackpots made by GSRs (for jackpots above a specified dollar-amount)[4]
- Daily scheduling of GSRs

Slot Shift Supervisors are the first mode of recourse for slot customer disputes and complaints, making diplomacy skills critical for those in this position. The majority of customer disputes are resolved at this level. Performing GSR duties and customer dispute resolution represents the bulk of activity for the Slot Shift Supervisor.

Slot Floor Persons (or GSRs)

The duties of the GSRs are characterized by frequent customer contact. That is, GSRs are on the front line of the Slot Department. These employees should be given to the notion of providing excellent customer service. As you will see from the following list, the scope of the GSR duties is considerable.

- Provide outstanding customer service
  - o Relationship building through courteous and helpful interaction
  - o Facilitate timely and effective cocktail service
  - o Provide directions to locations throughout the casino
- Jackpot processing
  - o Verify jackpots at the game level
  - o Enter jackpot amounts into the slot accounting system (via keypads on the slot machines)
  - o Assist in the completion of appropriate tax forms
  - o Pay the customers (i.e., hand-pay jackpots)
- Minor machine repairs
  - o Clear game malfunctions (a.k.a. tilts)
  - o Clear bill jams (i.e., currency jammed in the bill acceptor)
  - o Clear voucher jams (i.e., wagering vouchers (or tickets) jammed in the bill/voucher acceptor)
  - o Replace paper in the ticket printers

Slot Performance Analyst

As shown in Figure 4.2, this position usually reports directly to the Director of Slot Operations. The role of the Slot Performance Analyst is critical to the success of the slot operation. This position is responsible for the following duties.

- Produce slot performance reports at the game and floor levels
- Identify ways to improve the slot mix
- Analyze games to determine popular game characteristics
- Identify successful and unsuccessful slot machine locations and configurations[5]

---

[4] In most casinos, GSRs can pay low-limit jackpots without the involvement of the Slot Shift Supervisor.
[5] Configuration refers to the way in which games are arranged. For example, the analyst might examine differences in performance with respect to banks of games (a linear arrangement) vs. pods (a circular arrangement).

- Assist in lease-vs.-buy analyses with regard to the acquisition of games

The scope of the Slot Analyst is considerable, as this person will provide analytical support for a variety of projects initiated by senior management. As a result of this condition, it is difficult to provide an exhaustive list of job tasks.

Slot Technician Manager

Technicians have little or no interaction with customers. Their primary duties consist of installing, converting, and maintaining slot machines. The Slot Technician Manager is responsible for planning the work to be performed by the technicians. The paragraphs following the list of this position's responsibilities contain explanations of selected items.

- Plan and supervise the installation of new slot machines
  - o Schedule installation times and dates
  - o Ensure the appropriate peripheral technology is installed on the new games, including the following items:
    - Bill validators
    - Voucher printers
    - Player tracking units
    - Slot accounting and player tracking system connections (i.e., harnesses)[6]
- Coordinate game conversions[7]
  - o Replace the glass on the games[8]
  - o Replace the computer chips on the games (i.e., EPROMS)[9]
- Oversee the maintenance of the slot master database
- Produce computer-aided design (CAD) maps of the slot floor
- Recruitment, development, discipline, and termination of technical personnel

The slot master database contains game-level data describing the game type (e.g., video poker), minimum wagering unit (e.g., nickels), the game's installation date, and the game's serial number, among other items.

CAD maps are technical drawings of the slot floor. These maps are usually scaled and color-coded so that management can review layout and game characteristics such as bank

---

[6] A harness is cluster of cables that connects the slot machine to the casino's primary operating systems. In most cases, one harness would connect the game to the slot accounting system, and a second harness would connect the game to the slot marketing system. One end of the harness attaches to system cables, which are fed through ducts in the casino floor, while the other end attaches to the game at cable plug-in points.

[7] Game conversion kits transform an existing game into a new game. The cabinet and stand of the original game remain, but the game data, decorative glass, video, and audio components all change. The converted game appears as a new game to the customers.

[8] Game glass is the decorative glass that the players see when approaching the game. It is not the game screen that displays the outcome of a spin.

[9] Conversion kits usually contain three separate chips, one for the pay table and probability of possible events/outcomes, one for the graphics, and one for the audio files. Many game makers are moving toward the use of USB sticks to store game data, graphics, and audio files.

locations, the denomination of games in a bank, and shapes of banks (i.e., bank configurations).[10] The games are identified by codes so that game locations from the map can be matched with performance data. That is, distinct machine numbers or asset numbers are assigned to each game. These numbers often appear on both the CAD maps and the performance reports, allowing management to link specific results to specific locations.

Senior Slot Technician

This position serves in the capacity of a Shift Manager, overseeing the work of Journeyman Slot Technicians and Apprentice Slot Technicians. There is usually one Senior Slot Technician on each scheduled shift. Some describe this position as a working Foreman, as Senior Slot Technicians will often participate in the work they plan and supervise. The job duties of this position are as follows:

- Schedule and assign all work to be performed by Journeyman and Apprentice Technicians
    - Ensure subordinates have all materials/resources needed to complete the assigned tasks
    - Monitor progress of assigned tasks and ensure timely completion of the work
- Coordinate preventive maintenance on games
- Supervise game conversion work
- Replace broken monitors
- Reset frozen game screens (when operations staff are unable to do so)
- Troubleshoot all challenging electronic game malfunctions

Journeyman Slot Technicians

This position is essentially a Senior Slot Technician without the supervisorial and administrative responsibilities. That is, aside from planning and supervising the work, the Journeyman Technician performs the same basic job duties as the Senior Slot Technician.

Apprentice Slot Technician

This is an entry-level training position for those who wish to become Journeyman Technicians. Under the supervision of a Journeyman Technician, the Apprentice Technician works on the same jobs/tasks as the Journeyman Technician. As a Technician's scope of work is considerable and the tasks are complex, a substantial amount of on-the-job training is necessary.

Bench Technician

Bench Technicians are also known as Board Technicians. Unlike the Journeyman and Apprentice Technicians, Bench Technicians spend very little time working on the slot

---

[10] "Bank" usually refers to a linear arrangement of contiguous slot machines, e.g., two back-to-back rows of three games would form a six-unit bank. Pods and carousels usually refer to circular groupings of games.

floor. The tasks of this position entail almost no customer interaction. The primary job duties of the Bench Technician are listed next.

- Repair complex electronic devices, including the following items:
  o Slot machine video monitors
  o Slot machine mother boards
  o Power supply units from games

This section only lists a few of the Bench Technicians tasks. However, it is not difficult to imagine the value of a good Bench Technician, as successful repairs can lengthen the useful life of many expensive slot machine components.

Tables Game Operations

In terms of scope, the table game operation does not include the following areas: Poker room, bingo room (should one exist), and keno lounge. Of course, many other gaming areas fall outside the realm of table game operations, but the previously mentioned areas are often incorrectly assumed to be part of the Table Game Department.

The following table games are commonly found on U.S. casino floors:

- Blackjack and all of its many variations
- Craps
- Baccarat and all of its variations such as Mini- and Midi-baccarat
- Roulette
- Pai Gow
- Carnival games such as Pai Gow Poker, 3-card Poker, & Caribbean Stud

The structure of the organizational chart, job titles, and specific job duties will vary by property, according to variables such as the number of table games offered by the casino and management operating policies and procedures. For example, most Las Vegas Strip properties would have a VP of Table Games, while many smaller properties would have a Director of Table Games in the senior position. In any case, Figure 4.3 provides a framework for a discussion of the basic responsibilities associated with managing a table game operation.

Director of Table Games

This position reports directly to the VP of Casino Operations. In Figure 4.3, the Director of Table Games is the senior management position with regard to table game operations. The following bullet points summarize the responsibilities of this position.

- Strategic planning and implementation
- Recruitment, development, discipline, evaluation, and termination of table games management

- Represent interests of the Table Game Department at the property level
- Prepare capital and operating budgets
- Ensure that all games are operated according to the prescribed regulations
- Responsible for all activity within the table game operation
- Determine operating policies and procedures
- Authorize/grant credit to players
- Manage the table games operation within the financial guidelines set forth by the operating budget
- Participate in the development of the casino marketing plan and day-to-day casino marketing decisions

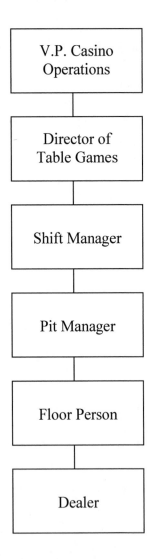

Figure 4.3. Sample Organizational Chart: Table Game Operations Department.

Shift Manager

In the absence of the Director of Table Games, the Shift Manager represents the senior management position, in terms of direct responsibility for the table game operation. Examples of the Shift Manager's job duties are listed next.

- Supervise Pit Managers
- Participate in the credit granting process
  - Shift Managers often have limited authority to grant credit
- Issue comps with full comp authority
- Address all incidents, conflicts, and crises that occur during the assigned shift
  - For example, customer issues related to comp awards must be addressed by a manager with comp authority (usually the Shift Manager)
- Contact and communicate with surveillance, regarding situations that occur in the pit areas
- Participate in policy decisions related to the table game operation
- Communicate all decisions related to disciplinary matters to subordinate positions
- Determine the number of games to open on the assigned shift
- Responsible for scheduling all positions on the shift (e.g., days off, start times, and vacation days)
- Participate in the payment of slot jackpots (over an identified critical value)

Pit Manager

In recent years, many U.S. casino executives have decreased the number of table games offered in their casinos. As a result of this trend, the Pit Manager position has been removed at some properties. However, we have included the Pit Manager in Figure 4.3, and show this position reporting directly to the Shift Manager. The following bullet points summarize the job duties of the Pit Manager.

- Directly supervise all Floor Persons and indirectly supervise the Dealers within his or her assigned area of responsibility (i.e., pit)[11]
- Track/estimate the cumulative win/(loss) of the assigned pit, noting any substantial player wins/(losses)
- Determine when to open or close games within his or her assigned pit
- Determine when to increase or decrease the dollar-amount of the required minimum wager on individual table games
- Issue comps
- Advise Shift Manager of any critical issues, incidents, or situations occurring in their assigned pit
- Game protection

---

[11] A pit is a grouping of table games. The individual tables are usually arranged to form a circular or rectangular shape. The interior of the pit is manned by employees, while customers occupy the exterior gaming positions. Customers are not permitted in the interior of a pit.

Floor Person

This position represents the front line of table game management. The following bullet points summarize the job duties of this position.

- Supervise the operation of one or more table games
- Customer dispute resolution (e.g., addressing customer claims of Dealer error)
- Request fills and credits as needed[12]
- Along with the dealer, ensure the accuracy of requested fills and credits
- Identify unknown players for the purpose of having their name added to the casino system and their play rated/tracked
- Responsible for estimating the following items related to the player rating process:
  - The player's average bet
  - The duration of a player's wagering session (e.g., 4 hours)
  - The player's actual win or loss
- Initiate credit requests for established players (i.e., those who have existing credit lines)
  - If approved, the Floorperson will obtain the player's signature on a marker in the amount of the approved credit request[13]
  - Once the marker is signed, the Floorperson authorizes the dealer to advance gaming cheques to the player
- Accept the repayment of previously issued markers, if permitted by the gaming regulations
- Issue comps (if authorized by the casino's comp policy)
- Identify and log all reportable cash transactions as required by U.S. Title 31
- Game protection
- Alert senior management and/or surveillance to any suspicious activity occurring on his or her assigned table(s)

Dealer

This position is the face of the Table Game Department, as Dealers interact directly with the players. As a result, people skills are critical. Dealers who can deal multiple games have increased value to management, as scheduling and operating flexibility both result from the expanded skill set of the multi-game Dealer. The following bullet points highlight the job duties of the Dealer.

- Deal the games in a technically proficient manner
- Provide a friendly gaming atmosphere
- Alert management to any suspicious act by a player

---

[12] Fills represent additions of gaming cheques to a table game's tray. Credits represent the removal of gaming cheques from a table game's tray. Fills and credits are discussed in detail in Chapter 6.
[13] Similar to counter checks in a bank, *markers* are negotiable instruments that represent the casino's claim against funds held in a player's bank account. Markers are further discussed in subsequent chapters.

- Ensure that players adhere to all game rules and casino policies (posted & otherwise)
- Ensure that the pace of game is sufficient, but not so rapid that players feel rushed.
- Verify the accuracy of game fills and credits

Poker Room

The organizational chart of a poker room can vary greatly by property. For example, as the number of tables in a poker room increases, the number of managerial levels in the organizational structure can be expected to increase. The managerial positions in smaller poker rooms are usually characterized by a wider scope of responsibility than those of larger rooms. The smaller rooms do not generate sufficient business volume to justify managerial positions with limited and/or very specific responsibilities. Figure 4.4 illustrates one possible organizational structure for a poker room, and provides a framework for further discussion of specific job duties within this hierarchy.

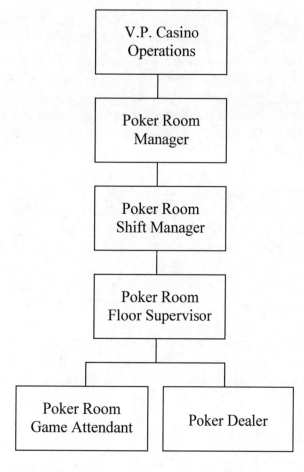

Figure 4.4. Sample Organizational Chart: Poker Room Operations.

Poker Room Manager

In Figure 4.4, the Poker Room Manager reports directly to the VP of Casino Operations. This is often the senior position in poker room management. Casinos featuring larger poker rooms sometimes have a Director of Poker Operations above the Poker Room Manager. The responsibilities of the Poker Room Manager are summarized by the following bullet points.

- Strategic planning
- Recruit, develop, discipline, evaluate, and terminate all poker room positions
- Represent interests of the poker room at property-level meetings
- Prepare capital and operating budgets
- Scheduling
- Issue comps
- Create promotions and tournaments
- Responsible for compliance with gaming regulations and Title 31 reporting requirements (although poker rooms do not typically generate an abundance of reportable transactions, under Title 31)

Poker Room Shift Manager

This position assumes the duties and responsibilities of the Poker Room Manager, when he or she is absent. The Shift Manager reports directly to the Manager and could be thought of as his or her understudy. However, when the Manager is present, the Shift Manager's duties focus on supervising the operation of the shift, as opposed to general administrative duties related to the poker room. A summary of the Shift Manager's responsibilities are provided next.

- Responsible for operations on a specific shift
- Participate in disciplinary matters (of employees)
- Provide input in the planning of promotions and tournaments
- Assist the Poker Room Manager with administrative matters as directed
- Issue comps

Poker Room Floor Supervisor

This position usually reports to the Poker Room Shift Manager. Overall, the Floor Supervisor could be thought of as a game facilitator. That is, he or she attends to the detailed tasks required for the successful operation of the poker games. The typical responsibilities of the Floor Supervisor are listed next.

- Direct supervision of Dealers
- Assign specific Dealers to each day's scheduled games
- Schedule breaks for Dealers

- Open and close games according to the schedule and customer demand for specific types of games
- Meet and greet customers
- Serve as the first line of customer dispute resolution
  - Very few disputes go unresolved (i.e., few disputes involve management beyond this level)

Poker Dealer

Dealers in most Las Vegas poker rooms are expected to proficiently deal Texas Hold 'em, 7-card Stud, and Omaha. Aside from dealing the games, Dealers are expected to be courteous and friendly to the players. In summary, this position calls for technical proficiency and the ability to pleasantly interact with customers.

Poker Room Game Attendant

This position takes direction from the Floor Supervisor. The Game Attendant position is also known as a Brush or a Chip Runner. The duties of this position are listed next, followed by a brief explanation of selected bullet points.

- Facilitate buy-ins by poker players
- Keep the poker room clean of debris
- Attend to the waiting list of players (for specific games)
- Recruit and encourage play by interacting with patrons standing near or passing by the entrance of the poker room

In poker, players sit at a game and buy-in with currency. The Game Attendant will take this currency and replace it with a lammer indicating the dollar-amount of the requested buy-in.[14] The Game Attendant will go to the Poker Room Cage or Cashier and exchange the player's currency for the requested denomination(s) of poker cheques. These cheques are then given to the player (at the table) and the lammer is taken down.

Race & Sports Book

The organizational chart of the Race and Sports Book Department can vary greatly depending on the size of the book and the property. That is, smaller properties will consolidate job duties into fewer positions. These properties lack the business volume needed to justify employees with highly specialized areas of responsibility. The organizational chart depicted in Figure 4.5 assumes a fairly typical structure for a race and sports book in a Las Vegas hotel-casino resort.

---

[14] A lammer is a plastic disk that is approximately the size of quarter. These disks have numbers printed on them that represent dollar-amounts. In poker, lammers simply serve as temporary receipts for customer buy-ins. Different types of lammers are also used in other games, such as craps.

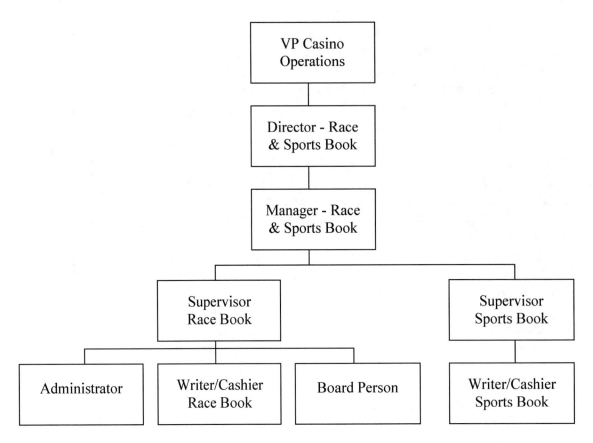

Figure 4.5. Sample Organizational Chart: Race & Sports Book Department.

The basic duties of each position in Figure 4.5 are described next. Use of industry terms is always necessary when discussing race and sports book operations. While every attempt will be made to define these terms here, detailed coverage of race and sports book operations is included in Chapter 15. The following sections are designed to provide a general sketch of the responsibilities and/or daily duties of each position in the book.

Director of Race & Sports Book

Some larger casinos may have a vice president over the race and sports book operation, but most do not. Typically, the Director of the Race & Sports Book is the senior position in this department. The Director usually reports to the Vice President of Casino Operations. In short, the Director occupies an executive position that is ultimately responsible for all matters concerning or affecting the operation of the Race and Sports Book. Specific job duties are listed next.

- Represent the department at the property level, regarding all matters involving the Race & Sports Book
- Develop strategic initiatives
- Produce operating and capital budgets
- Develop, initiate, and oversee all Race and Sports Book marketing activities

- Recruit, develop, discipline, evaluate, and terminate Race & Sports Book personnel

Race & Sports Book Manager

This position oversees the daily operation of the Race and Sports Book. The Manager's race book duties include the following tasks:

- Create promotional ideas and special events
- Execute and supervise all marketing activities
- Supervise all book supervisors and employees
- Review big-ticket wagers and ensure compliance with federal reporting requirements (i.e., Title 31)
- Participate in employee recruitment, hiring, termination, and discipline
- Resolve customer complaints

The Manager is responsible for these same tasks on the sports book side of the operation. However, the Sports Book brings additional responsibilities to the position. The Manager must establish or adjust the opening lines for each wagering proposition. Although most books subscribe to an external odds making service,[15] adjustments are often made to the opening lines to addresses the specific wagering tendencies of the book's clientele.

The line refers to the opening price/terms of the wager. For example, money line wagers such as those placed on boxing and baseball games have opening prices assigned to the fighters or teams. Consider the following example:

Reds (pitcher – Volquez)   -135
Cubs (pitcher – Zambrano)   +125

Here, a wager of $135 on the Reds (to win the game) would pay $235, resulting in a customer win of $100 ($235 - $135). A wager of $100 on the Cubs would pay $225, resulting in a customer win of $125 ($225 - $100). The -135 and +125 terms are referred to as the line for this game.

The Manager also oversees the bookmaking process for each line. For example, if the betting public continues to heavily wager on the Reds (but not the Cubs), the Manager will adjust the line to encourage more wagers on the Cubs. This type of adjustment is an example of bookmaking, which is one of the Manager's most critical responsibilities. The specific tactics and operating processes associated with sports book management will be covered in detail in Chapter 15.

Finally, the Manager reviews all wagers involving great sums of money to assess the book's exposure to substantial losses. That is, the book's premium players wager

---

[15] An external company hired to provide opening betting lines for sporting events. Also referred to as handicappers, these companies provide the wagering terms needed to offer bets to the public.

amounts of money that far exceed the sums wagered by typical patrons. The Manager reviews these wagers to identify the sporting events that could expose the book to great losses. The manager also verifies that these wagers are properly logged and/or reported per the federal reporting requirements (i.e., Title 31). These requirements will be thoroughly covered in Chapter 8.

✓ **Race Book Supervisor**

The following is an abridged list of the Race Book Supervisor's job duties.

- Create the work schedule for the writer/cashiers
- Direct supervision of writer/cashiers
- Cater to requests from premium players (e.g., comps)
- Ensure that wagers from premium players are tracked (i.e., recorded)
- Report and log transactions in compliance with federal cash reporting requirements (i.e., Title 31)
- Address customer complaints
- Establish relationships with customers and identify promising customers

✓ **Sports Book Supervisor**

The duties of the Sports Book Supervisor include all those mentioned in Race Book Supervisor Section. However, this position is also charged with routine bookmaking duties. That is, the Sports Book Supervisor will make routine adjustments to betting lines, as prescribed by book policy. Any potentially dangerous adjustments to lines would be made or approved by the Manager of the book.

Race Book Administrator

If the Race and Sports Book has electronic wall boards, the Administrators are responsible for reviewing and updating changes to the posted information. Wall boards post race information by track and race number. Examples of such information include horse and jockey names, horse weight, and the odds against each horse winning. The results of completed races and payoffs for winning wagers are also posted on the boards. For many Las Vegas books, this information is automatically fed into the race and sports system by the external disseminator. That is, casinos subscribe to an external dissemination service to provide race information, including the official results of horse races. Administrators make sure that revisions to the original information are input and displayed on the electronic wall boards. Examples of such updates are scratched horses, revised weight information, and horses that have received lasix injections.

If the Race Book does not have electronic wall boards, a full-time employee is needed to manually post and revise the information listed on the paper wall boards. The Race Book Board Person's duties are described in a subsequent section.

Race Book Writer/Cashier

The Writer/Cashier position reports to the Race Book Supervisor. An abridged list of the job duties is presented here, with further explanation offered in the paragraphs that follow.

- Responsible for balancing his/her bank
- Write tickets
- Pay winning tickets
- Sell racing forms
- Review and sign transaction logs in compliance with federal cash reporting requirements (i.e., Title 31)
- Record wagers from premium players for purposes of player valuation

Writer/Cashiers are issued a bank (i.e., cash drawer) at the beginning of their shift. Any change in the beginning cash balance of this drawer must be supported by the appropriate documentation.

Writer/Cashiers enter the details of each wager into the race and sports book system, including the amounts wagered on each proposition.[16] The system then prints a receipt (i.e., ticket) detailing the specific terms of the wager. This task is referred to as writing tickets. Before computerized systems, writers actually wrote this information on a paper ticket. Of course, the customer was given a copy of the ticket as evidence that the bet was accepted by the casino.

Customers claim winning wagers by presenting their tickets to the Writer/Cashier. When this occurs, the Writer/Cashier must access the system to verify that the ticket is indeed a winning ticket. If it is verified as a winner, the ticket is paid. In this case, the Writer/Cashier is performing a Cashier function.

The Writer/Cashier is asked to sell racing forms to the race book patrons. In general, this form lists information about the horses in each race, at each track covered by the form.

Finally, this position is also required to review and sign transaction logs required by Title 31. Each casino must record wagers which are in excess of its established threshold (for a single wager). The dollar-value of this threshold varies by property, but the reporting requirement does not. Writer/Cashiers must review and sign transaction logs, indicating their participation in and the accuracy of specific log entries. Writer/Cashiers also record wagering activity to the accounts of premium players to determine each player's value to the casino and his/her comp eligibility.

Writer/Cashiers perform other important tasks as well. The job duties covered here were limited to the more common tasks of the position.

---

[16] The term "Proposition" is used to represent the specific event on which a bet is placed.

95

Race Book Board Person

This position only exists in those casinos that do not have electronic wall boards. If the Race and Sports Book has an electronic board, these duties are performed by the Administrator. In the absence of an electronic wall board, the Board Person manually posts all pertinent race information (see Administrator Section for details). The Board Person is also responsible for updating revisions to the posted information such as taking down scratched horses and posting the results of completed races. These tasks are accomplished by printing this information with a dry marker on a paper wall board.

This is a full-time position in the Race Book, as Writer/Cashiers do not have time to perform these duties. On a given day, there could be races occurring at more than 15 different tracks, keeping the Writer/Cahiers engaged in wagering-related transactions. Further, horse races produce a considerable amount of information that must be posted. To the contrary, the Sports Book Writer/Cashiers perform the Board Person's duties, as the pace of updating information and posting results is much less demanding in the Sports Book.

Sports Book Writer/Cashier

The Writer/Cashier position reports to the Sports Book Supervisor. Aside from selling racing forms, the Sports Book Writer/Cashier performs the same essential duties as the Race Book Writer/Cashier. That is, the Sports Book Writer/Cashier accepts and records wagers, pays winning tickets, and is responsible for a bank/cash drawer. All of these duties are carried out in much the same way that the Race Book Writer/Cashiers perform their job tasks.

When the casino does not have an electronic wall board, the Sports Book Writer/Cashiers manually post the available information for the next day's games, on the previous night. On the following day, the day shift Writer/Cashiers post the morning line for the games. The morning line represents the initial payout for each wagering proposition listed on the board. As the casino accepts wagers, these lines can change. When changes in the lines occur, the Writer/Cashiers manually update the line on the wall board.

Casino Cage Department

Essentially, the cage functions as a bank. Although it is considered to be a critical component of any casino operation, the cage typically falls under the control of the Vice President of Finance. The rationale for this structure is based on the reality that the cage operation entails facilitating, recording, and accounting for the movement of cash through the casino. Finance personnel are trained in such matters, and, therefore, better suited to manage the cage operation. Figure 4.6 illustrates the reporting hierarchy and positions within the Cage Department. Of course, there are many possible organizational configurations for a cage operation. Figure 4.6 represents one of these possible structures.

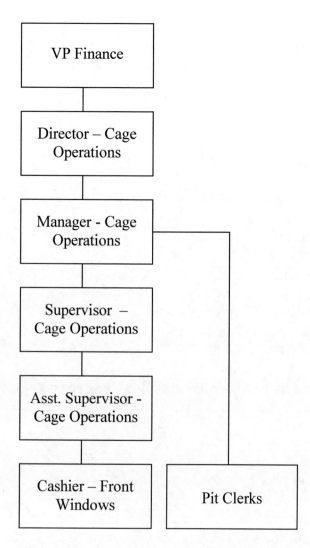

Figure 4.6. Sample Organizational Chart: Cage Department.

Director of Cage Operations

This position reports directly to the Vice President of Finance and is responsible for all matters concerning the cage operation. The Director's responsibilities are largely administrative, representing the Cage in meetings that address property-wide issues. This position is also responsible for the following tasks:

- Prepare the Cage Department's operating and capital budgets
- Recruit, hire, develop, discipline, evaluate, and terminate cage personnel
- Comply with federal reporting requirements for cash transactions (i.e., Title 31)
- Cash management:
  - Ensure that the cage meets the minimum bankroll requirements set forth in the gaming regulations (for cash on hand)
    - Order currency from the bank when necessary, to meet funding requirements

As no Credit Manager or Collection Manager is shown in Figure 4.6, the Director of Cage Operations would also review requests for credit (from gaming customers) and assist in the collection process. The collection process refers to the pursuit of outstanding debts, resulting from the extension of credit to gaming customers.

Cage Manager

This position is responsible for the following tasks:

- Manage the day-to-day operation of the cage
- Manage cage supervisors
- Address customer complaints/issues
- Schedule all cage staff
- Approve/review transactions such as: Customer check cashing, substantial cash-outs of gaming cheques, credit requests, cash-for-cash transactions above specified amounts
- Assume Cashier duties if necessary
- Supervise and schedule the Pit Clerks

This is an abridged list, as the responsibilities of this position are many and vary greatly by property.

Cage Supervisor

This position is responsible for the following tasks:

- Assume the responsibilities of the Cage Manager, in his/her absence
- Approve various transactions conducted by Cashiers
- Participate in the review/approval of small credit requests
- Assume Cashier duties if necessary

Assistant Supervisor of Cage Operations

The duties of this position mimic those of the Cage Supervisor. The Assistant Supervisor will also cover supervisor shifts. Essentially, this person is a Senior Cashier capable of covering Supervisor shifts when needed.

Cashier

An abridged list of Cashier job duties is offered here. The tasks are only briefly defined in this chapter. However, Chapter 7 includes additional details related to Cashier job duties.

- Cash customer checks
- Assist customers with credit card and ATM transactions (when a customer's daily activity levels are exceeded)

- Exchange cash for slot vouchers/tickets
- Exchange cash for gaming cheques
- Assist in the preparation of the paperwork required to extend credit to customers
- Sell and issue purchase tickets to slot players (i.e., exchange slot tickets for cash)
- Receive and process payments from customers (to retire their debt to the casino)
- Redeem marketing coupons that require the disbursement of gaming cheques or cash
- Record and log all reportable transactions in accordance with the federal cash reporting requirements (e.g., Title 31)
- Exchange foreign currency

The details of the cage operation are thoroughly covered in Chapter 7. That is, the processes related to the job duties listed in this chapter are described in Chapter 7.

Pit Clerks

This position reports to either the Cage Manager or the Director of Cage Operations, depending on the organizational structure of the property. Although all duties of the Pit Clerks are directly related to table game operations, they report to the Cage Department. This is because Pit Clerks are responsible for recording critical transactions that occur in the Table Game Department. As a result, the Pit Clerks must be independent from table game management to protect the integrity of these transactions. The following list describes some of the more common duties of Pit Clerks. Brief explanations of each listed job duty are provided in subsequent paragraphs.

- Input openers and closers
- Input fills and credits
- Input marker issue and redemption slips
- Input player rating slips
- Record transactions in the Multiple Transaction Log, in compliance with Title 31

Openers and closers are inventories of the cheques on each table game. These inventories are provided by supervisors from the Table Game Department. The Pit Clerks input these inventories into the casino accounting system.

Fills are requests for additional cheques to be transferred from the cage to a particular table game. Credits are requests to move cheques from a particular table game to the cage.

Marker issue slips record the issuance of cheques to table game players. Marker redemption slips record payments made by players against marker balances.

Player rating slips record the gambling activity of players, as observed by personnel from the Table Game Department. In general, these slips are the basis of comp awards and player valuation.

A Multiple Transaction Log (MTL) is required to comply with U.S. Title 31 of the 1970 Bank Secrecy Act. These and other logs will be described thoroughly in Chapter 8. Pit Clerks are responsible for recording certain types of transactions in the MTL.

Bingo Room

Although bingo is on the decline in most markets, many U.S. gaming properties continue to offer the game. This section offers a review of the positions commonly found in a bingo department, including a list of each position's primary responsibilities. Of course, differences in organizational structure and specific job duties will vary by property. As there are only three positions reviewed here, an organizational chart is not necessary.

Bingo Manager

The Bingo Manager holds the senior management position in the Bingo Department. As a result, he or she must manage all administrative matters at the departmental level. In most cases, the Bingo Manager would report to the VP of Casino Operations (as depicted in Figure 4.1). The job duties of this position are listed next:

- Ultimately responsible for all events occurring in the bingo room
- Direct and supervise all bingo personnel
- Safeguard company assets
- Develop and implement operating policies, procedures, and guidelines
- Provide a work schedule for all positions in the department
- Strategic planning and implementation at the departmental level
- Represent the interests of the Bingo Department at the property level
- Prepare capital and operating budgets
- Recruit, develop, discipline, evaluate, and terminate bingo personnel
- Explain operating results that are substantially different from budgeted amounts
- Create and market effective promotions
- Authorize payouts above a specified dollar-amount
- Address and attempt to resolve customer disputes
- Ensure compliance with all internal controls and external regulations
- Perform the duties of subordinates when necessary

Bingo Supervisor

This position provides a management presence in the absence of the Bingo Manager. The Supervisor shares many of the same duties as the Manager. This position's primary responsibilities are listed next.

- Assist the Manager with administrative tasks as needed
- Safeguard company assets
- Responsible for the bingo operation on his or her assigned shift

- Customer dispute resolution
- Direct supervision of Game Attendants and live games
- Authorize payouts above and below specified dollar-amounts
- Perform the duties of subordinates when necessary
- Complete pre-shift operating preparations:
    o Stock all stations with bingo packs (a.k.a. paper)
    o Verify the integrity of the bingo balls
    o Prepare the operating system for the upcoming shift
- Verify each station's beginning and ending inventory of bingo packs
- Reconcile the change in bingo pack inventory for each station (i.e., from the serial number of the first ticket to the serial number of the last ticket sold)
- Reconcile the change in the balance of each station's bank, over the course of the shift
- Compute operating statistics for each shift, including the game's win/(loss)

Bingo Game Attendant

Also known as Agents, the Game Attendants are operations generalists. That is, they perform a variety of duties, some of which are listed next. Further explanation of selected bullet points appears in the subsequent paragraphs.

- Call/Announce the live games (e.g., B-11, N-34, etc.)
- Verify winning tickets (of those that call Bingo)
- Pay verified winners
- Sell packs (the paper bingo cards are bundled and sold as packs)
- Serve as an information source for customers, answering questions about both bingo and the overall property
- Provide customer service consistent with management's expectation
- Set-up any bingo equipment/balls necessary to produce the game

The Game Attendant calling the game (i.e., the Caller) is responsible for controlling the pace of the game and reading the rules of the current game when necessary. The Caller usually operates the device that circulates the bingo balls. This device is known as a blower. Selected balls are displayed to the players and announced. In most cases, the caller will use a microphone to announce the results, as many bingo rooms are quite large.

With respect to the verification process, control/serial numbers on the pre-printed packs are entered into the system when they are sold to the players. This form of pack registration prevents players from introducing fraudulent cards into the game. Also, patrons sometimes make mistakes when daubing (i.e., marking) their cards, resulting in invalid declarations on bingo. Before a ticket is paid, the Game Attendants verify that all marked spots were actually called, and that the ticket was registered in the system prior to the onset of the current game.

The Game Attendants performing the cashier function must requisition imprest banks from the employee cage.[17] Such banks are nothing more than money drawers for use in the point-of-sale terminals located inside the bingo room.[18] Of course, imprest banks facilitate the sale of bingo packs. That is, the Game Attendants must be able to make change for those who pay with cash (in excess of the pack price). Also, most standard payouts are made from imprest bank funds. Progressive jackpot payouts require management approval. Checks are often issued when substantial jackpots are won.

Game Attendants are usually capable of performing all of the previously described job duties. In fact, they usually rotate from cashiering to calling the game, to verifying winning tickets (i.e., floor duties). There is no prescribed order to this rotation of jobs.

Keno

Keno is another game that is in decline in most U.S. gaming markets. In fact, many Nevada properties no longer offer keno games. There are relatively few positions in most current Keno Departments, so no organizational chart is needed in this section.

The **Keno Manager** is usually the senior management position in the Keno Department, reporting to the VP of Casino Operations (as shown Figure 4.1). This position represents the department at the property level and performs all administrative duties at the department level. Such duties are not different from those performed by previously described department head positions (e.g., Bingo Manager). Keno games do produce substantial payouts, requiring the Keno Manager to ensure compliance with all payout approval procedures and transaction reporting requirements.

The **Keno Shift Manager** provides a management presence in the absence of the Keno Manager. His or her responsibility for the operation is limited to the assigned shift. The Shift Manager directly supervises all Writer/Cashiers and Runners. The general scope of this position's responsibilities is not different from that of previously defined Shift Manager positions (e.g., Poker Room Shift Manager).

The **Writer/Cashier** typically works behind a counter, performing a variety of tasks. Aside from the standard customer-service-related functions, the primary tasks of this position are to write tickets, accept wagers, and pay winning tickets.

The Writer/Cashier accepts the ticket marked by the customer along with the associated wager. The selected numbers and the dollar-amount wagered are entered into the keno system to make an electronic record of the customer's bet. Prior to computerized systems, the Writers would mark the tickets by hand, hence the title "Ticket Writer," or "Writer," in short form.

---

[17] Imprest banks and the Employee Cage are described in detail in Chapter 7. This responsibility falls to the Bingo Supervisor at some properties.
[18] In simple terms, point-of-sale systems could be thought of as cash registers linked to an operating system.

Keno Runners are less common in modern games. Runners are charged with collecting tickets and wagers from players, submitting tickets and wagers to the Writer/Cashiers, returning the tickets to the players, and paying any winning tickets. That is, Runners canvas venues such as restaurants and lounges collecting tickets and wagers from customers. These tickets (and associated wagers) are then submitted to the Writers, where the ticket information (i.e., selected numbers and dollar-amounts wagered) is entered into the system. The Writer provides the Runner with hard copies of the customer tickets (printed from the system). The Runner returns the copies of the tickets to the customers, and pays winning tickets, up to a specified dollar amount.

The Management Pyramid

Although some are challenging the wisdom of the management pyramid structure in contemporary business settings,[19] it remains well established in the gaming industry. That is, casino properties are typically structured according to the classical top-down management model, whereby Supervisors report to Managers, who, in turn, report to Directors, and so forth. This vertical structure is evident in the organizational charts featured in this chapter.

Although job descriptions and communication channels are more clearly defined in top-down structures, there are disadvantages to this design. For example, rigid top-down structures work best when all members of the organization operate within their defined scope of responsibilities (i.e., inside the box). The strict command-and-control structure of the top-down model lacks flexibility and limits innovation and collaboration, especially with those at lower levels of the organization. To the contrary, team structures comprised of individuals with unique skill sets encourage innovation and collaboration, while increasing the organization's ability to adapt to today's complex and dynamic markets. In any case, the top-down model remains firmly entrenched in the gaming industry.

Management Skills vs. Technical Skills

In gaming, entry-level or front-line employees rely heavily on technical skills to perform their job duties. For example, Dealers must be able to proficiently deal the games. However, as Dealers are promoted to Floor Person and beyond, they rely much less on their technical skills, and much more on their management skills. That is, they no longer need to deal the game – they now have to manage it. Management skills can be described in terms of human skills and conceptual skills.

Human skills involve the ability to work cooperatively in layered environments to achieve specific goals. For example, managers must often motivate their employees to produce a desired outcome. The manager himself does not produce this outcome, but

---

[19] Nayar, V. (2008, October 8). It's time to invert the management pyramid. Retrieved October 28, 2009 from http://blogs.harvardbusiness.org/hbr/nayar/2008/10/its-time-to-invert-the-managem.html.

through leadership and clear communication he is able to motivate the employees to achieve the desired end. That is, the manager uses the skills of the employees rather than his own technical skills as the means to this end.

The ability to work well with others is a critical human skill for any manager. Moreover, in the hotel-casino industry, many projects cross departmental lines, requiring cooperation with mangers and employees from other departments to achieve goals and objectives. In this case, managers must work with personnel who do not report to them. That is, managers must be able to lead, manage, and motivate others without the aid of hierarchical authority.

In gaming, conceptual skills relate to one's ability to see the big picture at the property level. That is, managers need to understand how the actions of their department affect the ability of the larger organization to achieve its stated objectives. A manager with poor conceptual skills is likely to focus on departmental goals instead of company goals. Such a perspective could be characterized by the motto – All for one and none for all.

Let's summarize this section by extending a previous example. Consider the decision to promote an employee from Dealer to Floor Person. All too often, this decision is based on the technical proficiency of the candidate. While technical proficiency is critically important when dealing the games, such skills decline in importance as one ascends the management ladder. Therefore, executives should focus on the candidates (i.e., Dealers) who demonstrate the skills necessary to succeed as a manager. For example, executives should promote Dealers who demonstrate an abundance of conceptual and human skills. Of course, technical skills are important too, but they should not be the primary determinant of who is promoted to Floor Person. Alternatively stated, the best Dealers are not necessarily the best candidates for Floor Person.

Questions/Exercises:

1. Within the Slot Department, what is the primary difference between a Technician Manager and a Shift Manager?
2. When might the President/GM be concerned that Vice Presidents are striving to maximize departmental profits? That is, how could this possibly be a concern?
3. Which operating departments fall under the authority of the VP of Casino Operations?
4. What is the primary difference between the job duties of the Sports Book Supervisor and those of the Race Book Supervisor?
5. Why would Pit Clerks report the Manager of Cage Operations, as opposed to someone from the Table Game Department?
6. After reading this chapter, the job duties of which position most resemble those of a Bank Teller?
7. What are the advantages and disadvantages of a top-down management structure?
8. In general terms, how do the job duties of the Keno Writer/Cashier differ from those of the Keno Runner?

9. Without referencing the text, can you name the Poker Room positions listed in the sample organizational chart? Hint: There are five, excluding the VP of Casino Operations.
10. Per the text, which games are often incorrectly assumed to be part of the Table Game Department?
11. Within the Table Game Department, to whom does the Shift Manager report?
12. Across the various operating departments, would you say the job duties are more similar at the tops (i.e., just below VP) or the bottoms of the organizational charts? Explain your answer.
13. Are technical skills more important to those in positions at the top or the bottom of the organizational chart? Explain your answer.
14. Within the Bingo Department, which position would you say is most visible to the customer? Explain your answer.
15. Who is responsible for the installation of a harness? What is a harness?

Chapter 5
Nevada Gaming Regulations

Why is it important to understand gaming regulatory requirements?
Why do jurisdictions have strict requirements to obtain a gaming license?
Why is a gaming license in Nevada treated as a 'privilege'?
What are the primary responsibilities of the Nevada Gaming Commission?
What are the primary responsibilities of the Nevada Gaming Control Board?
How is a gaming license obtained in Nevada?

Scope

It is the regulatory structure of the gaming industry that drives much of a casino's operating protocol, making a thorough understanding of the regulations essential to anyone studying the gaming business. This chapter is designed to provide an overview of Nevada's gaming regulatory system. Nevada's system has been studied and closely copied by most gaming jurisdictions throughout the world. It is important to note that in each jurisdiction there will be differences, however, understanding Nevada's gaming control model will give casino managers a good understanding of the primary functions of gaming regulation in any jurisdiction. The chapter discusses the role of the Nevada Gaming Commission and Nevada Gaming Control Board in the regulatory process. Also addressed is the process of obtaining a gaming license, including a review of who must be licensed. Finally, the chapter addresses the current tax structure and how that structure has evolved throughout the history of Nevada.

Chapter Goals

- Discuss why a strong regulatory system is essential to the overall economic success of the gaming industry in Nevada
- Describe the primary goals of the Nevada Gaming Commission and Nevada Gaming Control Board
- Describe the gaming license application process in Nevada
- Describe the character traits the Nevada Gaming Commission looks for in gaming license applicants
- Understand the history of gaming control in Nevada and how the regulatory system evolved to the current model
- Describe the difference between a nonrestricted and restricted gaming license in Nevada
- Demonstrate the gaming tax structure in Nevada, and how credit play affects the tax calculation

The Modern Era of Nevada Gaming Control

The modern era of gaming in Nevada began on March 19, 1931, when then-governor Fred Balzar signed Assembly Bill 98 into law. Though gaming was originally legalized in Nevada in 1869, it was heavily restricted, and a strict ban was enacted in 1909. Assembly Bill 98 is often referred to as the "Wide-Open Gambling Bill" because almost all forms of gambling were made legal, including slot machines, table games, and race and sports betting.[1]

Despite legalizing gambling in 1931, Nevada did not make any effort to tax casinos until fourteen years later. From 1931 to 1945, a casino owner simply needed to receive a business license from the city or county in which he chose to operate and pay a small fee. This fee amounted to $10 per month for each slot machine and $25 per month for each table game. The regulation of gaming was left to these city and county officials. In 1945, Nevada lawmakers realized that a state gaming tax could replenish state coffers. Senate Bill 142 was passed, implementing a 1% tax on each gaming establishment's gross revenue. In addition, this bill made the Nevada Tax Commission the gaming industry's regulatory authority.[2]

In 1950, a freshman United States Senator from Tennessee, Estes Kefauver, was appointed to a special Senate subcommittee to investigate interstate gambling and racketeering activities. Kefauver, as a freshman senator, saw investigating organized crime as his route to national prominence. The subcommittee, formally titled the "Special Committee to Investigate Organized Crime in Interstate Commerce," held hearings in 14 cities, including Las Vegas.[3] The subcommittee found that "the caliber of men who dominate the business of gambling in the state of Nevada is on a par with that of professional gamblers operating illegal gambling establishments throughout the country."[4] Furthermore, and more damning to the regulatory system, the subcommittee noted, "the licensing system which is in effect in the state has not resulted in excluding the undesirables from the state, but has merely served to give their activities a seeming cloak of respectability," and "as a case history of legalized gambling, Nevada speaks eloquently in the negative."[5]

To remedy the problems of gaming regulation in Nevada, Kefauver recommended the federal government impose a 10% tax on all gaming. This proposition, which had potentially disastrous consequences for Nevada, caused a political uproar. U.S. Senator Pat McCarran argued fervently and successfully against Kefauver's recommendation. Even with Kefauver's gaming tax proposal rejected, Nevada's legislature was concerned about possible federal regulation of the Nevada gaming industry, and acted quickly to

---

[1] Gaming in Nevada: 2008-2009 Policy and Program Report. Legislative Counsel Bureau. Retrieved on February 1, 2010, from http://www.leg.state.nv.us/lcb/research/PandPReports/12-GNs.pdf.

[2] Parry, M. *2008). The Agony and the Ecstasy of Nevada's Gross Revenue License. *Nevada Lawyer* 16(5).

[3] Raab, S. *Five Families: The Rise, Decline, and Resurgence of America's Most Powerful Mafia Families.* New York, NY: Thomas Dunne Books, 2005. p. 96-97.

[4] Special Committee to Investigate Organized Crime in Interstate Commerce. *The Kefauver Committee Report on Organized Crime.* New York: Didier, 1951. p. 72.

[5] Ibid., p. 74, 75.

demonstrate that the state could effectively regulate the industry and remove the influence of organized crime.[6]

In 1955, to regulate the industry, the legislature organized the State Gaming Control Board (GCB) as a division of the Nevada Tax Commission. In 1959, the legislature passed the Gaming Control Act. This law created the Nevada Gaming Commission (NGC) to oversee activities of the GCB, eliminating the Tax Commission from the gaming control system. Finally, in 1961, the legislature created the Gaming Policy Committee, which has the authority to hold hearings on gaming policy, and serves as a recommending body to the NGC and GCB. This basic model has not changed to this day, which is a testament to its success.

Primary Objectives of Gaming Regulation

The state legislature, in the Gaming Control Act, declared the gaming industry vitally important to the economy of the state and the general welfare of its inhabitants.[7] To ensure the continued economic viability of the industry, the NGC and GCB are guided by two primary objectives:

1) Ensuring that gaming is conducted honestly, competitively and free of criminal and corruptive elements; and

2) Ensuring accurate and timely taxes are paid to the state.

In 1959, the Nevada legislature recognized that, for the industry to be successful, gaming must be conducted honestly and fairly and, most importantly, must be viewed as honest and fair by the public. The strict regulation of gaming was designed to ensure that the public could trust that a public agency was overseeing all operations, protecting the public from unsavory practices.

Two-Tier System of Nevada Gaming Regulation

Nevada's gaming industry is regulated through a two-tiered system consisting of the NGC and GCB, as required by the Gaming Control Act. This two-tiered system, in which the GCB makes recommendations to the NGC, which makes the final approval, was originally implemented to ensure the system avoided any appearances of corruption. The Nevada Attorney General is the legal advisor to both the NGC and GCB.[8] Figure 5.1 illustrates Nevada's regulatory structure.

---

[6] American Experience. "Las Vegas: An Unconventional History." Public Broadcasting System. Retrieved on February 16, 2010, from http://www.pbs.org/wgbh/amex/lasvegas/peopleevents/p_kefauver.html.
[7] Nevada Gaming Control Act, Nevada Revised Statutes (hereafter NRS) 1959, c.463 s.0129(1)(a)
[8] NRS 463.0199

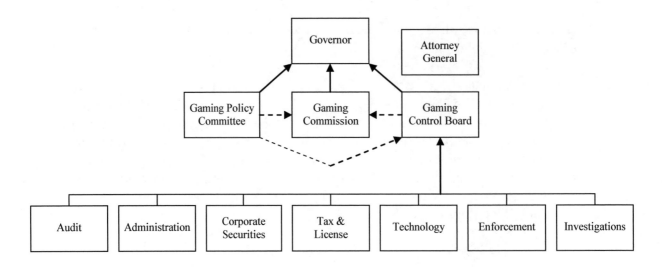

Figure 5.1. Overview of Nevada's Regulatory Structure.

Selection Criteria of Nevada Gaming Commissioners

The Nevada Gaming Commission is a five-member lay body appointed by the Governor. Commissioners are part-time employees of the state. Each Commission member is appointed to a four-year term and must meet the following criteria:

1) A U.S. citizen and resident of Nevada;

2) Not a member of the Nevada Legislature;

3) Not a person holding any elective office in the state government, nor any officer or official of any political party;

4) Commission members must not be actively engaged in or have a direct pecuniary interest in gaming activities; and

5) Preferably no two Commissioners shall be of the same profession or major field of industry.[9]

Moreover, not more than three members of the Commission shall be of the same major political affiliation.[10]

---

[9] While this is preferred, per NRS 463.023(3), it has not always been the followed by the Governor when making NGC appointments.
[10] NRS 463.023

Primary Responsibilities of the Nevada Gaming Commission

The NGC primarily functions to:

1) Act on recommendations of the GCB in licensing matters and ruling over gaming employee registration appeal cases;

2) Serve as the state's final authority to approve or deny the recommendations of the GCB on any license application;

3) Adopt regulations for the gaming industry. These regulations effectuate law or policy or describe the procedures and guidelines of the NGC or GCB;[11] and

4) Consider changes to public policies regarding gaming, including passing changes to the NGC regulations.

The NGC holds monthly public meetings, two weeks after the GCB public meetings, to consider license applications and policy matters, as recommended by the GCB.

Selection Criteria of Nevada Gaming Control Board Members

The Nevada Gaming Control Board is a three-member lay body appointed by the Governor. Board Members are full-time employees of the state. Each Board member is appointed to a four-year term and must meet the following criteria:

1) A U.S. citizen, and, or within six months of appointment, be a resident of Nevada;

2) Not a member of the legislature; and

3) Not a person holding any elective office in the State Government, nor any officer or official of any political party.

The Chairman of the Board, who is its Executive Director, must have at least five years of responsible administrative experience in either the public or business sector or possess broad management skills. One member must be a certified public accountant, have five years of progressively responsible experience in general accounting, and have a comprehensive knowledge of the principles and practices of corporate finance. The final member of the Board must be selected with special reference to his training and experience in the fields of investigation, law enforcement, law, or gaming.[12]

---

[11] NRS 463.145
[12] NRS 463.040

Primary Responsibilities of the Nevada Gaming Control Board

The GCB primarily functions to:

1) Provide for the effective investigation, licensure, and administrative approvals in conformance with applicable statutes and regulations, thereby promoting growth and stability of the gaming industry;

2) Issue recommendations to the NGC in licensing matters and gaming employee registration appeal cases; and

3) Establish rules and regulations for all tax reports submitted by Nevada gaming licensees.

The GCB holds monthly public meetings to consider license applications and policy matters, and make recommendations on those matters to the NGC. The GCB has offices located in Las Vegas, Reno, Carson City, Elko, and Laughlin. The GCB has approximately 420 employees throughout these five offices.

The GCB's staff is divided into seven divisions: 1) Administration; 2) Audit; 3) Tax and License; 4) Enforcement; 5) Investigations; 6) Corporate Securities; and 7) Technology.[13]

Administration Division

The Administration Division handles the day-to-day administration of the GCB. This includes resolution of personnel and budget issues as well as record retention. The Administration Division works closely with the state legislature regarding legislative issues and the Board's budget.

Audit Division

The Audit Division is responsible for auditing the largest gaming establishments (Group I licensees)[14] in Nevada to ensure all gaming revenue has been properly reported and all taxes have been remitted to the state. It also monitors the financial operations of gaming licensees. The Audit Division developed and periodically updates the minimum internal control standards (MICS), which define minimum controls to which each licensee must adhere.

Tax and License Division

The Tax and License Division is similar in many ways to the Audit Division. The Tax and License Division is responsible for reviewing the financial performance of the

---

[13] Nevada Gaming Commission and State Gaming Control Board. Retrieved on February 13, 2010, from http://gaming.nv.gov/.

[14] A Group I licensee is defined by NGC regulation 6.010, effective July 1, 2010, as a nonrestricted licensee having gross revenue of $5,870,000 or more for the 12 months ended June 30th each year.

smaller gaming establishments (Group II licensees)[15] in Nevada. In addition, the Tax and License Division is charged with the administration and processing of all tax collections from the gaming industry.

Enforcement Division

The Enforcement Division is the law enforcement arm of the GCB. Although not referred to as police officers, Enforcement Agents have full police powers, including arrest authority. Enforcement Agents are charged with investigating criminal violations of the state's gaming laws. In addition, the Enforcement Division handles customer disputes brought by gaming patrons against a licensee. As the Gaming Control Act declared that public confidence and trust in the gaming industry is vital to maintaining a prosperous economy, the Enforcement Division dedicates a large amount of their resources to arbitrating customer disputes, ensuring all games are conducted fairly, honestly, and free of corruption. Finally, the Enforcement Division inspects and approves new games, surveillance systems, and chips, cheques, and tokens to be used in casinos.

Investigations Division

The Investigations Division is responsible for the investigation of all individuals and privately held business entities that apply for a Nevada gaming license. Investigations personnel conduct an exhaustive examination of each applicant's personal and financial background, to ensure the integrity and suitability of the individual. Their exhaustive investigations, prior to licenses being issued, maintain the public's confidence that organized crime affiliates are not involved in the industry. Applicants are required to provide Investigations Division personnel with 'power of attorney,' allowing GCB staff to legally access all criminal and banking records of the applicant.

Corporate Securities

The Corporate Securities Division was previously an arm of the Investigations Division, as their missions are quite similar. The Corporate Securities Division is charged with conducting the background and financial investigations of publicly traded corporations that apply for a Nevada gaming license. Further, the division is responsible for ongoing reviews of publicly traded companies that hold gaming licenses. This includes monitoring Wall Street developments relating to gaming, and actions of licensees with regard to operations outside of Nevada.

Technology Division

The Technology Division is responsible for reviewing and testing all gaming devices and associated equipment before it is put into use on a casino floor. The division tests each game, ensuring the integrity of the machine in the GCB's laboratory. In addition, the

---

[15] A Group II licensee is defined by NGC Regulation 6.010, effective July 1, 2010, as a nonrestricted licensee having gross revenue of less than $5,870,000 for the 12 months ended June 30th each year.

Technology Division performs random field inspections of gaming devices to ensure integrity. The Technology Division assists the Enforcement Division with patron disputes by examining and analyzing gaming device electronics.

Gaming Policy Committee

The Gaming Policy Committee was created in 1961. It is an administrative body consisting of government, public, and industry representatives who are charged with making recommendations regarding gaming policy to the GCB and NGC. Unlike the NGC and GCB, the Gaming Policy Committee meets only when called by the Governor. Recommendations made by this committee are advisory in nature, and the recommendations are not binding on the GCB or NGC. The Gaming Policy Committee has not convened since 1984, when it was called to order by then-Governor Richard Bryan.

The Gaming Policy Committee consists of 11 members. Unlike the NGC and GCB, this committee is not entirely appointed by the Governor. The committee is composed of:

1) The governor;

2) One member of the NGC (designated by the Chairman of the NGC);

3) One member of the GCB (designated by the Chairman of the GCB);

4) One member of the Senate (appointed by the Legislative Commission);

5) One member of a Nevada Indian tribe (appointed by the Inter-Tribal Council of Nevada);

6) Two members of the general public (appointed by the Governor);

7) Two members who are representatives of nonrestricted gaming licensees (appointed by the Governor); and

8) One member who is a representative of a restricted gaming licensee (appointed by the Governor).[16]

Gaming Licensing

The Nevada legislature passed Senate Bill 142, in 1945, instituting a broad tax on gaming revenue. In effect, this bill made the Nevada Tax Commission the regulatory body of the gaming industry. At this time, however, the legislature was only interested in collecting taxes. That is, regulating gaming activity through licensing and employee registration

---

[16] NRS 463.021

was not a concern. Since the passage of the Wide-Open Gambling Bill, in 1931, gaming licensing and regulation had been left in the hands of local authorities, such as cities and counties. The Tax Commission was happy to leave the actual regulation of gaming with local officials, while collecting the tax for the state.[17]

This laissez-faire attitude toward regulation changed after Senator Kefauver issued his subcommittee report on gaming, and the Nevada legislature moved quickly to create the GCB, in 1955. While the GCB was just a division of the Tax Commission (until 1959, and the passage of the Gaming Control Act), the division took on formal regulatory responsibilities. At this time, the GCB was charged with the investigation of applications for state gaming licenses, enforcement duties, and reporting on applications for gaming licenses to the Tax Commission for final approval. Of course, today, the GCB's mission has not materially changed, however, the GCB now reports to the NGC for final approval in licensing matters.

Nevada Gaming License is a Privilege

The NGC has broad, though finite, authority, including full and absolute power to deny any application or revoke or suspend any license for any cause deemed reasonable.[18] In addition, no applicant has any right to a license. Any license issued, or other commission approval granted is a revocable privilege, and no holder acquires any vested right.[19]

These powers are the backbone of Nevada's system of gaming regulation. A license to operate gaming in Nevada is a privilege granted by the NGC, not a right. Had the operation of gaming been defined as a right, the state would have been powerless to eliminate organized crime influences from the industry. At the time the Gaming Control Act was passed, the casino industry was rife with members of the organized crime underworld, many of whom had not been convicted, or even charged, with crimes. The NGC was able to deny licenses to reputed organized crime members, based on the fact that a license was deemed a 'privilege' by the Gaming Control Act.

Types of Licenses

There are two broad categories of gaming licenses in Nevada, nonrestricted[20] and restricted.[21] Nonrestricted licenses do not restrict the number of machines, tables, etc. Restricted licenses allow 15 or fewer slot machines and no table games. For general purposes, bars, convenience stores, and grocery stores have restricted licenses, while casino-resorts have nonrestricted licenses. A slot route operator's[22] license is considered a nonrestricted license.[23] A distributor's license[24] and manufacturer's license[25] are two

---

[17] Parry, op. cit.
[18] NRS 463.1405(4)
[19] NRS 463.0129(2)
[20] NRS 463.0177
[21] NRS 463.0189
[22] Slot route operator is an individual or company that places slot machines in a licensed location, and shares in the revenue generated from those machines. This is common in restricted locations.
[23] Nevada Gaming Commission Regulation 4.030(1)(b)(2)

distinct licenses; however, for purposes of investigation and oversight, they are treated as nonrestricted licenses.

As of 1992, the NGC can only issue a nonrestricted license to a 'resort-hotel,' which is defined as an establishment with the following amenities:

1) More than 200 rooms available for sleeping accommodations;

2) At least one bar with permanent seating capacity for more than 30 patrons that serves alcoholic beverages sold by the drink for consumption on the premises;

3) At least one restaurant with permanent seating capacity for more than 60 patrons that is open to the public 24 hours each day and 7 days each week; and

4) A gaming area within the building or group of buildings.[26]

The Nevada Resort Association championed this change in 1992, which had the effect of protecting existing resorts from competition. To enter the casino market, a company now had to build an entire resort, which required a large capital investment. This increased the barrier to entry for any outside company, effectively insulating the major casino companies that dominated the Las Vegas market from smaller gaming-centric properties.

Local jurisdictions can implement additional restrictions for operating within a specific city or county. The above requirement that nonrestricted licenses can only be issued to resort-hotels is state law; therefore, a local jurisdiction can make its requirement more stringent, but cannot relax this requirement.

Who Must be Licensed?

In Nevada it is unlawful for any person or entity to make available for play any form of gambling without first having applied for, and been granted, a license by the NGC.[27] This includes, but is not limited to, the following:

1) Any beneficial owner or legally designated manager of a privately held company (no matter how small the percentage of ownership);[28]

2) Any institutional investor that owns 15% or more of a publicly traded corporate entity that holds a gaming license;[29]

---

[24] NGC Regulation 4.030(3)
[25] NGC Regulation 4.030(2)
[26] NRS 463.01865
[27] NRS 463.160
[28] NGC Regulation 15.1594-6 and NGC Regulation 15A.060 and NGC Regulation 15B.060
[29] NGC Regulation 15.430(1)

3) Any person or entity that acts as a manufacturer or distributor of gaming devices;[30] and

4) Any person or entity that acts as a slot route operator.[31]

In all cases, the company and/or individual must be licensed before gambling can be made available. In addition, the following individuals are required to file applications for a license; however, individuals holding these positions are allowed to serve in their designated capacity prior to being granted a gaming license. Each individual must have an application on file with the GCB within thirty days of being appointed to his/her respective position.

1) Any officer or director of a privately held company;[32]

2) Any officer, director, or employee of a publicly traded company that holds a gaming license, who the NGC determines is actively engaged in gaming operations;[33] and

3) Any "Key Employee" of a gaming licensee; whenever at least three members of the NGC deem such licensure necessary.[34]

A Key Employee is defined as "Any executive, employee, or agent of a gaming licensee having the power to exercise a significant influence over decisions concerning any part of the operation of a gaming licensee."[35]

Gaming employees whose job responsibilities do not require them to file a key employee application are still required to register with the GCB. Upon registration, the GCB checks criminal databases for any outstanding warrants and/or prior criminal convictions. Once an employee is successfully registered, the individual must notify the GCB within ten days of any change in employment. Because of this practice, the GCB knows where every gaming employee in the state is working, at all times.

In addition to positions for which gaming licensure is required, the NGC has the power to require any person in the gaming industry to file an application and go through the licensing process.[36] This power prohibits licensees from shielding employees from the licensing process. When organized crime influences operated much of the gaming industry in Nevada, a front man, or clean businessman, would file an application and be approved to own and operate the casino. The actual operators, organized crime members, would have titles such as 'Director of Food and Beverage.' This title would not carry the

---

[30] NRS 463.650 and NGC Regulation 14.020(1) and NGC Regulation 4.030(2) and NGC Regulation 4.030(3)
[31] NGC Regulation 4.030(1)(b)(2)
[32] NRS 463.530
[33] NRS 463.637(1)
[34] NGC Regulation 3.110
[35] NGC Regulation 3.110(1)
[36] NGC Regulation 3.110(2)

job responsibilities that would require a key employee license. The NGC, however, was able to require these people to file applications. Such authority played a critical role in eliminating organized crime from the industry.

Finding of Suitability Requirements

Any beneficial owner, officer, director, member, manager, etc., of a holding company of a gaming licensee, who is engaged in any way with the administration or operation of the gaming licensee must be found suitable by the NGC, and may be required to be licensed.[37] The NGC uses the exact same requirements in determining suitability for an individual as is used in determining licensure. Furthermore, the distinction does not include any difference in the investigative process. The distinction between suitability and licensure is made to determine direct control over a licensee. An individual working for a licensee and exerting day-to-day control over the gaming operations is required to be licensed. An individual found suitable serves in a position that does not include day-to-day control.

Application Process: Nonresticted License

The application process for receiving a nonrestricted license is lengthy and difficult. Further, the applicant must pay for the cost of the required investigation, which often is hundreds of thousands of dollars. Several colorful and anecdotal accounts of past applicants and current licensees have compared the licensing process to medical procedures such as root canal surgery and the colonoscopy.

An applicant begins the process by filing an application, submitting fingerprint cards, filling out an approximately 100-page personal history disclosure form, and signing paperwork giving the GCB power of attorney. In addition, the GCB requires every piece of financial paperwork, including bank statements, investment account statements, IRA statements, tax returns, real estate documents, and many other business/financial documents related to the previous five years of the applicant's life. GCB investigators will travel the world, if necessary, to pursue information on each applicant.

After the Investigations Division has compiled and analyzed all required information, a report on each individual applicant is written. The GCB holds its monthly open meeting to consider the application and issues a recommendation to the NGC. Two weeks later, the NGC holds its monthly public meeting, and votes on the GCB's recommendation. The process, from filing an application to the NGC's yay or nay vote, can take well over a year.

Application Process: Restricted License

The application process for a restricted license is much simpler. An applicant pays a flat fee, rather than footing the bill for all investigative costs. The scope of the investigation is narrower, primarily focusing on the applicant's source of funding for the business

---

[37] NRS 463.595(1)

118

venture. While a nonrestricted license investigation can take over a year, most restricted license investigations take only a few months.

Application: Approval Process

The NGC has final decision-making power in granting or denying a license to an applicant. The NGC's voting process, however, is determined by the recommendation of the GCB. If the GCB unanimously recommends approval, a simple majority rule vote by the five members of the NGC is needed for approval or denial. If the GCB is split 2-1, either for approval or denial, a simple majority rule vote by the NGC is needed for approval or denial. If the GCB unanimously recommends denial, the only way for the application to be approved is a unanimous approval vote from the Commissioners.[38] This two-tiered system has proven successful in guarding against political corruption in gaming regulation.

In addition to the state's licensing requirements, several local jurisdictions in Nevada require gaming license applications to be filed. This is primarily a way for these jurisdictions to collect license fees. Local jurisdictions do very little due diligence on proposed gaming licensees. Instead, they wait for the decision of the NGC and then follow suit.

NGC Licensing Decisions

While the NGC has the absolute power to make decisions on licensing matters, the Gaming Control Act and NGC Regulations provide guidelines and standards for determining the quality of individuals appropriate for a gaming license. These standards include, but are not limited to, the following:

1)   The applicant is a person of good character, honesty, and integrity;

2)   The applicant is a person whose background, reputation, and associations will not result in adverse publicity for the state of Nevada and its gaming industry; and

3)   The applicant has adequate business competence and experience for the role or position for which the application is made. [39]

In addition, the NGC makes a determination regarding the source of funds for an operation. The NGC must be satisfied that the source of funding for an operation was obtained from a reputable source.[40] This is, again, a tool to eliminate organized crime influences from the industry.

---

[38] NRS 463.220
[39] NGC Regulation 3.090(1) and NRS 463.170(2)
[40] NGC Regulation 3.090(2) and NRS 463.170(3)

Nevada Gaming Tax Structure

When the Nevada legislature passed the Wide-Open Gambling Bill in 1931, no effort was made to institute a state tax on the industry. Small fees were imposed by local jurisdictions, and the state received 25% of these fees. The state's total revenue from fees in the first year of legalized gaming amounted to $68,110, slightly more than 1% of the state's total income.[41]

In 1945, the Nevada legislature passed Senate Bill 142, instituting a 1% tax on gross gaming revenue. This bill defined gross gaming revenue as "The total sums received as winnings less only the total of all sums paid out as losses by a licensee under a state gambling license."[42]

Nevada's gaming tax structure has expanded from this one simple line, to several worksheets used to compute gaming taxes. At the heart of the tax structure is a percentage tax on gross gaming revenues. As of 2003, the nonrestricted gaming tax structure is as follows:

1) 3.5% of the first $50,000 of gross gaming revenue during each respective month;

2) 4.5% of the next $84,000 of gross gaming revenue during each respective month; and

3) 6.75% of revenue exceeding $134,000 of gross gaming revenue for each respective month. [43]

Gross gaming revenue is defined as:

	Cash received as winnings
Plus	Cash received in payment for past credit issuances
Plus	Cash received as a rake[44]
Less	Cash paid out as losses to patrons.[45]

While this definition is not overly convoluted, the tax structure has been complicated by the practice of wagering cheques, chips, tokens, or slot credits issued by way of markers.[46] Note that the definition of gross gaming revenue does not include wagering instruments issued to the player (via credit), and subsequently won by the casino, for which the casino has not received cash.[47]

---

[41] Kaufman, P. (1974). *The Best City of Them All: A History of Las Vegas, 1930 - 1960*. Ph.D. diss. (nonpublished), University of California Santa Barbara: p. 231

[42] Parry, op. cit.

[43] NRS 463.370(1)

[44] Rake is any compensation received by the gaming establishment in which the establishment is not party to a wager. The most common form of a rake in casinos is poker.

[45] NRS 463.0161(1)

[46] Refers to the practice of issuing credit (i.e., markers) to players in lieu of a cash buy-in.

[47] NRS 463.0161(2)(g)

Casino operators are not required to pay taxes on outstanding debt resulting from credit issued to players, until the money has been collected.[48] For example, assume a player wagered against a $1 million line of credit, and lost the entire line in March; however, the casino operator did not collect the $1 million until June. The operator's gaming tax liability on the $1 million would be deferred until June (i.e., the month in which it was collected). In addition, if the casino operator agrees to forgive the debt, or settle for a lesser amount, the operator only pays tax on the amount of cash received, which, in the extreme case, could be nothing.

In Nevada, Forms NGC-01 and NGC-31 are completed by the licensee each month (see Figures 5.2 and 5.3). These two forms accompany the licensee's monthly tax payment to the state. With regard to the example from the previous paragraph, Section B of NGC-31 provides a worksheet for licensees to report the monthly dollar-amounts of both credit issues and collections of credit issued in previous months.

Each licensee is also assessed quarterly and annual fees based on the number of slot machines and table games in-service. Licensees self-report the number of slot machines and table games in-service at their respective locations. The GCB Audit Division periodically inspects licensees for reporting accuracy. In addition, nonrestricted licensees are subject to a live entertainment tax of 10% on all sales occurring in venues in which live entertainment is taking place.

Restricted gaming licensees are not subject to a tax on gross gaming revenues. Rather, restricted licenses simply pay quarterly and annual fees based on the number of in-service slot machines at the location. As of this writing, the annual machine fee is $250 for each machine in-service (prorated on a monthly basis) and a quarterly fee of $81 per machine (with no proration).

Regulatory Structures in Other Jurisdictions

Given Nevada's long history of legal and regulated gambling, its general regulatory structure has been replicated in gaming jurisdictions throughout the world. Over the years, Nevada's regulators have endured many attempts to circumvent the state's regulation. Some of these attempts have been better orchestrated than others, but all have contributed to the collective experience of Nevada regulators. To a great extent, Nevada's gaming regulations represent a patchwork of solutions designed to foil specific attempts to avoid compliance.

Given the great number of regulated gaming jurisdictions across the globe, a review of each one's regulatory structure would be burdensome and quite lengthy. As noted, most of these jurisdictions have adopted a regulatory structure very similar to Nevada's two-tier system. This is a sensible approach, as it would be remiss for governments in other gaming jurisdictions to not consider Nevada's rich history of regulation. Therefore, to

---

[48] NGC Regulation 6.120 and NGC Form 1.

NGC-01 (04-07-05)

NEVADA GAMING COMMISSION
Monthly Gross Revenue Report

This report, together with your remittance payable to the order of the NEVADA GAMING COMMISSION, is required to be filed MONTHLY, NOT LATER THAN THE 24th DAY OF THE MONTH, covering the preceding calendar month.

For Gaming operations during the month of:
Filing Deadline:

Account No., Name, Address, Zip Code

For Office Use Only

Check Number _____

Batch Number _____

Entry Date _____

Please correct if in error

1. **GROSS REVENUE** before adjustments [from NGC-31] $ _____

2. **ADJUSTMENTS:**
   A. Cage credit issued $ _____
   B. Collections in areas other than the pit _____
   C. Net of return checks _____
   D. NET ADJUSTMENTS [Line 2A + 2B +/- 2C] _____

3. **LOSS CARRY-OVER:** from _____ Reg. 6.110(7) _____
   [not to exceed Line 1 + Line 2D]

4. **GROSS REVENUE $** [Line 1 +/- Line 2 – Line 3] $ _____

5. **LICENSE FEE COMPUTATION:** NRS 463.370(1)
   A. 3.5% of the first $50,000 on line 4 $ _____
   B. 4.5% of the next $84,000 on line 4 _____
   C. 6.75% of the remainder of line 4 _____

6. **ESTIMATED FEE DUE BASED ON GROSS REVENUE** [Line 5A + 5B + 5C] $ _____

7. **ESTIMATED FEE ADJUSTMENT** NRS 463.370(6)(b)
   A. Current month's actual FEE DUE [Line 6] $ _____
   B. Est. payment on _____ (_____)
   C. Estimated Fee Adjustment [Line 7A – 7B] _____

8. **SUBTOTAL** [Line 6 +/- Line 7C] _____

9. **CREDIT from PRIOR PERIOD** [not to exceed Line 8]
   Total CREDIT available _____ _____

10. **SUBTOTAL** [Line 8 – Line 9] _____

11. **ADVANCE ESTIMATED PAYMENT** NRS 463.370(3) [THREE (3) times the amount on Line 6] _____
    Note: Applies only to the first FULL month of operation for a NEW LICENSEE

12. **TOTAL DUE BEFORE PENALTY** [Line 10 + Line 11] _____

13. **PENALTY FOR LATE PAYMENT:** NRS 463.270(5)
    A. Fewer than 10 days late: 25% of line 12 but
       not less than $50 or more than $1000. $ _____
    B. Ten or more days late: 25% of line 12, but
       not less than $50 or more than $5,000. _____
    PENALTY DUE [Line 13A or Line 13B] _____

14. **TOTAL AMOUNT DUE:** [Line 12 + Line 13] $ _____

15. **TOTAL REMITTANCE** Check Number: _____ $ _____

**Please make remittance payable to the Nevada Gaming Commission and return to
State Gaming Control Board, Tax and License Division, P.O. Box 8004, Carson City, NV 89702-8004**

I, _____, certify and declare under the penalties of perjury that I am the
_____ of the business named above; that this is a true, correct and complete report
(Owner, Partner, President, Treasurer, Other-describe)
to the best of my knowledge, information, and belief; and that this application and report is made with the knowledge and
consent of all other individuals licensed.

Dated _____   Signed _____

Person to contact regarding this report: Name: _____   Phone: _____

RETURN ORIGINAL AND MAKE DUPLICATE FOR YOUR RECORDS

Figure 5.2. Form NGC-01 Monthly Gross Revenue Report.

NEVADA GAMING COMMISSION – MONTHLY GROSS REVENUE STATISTICAL REPORT

NGC-31
(03/12/09)

Group:

FILING DEADLINE FOR THIS REPORT:

For Gaming operations during the month of:

(For Commission Use Only)

SECTION A		NO. OF UNITS	COINS IN ($)	DROP ($)	GROSS REVENUE ($)
CODE	SLOT MACHINES				
010	1 Cent				
011	5 Cent				
012	10 Cent				
013	25 Cent				
014	50 Cent				
015	$1.00				
016	Megabucks				
017	$5.00				
018	$25.00				
020	$100.00				
021	$500.00				
022	Multi Denomination				
023	Mobile Gaming				
024	Other Denominations				
053	Adjustments				
	TOTALS				

SECTION B		NO. OF UNITS	PIT CREDIT ISSUES ($)	PIT CREDIT PAYMENT (CHIPS)($)	PIT CREDIT PAYMENT (CASH)($)	DROP ($)	WIN ($)	GROSS REVENUE ($)
CODE	TABLE GAMES							
002	Craps							
003	Roulette							
001	Twenty-One							
005	Wheel of Fortune							
007	Mini-Baccarat							
006	Baccarat							
056	Caribbean Stud							
057	Let It Ride							
037	Pai Gow							
043	Pai Gow Poker							
059	3-Card Poker							
009	Other Games (Describe Below):							
050	Adjustments							
	TOTALS							

PROGRESSIVE KENO (Check One)? ☐ Yes ☐ No

ACCOUNTING METHOD USED FOR RECORDING RACE AND SPORTS BOOK REVENUE (Please Check One):
☐ CASH: All cash wager received for the day less all cash paid out for day.
☐ MODIFIED ACCRUAL: All wagers for the events completed for the day less cash paid out.

The HASH TOTAL is a number comprised of the following subtotals added together.

SECTION A: ("NO. OF UNITS" TOTAL CONVERTED TO DOLLARS)
　　　　　　 ("COINS IN" TOTAL)
　　　　　　 ("DROP" TOTAL)

SECTION B: ("NO. OF UNITS" TOTAL CONVERTED TO DOLLARS)
　　　　　　 ("PIT CREDIT ISSUES" TOTAL)
　　　　　　 ("PIT CREDIT PAYMENTS" (CHIPS) TOTAL)
　　　　　　 ("PIT CREDIT PAYMENTS" (CASH) TOTAL)
　　　　　　 ("DROP" TOTAL)
　　　　　　 ("WIN" TOTAL)

SECTION C: ("NO. OF UNITS" TOTAL CONVERTED TO DOLLARS)
　　　　　　 ("WRITE" TOTAL)

SECTION D: ("NO. OF UNITS" TOTAL CONVERTED TO DOLLARS)

SECTION C		NO. OF UNITS	WRITE ($)	GROSS REVENUE ($)
CODE	COUNTER GAMES			
025	Keno			
026	Bingo			
035	Race Book			
048	Race Parlay Cards			
052	Race Pari-Mutuel			
034	Sports Parlay Cards			
036	Sports Pool (other)			
004	Football			
008	Basketball			
033	Baseball			
051	Adjustments			
	Totals			

PERSON TO CONTACT REGARDING THIS REPORT

NAME

PHONE NUMBER

HASH TOTAL

SECTION D		NO. OF UNITS	GROSS REVENUE ($)
CODE	CARD GAMES		
030	Poker		
032	Other Card Games		
054	Adjustments		
	TOTALS		
TOTAL GROSS REVENUE (Add Sections A, B, C, D)			

Enter on Line 1 of Form NGC-1

I, _____, certify and declare under the penalties of perjury that I am the _____ (Owner, Partner, President, Treasurer, Other) of the business named above; that this is a true, correct and complete report to the best of my knowledge, information, and belief; and that this report is made with the knowledge and consent of all other individuals licensed.

Dated _____ Signed _____

**Please return to State Gaming Control Board, Tax and License Division
P.O. Box 8004, Carson City, NV 89702-8004**

Figure 5.3. Form NGC-31 Monthly Gross Revenue Statistical Report.

review Nevada's general regulatory structure is to review the basic structure of gaming regulation throughout the world. Of course, this is not to say that important differences do not exist.

One general difference in the regulations of other jurisdictions provides for increased onsite presence of gaming regulators. For example, New Jersey and Missouri regulations prescribe much more onsite presence and oversight of operations than that of the Nevada regulations. Another noticeable difference is the tax rate. Aside from tribal gaming, most, if not all regulated jurisdictions in the world tax gaming revenues at rates beyond that of Nevada's.

In addition, jurisdictions such as New Jersey and Macau do not allow licensees to defer tax liability on uncollected markers. For example, if management were to issue a player $1 million in gaming cheques, by way of credit, and the player subsequently lost the entire $1 million, the licensee must recognize the $1 million as win in the reporting period in which it occurred. Moreover, management must include the $1 million in the calculation of taxable gaming win, regardless of whether any part of the $1 million is ever collected from the player. In a jurisdiction with a 40% tax rate, this uncollected debt would increase the operator's tax liability by $400,000. In Nevada, the same series of events would have no effect on the licensee's tax liability. This example demonstrates how an operator's credit policy can be greatly affected by a jurisdiction's regulatory structure.

Questions/Exercises:

1. What are the two primary objectives of Nevada's Gaming Commission (NGC) and its Gaming Control Board (GCB)?
2. What are the responsibilities of the Gaming Control Board's Audit Division?
3. What are the responsibilities of the Gaming Control Board's Investigations Division?
4. What are the responsibilities of the Gaming Control Board's Enforcement Division?
5. Explain what is meant by *privilege*, with regard to the terms of a Nevada gaming license?
6. Why is the concept of a privileged license essential to Nevada's system of gaming control?
7. Describe the standards by which the GCB and NGC evaluate the character and personal attributes of gaming license applicants.
8. As of 2003, describe the nonrestricted gaming tax structure in Nevada.
9. How is gross gaming revenue defined in Nevada?
10. How is the Nevada gaming tax structure complicated by the practice of issuing gaming cheques by way of credit?
11. Describe the central premise of Nevada's two-tier system of gaming control.
12. Explain the difference between Nevada's nonrestricted and restricted gaming licenses.

Chapter 6
Casino Drop & Count Processes

Why are internal controls critical to the drop and count processes?
Why are the drop and count uniquely important to table games?
What are the primary steps of the slot drop and count processes?
What are the primary steps of the table game drop and count processes?
How is currency transferred from the count room to the cage?
How is a table game's win/(loss) computed?

Scope

This chapter is designed to provide an overview of a casino's drop and count processes. These processes and the regulations that govern them will vary by gaming jurisdiction. Certain aspects of the count and drop processes vary by property, within the same jurisdiction. For example, differences in the capabilities of systems and technology employed by resorts can produce procedural variations between resorts. However, the fundamental aspects of the drop and count processes are essentially the same across all jurisdictions. Most of the procedures and practices described in this chapter are based on those employed by Las Vegas Strip hotel casinos. Therefore, the Nevada Gaming Control Board's (NGCB) Minimum Internal Control Standards (MICS) serve as a guide for most of the process descriptions.[1] However, it should be noted that some casino operators employ internal controls that exceed the minimum requirements set forth by regulators.

The drop and count processes for slots, table games, and poker tables[2] are all addressed. The discussion of slot procedures is limited to currency processing, as coin-operated devices account for only a small fraction of the total slot drop in a modern casino.

Chapter Goals

- Define terminology central to the discussion of the drop and count processes
- Describe the primary steps of the slot currency drop process
- Describe the primary steps of the table game drop process
- Describe the primary steps of the currency count and transfer processes
- Review key control procedures as they apply to the drop and count processes
- Provide a managerial overview of the drop, count, and transfer processes: Describe how the currency makes its way from the games to the casino's vault
- Demonstrate how to compute a table game's win/(loss)

---

[1] All MICS cited in this chapter are available online at http://gaming.nv.gov/audit_mics.htm.
[2] In most casino properties the poker room is not part of the Table Game Department.

Terminology

There is a considerable amount of industry jargon related to the drop and count processes. While some of these terms have been defined as they appear in the text, the terms that are most critical to the discussion have been defined in this section. Upfront knowledge of the terms defined here should make discussions related to drop and count procedures easier to follow.

Drop

This term refers to the act of collecting the various cash containers from gaming devices or locations on the casino floor. The group of employees responsible for this task is referred to as the *drop team*. Alternatively, drop represents the net dollar-value of certain items found in the cash containers. To avoid confusion, any reference to or use of the latter definition of drop will be clearly stated.

Count

This term refers to the process of counting the contents of the cash containers collected by the drop team. The group of employees responsible for counting the contents of these containers is referred to as the *count team*. It is not uncommon for some of the same employees to be members of both the drop and count teams.

Bill Validators

Also known as *currency acceptors*, bill validators are devices that are either imbedded into a slot machine or attached to one, in a peripheral sense. These devices allow currency to be directly inserted into a slot machine. The slot system then converts the currency into game credits. Once the customer inserts the currency into the bill validator, it resides in the *currency container*. Prior to bill validators, customers with currency were required to obtain change or gaming tokens from a slot attendant. Bill validators also accept wagering vouchers, which are defined next.

Wagering Vouchers

These are tickets used in a *VIVO* system. VIVO stands for voucher-in – voucher-out technology. This technology allows slot players to receive paper tickets when they cash-out slot credits, as opposed to buckets full of coins or tokens. If players decide to play again or just switch machines, they simply insert the bar-coded voucher (or ticket) into the machine's bill validator, and the credit balance from the voucher is recognized by the game.

VIVO is the generic acronym for this technology. The companies that produce this technology have various names for their voucher-based systems such as ticket-in – ticket-out (TITO). Another company refers to its voucher-based gaming instrumentalities as Qwikets.

Hot Cans & Cold Cans

As the drop team moves across the casino floor it collects currency containers from slot machines. These containers are referred to as hot cans. They are called hot cans because they are warm to the touch when they are removed from the interior of the machines. The metal can absorbs the heat produced by the game's electronics. Hot cans usually contain currency and wagering vouchers when they are removed from the game. The drop team replaces the hot can with a new empty currency container, which is referred to as a cold can. As you might have guessed, cold cans are stored in air conditioned metal carts and are relatively cold to the touch, hence the name.

Drop Boxes

The drop team also collects cash containers from table games. These containers are referred to as *drop boxes*. Each table game has a drop box. Although drop boxes certainly do contain currency, they contain other items as well. These items will be listed and defined in a subsequent section of this chapter. When discussing the drop and count processes, drop boxes are also referred to by some as hot and cold cans.

Wand

Also known as a *dolphin*, this device is used to match cans to specific slot machines. That is, a wand functions as a bar code reader. For example, the cold can bar code is read before it is placed in the slot machine. The slot machine bar code is also read to match the cold can to that game. The wand or dolphin stores these can-machine pairings. The count team eventually uses the wand to upload this stored information to the slot accounting system.

Currency Counter

This device counts and straps currency. A *strap* is a 100-note bundle. That is, 100 notes of the same denomination are bundled together by the currency counter using a strap to secure the bundle. Some currency counters are also able to *bag* the counted bills. The transparent bags usually consist of 2,000-note bundles. In appearance, bagged currency resembles a brick or small block of notes wrapped in transparent plastic.

In general, currency counters are expensive. It is not uncommon to pay $240,000 for a currency counter, with the cost of some models ranging well beyond this amount. Additionally, management can expect to pay another $35,000 per year for the machine's service contract. However, it is well worth it, as the labor savings provided by the device far exceed these costs.

Transport Carts

These carts are also known as *money carts, drop carts, storage racks*, and *trolleys*. The transport carts (or carts) are used by the drop team to transport cold cans and empty drop boxes to the casino floor. They are also used to transport full drop boxes and hot cans from the casino floor to the count room.

Common Elements of Drop & Count Processes

Drop & Count Schedules

Management must file drop and count schedules with the gaming regulators. These schedules are usually filed annually in Nevada. A drop or count may not begin before or after the scheduled time, unless management notifies the board in writing, in advance of any change in the schedule. With regard to schedule changes, gaming regulators would like to be given as much notice as possible. However, in practice, there are times when management notifies regulators of delays on the day of the affected drop/count.

The purpose of the schedules is to allow gaming regulators to observe the drop and/or count without notifying management. In this sense, the schedules themselves serve as control mechanisms, as management will not know if or when gaming regulators will choose to observe a drop or count.

Count Room Surveillance

Count rooms are heavily regulated and monitored, as tremendous amounts of unverified cash and gaming cheques are handled by those inside. Nevada count rooms are equipped with cameras to record the counts. Many are equipped with technology that allows surveillance personnel to listen to the conversations of the count team members during the count process. The video and audio records are stored by the Surveillance Department and available for review should there be any discrepancies in the count process. In many jurisdictions, a security officer must be present during the count, while others require the presence of a gaming regulator to witness the count.

Count Team Uniforms

Count teams wear either special jumpsuits or pocketless smocks. The purpose of the uniform is to deter theft. Specifically, the uniforms are designed to prevent employees from stealing cash and/or gaming cheques by putting these items in their pockets or inside articles of clothing.

Reporting Structure

The drop and count teams usually report to the Finance Department or some other department independent of the revenue-producing and security departments. This reporting structure is designed to reduce the likelihood of theft by way of employee collusion. For example, if the drop and count teams reported to either a revenue-producing department or the Security Department, they could be pressured by management to conceal or participate in theft, to avoid losing their jobs. Count teams must be comprised of employees who are independent of revenue producing departments (e.g., Table Games and Slots) and the department that assumes subsequent responsibility for the counted currency (e.g., Cage).[3] The Nevada regulations do permit certain exceptions to this standard.

Number of Count Team Members

Both the currency container count and table game drop box count must be performed by a minimum of three employees.[4] That is, at least three employees must be in the count room until the count is completed. Of course, these employees must meet the requirements for count team membership set forth in the regulations.[5] For the table game count, three-member count teams must be rotated on a consistent basis.[6] Specifically, the count team can be comprised of the same three individuals on no more than four days per week.

Currency Counter Test

Prior to both the currency container count and the table game drop box count, the currency counting machine must be tested.[7] That is, an authorized count team member feeds a known sum of money through the counter to ensure that it produces the correct count. This test is repeated by a second count team member. The test currency must be from a source that is separate from the currency to be counted on that day. For example, the test currency cannot be taken from a drop box that will be counted on that day. The accuracy of the currency counter is tested for each denomination of currency to be counted. Such tests are required for all forms of wagering instruments (e.g., vouchers).

Theft

Despite the surveillance equipment, special uniforms, reporting structure, and all the regulations and controls, theft is not uncommon in count rooms. Management teams battle theft regularly. These battles are usually not publicized, as management does not want to project the idea that it is difficult to deter theft.

Slot Drop

Given the predominance of bill validators/currency acceptors, only the procedure for dropping the currency containers will be covered here. Bill validators have become so common they have essentially eliminated coin from casino floors.[8]

---

[3] NGCB (2009). MICS, Group 1 Licensees, Slots, #38; and Table Games, #89.
[4] NGCB (2009). MICS, Group 1 Licensees, Slots, #37; and Table Games, #87.
[5] NGCB (2009). MICS, Group 1 Licensees, Slots, #38; and Table Games, #89.
[6] NGCB (2009). MICS, Group 1 Licensees, Table Games, #88.
[7] NGCB (2009). MICS, Group 1 Licensees, Table Games, #90; and Slots, #42.
[8] For more on the drop procedures of coin-operated devices, see Kilby, J., Fox, J., & Lucas, A.F. (2004). *Casino Operations Management*, 2nd ed., Wiley: New York, pp. 195-197.

Managers of Las Vegas Strip resorts rarely have all slots dropped on the same day. In fact, most drop between 400 and 500 machines per day. Many attempt to drop each machine a minimum of one time per week. Nevada gaming regulations require that all currency containers must be dropped and counted at least one time per month.[9]

Maximizing the Drop

Traditionally, the drop schedule was based on section/area of the floor. However, when the areas of the floor receiving little play were the only sections dropped, the amount of currency collected was minimal. That is, despite having conducted the daily drop, a great amount of cash remained on the casino floor uncollected and unrecorded.

Nevada's MICS do not require casino management to identify which particular slot machines will be dropped on a particular day. However, management is required to report whether slots will be dropped by denomination, section of the floor, or percentage of the floor.[10] By choosing the percentage-of-the-floor option, management is afforded the most latitude with respect to which specific machines will be dropped.

To minimize the number of days that money sits uncollected on the floor, managers at some properties query the slot system to identify the games with the most cash in them. Once these cash-heavy machines are located they are dropped. This system/process results in collecting and recording cash sooner rather than later. This is considered to be a best demonstrated practice, with respect to drop procedures.

Drop Team

In practice, the drop team is usually comprised of three members, which meets the minimum procedural requirement.[11] One member is from the Security Department, while the other two are usually from the Finance Department (i.e., count room). This assumes that the count room personnel dedicated solely to the drop and count functions report to management within the Finance Department. In the slot drop, the security guard is primarily an observer, although he is also responsible for guarding the cart that contains the cash cans. The other two team members are doing most of the manual labor. That is, one of the remaining two team members uses the door key to open the games, while the other uses a release key to remove the hot cans and loads them on the transport cart. Of these two jobs, opening the games is the preferred assignment, as removing the cans and loading them on the carts is much more difficult work.

Drop Day Staging

The slot drop for a given day actually begins on the previous day. That is, on the day before the scheduled drop, the carts are loaded with the appropriate complement of cold

---

[9] NGCB (2009). MICS, Group 1 Licensees, Slots, #31.
[10] NGCB (2009). MICS, Group 1 Licensees, Slots, #218, Note 4.
[11] NGCB (2009). MICS, Group 1 Licensees, Slots, #32.

cans and secured in the count room. Larger casinos will prepare three to four carts for a 400- to 500-machine drop.

Before the actual drop can begin, the appropriate keys must be obtained from the main cage.[12] Key control is a significant issue in the gaming industry, as unrestricted access to cash containers would invite theft.[13] Several controlled keys are needed to complete the slot drop and count. Two keys are needed to access the count room. One is issued to an officer from the Security Department and the second is issued to a count team member from the Finance Department. Slot machine access keys are issued to count team members from the Finance Department.[14] Keys to the transport cart padlocks are issued to a count team member from Security and a count team member from the Finance Department. There are two separately keyed padlocks that secure the doors of the transport cart, so both keys are required to unlock a properly secured cart.

Once the count room door is opened, a cart loaded with cold cans is removed and wheeled to the casino floor. Due to the tremendous weight of a loaded cart, only one cart can be deployed. If multiple carts were to reside in the same area of the casino, substantial damage could be done to the floor. The weight of the loaded carts can fracture even a concrete surface. Because of their design and weight, the carts often tear the carpet on the casino floor when they are pushed or pulled across it. In fact, in resorts with expensive flooring, cart paths are often restricted to specific areas of the casino floor. Motorized vehicles known as *tuggers* are used by some to pull the heavy transport carts through the drop process, alleviating the physical strain of manual locomotion.

Slot Drop Process

With a fully assembled count team and a cart loaded with cold cans on the casino floor, the remaining steps of the drop process are listed here. Further explanation of selected steps appears in the paragraphs following the list.

- Slot machine door is opened by count team
- Hot can is pulled and placed in the transport cart
- Cold can is wanded
- Machine is wanded
- Cold can is inserted into the machine
- Machine is closed/locked
- Process is repeated until the cart is full
- When the cart is full, the wand is placed inside the cart
- Cart is padlocked and wheeled to the count room

---

[12] The main cage is described in detail in Chapter 7. It serves as a secure storage facility/vault for the casino's cash and gaming cheques. Keys to cash containers are secured within the main cage as well.

[13] For more on key controls see: NGCB (2009). MICS, Group 1 Licensees, Slots, #144 – 152(b).

[14] Three separately keyed access keys are required to drop and count currency: (1) Slot machine door key; (2) Currency can release key; and (3) Currency can contents key [*Ibid, #141*]. Simultaneous access to the release key and the contents key is prohibited [*Ibid, #145*]. Physical custody of the currency can contents key requires the presence/involvement of employees from three separate departments [*Ibid, #144*].

- Once the cart arrives at the count room, a cage employee counts the number of hot cans on the cart
- Count team member counts the number of hot cans on the cart
- Information on the wand is uploaded to the slot accounting system
- Cart is padlocked and locked inside the count room for the duration of the drop
  - Count can begin (for this cart's contents), if three count team members are present in the count room
- Next cart is wheeled onto the casino floor
- The process is repeated until the last cart has completed its journey

When the hot can is pulled from the machine the slot accounting system is automatically alerted. The cold can and machine are both wanded to match these items in the slot accounting system. That is, the system records that a specific can was inserted into a specific machine. Again, the cold can is the empty replacement container for the hot can removed from the machine. After the last game has been dropped, the wand is locked inside the transport cart with the hot cans removed from the games. Of course, the hot cans were wanded and paired with the same slot machines when they were inserted as cold cans on the previous drop. Therefore, the machine, the hot can, and the cold can are all linked together in the slot accounting system.

Once the cart arrives at the count room, someone from the Cage Department counts the cans and verifies that the number of hot cans on the cart is not different from the number listed on the drop schedule for that day. A member of the count team, other than the security guard, does the same. This is an internal control that goes beyond Nevada's Minimum Internal Control Standards (i.e., MICS).

In most cases, multiple transfer carts are needed to complete the daily drop. Once the cart's supply of cold cans has been exhausted, regulations require that a minimum of two employees escort the cart (full of hot cans) to the count room, where it is locked inside until the count takes place.[15] This process must be repeated until the drop is completed. However, if three count team members are present (in the count room) when a loaded cart returns from the casino floor, the count may begin for this cart's contents. This is important to note, as the speed of the drop and count process is increased by beginning the count as the carts arrive in the count room.

Slot Count & Cage Transfer

Before the count begins, the members of the count team assemble in front of the count room door. A count team member and the security officer must both use their keys to unlock the count room door. Once inside the count room, the count process can be summarized by the steps listed here.[16] Further explanation of selected steps can be found in the subsequent paragraphs.

---

[15] NGCB (2009). MICS, Group 1 Licensees, Slots, #32(d).
[16] For more on the regulations governing the currency drop and count processes see: Nevada Gaming Control Baord (2009). MICS, Group 1 Licensees, Slots, #31 - #57.

- Hot cans are removed from the transport carts
- Hot cans are arranged on the counter top to be scanned
- Hot cans are scanned to create header tickets to be read by the currency counter
- Header tickets, currency, and wagering vouchers from the corresponding cans are placed in a plastic tray
- Contents of plastic trays are fed through the currency counter
- The currency is counted manually by count team members
- The currency counter uploads the counts to the slot accounting system
- The currency counter's count sheet is signed by all who participated in the count
- A transfer slip is completed to move the currency from the count room to the cage

The hot can contents include only two items: Wagering vouchers and currency. Although the wagering vouchers are fed through the currency counter, it does not recognize them as cash. When a hot can is opened and emptied, the empty can is shown to another member of the count team and to a count room surveillance camera.[17]

The header tickets identify each machine to the currency counter. This is important, as the currency counter automatically uploads the currency count for each machine to the matching machine record in the slot accounting system. The plastic trays will contain the contents of multiple cans. For example, a plastic tray may hold the contents of 20 hot cans, and, of course, 20 corresponding header tickets. If the header tickets did not separate the contents of the 20 cans, the currency counter would not be able to identify which currency belonged to which machine.

At least one count team member reconciles the count produced by the currency counter to a physical count of the currency.[18] This physical count is often independently performed by two count team members. To clarify, each note (of currency) is not physically counted. The manual counts are performed on bagged and strapped currency. That is, the bundles of notes are counted and multiplied by their respective denominations to arrive at a grand total, which is then compared to the machine count. The physical counts must match the machine count. However, the currency counter uploads its count to the slot accounting system without regard for the physical counts. Any variance between the physical and automated counts must be reported to the Accounting Department, where slot auditors must investigate and reconcile the difference.

Transfer to Cage

Before the currency can be transferred to the cage, everyone who participated in the count signs the count sheet, which is nothing more than a receipt/tape produced by the currency counter. The participants could sign other reports to document their involvement in the count; however, most casinos use the count sheet to record participation. Finally, a transfer slip is prepared, which includes the total dollar-amount of money to be transferred to the cage. The transfer slip accompanies the money to the cage, but not

---

[17] NGCB (2009). MICS, Group 1 Licensees, Slots, #48.
[18] Pursuant to NGCB (2009), MICS, Group 1 Licensees, Slots, #52.

before a cage representative completes an independent count of the money to be transferred and verifies that her count matches the dollar-amount listed on the transfer slip.[19] Once the dollar-amount of the transfer has been verified, the cage representative certifies the transfer by signing the transfer slip. Only then is the money accepted by the cage, as the transfer slip not only documents the physical relocation of the money, it documents the transfer of responsibility for the funds.

Bagging & Strapping Money

Depending on the specific capabilities of the currency counter, it automatically bags and/or straps the counted currency in bundles of the same denomination. The best currency counters are able to bag the counted bills in such a way that the contents of the bags can be loaded directly into the *cash cassettes* used in the *kiosks*. The cash cassettes are usually stored in the main bank area of the main cage.[20] They are essentially a plastic cartridge that can be inserted into an all-purpose cash-dispensing machine referred to as a kiosk. These kiosks are strategically located throughout the casino floor and can be accessed by customers for the following purposes:

- Break bills, e.g., receive five $20-bills for a $100-bill
- Redeem slot machine wagering vouchers
- ATM transactions
- Credit card cash advances

Table Drop

Unlike most other business settings, many table game transactions go unrecorded. In most cases, management does not know how much a table game has won or lost on a given day. To know this, the game must be dropped and counted. However, most casino shift managers do track pit transactions above a specified dollar amount, allowing them to estimate the results.

In most jurisdictions, the bulk of tax revenue provided by casino resorts is based on gaming win. In the case of table games, win can only be computed after the drop and count are conducted. This sequence causes gaming regulators to be very interested in the integrity of the drop and count processes. If these processes are not regulated, the state may not receive its share of the casino's revenues. That is, any theft during the drop and count would reduce the state's tax base.

Management is also very interested in protecting the integrity of the drop and count processes, as the casino's cash is exposed to many employees during these tasks. Well-conceived internal controls help prevent employee theft. Without these controls the likelihood of theft increases, resulting in reduced casino revenues.

---

[19] Per NGCB (2009), MICS, Group 1 Licensees, Slots, #54.

[20] The main bank area of the main cage serves as the casino's vault, i.e., the primary cash storage facility. All areas of the main cage are covered in detail in Chapter 7, including the main bank.

Table Game Drop Team

The table game drop team can consist of as few as two employees. For example, the drop team of many casinos is comprised of a security officer and a table game floor supervisor (i.e., floorperson). The security officer performs the manual labor in the table game drop process. This is quite different from the role of the security officer in the slot drop, where he is essentially an observer. In the table drop process, the floorperson assumes the role of observer.

Drop Frequency

Most Nevada casino operators drop the table games once daily. However, it was once common to drop each game after each shift, or three times daily. As casinos began to offer greater numbers of table games, completing three drops per day became expensive and difficult to execute. In 1993, the MGM Grand Hotel Casino opened its doors and became the first Nevada casino to implement a 24-hour table game drop. That is, it was the first casino to abandon the practice of dropping each game after each shift. Of course, the 24-hour drop was first approved by the Nevada gaming regulators.

Nevada gaming regulators no longer require management to drop table games that have not been played in the 24-hour period preceding the scheduled drop time. This exemption saves time and money, as pulling empty drop boxes benefits no one.

Drop Time

The table game drop time is the same time as the gaming day rollover time. Per Title 31, the drop must correspond with the end of the gaming day.[21] That is, management must designate a specific rollover time, which represents the end of one gaming day and the beginning of another. All transactions that occur prior to the rollover time are assigned to the current gaming day, including player ratings.[22] All transactions that occur after the rollover time are assigned to the next gaming day.

Table Drop Process

The primary steps of the drop process are listed here. Some industry jargon is used in the list, but further explanation of the steps and terms appears in the subsequent paragraphs.

- Floorperson manually counts the cheques in the trays and creates closers
- Appropriate keys are obtained by the drop team
- Transfer carts loaded with empty drop boxes are retrieved from the count room
- Security guard places empty boxes next to the appropriate games

---

[21] Title 31 of the U.S. Code (aka the Bank Secrecy Act) is federal regulation that addresses currency reporting issues. Title 31 is covered extensively in Chapter 8.

[22] Player ratings are estimates of a player's wagering activity. A floorperson's observations are the basis of these estimates/ratings. The ratings are entered into the casino system to create an electronic record of each player's estimated value.

- Closers are dropped into the table game drop boxes and the boxes are pulled
- The boxes pulled from the games are loaded on the transfer cart
- New empty boxes are placed in the table games
- Openers are dropped into the new empty drop boxes
- Once the last drop box has been loaded on the transfer cart, the cart is returned to the count room where it is secured

Creating Closers. The gaming cheques[23] for each denomination on each table game are counted by a floorperson and recorded on a multi-part form called a closer.[24] The closer includes the total dollar-value of cheques in the table game's tray.[25] A closer is completed for each table game and placed on its surface. When the floorperson creates the closer, a carbon copy of the closer is created. This copy will serve as the opener for the next gaming day. That is, when a floorperson eventually opens the game, the opener contains the beginning dollar-value of the tray for that gaming day.[26] The opener will be discussed further as we move through the drop process.

Keys. Several controlled keys are needed to complete the drop process.[27] That is, access to these keys is controlled either electronically or by way of a key control log. The following keys are accessed by the drop team:

- Two count room door keys
- Drop box release key
- Two transfer cart keys (for padlocks)

The count room door has two separately keyed locks. One count room key is controlled by the Security Department and issued to the security officer participating in the drop. The second count room key is controlled by the Cage Department and issued to members of the count team from the Finance Department. Both keys are required to access the count room. Before the drop can begin, the count room is accessed to retrieve the transfer carts loaded with empty drop boxes.

The drop box release key is used to remove the drop box from the table game. The drop release key must be separately keyed from the table game drop box contents key and the slot machine cash can release key.[28] The drop box release key is usually controlled by the

---

[23] In practice, gaming cheques are often incorrectly referred to as chips. Cheques have a face value, but chips do not. For example, chips appear primarily on roulette games.

[24] As the closer serves as an inventory form in this example, the accuracy of the closer is verified by two pit supervisors, or equivalent personnel, per NGCB (2009). MICS, Group 1 Licensees, Table Games, #72.

[25] The tray is the metal square housed in the playing surface of a table game (directly in front of the dealer position). Within the tray there are corrugations called tubes, which hold the gaming cheques in place. Craps and roulette games do not have trays.

[26] Many casinos no longer drop openers and closers. Instead, the cheques on each game are counted and recorded on an inventory form. Pit clerks enter the dollar-value the opening/closing inventories directly into the casino system.

[27] For more on key control standards see: NGCB (2009). MICS, Group 1 Licensees, Table Games, #111 - #122(c).

[28] NGCB (2009). MICS, Group 1 Licensees, Table Games, #111.

Security Department and issued to the security officer participating in the drop.[29] Although not specifically required by regulation, most Nevada casinos require the participant from the Table Game Department to accompany the security officer to obtain this key. That is, the security officer participating in the drop is not permitted to obtain the drop box release key in the absence of the drop team member from the Table Game Department. Lastly, the drop team members are not be permitted to simultaneously access the drop box release key and the drop box contents key.[30]

The transfer carts are secured by two separately keyed padlocks. One padlock key is controlled by the Security Department and issued to the officer participating in the drop. The second padlock key is usually controlled by the Cage Department and issued to the floorperson participating in the drop. Drop team members authorized to access the transfer cart keys are not permitted to access the drop box contents key.[31]

Not all key controls are the result of external regulations. Gaming management has developed many effective security procedures that go beyond that of the minimum controls set forth in the regulations.

Transfer Carts Retrieved. On the day before the current day's drop, the transfer carts are loaded with the empty drop boxes. These loaded carts are padlocked and locked inside the count room until they are retrieved on the following day (i.e., the current drop day). These carts are wheeled to the casino floor and opened.

Placement of Empty Boxes. Once the transfer carts are unlocked on the casino floor, the security officer unloads the empty drop boxes and places them next to the appropriate table games. That is, each drop box has a table game number painted on it, indicating the table game to which the drop box belongs. The table games are marked with the same number. For example, both the drop box and the table game would be marked with "01BJ04", indicating Blackjack 4 in Pit 1.[32] There is only one "01BJ04" on the casino floor. Additionally, Nevada regulations require that drop boxes and table games are permanently marked with their corresponding identification labels (e.g., 01BJ04), which must be visible from a distance of at least 20 feet.[33]

Closers Dropped. The closer is dropped into the drop box on the game and the paddle is not replaced in the drop slot.[34] The security officer then inserts the release key and pulls

---

[29] The drop box release key can also be controlled by the Cage Department. Nevada's MICS only require the department that controls this key to be independent of the Table Game Department, per NGCB (2009). MICS, Group 1 Licensees, Table Games, #114.

[30] NGCB (2009). MICS, Group 1 Licensees, Table Games, #115.

[31] NGCB (2009). MICS, Group 1 Licensees, Table Games, #117.

[32] A pit is a grouping of table games. The individual tables are usually arranged to form a circular or rectangular shape. The interior of the pit is manned by employees, while customers occupy the exterior gaming positions. Customers are not permitted in the interior of the pits.

[33] Nevada Gaming Commission (2009). Nevada Gaming Statutes & Regulations, Regulation 1, Issuance of Regulations; Construction; Definitions, § 1.1.

[34] The closer must be dropped by someone other than a pit supervisor, per NGCB (2009). MICS, Group 1 Licensees, Table Games, #73.

the box from the game. If the paddle were in the drop slot, the box could not be removed. The act of pulling the drop box from its housing automatically closes the drop slot on the game's playing surface. That is, nothing can be inserted into the drop slot without a drop box in the game.

Again, the drop slot is located on the playing surface of the table game and serves as access to the drop box. A paddle is placed in the slot when it is not in use. When players exchange currency for gaming cheques, the dealer lifts the paddle from the drop slot and inserts the currency into the drop box. The dealer then places the paddle back into the slot to block access to the drop box. Other items besides currency are placed in the drop box, but these items will be discussed in the section that describes the table game count process.

Loading the Cart. Once the active drop box has been removed from the game, the security officer loads it on the transfer cart.

Empty Boxes Inserted. Once the game's active drop box has been removed, it is replaced with a new empty drop box. This empty box is the one that the security officer placed next to the game at the beginning of the drop process.

Openers Dropped. Once the new empty box is inserted into the game, the drop slot is automatically opened. The opener (formally the closer) is the first item placed in the new drop box. The paddle is then returned to the drop slot and the game is open for business on the new gaming day.

Transfer Cart Returned. Once the last box has been pulled from the game and loaded on the cart, the transfer cart is padlocked and wheeled back to the count room. Should more than one transfer cart be needed to complete the drop, regulations require that any full cart be escorted to a secure location by at least two employees, at least one of whom is independent of the Table Game Department.[35] In fact, any full cart must remain in a secured location until the count takes place.[36]

Table Game Count Process

The primary steps of the table game count process are listed here.[37] Some industry jargon is used to describe these procedures, but further explanation of the steps and terms appears in the paragraphs that follow the list.

- Count team assembles outside the count room
- Controlled keys needed to complete the count process are obtained
- Count team accounts for all drop boxes listed on that day's drop schedule
- Drop boxes are opened

---

[35] NGCB (2009). MICS, Group 1 Licensees, Table Games, #81.
[36] NGCB (2009). MICS, Group 1 Licensees, Table Games, #80.
[37] For more on table game count regulations see: NGCB (2009). MICS, Group 1 Licensees, Table Games, #83 - #102(b).

- Drop box contents are sorted (currency and paperwork)
- Currency is fed through the counter
- Paperwork is reconciled to the casino system
- Currency is manually counted by count team members
- Once the contents of all boxes have been counted, the count team signs the Master Game Report (MGR)

Assembly. The count team must be fully assembled outside of the locked count room before the controlled keys can be released and the count can begin. The count team usually consists of three members from the Finance Department, including a lead member or supervisor.

Keys. The following controlled keys are needed to complete the table game count process:

- Two count room door keys
- Drop box release key
- Two transfer cart keys
- Drop box contents key

The only new key here is the drop box contents key. This key is used to open the drop boxes. Once the count team has assembled and is ready to begin the count, the cage will issue this key to a member of the count team from the Finance Department. However, a member of the Security Department and a member of the Cage Department must be present when the drop box contents key is issued. More specifically, Nevada's Minimum Internal Control Standards require members of three different departments to be present when this key is issued.[38]

The door keys are used to enter the count room, and the cart keys are used to remove the drop boxes from the locked transfer carts. The need for the drop box release key during the count is less obvious. This key is used to reset the drop box mechanism that allows an empty box to be inserted into a table game. The drop boxes must be reset before they can be used in the next drop. This key is issued to a count team member from the Finance Department.

Box Inventory. Once inside the count room, the carts are opened and the count team accounts for all boxes listed on that day's drop schedule. No extra boxes should be on the carts and there should be no missing boxes.

Boxes Opened. This step is somewhat self-explanatory. The drop box contents key is used to open the drop boxes. However, once the box has been emptied, the count team member who emptied the box must show the empty box to another member of the count

---

[38] NGCB (2009). MICS, Group 1 Licensees, Table Games, #114.

team and to the count room camera.[39] The interior of the empty box is shown to the camera to make a video record of the empty box.

Box Contents Sorted. Once the boxes are opened, the currency is separated from the paperwork. The paperwork consists of the following items:

- Marker issue slips[40]
- Marker redemption slips[41]
- Openers
- Closers
- Fills[42]
- Credits[43]

There are other items found in drop boxes that are not considered to be paperwork, as previously defined. For example, the casino's own high-denomination cheques (e.g., $100,000 cheques) and poker cheques can both be found in drop boxes.[44] Additionally, gaming cheques from other nearby casinos are sometimes found in the drop box,[45] along with promotional items such as match-play coupons and promotional chips.[46] Neither of the latter two items is used in the calculation of a table's win. However, the value of the previously described cheques is included in the table win calculation.

All of the items listed as paperwork along with gaming cheques from other casinos are included in the table win formula. To compute a table game's win (i.e., revenue), the metric referred to as drop must first be calculated. The following formula is used to compute drop:

> Drop = Dollar-value of Currency in the Drop Box + Dollar-value of Gaming Cheques in the Drop Box + Dollar-value of Marker Issue Slips in the Drop Box – Dollar-value of Marker Redemption Slips in the Drop Box

To compute a table game's win, the dollar-value of the cheques missing from its tray must also be calculated. The following formula is used to compute this metric:

> Cheques Missing = Dollar-value of Opener + Dollar-value of Fills – Dollar-value of Credits – Dollar-value of Closer

---

[39] Pursuant to: NGCB (2009). MICS, Group 1 Licensees, Table Games, #97.

[40] A record of the casino's claim against funds held in a player's bank account.

[41] A record of payment to the casino to retire all or part of a player's debt.

[42] A record of gaming cheques transferred from the cage to the game.

[43] A record of gaming cheques transferred from the game to the cage.

[44] Policy dictates that these cheques are dropped, as there is no logical place for them in the game's tray.

[45] Many casinos honor gaming cheques from nearby competitors. Policy usually permits only the lower denominations of such cheques to be wagered on table games. Dealers are often instructed to drop these cheques when they are won by the casino or exchanged for house cheques.

[46] Promotional chips are usually awarded to established premium players as play incentives. Match-play coupons are also play incentives, which are typically offered to entry-level table game players.

The following equation uses the results of the previous two equations to compute a table game's win:

$$Win = Drop - Cheques\ Missing$$

Currency Counted. Header cards are created that identify the origin of each bundle of cash fed through the currency counter. In this case, the origin is a specific table game. The currency extracted from the drop boxes and the corresponding header cards are fed through the currency counter. The header cards also allow the currency counter to automatically upload each game's currency total to the casino system.

Paperwork Reconciled. While one count team member is feeding the currency through the counting machine, another is reconciling the drop box paperwork. All the paperwork items extracted from the drop box have been previously entered into the casino system by personnel from the Table Game Department. The count team counts and sums the dollar-value of the paperwork items for each of the following categories: Markers issued, markers redeemed, fills, and credits. The sum of the physical count must match the casino system total in every case. Each game has only one opener and one closer, so, for these items, the total on the paperwork records is simply compared to the value entered in the casino system.

In short, the count team makes sure that the physical items recovered from each game's drop box support the corresponding totals entered into the casino system. Any difference between these totals must be investigated and reconciled. Of course, the one exception is currency. That is, the casino system has no record of the currency residing in each table game's drop box. The game must be dropped and counted to know the value of the currency in its drop box.

Manual Count. At least one count team member reconciles the count produced by the currency counter to a physical count of the currency.[47] This physical count is often independently performed by two count team members. To clarify, each note (of currency) is not physically counted. The manual counts are performed on bagged and strapped currency. That is, the bundles of notes are counted and multiplied by their respective denominations to arrive at a grand total, which is then compared to the total produced by the machine count.

Signatures. The count team signs the MGR to document each team member's participation in the count process. If there are any issues with the integrity of the count process, management has a record of the participants. The signatures represent a step toward personal accountability for the count process and result.

Transfer of Table Game Currency to the Cage

A transfer slip is produced to move the currency from the cage to the count room. This form includes the total dollar-amount of money to be transferred to the cage. The transfer

---

[47] Pursuant to NGCB (2009), MICS, Group 1 Licensees, Table Games, #106.

slip accompanies the money to the cage. However, the currency is not accepted by the cage until a cage representative manually counts the money to be transferred and verifies that the total matches the amount listed on the transfer slip.[48] The cage employee then signs the transfer slip, certifying the transfer. Only then is the money transferred to and accepted by the cage. The transfer slip not only documents the physical relocation of the money, it documents the transfer of responsibility for the funds.

Poker Drop

The poker drop and count processes are similar to those of the table game drop and count processes. However, there are a few interesting differences. Although it is much more costly in terms of labor expense, poker tables are often dropped at the end of each shift. This practice occurs in casinos that drop other table games once a day. Also, poker cheques have different face values than cheques used on most table games. In spite of their unusual face values, poker cheques are negotiable and can be wagered on other table games.

The different face values of poker cheques are most helpful to the drop team. That is, management issues denominations of poker cheques that are consistent with the expected rake. In most cases, the rake is based on a percentage of the pot, up to a maximum dollar amount (e.g., $4). The pot refers to the aggregate dollar-value of all wagers placed on a hand of poker. By tailoring the face value of poker cheques to the rake structure, management reduces the number of cheques collected and deposited in the poker drop boxes.

Why would management be concerned with reducing the number of cheques in the poker drop boxes? Assuming all cheques are made from the same materials, four, $1-cheques will weigh four times that of a single $4-cheque. Reduced drop box weight is much easier on the drop team and the casino floor. Cheques are by far the heaviest items in a drop box, and poker drop boxes contain nothing but cheques. Managing the weight of these boxes by offering rake-friendly gaming cheques is no trivial matter.

Most importantly, great numbers of $1 cheques in drop boxes could cause them to fill before the scheduled drop time, creating several operational issues. For example, management would be required to conduct an emergency drop, using spare drop boxes. This is a costly interruption on several levels. Alternatively, management does not want too much of its poker cheques inventory in the drop boxes, as a minimum number of cheques are required to keep the games in operation. Once the cheques are in the drop box, the box must be dropped and counted before the cheques can return to circulation on the casino floor.

In summary, the risk of game interruption, emergency drop costs, and the potential weight of the active drop boxes are all reasons for the different face values of the poker cheques and for dropping the poker games each shift, as opposed to once daily.

---

[48] Pursuant to NGCB (2009), MICS, Group 1 Licensees, Table Games, #108.

Poker Count

Although the process is only briefly addressed here, the poker count is as tightly regulated as any other count process. This section is limited to a discussion of the unique aspects of the poker count procedures. For example, poker drop boxes only contain cheques, so there is no need for the currency counter. Further, there is no paperwork to reconcile. In short, the cheques are racked and transferred from the count room to the fill bank, by way of a transfer slip. The racks are plastic containers that hold five rows of twenty cheques, for a total of 100 cheques. Multiple denominations of cheques are never placed in the same rack. The value of a full rack is equal the product of the denomination of the cheques in the rack and 100. For example, a full rack of $4 cheques is equal to $400 (i.e., $4 x 100).

The unique denominations of poker cheques also reduces the time required to rack the cheques in the count process. For example, 100, $4-cheques can be racked in one fourth the time it takes to rack 400, $1-cheques. By increasing the speed of the racking process, management reduces the labor costs associated with the poker count process.

Questions/Exercises:

1. Name the items likely to appear in a table game drop box? Assume that data from table game cheques inventory forms are not entered into the casino system by pit clerks.
2. List the alternative names of the device used to match cans to specific slot machines, within the slot accounting system.
3. Based on the example provided in the text, interpret the following alpha-numeric code: 04BJ01.
4. Name the keys needed for a table game drop.
5. Describe the membership of both the slot and table game drop teams (as described in the chapter).
6. List the alternative names for the transport carts used to carry the cash containers from the casino floor to the count room.
7. Briefly describe the primary purpose of the drop.
8. Why does management offer poker cheques in denominations different from other table game cheques?
9. Briefly describe the primary purpose of the count.
10. What is unique about the poker count process?

Use the following information to complete the next three exercises.

Currency in the drop box	$50,000
Cheques in the drop box	$5,000
Markers issued in the drop box	$100,000
Markers redeemed in the drop box	$80,000
Opener	$120,000
Closer	$99,000
Fills	$40,000
Credits	$15,000

11. Compute the dollar-value of this table's drop.
12. Compute the dollar-value of the cheques missing from the table game.
13. Compute the win (i.e., revenue) produced by this table game.
14. How do the following items protect the integrity of the drop and count process?
    a. Mandatory drop and count schedules
    b. Count team uniform design
    c. Count room surveillance equipment
    d. Reporting structure (with respect to the count team)
15. How does the task of dropping poker games differ from that of dropping table games?

Chapter 7
Cage Operations

What is a casino cage?
What are the key areas within the main cage?
What are the functions of these key areas?
Where should management locate the cage?
What is the Daily Cash Summary Report?

Scope

This chapter is designed to provide an overview of a casino resort's cage operation. The primary banking areas of the main cage are identified and the basic functions of each of these areas are described in greater detail. Although the cage operation is heavily regulated and many internal control procedures are mandated, detailed descriptions of these regulations and procedures are not offered here. The focus of this chapter is on the managerial facets of a casino's cage operation.

Chapter Goals

- Provide a general description and overview of cage operations
- Provide a sample layout of a main cage
- Identify the primary functions of each bank/cage area within the main cage
- Explain the imprest banking process
- Describe the electronic key control process
- Provide recommendations for main cage location and configuration.

Terminology

There is a tremendous amount of industry jargon related to the cage operation. These terms of the trade have been defined as they appear throughout the chapter. The footnotes also contain definitions and additional information related to key terms.

Overview

There are several ways to configure and manage a casino cage. We have chosen one of these forms to serve as the framework for our explanation of cage operations. However, readers should know that other equally effective operating structures do exist.

In essence, the cage is the central hub for all cash transactions, serving in the capacity of a bank. In fact, in 1985, casinos were determined to be financial institutions per U.S. Title 31.[1] The intent of this determination was to prevent illegal money laundering activities within casinos.

Because gaming is a cash business, the cage interacts with each gaming department on a daily basis. The cage also has daily interaction with all major non-gaming revenue centers. With all the cash transactions, the cage is a heavily monitored and regulated operation. Although Title 31 applies to many transactions that take place in all major U.S. casino cage operations,[2] other specific regulations and methods of operation vary by jurisdiction.

Key Areas of the Main Cage

As some casinos have annex, auxiliary, or satellite cages, the term "main cage" is used here to collectively represent the following areas of operation:

- Front Windows
- Main Bank
- Marker Bank
- Fill Bank
- Employee Cage/Bank

The employee cage is sometimes referred to as an annex, auxiliary, or satellite cage. It is also sometimes referred to as the employee bank. However, in the cage structure we have chosen for this chapter, it is part of the main cage operation. Figure 7.1 depicts the layout of the main cage.

Front Windows

The front windows of the cage are located in Area 1 of Figure 7.1. This is the area of the cage that customers would approach from the casino floor. Although not a formal cage function, the front windows often serve as a customer information center. That is, patrons

---

[1] United States Code (2008), Title 31, Subtitle IV, Chapter 53, Subchapter II, § 5312, Subsection (a), Paragraph 2, Subparagraph (X).
[2] Ibid. The term "major" is intended to refer to all U.S. gaming establishments with annual gaming revenues of more than $1,000,000. This includes Indian gaming establishments, other than those limited to Class 1 gaming as defined by the Indian Gaming Regulatory Act.

often ask cashiers how to find various locations on the property. Cashiers also field many questions about the property's marketing and promotional activities. The front windows are usually staffed by cashiers, with supervisors and managers covering windows during peak business periods.

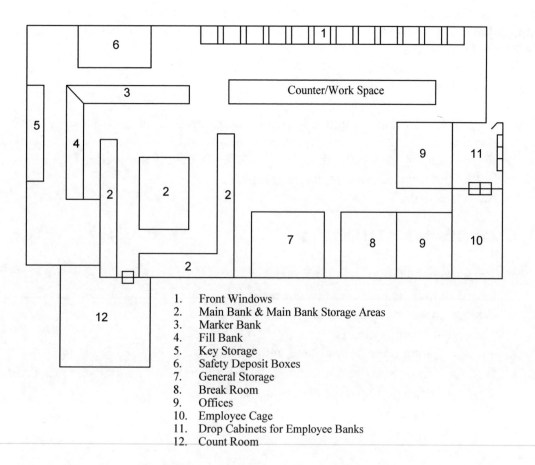

1. Front Windows
2. Main Bank & Main Bank Storage Areas
3. Marker Bank
4. Fill Bank
5. Key Storage
6. Safety Deposit Boxes
7. General Storage
8. Break Room
9. Offices
10. Employee Cage
11. Drop Cabinets for Employee Banks
12. Count Room

Figure 7.1. Main Cage Layout.

Imprest Banks

The banks or money drawers for the front windows are known as imprest banks. Imprest banks are issued to cashiers at the beginning of their shift. A typical imprest bank for a cashier at a Las Vegas Strip resort would contain $100,000. If the ending cash value of the bank is different from the beginning cash value, the variance must be reconciled. For example, let's assume the beginning balance of a cashier's imprest bank is $100,000 (in cash). Further, let's assume only one transaction occurs over the course of the cashier's shift. This transaction consists of a customer exchanging $2,000 in gaming cheques for cash. At the end of the shift, the cashier's imprest bank would contain $2,000 in gaming cheques and $98,000 in cash, for an ending value of $100,000. In this case, the difference between the beginning and ending cash balances is easily explained. When the change in the cash balance cannot be reconciled it results in one of two possible conditions: A cash shortage or a cash overage. This is a serious issue, as cashiers are permitted a limited number of irreconcilable banks.

In most casinos, at the end of the cashier's shift, the $2,000 in gaming cheques would be exchanged for cash to return the cash balance of the imprest bank to $100,000. The imprest bank (i.e., drawer) would then be returned to the main bank area of the cage to be stored until it is reissued.

Transaction Types

This section begins by listing frequently occurring transactions at the front windows of the main cage. Given the wide variety of transactions conducted at the front windows, a complete list would be very difficult to compile. The following transactions are defined and/or further described in subsequent paragraphs:

- Check cashing
- Credit card and ATM transactions
- Exchange slot vouchers for cash
- Exchange of gaming cheques for cash
- Assist in the issuance of cage markers
- Sell purchase vouchers to slot players
- Receive marker payments
- Process front money deposits and withdrawals
- Redeem marketing coupons that require disbursement of gaming cheques or cash
- Process Title 31 compliance transactions
- Exchange foreign currency
- Facilitate table game buy-ins (although rare)

Check cashing. Cashiers cash many forms of checks such as personal checks from customers, payroll checks, social security checks, travelers' cheques, and more.

Credit card and ATM transactions.[3] Although it would seem unnecessary, as these types of transactions are thought to be automated, there are instances requiring cashier involvement. For example, cashiers must assist customers who do not have a PIN assigned to their credit cards.[4] In this case, the customer must bring the receipt from the cash-advance machine to the cashier to receive her money. Also, cashiers must assist customers who exceed the bank-imposed ATM withdrawal limit. That is, these limits can be exceeded with assistance from the cashier.

---

[3] ATM stands for automated teller machines. External banks place these machines throughout hotel-casinos, with at least one located near the cage.

[4] PIN stands for personal identification number. Most credit card companies require customers to create a PIN before they are able to receive cash advances without contacting the credit card issuer.

Exchange slot vouchers for cash. VIVO stands for voucher-in – voucher-out technology. The vouchers are also referred to as tickets. When slot players finish playing and they have credits remaining on the game, they cash-out their credits. Instead of spitting coins into a metal tray, the ticket printer attached to the slot machine prints a voucher which includes the player's balance (in dollars). To convert the balance of the voucher to cash, slot players can present these vouchers to the cashiers at the front windows. The cashiers verify and pay the vouchers.

Exchange gaming cheques for cash. This may seem simple enough, if not self-explanatory. However, this is not always the case. For example, management determines critical values for cashing-in gaming cheques. These critical values are usually based on the wagering habits of the clientele. For a Las Vegas Strip resort, the critical value might be $4,000, while the management of an off-Strip property might deem $1,000 exchanges as critical. In any case, when players cash-in cheques equal to or greater than the established critical value, the cashiers must perform the following duties:

- Determine whether the player has an outstanding marker balance
- Verify that the player actually made wagers on a table game
- Record the transaction in the Multiple Transaction Log (MTL), per Title 31

Markers are counter checks held by the casino as evidence of money owed to the casino by a specific player.[5] Management does not want to give players cash when they owe the casino money, hence the marker-balance review.

The second task, verifying wagering activity, is an issue of compliance with the 2001 U.S.A. Patriot Act. That is, buying gaming cheques, placing no wagers (or very few wagers), and redeeming the cheques for cash is considered suspicious activity, and consistent with the act of money laundering.[6]

Casinos are required to log all transactions that meet the established critical value, and issue a Currency Transaction Report (CTR-C) to any customer who produces more than $10,000 in cash-in or cash-out transactions within a single gaming day.[7] While cashiers are not required to personally issue a CTR-C, they are required to log any transaction that meets or exceeds the established and applicable critical value. When cashiers accept gaming cheques in exchange for cash, they must report the transaction in the Multiple Transaction Log (MTL), assuming the dollar-amount of the exchange exceeds the critical value.

In review, any attempt to cash-in cheques equal to or greater than the established critical value, requires the cashier to review the casino system for outstanding marker balances and sufficient wagering activity. Cashiers must also log the transaction in the MTL. The

---

[5] Markers are not just evidence of debt. These instruments can be presented for payment at the customer's bank.
[6] 2001 U.S.A. Patriot Act, Title III, Subtitle B. See Suspicious Activity Reporting (SARC).
[7] Code of Federal Regulations (2009), Title 31, Subtitle B, Chapter 1, Part 103, Subpart B, §103.22.

Title 31 reporting requirements are discussed in greater detail in another chapter. For now, let's just say that cashing-in gaming cheques can be far from a routine procedure.

The cage cashiers are not permitted to exchange roulette chips for cash, as these chips have no face value. That is, these chips are assigned a unit value at the roulette table, when the player purchases them (i.e., buys-in). Although these chips are labeled by table, their value is established and maintained only on the table where they were purchased. Therefore, roulette chips may only be exchanged for standard gaming cheques at the roulette table on which they were purchased.

To avoid an excessive amount of Title 31 reporting, race and sports players who win substantial sums are sometimes paid in a special series of gaming cheques. These cheques are issued when the winning player has indicated that he would like to place additional race or sports wagers. Although these cheques do have a face value, they are to be redeemed at the race and sports book only. However, cage cashiers can redeem these special cheques when the race and sports book is closed.

Issue cage markers. Cashiers process marker issue slips for credit players, once such a transaction is approved by the appropriate personnel. Credit players are customers who have established lines of credit with the casino. A marker issue slip is the internal form used to document the credit player's debt to the casino and to reconcile the issuance of funds from the cage.[8] When a marker is issued to a credit player, his credit line must be reduced by the dollar-amount of the marker. In most cases, the cage issues markers to slot players. In Nevada, table game players are encouraged to buy gaming cheques at a table game. Again, cashiers only process marker transactions, as they do not have the authority to approve the extension of credit or to issue markers against a player's existing line of credit.

Sell purchase vouchers. With VIVO technology, players can purchase vouchers with values greater than the amount of cash they would feel comfortable carrying in their wallet or purse. That is, a slot player could purchase a $2,500 voucher from the cashier. When inserted, this voucher would register $2,500 worth of credits on the slot machine's credit meter. Purchase vouchers are usually sold through the front windows of the cage. A purchase voucher is not a marker, as no credit line is needed to purchase one. These vouchers can be purchased with any form of payment the casino is willing to accept, including a marker.

Receive marker payments. Markers can be redeemed at the front windows of the cage. That is, credit players can repay all or part of their outstanding markers at the front windows.

Process front money transactions. Players sometimes wire money from another bank to the casino's cage, to serve as a bankroll for substantial wagering activity. Such deposits are referred to as front money. Front money can be deposited or withdrawn at the front

---

[8] Markers are negotiable instruments. That is, casino executives can present a marker for payment at the customer's bank. Markers are counter checks.

windows of the cage. Of course, withdrawals would be made against a player's front money deposit. Markers can be issued against the balance of the front money deposit in the cage. Front money deposits remove the credit risk for the casino.

Redeem marketing coupons. The cashiers redeem coupons when the offers require cash or gaming cheques to be disbursed. This is not uncommon, as many offers direct customers to the cage for purposes of redemption.

Title 31 compliance transactions. Title 31 is part of the federal Bank Secrecy Act, which designates casinos as financial institutions.[9] With this designation comes the responsibility of logging and reporting many different kinds of transactions to the federal government. A great number of such transactions occur at the front windows of the cage. Rather than describing these transactions here, an entire chapter has been devoted to compliance with Title 31 and related acts.

Exchange foreign currency. Cashiers access the casino's posted currency exchange rates to exchange U.S. currency with currency from other countries. However, such transactions are limited in many ways. For example, most casinos will not exchange any foreign coins, despite the denomination. Some casinos will only buy foreign currency. That is, the casino will not sell foreign currency. For example, customers can exchange Euros for U.S. dollars, but they are not permitted to exchange U.S. dollars for Euros. Such policies vary greatly by property.

In most cases, the currency exchange rates are downloaded daily from the casino's external bank to the casino's cage operating system. Cashiers are provided with a reference book containing examples of each country's currency. The purpose of this book is to reduce the likelihood of exchanging cash for counterfeit foreign currency. In spite of this visual aid, most casinos do not accept currency from all countries.

Facilitate table game buy-ins. As noted earlier, the management of most Nevada casinos prefers that table game players buy cheques or chips on one of the table games. As cheques and chips are issued for the sole purpose of gaming, management would prefer that players buy them where they wager them – on the tables. However, there are rare cases where table game cheques are issued at the front windows of the cage.

Main Bank

The main bank and its associated storage areas are located in Area 2 of Figure 7.1. As this is one of the larger areas of the cage, three different counters/storage areas exist within Area 2. This bank is a floating bank, as opposed to an imprest bank. That is, the daily balance of the main bank can increase or decrease, based on the day's activity.

---

[9] United States Code (2008), Title 31, Subtitle IV, Chapter 53, Subchapter II, § 5312, Subsection (a), Paragraph 2, Subparagraph (X).

The primary functions of the main bank are listed next. Further description of these functions is provided in the subsequent paragraphs.

- Serves as the primary storage/vault area in the main cage
- Supplies funds to all other banks within the casino (including the front windows)
- Funds satellite windows/cages
- Accepts transfers of funds from gaming areas, the count room, and all other banks
- Supplies funds to pay substantial jackpots/customer pay-offs

These are the central functions of a main bank. However, smaller casinos sometimes expand the scope of the main bank to include marker bank and/or fill bank functions.

Storage/Vault Area

The main bank stores all of the reserve gaming cheques. That is, the cheques which are not in circulation. Reserve gaming cheques are a unique registered series of cheques[10] which can be pressed into service to combat attempts by customers to pass counterfeit gaming cheques. The reserve roulette chips are an exception, as these chips are not usually stored in the main bank.

The cash cassettes are also stored in the main bank. These are cartridges which are preloaded with cash for use in the casino kiosks. These kiosks are located at strategic points on the casino floor, serving as all-purpose cash dispensers. They can be used as ATM's, cash-advance machines, slot voucher redemption points, and bill breakers. Bill breakers simply make change. For example, a customer may insert a $100 bill into the kiosk and request five $20 bills in return.

Finally, the main bank stores currency ordered from an external bank and it stores currency received from the count room. As casinos are required to meet minimum bankroll requirements, it is sometimes necessary to order currency from external banks. That is, the Nevada gaming regulations require casinos to have a minimum amount of cash on site to cover the property's potential liability to winning players.[11] When cash reserves near this critical point, the appropriate cage personnel must order cash from an external bank. As for the count room transfers, the main bank simply serves as a vault. That is, once the count room personnel finish counting the money from sources such as the table game drop boxes and slot machine cash cans, it makes its way to the main bank.[12] Drop and count procedures will be covered in detail in another chapter.

---

[10] All gaming cheques must be registered and approved per the Regulations of the Nevada Gaming Commission & State Gaming Control Board (May, 2009). Regulation 12, Chips & Tokens, §12.020.

[11] Nevada Revised Statutes (2009). Gaming Control Act, Gaming Statutes & Regulations, Regulation 6.150, Minimum bankroll requirements, part 5.

[12] Slot machine *cash cans* are containers that store all of the currency inserted into the bill acceptors. The bill acceptors are devices that allow slot players to insert currency directly into the slot machine, in exchange for wagering credits.

In summary, the main bank stores the following items:

- Reserve gaming cheques
- Cash cassettes for casino kiosks
- Currency
  - Currency on hand
  - Currency ordered from external banks
  - Currency received from the count room

Of course, it is possible that the main bank at other casinos could serve as a storage facility for other sources of funds.

Supplies Funds to Other Banks

The main bank serves as a central bank, supplying funds to the following areas:

- Front Windows
- Employee Cage
- Satellite Cages
  - Poker
  - High-limit Table Games
  - High-limit Slots

These transaction points all require bankrolls. For example, the main bank would supply currency to a satellite poker cage so that poker players could exchange their poker cheques for cash. This cage is offered as a convenience to poker players. The high-limit cages are full-service operations designed to provide enhanced customer service and convenience to the casino's most valuable players. The employee cage prepares and issues imprest banks to employees in gaming and non-gaming areas, with funds supplied by the main bank. The functions of the employee cage will be covered in detail in a subsequent section of this chapter. Finally, the funds for the imprest banks issued to the front-window cashiers are supplied by the main bank.

Transfers

The main bank accepts transfers from the following areas:

- Slots
- Table Games
- Other Gaming Areas
- Count Room
- Other Banks/Satellite Cages

The best way to explain a transfer is by way of example. On each day, the casino's drop team collects the cash from table games and slot machines. This cash is transported to the count room where it is counted and wrapped. Once the cash is counted, it is physically transferred from the count room to the main bank. This last act is considered to be a *transfer in*, from the perspective of the main bank. In fact, a transfer slip is completed to document the movement of the cash and the transfer of accountability from the count room to the main bank. The transfer slip accompanies the cash, as it is passed through the window between Area 12 (count room) and Area 2 (main bank) of Figure 7.1.

As the main bank serves as the cage vault, it provides a secure location for storing great sums of money and gaming cheques. It provides a secure location for incoming cash (transfers in) and the capacity to store great sums of money to fund the cash needs of other banks/cages (transfers out). The main bank functions as a control point for all cash transfers into and out of the cage.

Marker Bank

The marker bank is located in Area 3 of Figure 7.1. This bank is a floating bank, as opposed to an imprest bank. That is, the daily balance of the marker bank can increase or decrease, based on the day's activity.

The primary functions of the marker bank are listed here (see bullet points). Further explanation of the functions can be found in subsequent paragraphs.

- Stores all outstanding markers
- Stores return-to-maker (RTM) checks
- Stores front money deposits
- Stores gaming-related wire transfer documentation
- Accepts the daily mass marker transfer

Of course, the functions of the marker bank could vary by property. This list merely provides readers with a sketch of common marker bank functions.

Storage Functions

The marker bank stores all unpaid markers (a.k.a. outstanding markers). The markers represent uncollected gambling debts owed to the casino by its customers. The marker bank provides casino executives with an orderly and centrally-located means of managing their accounts receivable.

All RTM checks are also stored in the marker bank. These checks have been presented by the casino to the customer's bank for payment; however, these checks were not honored by the bank. In most cases, the customer's checking account balance is less than the amount of the check presented for payment. These RTM checks are stored in the marker bank so that casino executives know the debt is still outstanding and that one unsuccessful attempt has been made to collect it. Further, such a record reminds management not to accept additional checks from these customers. The RTM check would also affect the customer's eligibility for casino credit (i.e., new markers).

154

All front money deposits are logged in the marker bank and stored with any associated wire transfer documentation. Front money funds are usually wired from a customer's bank to the casino's account. However, wire transfers do occur for other reasons as well. For example, marker payments are sometimes made via wire transfer. Also, casino executives sometimes pay players who win substantial sums of money by wiring funds to the customer's bank account. In any case, all wire transfer documentation is stored in the marker bank.

Marker Transfers

In Nevada, the marker bank accepts what is known as a daily mass marker transfer from the pit(s). The term "pit" refers to a grouping of table games in a given area of the casino floor. Many casino floors can have more than one pit. This mass transfer entails moving all outstanding markers from the pit(s) to the marker bank. This task is performed at the end of each gaming day. The gaming day ends at the same time each day, usually in the early hours of the morning.

Only management knows the precise time of the gaming day rollover. Federal law prohibits management from sharing this information with customers of the casino. The concern is that such knowledge would allow money launderers to avoid critical reporting processes by spreading transactions over two days. That is, transactions could be timed to occur just before and just after the rollover time. The chapter on federal reporting requirements discusses this specific issue in more detail.

Fill Bank

The fill bank is located in Area 4 of Figure 7.1. This bank is a floating bank. The daily balance of the fill bank can increase or decrease, based on the day's activity. Given the advent and widespread adoption of coinless slot machines, the fill bank rarely interfaces with the slot operation.

The fill bank is also often referred to as the chip bank. However, this alternative name may be confusing to some, as the fill bank usually does not store chips. Fill banks store gaming cheques. Cheques have a face value.[13] Chips do not have face values. For example, roulette chips cannot be exchanged for cash at the cage, as the value of these chips is maintained on the game where they were purchased and nowhere else. Due to this technicality, this bank will be referred to as the fill bank throughout this text.

The primary functions of the fill bank are listed next, with additional explanation of each function appearing in the ensuing paragraphs.

- Stores in-service gaming cheques
- Facilitates table games fills & credits
- Stores cheques received from front windows

---

[13] The face value of a gaming cheque is equal to the dollar value printed on its surface (i.e., its face).

Storage of In-service Cheques

These are the gaming cheques in circulation, as opposed to excess cheques held in reserve. Reserve cheques are stored in the main bank. As previously mentioned, roulette chips are not typically stored in the fill bank.

Fills & Credits

The fill bank supplies cheques to table games when needed. That is, gaming activity can deplete a game's inventory of cheques. When this occurs, a fill is ordered by table game personnel. A fill order requests specific numbers of specific denominations of gaming cheques to be transferred from the fill bank to a specific table game. The form used to place this order is usually referred to as a fill slip. The term "fill" is used, as the order refills the depleted tubes within the table game's tray. The tubes house the cheques; the tray houses the tubes; and the table houses the tray.

Credits are issued when a table game's tubes are overflowing with cheques. Such a condition also occurs from gaming activity. In this case, the cheques are transferred from a table game to the fill bank. The fill bank stores the cheques until they are needed elsewhere. Credits are also initiated when a table has an overabundance of one value of cheques and a shortage of another value of cheques.

Front Window Cheques

As mentioned in the Front Windows section of this chapter, customers often exchange gaming cheques for cash via the front window cashiers. However, these cheques are only temporarily stored at the front windows. The fill bank serves as the final storage destination of these cheques, within the main cage.

Employee Cage

This cage is located in Area 10 of Figure 7.1, with employee access through the door on the top-side of Area 11. The employee cage is referred to by other names such as the employee bank, annex cage, and the auxiliary cage. It is also referred to by some as a satellite cage. In Figure 7.1, the employee cage is located adjacent to the main cage, but this is not always the case. As mentioned previously in this chapter, the employee cage is considered to be a component of the overall main cage operation.

The primary functions of the employee cage are listed next, with further explanation of each function provided in the subsequent paragraphs.

- Supplies imprest banks to employees
- Provides a secure drop box for ending employee banks
- Replenishes imprest banks (mid-shift)
- Provides an exchange venue for tip earners

Imprest Banks

The employee cage supplies imprest banks to workers from many different departments. The following list provides a sample of areas that require these imprest banks:

- Restaurants
- Retail Shops
- Box Offices
- Slot Operations

Points of sale such as restaurants, retail shops, and box offices require imprest banks to fund opening drawers for cash registers. Slot attendants use imprest banks to redeem routine jackpot tickets or tickets with nominal credit balances. That is, slot players exchange their credit vouchers for cash, which is supplied by the imprest bank of the slot attendant. Slot attendants use imprest banks for a variety of other transactions, stemming from events such as slot machine and ticket printer malfunctions.

Drop Box

Imprest banks are issued to employees for use during a single shift. At the end of their shift, the employees return the remaining cash and receipts/documentation to secure drop boxes located in the employee cage. These drop boxes are shown on the right side of Area 11 in Figure 7.1.

Replenish Banks

The imprest bank issued to a slot attendant is limited. That is, players sometimes win jackpots in excess of the funds available in an attendant's bank. In these cases, the slot attendant would be able to replenish his imprest bank in the employee cage (during the same shift). Of course, some jackpots are so great, only the main bank is able to supply the funds necessary to pay the customer.[14] Imprest banks would not be used to pay such jackpots.

Tip Exchange

As a convenience to employees who earn tips, the employee cage serves as a tip exchange. For example, positions such as cocktail servers, valet attendants, and bartenders often receive gaming cheques as tips. These cheques can be exchanged for cash at the employee cage. Employees who receive a considerable number of small bills as tips can also use the employee cage to exchange the small bills for greater denominations.

---

[14] Many larger casinos would be able to pay such jackpots from funds stored in high-limit slot cages (a.k.a. satellite cages).

Three-bag Banking System

This system is used to issue and account for the employee imprest banks. The cash for the bank is prepared and issued in Bag 1 of a three-bag plastic pouch system (see Figure 7.2). When the bank is issued to the employee the three transparent bags are connected to one another, appearing as a single sheet of plastic. However, the bags can be separated by tearing them along the perforated seems.

CASHIER'S TRANSACTION REPORT
Bag 1
DATE: SHIFT TIME: FROM: TO:
SHIFT: G D S
CASHIER (Print name):
DEPARTMENT/OUTLET:
CASHIER (Signature):
CASHIER ID #:

I III II II I III II I 004333951

CASHIER'S TRANSACTION REPORT
Bag 2
DATE: SHIFT TIME: FROM: TO:
SHIFT: G D S
CASHIER (Print name):
DEPARTMENT/OUTLET:
CASHIER (Signature):
CASHIER ID #:

I III II II I III II I 004333951

CASHIER'S TRANSACTION REPORT
Bag 3
NO CASH IN THIS POUCH – PAPERWORK ONLY
DATE: SHIFT TIME: FROM: TO:
SHIFT: G D S
CASHIER (Print name):
DEPARTMENT/OUTLET:
CASHIER (Signature):
CASHIER ID #:

I III II II I III II I 004333951

Figure 7.2. Three-bag Imprest Bank Pouch.

As shown in Figure 7.2, all three bags are imprinted with a bar code and the same control number. Bag 2 contains any cash remaining at the end of the employee's shift. Bag 3 contains all receipts and/or documentation needed to reconcile the change in cash value from Bag 1 to Bag 2.

At the end of the employee's shift, Bag 1 is empty, and Bags 2 and 3 are deposited in secure drop boxes located in the employee cage. Both Bag 2 and Bag 3 are dropped in specific and separate boxes. Because Bag 2 contains cash, the count team accesses the Bag 2 drop box and counts the contents of all Bag 2 deposits. The count team is comprised of the same employees who count the money in the table game drop boxes and slot machine currency containers.

Not all casinos use the three-bag plastic pouch system. In fact, many use reusable canvas bags to achieve the same end, as the three-part plastic bags are more expensive.

Cage Accountability

Given the number and magnitude of cash transactions that occur in the cage on a daily basis, cage accountability is a chief concern for management. Accountability is also at the heart of the considerable number of state and federal regulations that govern cage operations. To these ends, all banks within the cage must be reconciled at the close of each shift. That is, documentation must be supplied to explain any difference between an opening and closing bank balance.

Signature Card & Photo ID Storage

The Nevada gaming regulations require that the licensee (i.e., casino) maintain a signature card and copy of each credit player's picture identification card. Examples of acceptable identification cards are a valid U.S. driver's license, state-issued I.D., military I.D., or a current passport (i.e., not expired). These materials are used to verify the identity of players when they request markers. Management must be sure that other parties do not access the credit line of their players. These signature cards and copies of player identification cards are stored in the cage.

Key Control/Storage

The key control system is located in Area 5 of Figure 7.1. Key access is electronically controlled within the cage, for keys to most cash containers. For example, keys to the following items are electronically controlled:

- Slot machines
- Table game drop boxes
- Kiosks
- Money carts

Such keys are controlled by assigning access profiles and passwords to those who access these containers as part of their job duties. For example, gaming keys require three different people to enter passwords before access is granted by the key control system. That is, someone from each of the following departments must enter their password to access such a key: Cage, Security, and Count Room. Most electronic key control systems will alert management when keys are not returned promptly, as outstanding keys represent a security risk.

Cage Location & Configuration

It is recommended that the cage be located near the middle of the casino. The security of the funds stored in the cage is increased when it is located away from casino entrances/exits. Those with criminal intentions may be less likely to attempt a cage robbery if they are required to travel a great distance to and from the cage. The greater travel distance increases the likelihood of witnesses and exposure to cameras. Additionally, a central location eliminates the possibility of accessing the cage by penetrating an exterior/perimeter wall of the casino.

It is also recommended that the count room be located adjacent to the main cage. Figure 7.1 illustrates such a configuration. Notice that Area 12 (Count Room) is located adjacent to Area 2 (Main Bank). These two areas are connected by a window depicted on the top side of Area 12. This set-up allows for money to be transferred from the count room to the main bank without traveling across the casino floor. This configuration eliminates one exposure of the money to a public area. Labor is also reduced by eliminating one leg of the transportation process (i.e., from the count room to the main bank).

A centrally located cage/count room also decreases the maximum transport distance for the money carts. That is, once the drop boxes and currency containers are loaded on to the transport carts, these carts are wheeled across the casino floor to the count room. A centrally located cage/count room prevents the money cart from travelling the entire length of the casino floor. Wheeling money carts across the casino floor introduces a number of safety and security risks. Further, customers are often bothered by making way for the money carts, especially when the casino floor is crowded. For all of these reasons, shorter trips are desirable.

Daily Cash Summary

The cage operation generates many reports. However, the Daily Cash Summary is the most comprehensive report produced by the cage. In short, this report provides a record of all the ins and outs, with respect to cage transactions/activity. Alternatively, this report could be thought of as a summary of all increases and decreases in cage accountability. In this case, accountability represents the change in all cage balance sheet accounts. That is, the Daily Cash Summary documents the changes in the balances of key cage accounts such as:

- Cash
- Gaming Cheques
- Markers (i.e., Accounts Receivable)
- Front Money

Further, this report includes items of interest to management such as the number and dollar-amount of coupons redeemed through the cage. This information allows management to measure the changes in key business volumes against coupon redemption activity. As you can imagine from this one example, the physical support material for this report is considerable. That is, all the coupons redeemed by the cashiers would be bundled and stored by the casino, as support for that day's Daily Cash Summary.

Even casual consideration of the support material requirements for this report gives rise to the idea of electronic storage technology. This technology allows for support materials to be scanned, stored, and viewed electronically, as opposed to physically. Such technology improves the accessibility of these support materials and reduces ongoing storage costs. However, many managers continue to store these physical records and documents in warehouses.

Questions/Exercises:

1. Per the example provided in the chapter, name the primary areas of the main cage.
2. How would you describe the imprest banking process, as it applies to cashiers at the front windows of the main cage?
3. Name five types of transactions conducted by cashiers at the front windows of the main cage.
4. Are slot purchase tickets considered to be markers? Explain your answer.
5. Per the example in the chapter, what are the primary functions of the main bank?
6. In general, which kinds of items are stored in the main bank?
7. Which types of banks does the main bank fund?
8. Per the example provided in the chapter, what are the primary functions of the marker bank?
9. What is the difference between the main cage and the main bank?
10. Per the example provided in the chapter, what are the primary functions of the fill bank?
11. Why is the fill bank not referred to as the chip bank, within this text?
12. Per the example provided in the chapter, what are the primary functions of the employee cage?
13. Name three operating areas of a hotel-casino property that regularly request imprest banks from the employee cage? Explain the use/purpose of the imprest bank for each area named.
14. What is the purpose of each bag in the three-bag imprest banking system?
15. Why are signature cards and photo ID's stored in the main cage?
16. Name three items for which the access keys are electronically controlled?
17. What recommendations were offered regarding the main cage layout and location within the casino?

Chapter 8
Currency & Suspicious Activity Reporting

How does compliance with Title 31 affect the daily operation of a casino?
Could a casino be operated without extensive knowledge of Title 31 regulations?
How does compliance with Title 26 affect the daily operation of a hotel-casino resort?
What is suspicious activity reporting?
What is the most common cause of suspicious activity reporting in casinos?
What are the responsibilities of casino employees who witness a suspicious activity?

Scope

Title 31 of the Code of Federal Regulations and Title 26 of the Internal Revenue Code are covered to the extent that these regulations apply to the hotel-casino industry. These federal reporting requirements are critical to the operation of a major hotel-casino property. Title 31 and/or Title 26 apply to all U.S. hotel-casinos, including properties operated by sovereign Indian tribes. This chapter provides detailed discussions of recommended compliance policies and procedures, IRS[1] compliance expectations, and the spirit of these regulations. Additionally, the chapter includes examples of the forms casino operators file to comply with federal currency reporting requirements and suspicious activity reporting. The depth of the material contained in this chapter is on par with that of a training program aimed at currency and suspicious activity reporting.

Chapter Objectives

- Explain the purpose of currency and suspicious activity reporting requirements
- Define Title 31, Title 26, & suspicious activity reporting requirements
- Describe the common types of suspicious transactions occurring in hotel-casino resorts
- Review the critical elements of compliance with federal reporting requirements
  - o Define key terms specified in the regulations, such *cash in* and *cash out*
  - o Describe multiple transaction and negotiable instrument logging processes
  - o Provide recommended policies and procedures
  - o Describe common IRS objections
  - o Illustrate the forms filed by operators, in compliance with reporting requirements

---

[1] Internal Revenue Service.

Regulatory Overview

In 1985, casinos and card clubs were deemed financial institutions by the U.S. Treasury Department, in an effort to prevent and/or expose money laundering activities taking place in these businesses.[2] This distinction made casinos subject to the 1970 Bank Secrecy Act (BSA).[3] This act is part of Title 31 of the U.S. Code, making it a federal law. Essentially, Title 31 requires the reporting of cash transactions in excess of $10,000, as well as the reporting of suspicious transactions or attempts to conduct a suspicious transaction.[4]

Prior to July 1, 2007, Nevada casinos with annual gross gaming revenue in excess of $10,000,000 had an exemption from Title 31, but were required to comply with similar currency reporting guidelines under Nevada's Regulation 6A.[5] On July 1, 2007, compliance with Title 31 became mandatory for all Nevada casinos with annual gross gaming revenues in excess of $1,000,000. This was a big change for casino operators as well as Nevada regulators, as they no longer had jurisdiction over currency reporting procedures. This meant that Nevada regulators would no longer provide oversight and guidance with respect to currency reporting and record keeping requirements for casinos.

The U.S. government requires certain cash transactions occurring within or connected to the United States to be reported on a Currency Transaction Report (CTR). More specifically, pursuant to Title 31, gaming management must report all casino-related cash transactions exceeding $10,000. Casino operators report these transactions to the U.S. Department of Treasury's, Financial Crimes Enforcement Network (FinCEN) on Form 103 (See Figure 8.1). This form is also known as a CTR-C, which stands for Currency Transaction Report by Casinos. Non gaming areas of a hotel-casino resort as well as casinos and card clubs with annual gross revenue of $1,000,000 or less are subject to different reporting requirements.[6] The management of these operations must report all cash payments over $10,000 to the IRS.[7]

Many major gaming companies have branch offices located in U.S. cities and abroad. The branch offices located within the United States are also required to comply with the requirements of Title 31. Each U.S. branch office is considered an extension of the primary property with respect to Title 31 compliance. The branch offices located outside of the U.S. are not required to report transactions that occur abroad. However, many casino operators elect operate foreign branches according to the same record keeping and reporting requirements of U.S. branch offices.

---

[2] See 31 Code of Federal Regulations (C.F.R.) Part 103.22 and Kilby, J., Fox, J. & Lucas, A.F. (2004). *Casino Operations Management* (2nd ed.). New York: Wiley, pp. 61-62.
[3] See 31 U.S. Code § 5311 et seq.
[4] See 31 C.F.R. Part 103 et seq.
[5] NGC Regulation 6A (repealed).
[6] See 26 U.S.C. Subtitle F, CHAPTER 61, Subchapter A, PART III, Subpart B, § 6050i.
[7] Only cash payments received from customers are reported to the IRS.

Figure 8.1. FinCEN Form 103: Currency Transaction Report by Casinos (CTR-C).

Prohibited Transactions under Regulation 6A

As previously noted, prior to July 1, 2007, certain casinos in Nevada had an exemption from Title 31. Prior to Title 31, the Nevada Gaming Control Board (GCB) oversaw compliance with the Nevada Gaming Commission's (NGC) currency reporting requirements, as specified under Regulation 6A. As such, certain transactions and activities were prohibited. If casino operators engaged in these prohibited activities whether knowingly or by accident, they were subject to disciplinary action by the GCB. Like federal regulators, Nevada regulators also wanted to ensure that people were not laundering money through Nevada casinos.

In the judgment of the regulators, the transactions that were prohibited under Regulation 6A either lacked a legitimate business purpose or were riskier than other common transactions. These prohibited transactions had a dollar threshold of only $3,000, which made it cumbersome, if not difficult, to successfully launder money through Nevada casinos. However, the aggressive $3,000 reporting threshold also triggered a considerable amount of paperwork, which negatively impacted the customer experience.

The prohibited transactions under Regulation 6A included exchanging cash for other cash, and issuing a check, or an electronic funds transfer, in exchange for cash. Essentially, Nevada regulators did not want patrons to bring "dirty" (illegitimately obtained) money to casinos and leave with "clean" or "laundered" money.

Exchanging cash for cash can be as simple as exchanging a tremendous number of small-denomination bills for a lesser number of large-denomination bills, making it easier to physically transport the money. Alternatively, there are those who simply wish to exchange marked bills for unmarked bills. Casino checks and wire transfers can be used to accomplish similar results.

If someone exchanges "dirty" cash in return for a casino check or uses the "dirty" money to fund a wire transfer, they have accomplished several things. First and foremost, they have unloaded the "dirty" cash at the casino. Second, they now have a paper trail, which, on the surface, appears as though the casino was the source of the cash. Of course, this adds the appearance of legitimacy to the money. Third, with a wire transfer, they are able to transport the funds out of the U.S.

While Title 31 does not expressly *prohibit* any specific transactions, casino operators are expected to exercise caution when conducting transactions which may appear to lack a legitimate business purpose. For example, accepting cash from a customer for the sole purpose of wiring it to another location. Such a transaction would lack a legitimate business purpose for a casino operator, as no part of it pertains to gaming or the facilitation of gaming.

Working Definitions

Before discussing the details of Title 31 and Title 26 reporting protocol, it may be helpful to generally define some of the key terms. Of course, any discussion of federal regulation as it applies to the gaming industry is bound to include a considerable amount of jargon. The definitions provided here are intended to ready the reader for a somewhat technical discussion of currency reporting procedures. With the exception of *gaming day*, the definitions of the listed terms were intended to generally apply to both Title 31 and Title 26 compliance.[8] Other key terms will be defined as they appear in the text.

- *Reportable* – Cash transaction(s) exceeding **$10,000.**
- *Loggable* – Cash transaction(s) of a predetermined amount that will be recorded and aggregated with subsequent transactions. This amount varies by property, but it typically ranges from **$3,000** to **$5,000.**
- *Customer (patron)* – A person involved in a transaction governed by federal currency reporting requirements, whether or not that person directly participates in the transaction.
- *Agent* – A person who conducts a cash transaction on behalf of another individual or organization.
- *Multiple persons* – This term is used when discussing instances where more than one person benefits from a cash transaction. For example, multiple parties working from a common bankroll.
- *Gaming day* – A specified 24-hour period for which revenue is calculated. All gaming departments must abide by a common gaming day. The gaming day also defines the cut-off point for currency reporting requirements.

The Title 31 Record Keeping & Reporting Process

Currency Transaction Reports

Management must file a Currency Transaction Report by Casinos (CTR-C) to report currency transactions involving either cash in or cash out (from the casino's perspective) of more than $10,000 in a gaming day.[9] Next, the key terms of this requirement are defined.

In general, *cash in* refers to currency received by the casino. More specifically, cash-in transactions include, but are not limited to the following items:[10]

- Purchase of gaming cheques, chips, tokens, or other gaming instrumentalities
- Front money/safekeeping deposits
- Payments on any form of credit, including markers and counter checks
- Bets of currency, e.g., *money plays*[11]
- Currency received from a patron for the sole purpose of transmitting the funds to another location by way of wire transfer
  - For example, a customer brings cash to the casino cage for the sole purpose of wiring it to another location
- Purchases of a casino's check

---

[8] There are some subtle, yet important, distinctions in the definitions as they apply to Title 31 and Title 26, separately. However, these differences/distinctions are explained in subsequent sections of this chapter.
[9] 31 C.F.R. § 103.22 (b) (2).
[10] 31 C.F.R. § 103.22 (b) (2) (i).
[11] Actual currency/bills are placed in a betting area of a table game in lieu of gaming cheques or chips.

      o For example, a customer exchanges cash for a check drawn on the casino's account
- Currency-for-currency exchanges, including foreign currency exchanges

Cash out refers to cash payments made by the casino to patrons of the casino. More specifically, cash-out transactions include, but are not limited to the following:[12]

- Redemption of gaming cheques, chips, tokens, or other gaming instrumentalities
- Front money/safekeeping withdrawals
- Advances on any form of credit, including markers and counter checks
- Payments on winning wagers, excluding slot jackpots[13]
- Payments to customers accessing their credit lines, based on receipt of funds from wire transfers
- Cashing of checks or other negotiable instruments received from customers
- Currency-for-currency exchanges, including foreign currency exchanges
- Reimbursements for travel and entertainment expenses incurred by customers

Cash-in and cash-out transactions are aggregated separately. That is, they are not netted against each other. For example, if a customer buys gaming cheques (cash in) for $20,000 and later redeems the cheques (cash out) for $10,000, it would not result in a single transaction of $10,000 in cash in. The two transactions must be treated separately. In this case, a CTR-C would be issued for the $20,000 in cash in, but not the $10,000 in cash out, as the cash-out value did not *exceed* $10,000.

Submitting CTR-Cs

Manually generated CTR-Cs must be submitted within the 15-day period following the reportable transaction date.[14] Electronically generated CTR-Cs must be submitted within the 25-day period following the reportable transaction date.[15]

Prior to conducting a transaction that will require the submission of a CTR-C, casino employees must either ask the patron for the required identification information or ensure that it is on file with the casino. If the customer refuses to provide the required identification data/credentials, the transaction should not be conducted. By obtaining this information before conducting the transaction, casino employees protect themselves and the casino from liability arising from potential violations of Title 31.

The identification information and credentials required to properly complete a CTR-C include the following items:

- Customer's first & last name
- Permanent address (not a Post Office box)

---

[12] 31 C.F.R. § 103.22 (b) (2) (ii).

[13] Slot jackpots $\geq$ $1,200 are reported on a W2-G tax form.

[14] 31 C.F.R. § 103.27 (a) (1).

[15] Ibid.

- Social security number (for U.S. Citizens)
- Date of birth
- Identification credential (passport, drivers license, or some other form of government issued identification)
- Customer's account number (e.g., a slot club number)

Multiple Transaction Log (MTL)

Title 31 does not specifically define a logging threshold for tracking cash transactions. However, management must design and implement a logging process and establish a dollar threshold for recording and aggregating transactions conducted by patrons and/or an agent of a patron. Typically, operators will set the minimum loggable value within the range of $3,000 to $5,000.[16] The minimum dollar-value of a loggable transaction will vary by property. An MTL can be either manual or electronic. Many of the larger resorts use sophisticated software packages to facilitate the MTL process.

Once a minimum dollar-value is determined, casino operators use a multiple transaction log (MTL) to record and aggregate cash transactions conducted by or for individual patrons. The MTL is used to determine whether patrons have exceeded the $10,000 reporting threshold, over the course of a designated 24-hour period (i.e., the gaming day). That is, a CTR-C must be filed for a patron if the sum of his logged transactions exceeds $10,000 in cash in or cash out, over the course of any gaming day. In such a case, a CTR-C would be filed in spite of the fact that the customer participated in no single transaction that exceeded the $10,000 reporting threshold.

As previously noted, management must establish a minimum dollar value or threshold for logging transactions in the MTL. However, casino employees must also log *like-kind* transactions that fall below the established logging threshold, provided that the aggregate value of these transactions exceeds the established logging threshold and that the employees have knowledge of the transactions. For example, let's assume management has imposed a logging threshold of $3,000 for the MTL. Further, let's assume a customer purchases $2,500 in gaming cheques from a cashier named Sarah. Later, in the same gaming day, the customer returns to Sarah and purchases an additional $2,500 in cheques. Taken separately, both transactions would be less than the $3,000 logging threshold; however, because Sarah had knowledge of the *like-kind* transactions she must ensure that the aggregate amount (i.e., $5,000) is recorded in the MTL.

At the conclusion of the gaming day, the logging of transactions is ceased, and a new MTL is started for the next gaming day. Transactions are not aggregated across different gaming days. For example, let's assume a customer produces $12,000 in cash-in transactions which are *reported* on Monday. On Wednesday, of the same week, he produces an additional $6,000 in cash-in transactions which are *logged* in the MTL. The transactions from Wednesday would not be reported or added to the $12,000 reported on Monday.

---

[16] No maximum logging values apply; however, it should be noted that cash transactions in excess of the $10,000 CTR-C reporting threshold are also logged in the MTL.

Each entry on the MTL generally contains the following information:

- Name of the patron(s) and/or agent
- Known patron status (i.e., Do they have a complete ID on file?)
- Casino account number (e.g., a slot club or player's club number)
- Time and date of transaction
- Dollar amount and type of transaction (e.g., $6,000 redemption of gaming cheques)
- Transaction location (i.e., cage, pit, etc.)
- Name of employee conducting/recording the transaction

Management can claim that a customer is *known*, when the following information and credentials are on file:

- A physical or permanent address
  - o P.O. boxes do not satisfy this requirement
- A valid government-issued identification credential
  - o This identification credential must have been previously verified, and not expired when it was accepted[17]
  - o When employees discover that the ID on file has expired, an attempt to verify the customer's current ID should be made
    - ▪ Note: An expired ID is not acceptable when opening a deposit account or an account with marker signing privileges
- A social security number (for all domestic customers)

It should be noted that ID information and credentials are not required for MTL entries, when the dollar-amount of the transaction is less than the $10,000 reporting threshold. For example, the employee is not required to obtain a customer's complete ID when logging a $6,000 transaction in the MTL.

Some players will not provide their name to employees attempting to complete an MTL entry. It is recommended that management develop a comprehensive method for tracking these refused-name customers. The following suggestions are provided to help management identify such players and prevent the occurrence of reportable transactions by unidentified patrons.

- Call surveillance and request to have the customer's picture taken
  - o Such a tactic might be reserved for refused-name patrons with transactions above a predetermined dollar amount
- Log refused-name customers based on their sex and physical description/attributes[18]

---

[17] Where *verified* means physically examined by an employee (and noted in the system). In some casinos, IDs are also verified by way of ID readers and verification software.

[18] One casino created a preset list of accounts named by ethnicity and sex. For example, there was an account for refused-name patrons who were Caucasian males.

- Do not use a common (or single) account to log all cash ratings (in table games) for refused-name players
  - Management must establish a protocol for describing refused-name players to the extent that one can be distinguished from another
    - The use of a single account for refused-name players will likely result in transactions totaling in excess of $10,000 in a gaming day, signaling the need to file a CTR-C
      - The burden of proof will be on management, should they claim that multiple customers contributed to the aggregate dollar-amount of transactions in the refused-name account

Negotiable Instrument Log

In addition to the cash MTL, casinos must also log negotiable instruments with a face value of $3,000 or greater.[19] The bulk of negotiable instruments are some form of a check. The logging requirement applies to both checks received by the casino and checks issued by the casino (i.e., checks in & checks out). Again, it is important to define *negotiable instrument* as it applies specifically to Title 31. A negotiable instrument includes but is not limited to the following items:

- Personal checks
- Cashier's checks
- Money orders
- Bank drafts
- Official checks (similar to a cashier's check)
- Promissory notes
- Business checks (e.g., from customers who own businesses)
- Casino checks (e.g., checks issued by a casino that are payable to a customer)
- Checks cashed through third-party services such as Global Cash Advance, Certegy, or any other third-party check cashing vendor
- Checks received in the mail from customers for payment on their outstanding marker balances
- Checks mailed to customers who have mailed-in winning race or sports tickets, or slot vouchers with credit balances[20]

In most cases, the negotiable instrument log (NIL) is maintained in the casino cage. The NIL is also known as a monetary instrument log (MIL). The NIL requires similar patron information to that required for MTL entries, as well as the specific information about the negotiable instrument. That is, all reference numbers and issuing bank information printed on the negotiable instrument must be recorded in the NIL.

---

[19] 31 C.F.R. § 103.36 (9) (A-H).
[20] Sometimes customers forget to cash-in slot vouchers with credit balances before leaving the casino. Management will accept these vouchers via mail, and send the customer a check for the balance.

A negotiable instrument does not have to be cashed or executed to be subject to the NIL requirements. NIL requirements are trigged by receipt of the instrument from the patron. For example, checks for marker payments and front money deposits held by management must be logged upon receipt.

The NIL entries must be in chronological order and contain the following information:

- Date of receipt
- Time of receipt
- Dollar amount of transaction/instrument
- Customer's name
- Permanent address of customer
- Type of instrument
- Name of the drawee or issuer of the instrument (e.g., the name of the bank)
- All reference numbers (e.g., a casino account number or personal check number)
- Name & employee number of the casino employee who conducted the transaction

Monitoring Compliance with Title 31

With respect to Title 31 compliance, management must implement a written system of internal controls and a risk-based analysis of casino transactions.[21] A record of best practices with respect to compliance should also be maintained. Each of these documents should be used as road map for compliance, reducing the casino's exposure to regulatory violations. Additionally, management should establish an audit department whose personnel conduct daily reviews of all compliance paperwork and issue notices of exception for non-compliance and record retention. Operators can expect compliance reviews from the casino's Internal Audit Department, and an intense 3-year review from the IRS. The U.S. Treasury's Financial Crimes Enforcement Network (FinCEN) delegated the authority to enforce Title 31 to the Small Business/Self Employed Division of the IRS. Given this authority, the 3-year compliance review from the IRS is not something to be taken lightly.

Management must also implement a comprehensive training program for all employees who may encounter a transaction governed by Title 31. This training should be department specific, as the scope of duties vary considerably by department and greatly influence the exposure to specific Title 31 issues. Management should have a means of documenting the content of the training, training dates, and the names of employees who were trained. Employees should be trained when they are newly hired, with annual training updates. Again, there is no specific provision for training in Title 31, but there is an expectation that employees are trained. Compliance is virtually impossible without proper training and a thorough understanding of required procedures. Establishing awareness and understanding of money laundering issues and risks is critical to the success of any casino compliance program. This awareness and understanding can only be gained through training.

---

[21] Management must identify, analyze, and rank casino transactions with respect to the relative compliance risk associated with each transaction.

The IRS has been known to take exception with the following compliance-related issues and items:

- Player ratings that indicate cheques/chips issued to or bought by one customer were given to another customer
- P.O. boxes listed on the NIL or CTR-C, in lieu of a street address
- Absence of social security number for patrons with a U.S. driver's license on file
- Patrons whose transactions consistently stay at or just below the $10,000 reporting threshold
- The absence of a comprehensive and written anti money laundering (AML) program[22]
- The absence of an honest risk assessment for each product or service offered
- Internal control standards that do not go beyond the framework of Title 31
- The absence of a well written training program
- No independent testing for compliance
- No compliance officer
- No procedures for using computer systems to aid in assuring compliance, if the casino has computerized systems
- The absence of procedures to remedy incorrect patron information and collect missing patron information
- The absence of a method to communicate the need to obtain missing patron information
- The absence of a log to document accounts opened for patrons who refused to provide a social security number
- The absence of a system-generated notice for incomplete CTR-C forms
    - For example, when a customer exceeds the reporting threshold and management does not have all of the required patron information on file, the casino's system should have a method of indicating an incomplete CTR-C
- Improper handling of transactions involving patrons who refuse to provide required information
    - For example, when a patron refuses to provide required information, and he has already exceeded the reporting threshold, the employee should terminate the transaction, bar the patron from the casino, and document the facts and circumstances related to the incident
    - While there is no exact language that mandates barring a customer's play for not providing proper identification, doing so is recommended

Although not usually a specific concern of the IRS, many internal audit departments strongly suggest that management maintain a barred patron log. Such a log would list every individual that has been barred from the casino. Although a barred patron log is not

---

[22] Required per 31 C.F.R. § 103.64. Management must produce written anti money laundering procedures defining the risks and processes associated with conducting, reporting, and detecting transactions related to Title 31.

required by Title 31, management could certainly assess the costs and benefits of creating and maintaining one.

Suspicious Activity Reporting

Title 31 also requires the reporting of any suspicious activity by casino patrons. Further, the reporting of such matters is pursuant to the USA Patriot Act.[23] For a casino-related transaction, a Suspicious Activity Report (a.k.a. SARC) is submitted to the U.S. Department of Treasury's Financial Crimes Enforcement Network (FinCEN), by way of FinCEN Form 102 (See Figure 8.2 (a) & (b)).

Money launderers often try to use financial institutions to conceal their illegal profits or to move these funds beyond the reach of law enforcement. Individuals working within the financial institutions are often more likely than government officials to have a sense of transactions that appear to lack justification or do not fall within the usual methods of legitimate business. The creation of an effective system for the detection and prevention of money laundering is impossible without the cooperation of financial institutions, including casinos.

Management must report every transaction or group of related transactions totaling $5,000 or more, when a casino employee knows, suspects, or has reason to suspect that the transaction falls into any of the following categories:

- Involves funds derived from illegal activity, or is intended to conceal funds derived from illegal activity;
- Is intended to avoid or prevent the filing of a Currency Transaction Report by Casinos (CTR-C);
- Has no apparent business or lawful purpose, or is not the sort in which a particular customer would normally be expected to engage; or
- Involves the use of the casino to facilitate criminal activity.

There are many types of transactions that may be deemed suspicious activity, including, but not limited to the following items:

- **Bribery**. Customers may offer employees incentives such as a large tip or a percentage of the transaction to launder money through the casino and avoid a currency transaction report.

- **Counterfeit/fraudulent checks.** Checks presented to the casino for payment, which have been altered, stolen, or do not represent a valid instrument for any other reason.

---

[23] USA Patriot Act (2001), Title III, Subtitle B.

174

FinCEN Form 102	Suspicious Activity Report by Casinos and Card Clubs	
April 2003 Previous editions will not be accepted after December 31, 2003	▶ Please type or print. Always complete entire report. Items marked with an asterisk * are considered critical (see instructions).	OMB No. 1506 - 0006

1 Check the box if this report corrects a prior report (see instructions on page 6) ☐

Part I   Subject Information   2 Check box (a) ☐ if more than one subject   box (b) ☐ subject information unavailable

*3 Individual's last name or entity's full name   *4 First name   5 Middle initial

6 also known as (AKA- individual), doing business as (DBA- entity)   7 Occupation / type of business

*8 Address   *9 City

*10 State   *11 ZIP code   *12 Country (if not U.S.)   13 Vehicle license # / state (optional) a. number b. state

*14 SSN / ITIN (individual) or EIN (entity)   *15 Account number   No account affected ☐   Account open ? Yes ☐ No ☐   16 Date of birth MM / DD / YYYY

*17 Government issued identification (if available)   a ☐ Driver's license/state ID   b ☐ Passport   d ☐ Alien registration
d ☐ Other _____
e Number: _____   f Issuing state or country _____

18 Phone number - work   19 Phone number - home   20 E-mail address (if available)

21 Affiliation or relationship to casino/card club
a ☐ Customer   b ☐ Agent   c ☐ Junket / tour operator   d ☐ Employee   e ☐ Check cashing operator
f ☐ Supplier   g ☐ Concessionaire   h ☐ Other (Explain in Part VI)

22 Does casino/card club still have a business association and/or an employee/employer relationship with suspect?   23 Date action taken(22) MM / DD / YYYY
a ☐ Yes b ☐ No If no, why? c ☐ Barred   d ☐ Resigned   e ☐ Terminated   f ☐ Other (Specify in Part VI)

Part II   Suspicious Activity Information

*24 Date or date range of suspicious activity
From ___ / ___ / ___ MM DD YYYY   To ___ / ___ / ___ MM DD YYYY
*25 Total dollar amount involved in suspicious activity $ _____ .00

* 26 Type of suspicious activity:
a ☐ Bribery/gratuity
b ☐ Check fraud (includes counterfeit)
c ☐ Credit/debit card fraud (incl. counterfeit)
d ☐ Embezzlement/theft
e ☐ Large currency exchange(s)
f ☐ Minimal gaming with large transactions
g ☐ Misuse of position
h ☐ Money laundering
i ☐ No apparent business or lawful purpose
j ☐ Structuring
k ☐ Unusual use of negotiable instruments (checks)
l ☐ Use of multiple credit or deposit accounts
m ☐ Unusual use of wire transfers
n ☐ Unusual use of counter checks or markers
o ☐ False or conflicting ID(s)
p ☐ Terrorist financing
q ☐ Other (Describe in Part VI)

Part III   Law Enforcement or Regulatory Contact Information

27 If law enforcement or a regulatory agency has been contacted (excluding submission of a SARC), check the appropriate box.
a ☐ DEA
b ☐ U.S. Attorney (** 28)
c ☐ IRS
d ☐ FBI
e ☐ U.S. Customs Service
f ☐ U.S. Secret Service
g ☐ Local law enforcement
h ☐ State gaming commission
i ☐ State law enforcement
j ☐ Tribal gaming commission
k ☐ Tribal law enforcement
l ☐ Other (List in item 28)

28 Other authority contacted (for box 27 g through l) ** List U.S. Attorney office here.   29 Name of person contacted (for all of box 27)

30 Telephone number of individual contacted in box 29   31 Date Contacted MM / DD / YYYY

Catalogue Number 35636U

Figure 8.2. FinCEN Form 102: Suspicious Activity Report by Casinos & Card Clubs (a).

Part IV	Reporting Casino or Card Club Information		2
*32 Trade name of casino or card club	*33 Legal name of casino or card club	*34 EIN	

*35 Address

*36 City	*37 State	*38 ZIP code

39 Type of gaming institution

a ☐ State licensed casino   b ☐ Tribal licensed casino   c ☐ Card club   d ☐ Other (specify)_____

Part V	Contact for Assistance

*40 Last name of individual to be contacted regarding this report	*41 First name	42 Middle initial

*43 Title/Position	*44 Work phone number	*45 Date report prepared
	(___) ___ — ____	___/___/___ MM DD YYYY

Part VI	Suspicious Activity Information - Narrative*

Explanation/description of suspicious activity(ies). This section of the report is critical. The care with which it is completed may determine whether or not the described activity and its possible criminal nature are clearly understood by investigators. Provide a clear, complete and chronological description (not exceeding this page and the next page) of the activity, including what is unusual, irregular, or suspicious about the transaction(s), using the checklist below as a guide as you prepare your account.

a. **Describe** the conduct that raised suspicion.
b. **Explain** whether the transaction(s) was completed or only attempted.
c. **Describe** supporting documentation and retain such documentation for your file for five years.
d. **Explain** who benefited, financially or otherwise, from the transaction(s), how much and how (if known).
e. **Describe and retain** any admission or explanation of the transaction(s)provided by the subject(s), witness(s), or other person(s). Indicate to whom and when it was given. Include witness or other person ID.
f. **Describe and retain** any evidence of cover-up or evidence of an attempt to deceive federal or state examiners, or others.
g. **Indicate** where the possible violation of law(s) took place (e.g., branch, cage, specific gaming pit, specific gaming area).
h. **Indicate** whether the suspicious activity is an isolated incident or relates to another transaction.
i. **Indicate** whether there is any related litigation. If so, specify the name of the litigation and the court where the action is pending.
j. **Recommend** any further investigation that might assist law enforcement authorities.
k. **Indicate** whether any information has been excluded from this report; if so, state reasons.
l. **Indicate** whether any U.S. or foreign currency and/or U.S. or foreign negotiable instrument(s) were involved. If foreign, provide the amount, name of currency, and country of origin.

m. **Indicate** whether funds or assets were recovered and, if so, enter the dollar value of the recovery in whole dollars only.
n. **Indicate** any additional account number(s), and any domestic or foreign bank(s) account numbers which may be involved.
o. **Indicate** for a foreign national any available information on subject's passport(s), visa(s), and/or identification card(s). Include date, country, city of issue, issuing authority, and nationality.
p. **Describe** any suspicious activities that involve transfer of funds to or from a foreign country, or any exchanges of a foreign currency. Identify the currency, country, sources and destinations of funds.
q. **Describe** subject(s) position if employed by the casino or card club (e.g., dealer, pit supervisor, cage cashier, host, etc.).
r. **Indicate** the type of casino or card club filing this report, if this is not clear from Part IV.
s. **Describe** the subject only if you do not have the identifying information in Part I or if multiple individuals use the same identification. Use descriptors such as male, female, age, etc.
t. **Indicate** any wire transfer in or out identifier numbers, including the transfer company's name.

u. **If correcting a prior report, complete the form in its entirety and note the changes here in Part VI.**

NOTE: Information already provided in earlier parts of this form need not necessarily be repeated if the meaning is clear.

Tips on SAR Form preparation and filing are available in the SAR Activity Review at www.fincen.gov/pub_reports.html.

Supporting documentation should not be filed with this report. Maintain the information for your files.

Do not include legal disclaimers in this narrative. Continue on next page as necessary.

Figure 8.2. FinCEN Form 102: Suspicious Activity Report by Casinos & Card Clubs (b).

- **Counterfeit/fraudulent credit/debit card use**. In the modern world, identity theft has become increasingly widespread. In casinos, employees frequently encounter patrons engaging in credit or debit card transactions with cards that belong to someone else. Generally, these customers will conduct a fraudulent credit card cash advance for a small amount, as a test run. If the test run proves successful, subsequent advances will be attempted for greater sums.

- **Embezzlement/theft.** Employees are certainly not exempt from suspicious activity reporting. For example, if a count room employee is stealing, this is considered embezzlement. In this case, the employee could face a felony charge for embezzlement and risk alerting the federal government to their criminal acts, by way of a SARC filing.

- **Minimal gaming activity with large transactions**. Identifying this form of suspicious activity is somewhat subjective. That is, minimal gaming is not defined per se. These transactions occur in many forms with varying degrees of severity. An example of a more obvious form would be a customer who uses cash to purchase $10,000 in gaming cheques and leaves the game without making a single wager. Alternatively, a customer could access $50,000 from his credit line and only wager $200 per hand for ten minutes.

- **Money laundering.** In general, the goal of money launderers is to convert money obtained from illegitimate sources into money that appears to have been supplied through legitimate means. In all cases, money launderers wish to conceal the previous and/or original sources of the funds they are laundering. Money laundering can take on many forms, such as simply exchanging bills for different denominations of bills or cash-for-cash exchanges to unload marked bills. These acts can be accomplished in several ways. For example, let's say you just robbed a bank, and some of the money you obtained has red ink on it (put there by the bank). To avoid a person-to-person transaction with those marked bills, you feed them into a slot machine. The bills go into the currency acceptor and you can either play or immediately hit the cash-out button.[24] It is important to note here that the bills that go into a slot machine or table game are never paid-out. This money stays on the games until the games are dropped and counted.

- **No apparent business or lawful purpose**. In this case, *business purpose* is used in reference to the business of running a casino. As casino managers are in the gaming business, all transactions under their purview should be closely related to the business of gaming. In the case of integrated resorts, managers would also expect to regularly encounter transactions involving the property's non-gaming amenities. To clarify, let's consider an example of a transaction that lacks a direct business purpose in a casino. A customer wires $500,000 from a bank in China to

---

[24] If a considerable dollar-amount of bills were fed into a slot machine followed by little or no associated wagering activity, it is likely that such behavior would also be deemed "Minimal gaming with large transactions", which is a box on the SARC form. Management should have a process for detecting such behavior.

the casino, and then asks to have the money wired from the casino to a bank in Russia. As this transaction is not related to gaming or the facilitation of gaming, it would not be considered a business transaction related to the operation of a casino. It may help the customer with their personal business, but that is not the test. The purpose of the transaction must be directly related to the business of operating a casino resort. Many casino executives are too willing to facilitate international wire transfers, never considering whether such activities meet the business/lawful purpose test.

- **Structuring.** This is clearly the most common cause of suspicious activity reporting. Customers will try to conduct (i.e., structure) transactions in dollar-amounts that will not trigger the filing of a currency transaction report. This practice is quite common when customers win amounts greater than $10,000 on table games or in the race and sports book.

    o For example, let's assume a customer wishes to cash-in a winning ticket from a wager on a sporting event. The value of this ticket is $25,000. When the customer presents the ticket for payment, he requests $10,000 in cash and the remaining $15,000 in gaming cheques. Then, he returns the following day and cashes-in $8,000 in gaming cheques. He waits yet another day to cash-in the remaining $7,000 in gaming cheques. Notice that no part of this three-day transaction includes a cash payment from the casino that exceeds $10,000.

    o People have been known to engage in similar behavior, after leaving a table game with gaming cheques in excess of $10,000. That is, they never cash-in more than $10,000 in gaming cheques, in the same gaming day. Alternatively, they may rely on a companion to cash-in a portion of their cheques to avoid reporting. Some patrons have actually employed other people to make cash purchases of gaming cheques on their behalf. For example, let's say you have $15,000 in cash. You sit down at a table game and buy $10,000 in gaming cheques. At this point, the floor supervisor may ask you for your name and/or player card, for the purpose of tracking your wagering activity. If you refuse to provide your name, they will still track your gambling activity, and identify you by your physical description. Let's assume you lose the $10,000 in gaming cheques, and you wish to buy an additional $5,000 in cheques with your remaining cash. However, you don't want to identify yourself and you know that the $5,000 buy will trigger a CTR-C. You decide to circumvent Title 31 by giving the $5,000 to your friend, so that he can buy the gaming cheques for you. If a casino employee had knowledge of this agreement, such acts would be considered suspicious activity in the form of structuring transactions. Both you and your friend would be subject to federal reporting requirements (i.e., SARC).

- **Use of multiple credit or deposit accounts.** Customers may change their name slightly, assume a relative's identity, or simply use a stolen identity to open a credit account. This usually happens when they owe the casino money from a previous trip and they either cannot pay the debt, or simply do not want to pay it. Alternate/false identities are also assumed when a customer has exhausted his established line of credit, and he either knows or believes that management will not extend him additional credit. When a customer assumes the identity of another person, he clearly has no intention of paying any debt incurred from gambling losses. With each of these alternate-identity scenarios, management usually detects the fraud well after the patron's gaming trip has ended. Those who engage in the name game are quite adept and practiced at this form of fraud. Further, a considerable amount of research is required to determine just how many accounts such individuals have established.

- **Use of multiple monetary instruments**. Typically, this occurs when customers are making payments to the casino. In order to avoid reporting requirements at banks, customers purchase cashier's checks or money orders from several different financial institutions, for amounts that do not exceed $10,000. By not exceeding $10,000, the customer dodges the mandatory filing of a currency transaction report by the banks. For example, a customer may pay his $80,000 debt to the casino with ten, $8,000 cashier's checks, purchased from ten different banks.

As previously noted, casino employees are required to report suspicious activity on FinCEN Form 102, commonly referred to as a SARC (Suspicious Activity Report - Casinos). This form must be filed within 30 days of the day on which the suspicious activity was observed. Casino management may take up to 60 days to file a SARC, if additional time is needed to determine the subject's true identity. Quite often management is not able to determine the true identity of the patrons conducting suspicious activities in the casino. After all, concealing one's identity usually lies at the heart of most suspicious activity.

Once a SARC form has been filed, casino employees are prohibited from alerting anyone involved in the incident to the filing. Because employees are prohibited from notifying the patron that the form is being completed, it is not always possible to meet all of the form's requirements. That is, some sections of the form must be left blank to avoid alerting the subject to the filing. In these cases, casino employees are to complete the form to the best of their ability.

Currency Reporting for Non-Gaming Areas - Title 26

Title 31 addresses the reporting requirements for casinos with gross gaming revenue greater than $1,000,000. However, Title 26 of the Internal Revenue Code sets forth reporting requirements for non-gaming areas.[25] Casinos and card clubs with revenues of

---

[25] See Title 26, Subtitle F, CHAPTER 61, Subchapter A, PART III, Subpart B, § 6050i.

$1,000,000 or less are also subject to the reporting requirements of Title 26.[26] Similar to Tile 31, Title 26 requires a report to be filed for transactions in excess of $10,000. However, Title 26 only applies to transactions where cash is received by the business, whereas Title 31 requires businesses to report both cash in and cash out.

Title 26 also has a provision for reporting suspicious transactions. IRS Form 8300 is used to report both purchases in excess of $10,000 and/or suspicious activity in non-gaming areas (See Figure 8.3). With respect to Title 26, non-gaming areas include, but are not limited to the following:

- Hotel
- Retail stores
- Ticket office
- Restaurants
- Bars/lounges/night clubs
- Wedding chapel
- Convention/banquet

Management must develop a process for logging non-gaming transactions. This includes establishing a minimum dollar value. That is, not all transactions will be logged, only those above a prudent threshold. This threshold, or minimum dollar value, must be defined by management. Also, management must ensure that the employees of the relevant non-gaming areas are trained and aware of the Title 26 reporting requirements.

Title 26 requires that all cash purchases (by patrons) in excess of $10,000 are reported to the IRS on a currency transaction report (i.e., IRS Form 8300). Any non-casino employee who receives more than $10,000 in cash, in a single transaction or series of related transactions, must report the transaction(s) by completing IRS Form 8300.

As it relates to Title 26, cash is defined as:

- United States coin or currency
- Foreign currency
- Negotiable instruments: Cashier's checks, bank checks, treasurer's checks, bank drafts, Travelers Cheques, and money orders (if they have a face value of $10,000 or *less*).

If the face value of any of the previously listed negotiable instruments were in excess of $10,000, it would not be considered cash, within the scope of Title 26. Additionally, cash does not include a check drawn on an individual's personal account, or the use of a credit card. The following examples are provided to clarify these distinctions.

---

[26] Ibid.

IRS Form 8300
(Rev. March 2008)
OMB No. 1545-0892
Department of the Treasury
Internal Revenue Service

Report of Cash Payments Over $10,000
Received in a Trade or Business
► See instructions for definition of cash.
► Use this form for transactions occurring after March 31, 2008. Do not use prior versions after this date.
For Privacy Act and Paperwork Reduction Act Notice, see page 5.

FinCEN Form 8300
(Rev. March 2008)
OMB No. 1506-0018
Department of the Treasury
Financial Crimes
Enforcement Network

1   Check appropriate box(es) if: a ☐ Amends prior report;   b ☐ Suspicious transaction.

Part I   Identity of Individual From Whom the Cash Was Received

2   If more than one individual is involved, check here and see instructions . . . . ► ☐

3 Last name	4 First name	5 M.I.	6 Taxpayer identification number

7 Address (number, street, and apt. or suite no.)	8 Date of birth . ► M M D D Y Y Y Y (see instructions)

9 City	10 State	11 ZIP code	12 Country (if not U.S.)	13 Occupation, profession, or business

14 Identifying document (ID)	a Describe ID ►	b Issued by ►
	c Number ►	

Part II   Person on Whose Behalf This Transaction Was Conducted

15   If this transaction was conducted on behalf of more than one person, check here and see instructions . . . . ► ☐

16 Individual's last name or Organization's name	17 First name	18 M.I.	19 Taxpayer identification number

20 Doing business as (DBA) name (see instructions)	Employer identification number

21 Address (number, street, and apt. or suite no.)	22 Occupation, profession, or business

23 City	24 State	25 ZIP code	26 Country (if not U.S.)

27 Alien identification (ID)	a Describe ID ►	b Issued by ►
	c Number ►	

Part III   Description of Transaction and Method of Payment

28 Date cash received M M D D Y Y Y Y	29 Total cash received $ .00	30 If cash was received in more than one payment, check here . . . . ► ☐	31 Total price if different from item 29 $ .00

32   Amount of cash received (in U.S. dollar equivalent) (must equal item 29) (see instructions):

a U.S. currency $ _____ .00   (Amount in $100 bills or higher $ _____ .00   )
b Foreign currency $ _____ .00   (Country ► _____)
c Cashier's check(s) $ _____ .00   Issuer's name(s) and serial number(s) of the monetary instrument(s) ►
d Money order(s) $ _____ .00   _____
e Bank draft(s) $ _____ .00   _____
f Traveler's check(s) $ _____ .00

33   Type of transaction

a ☐ Personal property purchased   f ☐ Debt obligations paid
b ☐ Real property purchased   g ☐ Exchange of cash
c ☐ Personal services provided   h ☐ Escrow or trust funds
d ☐ Business services provided   i ☐ Bail received by court clerks
e ☐ Intangible property purchased   j ☐ Other (specify in item 34) ►

34   Specific description of property or service shown in 33. Give serial or registration number, address, docket number, etc. ►
_____
_____
_____

Part IV   Business That Received Cash

35 Name of business that received cash	36 Employer identification number

37 Address (number, street, and apt. or suite no.)	Social security number

38 City	39 State	40 ZIP code	41 Nature of your business

42   Under penalties of perjury, I declare that to the best of my knowledge the information I have furnished above is true, correct, and complete.

Signature ► _____   Title ► _____
                   Authorized official

43 Date of signature M M D D Y Y Y Y	44 Type or print name of contact person	45 Contact telephone number ( )

IRS Form 8300 (Rev. 3-2008)   Cat. No. 62133S   FinCEN Form 8300 (Rev. 3-2008)

Figure 8.3. Internal Revenue Service - Form 8300.

Example 1: A customer purchases an item for $13,200. The customer pays the clerk with $6,200 in U.S. currency and $7,000 in Travelers Cheques. The Travelers Cheques would be treated as cash, as their aggregate face value is less than $10,000. This transaction would require the clerk to ensure that proper identification was obtained from the customer and that IRS Form 8300 was completed, reporting the amount of the transaction at $13,200.

Example 2: A convention group owes the hotel $12,000. The meeting planner who organized the convention settles the bill by paying $10,000 of the balance with a credit card and the remainder with $2,000 in cash. Because credit cards are not treated as cash, the hotel has not received more than $10,000 in cash. Therefore, there is no reporting requirement for this transaction.

Logging/Aggregating Transactions

Cash transactions occurring in non-gaming areas are logged in a multiple transaction log (MTL), just as they are in the casino. Like its casino counterpart, the non-gaming MTL contains critical information about the patron and the transaction. Again, management must determine the minimum dollar value of an MTL entry. While this threshold will vary by property, most gaming resorts range between $3,000 and $5,000.

Each MTL entry generally contains the following information:

- Name of the patron(s) and/or agent
- Time and date of the transaction
- Dollar amount and type of transaction
- Location of the transaction (i.e., the outlet in which it occurred)
- Name of the employee conducting/recording the transaction

The purpose of maintaining the MTL is to determine if a customer exceeds the $10,000 reporting threshold through some combination of related transactions. Related transactions will be aggregated for up to one year, if an employee of the company knows or has reason to believe that individual transactions are part of a series of connected transactions. For example, let's assume that a customer makes a cash deposit of $10,000 in March, for a July wedding. In July, when the wedding takes place, the customer pays the remaining balance of $5,000 in cash. The employee handling this customer's account would know that the guest paid a total of $15,000 for the wedding. Separately, neither of these two transactions would be directly reportable (i.e., > $10,000); however, when combined, the sum becomes reportable on IRS Form 8300. Here's another example. On Wednesday, a hotel guest pays you $5,000 in cash for a deposit on a poolside cabana. Two days later, the same guest returns, uses the cabana, and pays you an additional $6,000 to settle his bill. These would be related transactions, and would be reported in the aggregate (i.e., $11,000) on IRS Form 8300.

Identification

Like Title 31, customer identification is a critical element of the Title 26 reporting requirements. Employees must ensure that they have satisfied the identification requirements of Title 26 *before* conducting a transaction that will exceed the $10,000 reporting threshold. The Title 26 identification requirements are as follows:

- A government issued identification credential such as a driver's license or passport; and
- A taxpayer identification number (TIN) or a social security number (SSN)
  - Employees must obtain the SSN of any U.S. resident who attempts to conduct a reportable transaction.

These ID requirements apply to customers, agents, and multiple persons conducting transactions. Casinos are subject to penalties when IRS Form 8300 is submitted with an incorrect or omitted SSN/TIN. Any time a SSN/TIN is requested, but not obtained or recorded, a written statement must be attached to Form 8300 explaining why the SSN/TIN has been omitted. Of course, there are exceptions. Nonresident aliens and foreign organizations are not required to provide a TIN; however, they must be able to produce a foreign passport or other legitimate identification credential as proof of foreign residency.

Reporting Suspicious Activity

Similar to the requirements for reporting suspicious activity in the casino, Title 26 also requires the reporting of suspicious activity. If an employee witnesses a transaction that she considers suspicious, she is required to complete IRS Form 8300 to the best extent possible. In section 1(b) of Form 8300, she must indicate that the transaction was suspicious, even if the cash portion was less than $10,000. A transaction is suspicious if it appears that a person is attempting to:

- Prevent an employee from filing a report;
- Cause an employee to file a false or incomplete report; or
- Engage in a questionable or illegal activity.

Let's consider some examples of suspicious transactions to clarify these points.

- A customer makes a purchase, and, a couple days later, it is discovered that the credit card used to make the purchase was fraudulent or stolen
- When asked for their identification, the customer objects to the request, and asks how to structure the transaction to avoid filing a report
  - Typically, a customer will ask, "How much cash can I use, without filing a report?"
- A customer provides fraudulent or conflicting IDs
- A customer structures transactions to avoid reporting. There are many forms of structuring, including the following:
  - Making multiple purchases at, or just below, the reporting threshold

- o Manipulating transaction costs by having agents or other persons assume a portion of the total transaction cost. By allocating the total transaction cost across multiple parties, the dollar-amount of the customer's purchases is reduced to a level below the reporting threshold

Failure to file Form 8300 or falsifying Form 8300 is a violation of Title 26. Failure to comply with U.S. currency reporting regulations, as prescribed under Title 26, may result in any or all of the following consequences:[27]

- Fines of $25,000 for an individual and $100,000 for the property
- Imprisonment of up to 5 years
- Payment of the costs of prosecution

Questions/Exercises:

1. Title 26 currency reporting requirements apply to tranasctions occurring in the _____ areas of the resort, while Title 31 currency reporting requirements apply to transactions occuring in the _____ areas of the resort.
2. The jargon used in discussions related to federal currency and suspicious activity reporting utilizes many acronyms. Provide the full name of the items represented by the following acronyms.
   a. CTR-C
   b. SARC
   c. MTL
   d. NIL
   e. MIL
   f. AML
   g. FinCEN
3. Currency transaction reports stemming from non-gaming areas of resorts are submitted by way of which form?
4. Currency transaction reports stemming from the casino are submitted by way of which form?
5. Suspicious activity reports stemming from the casino are filed by way of which form?
6. Suspicious activity reports stemming from non-gaming areas of the resort are filed by way of which form?
7. What is the primary function of the MTL used to record casino transactions?
8. What is the primary purpose of the NIL, with regard to Title 31 compliance?
9. As of July 1, 2007, all Nevada casinos with annual gross gaming revenue in excess of _____ are subject to the Title 31 reporting requirements.
10. True or False: Sovereign Indian tribes operating casinos within the U.S. are subject to federal currency reporting requirements.

---

[27] 26 U.S. Code, Subtitle F, CHAPTER 75, Subchapter A, PART I, § 7203.

11. Within a gaming day, assume a player produces $9,000 in cash-in transactions and $5,000 in cash-out transactions, with all transactions occurring in the casino. Based on this information, what is the appropriate course of action, with regard to the federal currency *reporting* requirements?

12. Describe the critical difference between *reportable* and *loggable,* as the terms relate to discussions of Title 26 and Title 31 compliance.

13. With respect to dollar-amount, describe the general reporting requirements for the following forms of transactions:
    a. Cash tranasctions in the casino
    b. Cash tranasctions in non-gaming areas
    c. Negotiable instruments (e.g., checks) received or issued by the casino

14. With regard to dollar-amounts, what are the logging thresholds for MTL entires?

15. A customer who spreads the redemption of $34,500 in gaming cheques, over the course of four days, without ever exceeding the $10,000 reporting threshold, may be engaging in behavior consistent with which form of suspicious activity?

16. A person feeding marked bills into a slot machine, and pressing the cash-out button without making a wager, would be engaging in behavior consistent with which form(s) of suspicious activity?

17. Per Title 26, a tranasction is suspicious if it appears that a person is attempting to _____, _____, or _____.

Chapter 9
Slot Operations I

Are the outcomes of slot machines random?
What are virtual reels?
What are the critical components of a slot machine's anatomy?
How is slot win calculated?
How do progressive games work?
What are the various forms of participation agreements?

Scope

This chapter is designed to provide an overview of the various forms of electronic gaming devices. After defining these basic forms, the internal and external anatomy of reel slot machine is explained in detail. Critical concepts such as virtual reels are examined to ready the reader for a discussion of par sheet metrics, which occurs in the next chapter. Topics central to slot operations such as progressive games, participation games, and operating system connectivity are also discussed in detail. Finally, the computations of slot win for tax purposes and the assessment of unit-level performance are covered.

It is important to mention that any discussion of slot operations will involve a considerable amount of industry jargon and technical terminology. As this is an introductory text, every effort has been made to explain these terms as they appear in the chapter.

Chapter Goals

- Define the primary forms of electronic stand-alone gaming devices
- Review terms and mechanics of products and processes central to slot operations
    - Examine various progressive game configurations and jackpot accumulation schemes
    - Review different forms of participation agreements between operators and game makers
- Describe the external and internal anatomy of a slot machine
- Describe the primary function of each key element of a reel slot machine
- Examine the formulas used to determine slot win

Types of Reel Slots

In this section we describe the various forms of reel slot game designs. In general, game design is discussed in terms of the relationship between the amount wagered, the amount of the jackpot, and the number of ways to win a jackpot. There are three primary types of reel slot machine game structures: Multipliers, line games, and buy-a-pay games.

Multipliers

Unlike line games, multipliers have only one pay line. These games are characterized by payouts that increase as the amount wagered increases. For example, if "7 – 7 – 7" were to appear on the pay line, with one coin wagered, the payout would be 100 coins. However, if "7 – 7 – 7" were to appear on the pay line, with two coins wagered, the very same outcome would pay 200 coins. Video poker games are also multipliers. For example, a full house might pay 10 coins (i.e., credits) with one credit wagered, and 50 credits, on a five-credit wager. Of course, a two-credit wager would pay 20 credits, and so forth.

Line Games

On these games, players buy additional lines, or ways to win, by wagering additional credits. For example, wagering a single credit would afford a player only one line (i.e., way) to win. Let's assume that a single-credit wager activates pay line 1, in Figure 9.1. In this case, the outcome of the spin would be determined by the symbols that stop on pay line 1. That is, if the top-award symbols all appeared on pay line 2, the player would not win because his minimal wager did not activate pay line 2.

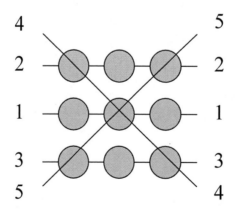

Figure 9.1. Pay Line Structure of a Line Game.[1]

Assuming all lines are equally activated, the payouts are identical from line 1 to line 5. Alternatively stated, there is only one pay table on a line game and it applies to each

---

[1] Adapted from Kilby, J., Fox, J., & Lucas, A.F. (2004). *Casino Operations Management* (2nd ed.). New York: Wiley. Of course, most modern line games feature additional reels and many more pay lines. For example, many modern video line games feature five reels and 50+ pay lines.

active line. Players are encouraged to increase their wagers to increase their chance of winning a payout. This differs from multipliers, where players increase their wagers to earn greater payouts on jackpots.

Buy-a-Pay

Also known as buy-a-symbol games, the structure of these games rewards players for buying or activating additional pay symbols by granting them additional ways to win. These games feature a single pay line (e.g., pay line 1 from Figure 9.1). To clarify this game design, consider the following example. On one-credit wagers, players activate the following pay symbols: Single Bars, Double Bars, and Triple Bars. On two-credit wagers, all the pay symbols activated on the one-credit wager remain in play, plus the following jackpot symbols: Red Sevens and Blazing Sevens. If Blazing Sevens were to appear in all three display positions of line 1, with only one credit wagered, the player would not receive a payout. However, the same outcome would produce a payout, if two credits were wagered. This example demonstrates the premise of the buy-a-pay structure. That is, players increase their chance of winning a jackpot by buying (i.e., activating) additional jackpot symbols.

Hybrid Forms

These games incorporate components of more than one game type. For example, a line game may offer a bonus payout on selected top awards, but only when the maximum wager is placed on all possible lines. This hybrid form incorporates a multiplier function into what is essentially a line game. Given the popularity of low-denomination line games (i.e., penny games), and the infrequency of maximum-bet wagers on these games, the number of hybrid games on slot floors is likely to increase. The bonus payout encourages maximum-credit wagering, which increases the game's dollar-contribution to the casino (i.e., theoretical win).[2]

Types of Reels

In this section we will describe the difference between mechanical and video reels. Also known as physical reels or steppers, mechanical reel games contain actual/physical spinning reels. These reels are motorized and receive their start and stop instructions from the game's processor.[3] Similar to the human eye ball, only a small portion of the reel's surface is visible. That is, the bulk of the physical reel is not visible through the game's glass. As is the case with the human eye ball, the size of the physical reel is much larger than most would imagine. It is not known whether the tendency to underestimate the physical size of the reels leads to overestimation of the likelihood of lining up the top award symbols. If there were any truth to this notion, it would certainly represent a little-known and possibly controversial enticement. Given the importance of the player's perceived chance of winning, this would certainly make for an interesting experiment.

---

[2] Theoretical win (a.k.a. t-win) is the product of the dollar-amount wagered and the house advantage associated with the wager(s).
[3] Each reel is powered by a stepper motor.

Video reel games have no physical reels. The physical spinning reels are graphically simulated by the game's processor. This technology provides many more opportunities to dazzle and entertain players by way of graphically-oriented effects. The animation and graphics of video reels more closely resembles that of video games than traditional slot machines.

Video reels were first released in the early 1980's, but failed to gain a place on the slot floor. Many cited trust issues stemming from the lack of physical reels as the primary reason for their demise. That is, many slot players were not sure that outcomes produced by computer-generated reels were legitimate. However, the acceptance and ensuing popularity of personal computers may have paved the way for the comeback of video reels. Today, these games enjoy both acceptance and popularity. Video reels have reached record numbers on many slot floors and represent an exciting platform for innovation with regard to the future forms of slot machines.

Video Poker Games

There are many forms of video poker games. For now, we will limit our discussion to describing the basic idea behind the game. Essentially, video poker machines are electronic stand-alone versions of 5-card draw poker, where the player plays against the house, and no other players. These games became popular in the 1980's, as their introduction appealed to players enticed by games of skill. That is, video poker games took coin-operated devices (i.e., reel slots) from games of chance to games of skill. The skill component of video poker made coin-operated games attractive to entirely new groups of gamblers, while enticing some existing reel slot players to crossover as well.

In short, the game deals the player five cards from a standard deck of 52 cards. From this original hand, players are permitted to hold all five cards, if dealt a winning hand, or discard and draw up to five new cards, to make their final five-card hand. The players are able to reference the posted pay table to learn the value of obtaining each winning hand/outcome. Typically, the least valuable winning hand is comprised of a single pair of Jacks or better. That is, a single pair of jacks, queens, kings, or aces. The most valuable hand is usually a royal flush, which is a suited straight beginning with the 10 and ending with the Ace. For example, the 10, jack, queen, king, and ace of hearts. Additionally, a royal flush can be comprised of the same ranks in clubs, diamonds, or spades. Of course, there are many variations on video poker pay tables, but in large part, the hands that are most difficult to obtain produce the greatest payouts.

Video Keno Games

These games are a video version of the live keno game. In short, the player chooses up to 20 numbers from a field of 80 numbers, ranging from 1 to 80. Early forms of video keno required players to select these numbers using a stylus attached to the game itself; however, most games now feature touch-screen technology, eliminating the need for a stylus. Once the player's numbers have been selected, the game then randomly selects 20 numbers from the same field of eighty numbers (i.e., ranging from 1 to 80). The players win or lose depending upon the extent to which the numbers they selected match those selected by the game's computer. Live keno is simply a form of a lottery, while video keno is nothing more than a stand-alone, coin/credit-operated, electronic version of the live game. However, to make video keno games more exciting, they are often enhanced with multi-card game functionality and special bonus payout features. [4]

Electronic Table Games

There are games such as dealerless roulette, which qualify as slot machines in the broader sense. This game differs considerably from its table game counterpart. It has much more in common with a slot machine. Players place their bets from terminals and there is no dealer to spin the ball, announce the outcome of the spins, mark the winning number, clear losing wagers, or pay winning bets. All of these tasks are performed by the game itself.

There are several versions of automated roulette. To date, the game has experienced varying degrees of success. One of the more successful implementations has been the Australian club market, where traditional table games are not permitted. In this market, dealerless roulette takes on added appeal, as there are no other live table games to compete against it.

Video blackjack is also available in many U.S. casinos. This game is nothing more than a stand-alone video version of the live game. This game is often offered on multi-game slot machine terminals. These terminals display multiple game icons on the machine's entry screen, allowing the player to choose from several different games. There are usually around eight different games offered on a multi-game terminal. Video blackjack's popularity and success is often affected by the presence of live blackjack, as a competing option for players.

Nontraditional Games

There are machines that feature no reels. These machines are neither video poker nor video keno games. For example, Atronic's *Deal or No Deal,*[5] based on the television game show of the same name, initially requires players to spin a single wheel (not a reel). This first round of interaction determines the possible payouts. At the second level of the game, players choose a specified number of numbered briefcases, which results in the elimination of possible payouts. After each round of briefcase selection, some payouts are eliminated. At this point, players are offered the option of accepting a payout that is based, in part, on the values of the remaining possible payouts. The point of this description is to demonstrate that this game resembles nothing but the bonus round of a contemporary game, offering no traditional base game (i.e., reel array).

---

[4] Multi-card game functionality allows bettors to play more than one keno ticket per game (i.e., per drawing).

[5] The game's full name is Deal or No Deal: What's Your Deal?

A description of a traditional game that offers a bonus round may help clarify the distinct game structure of *Deal or No Deal*. In general, traditional games that offer a bonus round have two structural components: A base game and a bonus round. Players begin in the base game, in which reels would appear on the game screen. They would most likely be video reels, as opposed to physical reels. The players would wager, and then spin the reels. Specific outcomes of the base game would be set to trigger a bonus round in which the player would most likely choose specific items from a field of choices. Only about two to four percent of all base game outcomes would trigger the bonus round. Once in the bonus round, the player would watch some form of video animation reveal the outcomes associated with his or her selections. Once the bonus round terminates, the player returns to the base game. As you can see, *Deal or No Deal* has no reel-oriented base game, making it a nontraditional slot machine.

Coinless Slots

Most games on the modern slot floor no longer accept coins. This is interesting, given that the original form of slot machines was based on wagering coins. Many factors have contributed to the extinction of coin-operated devices. For coin-based wagering to be economically attractive to management, a great numbers of coins must be wagered. Of course, great numbers of coins are heavy, making it difficult and burdensome for customers to transport them through the casino.

With respect to the customer experience, coin-operated games can run out of coins, causing unwanted interruptions in the gaming experience. Specifically, this happens when the hopper is emptied by payouts/jackpots paid by the game. The hopper is the slot machine's internal coin storage container, serving as the source of coins for the payment of most jackpots. Once the hopper is empty, the game shuts down until a slot attendant can answer the customer's service call and fill the hopper. The time required to answer and complete this service call is often lengthy.

The weight of the coins also affects the drop and count processes. As noted in Chapters 6 and 7, it is expensive and time consuming to transport, count, and process coins. It is much easier to process currency (i.e., bills).

So how were coins eliminated from the slot machine experience? The answer is technology, in the form of the bill validator/acceptor. This device allows customers to insert currency directly into the slot machine. The bill validator first validates the authenticity of the currency, then converts the currency into game credits, and finally, sends the inserted currency to the game's currency container (i.e., currency storage box).

Anatomy of a Standard Slot Machine: Exterior Features

Such a thing as a standard slot machine might not exist, or may be impossible to define. That said, we have attempted to describe what we believe to be a typical reel slot machine. Of course, the specific features and the location of the features will vary by game. Figure 9.2 is provided to identify the features discussed in the following paragraphs.

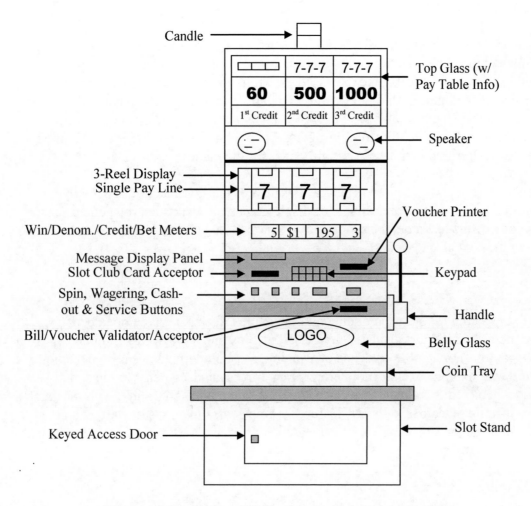

Figure 9.2. External Elements of a Reel Slot Machine.

Candle

This is the light that appears on the top of the slot machine. Historically, the candle was an important communication device. Slot attendants could read the candle to determine what action needed to be taken. For example, a solid light indicated that the player needed change (i.e., coin). As you can see from Figure 9.2, there are two parts of the candle. A single blinking light usually indicated that the game needed to be serviced. This could have meant anything from a coin jam to a hopper fill. Two blinking lights usually indicated the need for a hand-pay jackpot.

Due to the advent of online slot systems and technology such as bill validators, the candle may be the modern equivalent of the human appendix. That is, fewer players need change and all game malfunctions are communicated to the slot employees via the online operating system. Despite these advances, candles are still included on most new games.

Top Glass

The game's pay table is often displayed in the top glass. The top glass resides in the top box of a slot machine. The top box is the part of the game that sits above the game screen or reel display. In Figure 9.2, the pay table shown in the top glass is greatly abbreviated, as the size of the figure would not permit a readable version of a full pay table. On this game, an unabridged pay table would show each symbol outcome associated with a payout on one-, two-, and three-coin wagers. Although not shown in Figure 9.2, the top glass is often decorative, serving as "billboard" for the game.

Server-based games have no top glass, as this area of the slot machine is actually a LCD monitor.[6] These monitors are capable of displaying any downloaded image/data. Such technology offers operators great flexibility. Server-based games are discussed in greater detail in the next chapter.

Speakers

With today's coinless slots, producing audible game effects has taken on added importance. That is, most games no longer drop coins into a metal tray mounted above a hollow cavity.[7] For audible evidence of winning, most modern games rely on audio files played through the speakers. Audio effects range from enhancements to the sounds emitted when credits are increased to customized sound bites associated with the game's theme, specific outcomes, or bonus features. Some games feature subwoofers and premium sound packages, which take the audio experience well beyond that produced by a standard slot machine.

Reel Display

Also known as the game glass (on mechanical reel games) and the game screen (on video reels), the reel display allows the player to see the outcome of each spin. In Figure 9.2, this outcome is the top award, as "7 - 7 - 7" appears on the game's only pay line (i.e., its single pay line).

External Meters

The game illustrated in Figure 9.2 features four electronic meters located just below the reel display. The meter on the far left of the four-meter array displays the number of credits awarded, as a result of the most recent spin/outcome. In this case, the last spin produced a 5-credit payout. The meter to the immediate right of the win meter displays the denomination of the minimum betting unit, which is $1.00 in this case. The meter to

---

[6] LCD stands for liquid-crystal display.
[7] This configuration produced a distinct and remarkable amount of noise when the coins fell into the suspended metal tray.

the immediate right of the denomination meter displays the total number of credits remaining on the game. In this case, there are 195 credits remaining. As each credit is equal to $1.00, the value of the balance is $195.00. The meter on the far right of the four-meter array displays the number of credits wagered on the most recent/current spin. In this case, the wager was equal to three credits, or $3.00.

Voucher Printer

In concert with the bill/voucher acceptor, this technology removed the burden of transporting coin throughout the casino. A burden shared by players and management alike. When a player wishes to terminate play or switch machines, the game's cash-out button is pressed. Of course, this assumes the player has credits remaining. Pressing the cash-out button causes the voucher printer to produce a voucher for the corresponding dollar-amount. The game must convert the credits remaining on the meter to a dollar-amount before printing the voucher. In most cases, the players can insert these vouchers into the bill acceptor of any other slot machine on the premises. The bill acceptors recognize the dollar-amount of the vouchers as currency and issue the corresponding number of credits to the player.

Slot Club Card Acceptor

When players enroll in the slot club they are issued a club card. For the casino to credit or reward players for their gaming activity, the players must create a record of their patronage. This record is created by way of a club card, which is assigned to each member of the slot club. Once a player's club card is inserted into the card acceptor, also known as a card reader, a detailed electronic record of that player's gaming activity can be created and stored in the marketing module of the slot accounting system. Use of the club card allows management to measure the gaming value of each individual member. However, if a player's card is not inserted into the card reader, the gaming activity cannot be recorded to his or her account.

Keypad

The keypad shown in Figure 9.2 would have numbers and/or letters printed on each of the ten keys. After inserting their club card, players would use the keypad to enter their personal identification number (PIN). Provided that the PIN is kept confidential, it protects a player's point balance in the event of a lost or stolen card. That is, the PIN prevents others from accessing and redeeming the points accumulated on another player's card. The PIN is also used to access promotional offers such as free-play awards. For example, management may award a specific dollar-amount of credit to a particular player, as a play incentive or loyalty building gesture. Once the dollar-amount of the award has been electronically credited to a player's account, the keypad and PIN allow for secured access to the offer. Without a keypad and PIN, any awards credited to a player's account could be accessed by any person in possession of that player's card. Without this technology, those in possession of lost or stolen club cards could access and redeem the rewards of others. Not all slot clubs use PINs.

Message Display Panel

This small panel serves as a message crawler. Once a club card is inserted into the card acceptor/reader (shown Figure 9.2) the player is typically greeted by name. Once the player enters his or her PIN, the message display panel will provide detailed account balance information and details related to the redemption of rewards and/or play incentives. Information related to current promotional offers is also sent to the game and displayed on the message panel. Such offers can target specific players.

Operating Buttons

The following list provides examples of the types of operating buttons found on reel slot machines, with further description of these items offered in the subsequent paragraphs.

- Change/Service Button
- Cash-out/Print Voucher Button
- Bet Advancement Button
- Spin Button
- Maximum Wager/Spin Button

Although often labeled "change" this button is rarely pressed for the purpose of buying coins. Pressing this button activates the light in the game's candle and registers a service call in the slot system. Players would press this button for a variety of reasons, such as a frozen game screen or other game malfunctions. This button is also pressed to request cocktail service.

Pressing the cash-out button once triggered a cascade of coins into a metal tray. Pressing this button on most modern games initiates the printing of a voucher. The bet advancement button allows players to increase their wager each time it is pressed. Pressing the spin button simply sets the game's reels in motion. Of course, a player's wager cannot be changed once the spin button is pressed. Most games conveniently provide a maximum-wager button, encouraging players to make the greatest possible bet per spin. In fact, pressing this button not only places the maximum wager it usually finalizes it by setting the reels in motion.

Bill/Voucher Validator/Acceptor

This device accepts and verifies both currency and wagering instruments (i.e., vouchers). Of course, in U.S. casinos, the only currency accepted by these devices is U.S. currency. This technology eliminated the labor-intensive task of supplying change (i.e., coin) to slot players holding only currency. Again, the bill/voucher acceptors recognize the dollar-amount of vouchers as currency and issue the corresponding number of credits to the player.

Handle

Many games no longer feature handles. The spin button accomplishes the same task and can be housed on the face of the game. The handle must be mounted on the side of the game, expanding the cabinet width.

Belly Glass

Although pay table information sometimes appears on belly glass, it is usually only decorative. Server-based games replace this glass with a LCD monitor.[8] When the new game is downloaded, the belly glass monitor displays the associated graphics.

Coin Tray

Aside from its obvious function of holding dispensed coin, the metal coin tray added excitement to the slot experience. That is, the coin tray was typically mounted or housed above a hollow space, creating compelling and audible evidence of winning. A coin landing in this metal tray could be heard from a remarkable distance. Most games on the modern slot floor no longer feature coin trays. The bill/voucher acceptor and voucher printers have eliminated the need for coin. Sounds of winning are now created electronically.

Slot Stand

Many games rest atop stands, as shown in Figure 9.2. The stand elevates the game to a height that facilitates comfortable interaction with a seated player. Although the height of the stand is a function of the height of the game itself, most stands elevate the base of the game about 15 inches above the floor. Most stands feature a locking door. The interior of the stand can be used for a variety of purposes, such as storage compartment. For progressive games, the device used to divert portions of wagers to the jackpot meters (i.e., the progressive controller) is often mounted in the interior compartment of the slot stand.

Top Box/Cabinet Design

Although not expressly labeled, Figure 9.2 illustrates a standard top box. Remember, in general, the top box is the area of the slot machine above the reel display. The size, shape, and content of the top box can vary greatly. Games with elaborate and decorative top boxes can exceed ten feet in height. Such games are usually very expensive and must be located against a wall to preserve customer sight lines on the casino floor.

Slant-top games represent the other extreme, with respect to top boxes. That is, this particular style of game has an aggressively cropped top box. While this style preserves customer sight lines on the casino floor, the slant-top feature has been found to be

---

[8] Belly glass is also sometimes replaced by a static backlit general display or logo (e.g., the game maker or casino logo).

associated with decreased game performance.[9] There are a couple of theories as to why these games have performed poorly.

First, the cropped top box eliminates the billboard effect. There are those who believe that top boxes serve as a form of billboard advertising to players. Without a full-sized top box, players cannot easily identify the game, and therefore, it is played less than games that feature more prominent top boxes. Second, some believe that when slant-top games are configured in back-to-back banks, privacy and/or personal space issues arise. That is, in the absence of a top box, players sitting across from each other are able to look at each other, over the tops of the games. There are those who believe this potentially awkward eye contact decreases the appeal of slant-top games. Of course, these are just theories. There is no published empirical research that addresses the plausibility of either theory.

Anatomy of a Standard Slot Machine: Interior Features

Just as the exterior features of reel slot machines vary, so too do the interior components. There will be exceptions to any single example of the interior features of slot machines. Not surprisingly, much of the internal structure can be described in terms of the external features.

Processor Board

The most critical internal component of a slot machine is its processor board, also known as a machine processing unit (MPU) board. This could be thought of as the game's computer. The processor board resides inside of a locked box, which is mounted inside the game's main/central compartment. Of course, the slot machine's door is also locked. Therefore, access to two different controlled keys is required to reach the game's processor board.

Function of the Processor Board

The processor board serves as a memory/storage device and processing unit. In this capacity, the critical game files are stored on media such as a hard drive, flash memory, or an EPROM (for older games). The critical game files include data representing all possible outcomes from a spin and the associated payouts. The random number generator (RNG) and mapped virtual reels are also stored in the game's memory.[10] These mapped virtual reels determine the probability of each possible outcome. The game's video and audio files are often integrated into the processor unit, but not always.

All of the electronic peripherals shown in Figure 9.2 must be wired to the MPU. All player-initiated commands travel through the processor. For example, the spin button is

---

[9] Lucas, A.F., Dunn, W., Roehl, W.S., & Wolcott, G. (2004). Evaluating slot machine performance: A performance-potential model. *International Journal of Hospitality Management, 23*(2), 103-121; and Lucas, A.F., & Roehl, W.S. (2002). Influences on video poker machine performance: Measuring the effect of floor location. *Journal of Travel & Tourism Marketing, 12*(4), 75-92.

[10] RNG and mapped virtual reels are described in a subsequent section of this chapter.

wired to the processor. All marketing and accounting data resulting from the player's interaction with the game also must pass through the processor. As a result, items such as the card reader and the bill/voucher acceptor must be connected to the game's processor.

Harnesses

Due to the tremendous number of devices that must interface with the game's processor, harnesses are often used to efficiently accomplish this requirement. For example, many slot technicians will use a player tracking harness. On one end, this harness simply consists of three groups of wires which plug into peripheral devices. That is, one group of these wires plugs into each of the following three devices: The slot club card acceptor (a.k.a. card reader), the keypad, and the message display panel. The other end of this harness consists of two groups of wires attaching these three devices to both the game processor and the server that operates the marketing side of the slot operating system. Figure 9.3 provides a simple diagram of the player tracking harness and the devices it connects. The harness itself is represented by the bolded lines.

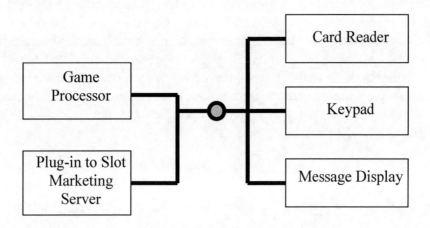

Figure 9.3. Simple Diagram of a Player Tracking Harness.

Casino Sub-floor

As you will notice from Figure 9.3, the player tracking harness attaches to the slot marketing server plug-in. This is one of the points where the game meets the casino sub-floor. In most cases, there are three such points. First, the game's power cord will plug into an electrical outlet (power supply) located beneath the casino floor. Second, the game will plug into the accounting module of the slot operating system. This will most likely occur by way of another harness, which will attach to the wiring in the sub-floor. Third, the game will plug into the marketing module of the slot operating system, as previously described. To accomplish the second and third connection points, the wiring for both the accounting and marketing modules of the slot operating system must be pulled throughout the entire sub-floor. Many modern systems combine the second and third connection points by way of a single wire that connects the game to both the accounting and marketing modules.[11]

Additional external connectivity is necessary for progressive games. For example, all Megabucks games are connected to the game maker's external server (located outside the casino). This connection allows the game maker to monitor coin-in rates, respond to error codes, send a lock-out signal, and more.[12] In the case of Megabucks, the game maker receives a portion of the game's coin-in. In return for this fee, the game maker assumes most of the costs of ownership. For example, the game maker is responsible for repair and maintenance of the games. They are also responsible for paying the progressive jackpots.

Sub-floor Wiring

Technological advancements in slot machines, peripheral devices, and slot operating systems all require a greater amount of data to be transmitted through the sub-floor wiring network. Such advancements have required increases in the capacity (i.e., band width) of the sub-floor wire. For example, many modern casinos use category 5 & 6 cable, which offers considerable band width. However, the casino in MGM's CityCenter project uses fiber-optic cable in the sub-floor to accommodate increased data transfer needs and connectivity associated with server-based slot machines. The fiber-optic cabling far exceeds the data transfer capacities of category 6 wire. Given the trends in slot machine technology, it makes sense to wire any new casino project to accommodate increases in connectivity to operating systems and increases in the amounts of data to be transferred to and from slot machines.

Virtual Reels

The creation of the contemporary virtual reel stems from a patent granted to Inge Telnaes in 1984.[13] Prior to this, the magnitude of jackpots was limited by the number of reels and the number of possible stopping positions on each reel. Given that it was difficult to fit more than 22 stops on a reel and that most games featured three-reels, the top award would be expected to occur once in every 10,648 spins (i.e., 22^3). This assumes that only one top-award symbol appears on each reel and that each reel's stop position is randomly selected. It is important to note that as the expected number of spins between top-award jackpots increases, the magnitude of the top award can be increased. That is, as the number of spins between top-award jackpots increases, the game is afforded a greater number of opportunities to win wagers. Of course, these winnings fund jackpots.

---

[11] Such technology is often referred to as a one-wire system.

[12] Once a progressive jackpot is hit by a player, a lock-out signal is immediately generated. This signal prevents the same jackpot from occurring on another game in the same link, before the meter can be reset. That is, the lock-out signal triggers a simultaneous meter reset to the beginning balance of the progressive award, on all linked games.

[13] Telnaes, Inge S. (May 15, 1984). Electronic gaming device utilizing a random number generator for selecting the reel stop positions. U.S. Patent #4448419. Retrieved May 1, 2010 from http://www.patent storm.us/patents/4448419/fulltext.html.

Although a top-award cycle of 10,648 spins allows for an impressive return on a 3-coin wager, state lotteries were offering life-changing jackpots well beyond those of Nevada's slot machines. The invention of the virtual reel changed Nevada's fortune. By mapping the stops on physical reels to ranges of randomly selected numbers that corresponded to virtual reel stops, slot machines could offer very attractive top awards. For example, the same 3-reel, 22-stop game could, in effect, become a 3-reel, 32-stop game. By increasing the "size" of the reels, this game's top award would be expected to occur once in every 32,768 spins, affording the possibility of a greatly increased top award. This assumes only one top-award symbol per reel and that each stop on the virtual reel has an equal chance of selection (i.e., 1/32).

The impact of the mapped virtual reel on top-award jackpots may be best explained by way of example. Let's assume only one top award symbol appears on each of three reels. Let's assume further that there are 22 stops on each physical reel. As previously noted, one could expect the top-award jackpot to occur once in every 10,648 spins (i.e., 22^3). Continuing the example, let's assume there were 12 blanks on each physical reel. To decrease the frequency of the top-award jackpot let's increase the number of stops on each reel to 32. How do we do this? We use a random number generator (RNG) that produces a number ranging from 1 to 32. But we only have 22 actual stops on each physical reel. What happens when the RNG produces the number 26? What will the game display for that reel? These problems are addressed by the mapping process, which is covered next.

Think of the mapping process in terms of a look-up table. For example, if the RNG produces numbers 1, 2, or 3 (from 32 possible numbers), the game will be mapped to stop the reel such that Blank #1 is displayed. If the RNG produces numbers 30 or 31, the physical reel will display Blank #12, and so forth. By mapping the physical stops to a *range* of numbers, the probability of selecting these symbols can be increased. When the selection of non-paying symbols increases, the frequency of jackpots decreases. When the frequency of jackpots decreases, the magnitude of the top-awards can be increased. In conclusion, by expanding the size of the reels and mapping the physical stops to the virtual stops, the magnitude of jackpots can be greatly increased.

Video Reels

What about video reel games? That is, these games are not constrained by physical reels. Just the same, many video reel games are constructed using these same principles. For example, video reel games have a defined set of symbols which can be displayed. The number of symbols in this set is usually much smaller than the number of stops on the game's virtual reel. Remember, the game maker must display a pay table somewhere on the game. A tremendous number of discrete symbols would be difficult to display in a pay table format, and is likely to confuse players. As a result of these conditions, the virtual reel process is also applied to video reels.

Are Outcomes Random?

Whether you are looking at all of the possible stops on a physical reel or all of the discrete symbols in a video reel game, if a weighted mapped virtual reel is employed, the game's outcomes are not random. However, the process of selection is randomized by way of the RNG. That is, for a sampling process to be random, each element of a population of elements must have an equal chance of being selected. Because all of the symbols on a virtual reel are not weighted equally (i.e., assigned to the same number of virtual stops), each of the symbols does not have the same chance of being selected. Because of this condition, games employing unequal weights in the virtual reel mapping process are not random. Of course, the primary purpose of mapping outcomes is to weight them unequally.

Progressive Games

Progressive games feature top awards that increase with play. In part, the progressive jackpots are a function of wagering activity. More specifically, progressive games divert a portion of the credits wagered to the progressive jackpot meters. Operators employ a device known as a progressive controller to divert a specific portion of the wager to the appropriate meters. Progressive games often have multiple progressive jackpots, so the controller diverts different percentages of the amounts wagered to different jackpot meters. The top progressive jackpot meter usually receives the greatest percentage contribution. The lesser jackpot meters are known as secondary meters.

Configurations

Many different types of games can be converted into a progressive game, including all forms of reel slots[14] and video poker games. However, not all pay tables are ideally configured to accommodate progressive jackpots. Although alternative configurations do exist, we will first describe the three traditional configurations of progressive games:

- Stand-alone progressives
- Local area progressives (LAPs)
- Wide area progressives (WAPs)

The stand-alone progressive jackpot meters are fed by wagers placed on a single game, hence the name stand-alone. Local area progressive jackpots are fed by wagers placed on multiple games, which are wired together. These games all reside on a single casino floor. Wide area progressive jackpots are also increased by wagers placed on multiple games, which are wired together. However, these games reside on multiple casino floors. Nevada's Megabucks games were the first and probably best known example of wide area progressive games.

---

[14] Where "forms" refers to multipliers, buy-a-pay games, and line games.

Jackpot Accumulation

Management usually determines the percentage of the wager that is diverted to the progressive jackpot meters. For example, if the house advantage of the game is 8% (given a maximum-unit wager) and management decides to divert 1% of maximum-unit wagers to the progressive meters, the house advantage of the game is reduced to 7%. Once any portion of a wager is diverted to a progressive meter it becomes the public's money. The gaming operator cannot later decide to take progressive games off the floor and recognize the unpaid jackpots as revenue.

As previously noted, a device known as a progressive controller is used to divert specified percentages of maximum-unit wagers to the appropriate jackpot meters. The controller is usually mounted below the game, inside the game's stand.[15] The controller is wired directly to the game's computer. It also connects all games linked to a common jackpot. When a progressive jackpot is won, the controller sends a signal to any and all linked games to reset the affected jackpot meters.

When linking games together, operators must consider the frequency of the top award jackpot. That is, top awards that occur frequently will limit the ability of the games to accumulate monetarily attractive top-award meters. After all, progressive games were founded on the theory that the balance of the top-award meter is directly related the ability of the linked games to attract players.

Hidden Meters

These are neither top-award meters nor secondary jackpot meters. A portion of a maximum-unit wager can be diverted to a hidden meter in the same manner that it is diverted to any other meter. The critical difference is that the players cannot see the balance of a hidden meter. At this point, one may wonder why operators would use hidden meters. If no one can see the balance, what good could come of it? The answer to this question lies in the reset value.

When a top-award progressive jackpot is won the meter resets to the game's top award, as designed by the game maker. Alternatively stated, the top-award meter's reset value is the game's normal top award, without any additional accrued jackpot funds. Because the top-award of most games is easily recognizable to players, they can deduce from the reset value displayed on the top-award meter that the progressive jackpot has been recently won. As many gaming operators believe gamblers to be superstitious, the balance of the hidden meter is added to the game's standard top award, creating an enhanced and disguised reset value. This increased reset value disguises the fact that the game's top award was just won. Many gaming operators believe that hidden meters help reduce the lull in play that often follows top-award jackpots.

---

[15] The stand is nothing more than a box that serves to elevate the game from the floor. Most stands are built on site to accommodate the specific dimensions of the games resting on them. Most stands are approximately 15 inches in height with the width and depth needed to accommodate two standard upright games.

Hidden meters are often used in markets catering to a repeater clientele. The thinking here is that players who visit a casino frequently are more likely to be aware of daily top award balances on progressive games. For example, Nevada bar owners often cite a decline in play following top award jackpots. They employ hidden meters in the hope of minimizing such a decline.

Alternative Configurations

For a player to win a progressive jackpot in any of the three traditional configurations, the top-award symbols must be aligned on the designated pay line. However, an alternative form of progressive configuration does not require the alignment of any symbols to win the jackpot. This alternative process randomly and anonymously selects a dollar-amount within a specified range of dollar-amounts (e.g., from $125k to $150k). Similar to the traditional configurations, a portion of the wagers from all linked games is diverted to the jackpot meter(s). The jackpot is won when the progressive contribution from a player's wager causes the progressive meter balance to meet or exceed the randomly selected dollar-amount.

To clarify, the alternative process begins with the selection of a randomly selected dollar-amount. The dollar-amount on the progressive meter continues to increase until a player's wager causes it to meet or exceed the predetermined dollar-amount. It could take days or months for the meter to increase from its reset value to the randomly selected dollar-amount (i.e., the jackpot amount). The number of spins between winners depends, in part, on the distance between the top award's reset value and the randomly selected dollar-amount.

This alternative progressive configuration is ideally suited for the low-denomination, multi-line, video reel games. Such a game may feature 25 pay lines and allow players to wager 20 units per line. This game would require a player to wager 500 units on a single spin to be eligible for the top progressive jackpot. These games are popular on many casino floors, but rarely receive the maximum-unit wagers necessary to qualify players for the progressive jackpot. This may be due to the considerable difference between the minimum and maximum wagers afforded by these games.

This lack of maximum-unit wagers results in an extended top-award cycle. That is, the top award symbols are aligned several times between jackpot winners. Alternatively stated, the games produce the winning outcome, but the players don't place the maximum-unit wager required to actually win the jackpot. This creates disappointment for the players who fail to place the required wager. It also results in long stretches of time between top award winners, which many believe makes the jackpots appear unwinnable to the players. Neither of these outcomes is desirable.

The alternative progressive configuration discussed in this section circumvents the lack of maximum-unit wagers on low-denomination, multi-line, video reels, as winning is not contingent on the alignment of top award symbols. This alternative configuration goes by several names and is increasing in popularity. One Las Vegas gaming operator has used this technology to link games across multiple casino floors. This configuration allows them to offer very attractive jackpots without requiring players to place maximum-unit wagers. Additionally, by linking so many games together, a remarkably minimal percentage of the dollar-amount wagered funds these attractive six-figure jackpots.

Purpose

Now that you understand how the progressive games work, you may be wondering why casinos offer them. For starters, progressive games offer jackpots that other games cannot provide. The progressive jackpots are well beyond those offered by games without a progressive feature. The magnitude of progressive jackpots is theorized to attract patrons that might not otherwise play slot machines. Similar to the notion of price points in retail, gaming operators must be conscious of managing prize points (i.e., jackpot magnitudes). Although the dollar-amount of progressive jackpots most certainly varies, these games represent important prize points.

Effectiveness

Do progressive games outperform their non-progressive counterparts? It may be surprising, but little is known about the relative performance of games featuring progressive jackpots. The question quickly becomes difficult to answer, as games are comprised of so many potentially critical components. To determine the unique contribution of the progressive feature, the effects of all other game features/components must be addressed. Most operators are not trained in the analytical techniques required to perform such an advanced analysis.

Only one academic study has addressed the effect of the progressive feature on game performance, and it was not the primary objective of the research.[16] The authors of the study examined the unit-level performance of $1.00 reel games in a Las Vegas Strip casino. In short, the presence of the progressive feature failed to affect coin-in levels. However, much more research is needed before any foundation of a theory can be established regarding the effect of progressive features on wagering volume.

Aside from the example described in the *Alternative Configurations Section* of this chapter, most games on slot floors do not include progressive features. However, without the aid of additional research, it is difficult to estimate the effectiveness of the progressive feature. That is, operators cannot know whether progressive games are over- or under-represented on their slot floors. Further, operators have little insight into related issues such as the relative effectiveness of the various forms of progressive features and the effect of jackpot magnitude on game performance.

Win Formulas

This section addresses the formulas that management would employ to compute win for an individual slot machine over a specific duration such as a day, month, or year. Of

---

[16] Lucas et al. (2004), op. cit.

course, all variables would represent activity for the same period of time (i.e., a day, month, or year). We will define each element of the following formula in the subsequent paragraphs.

$$\text{Win} = \text{Coin-in} - \text{Coin-out} - \text{Hand Paid Jackpots} - \text{Fills} - \text{Progressive Accrual}$$

Coin-in represents the dollar-amount of money wagered by players, including bets made by way of coins, currency (i.e., bills), and vouchers.[17] *Coin-out* is the dollar-amount of all payouts resulting from wagers, except for those that trigger hand paid jackpots. *Hand Paid Jackpots* represents the dollar-amount of all jackpots paid by a representative of the casino. Again, such payments occur when the game does not pay the jackpot by way of coin-out.[18] *Fills* is the dollar-value of all coin used to replenish a depleted hopper.[19] Fills are rare in modern casinos, as coinless games have no hoppers to fill. If a game has a progressive feature, a portion of each credit wagered is diverted to the game's progressive jackpot meters. *Progressive Accrual* represents the dollar-value of all credits diverted to the game's progressive jackpot meters. When the progressive jackpot is eventually won, the cumulative dollar-amount of all related accruals is reversed and the dollar-amount of the jackpot would be included in *Hand Paid Jackpots*. The accrual process simply allows management to recognize/record the jackpot liability in the period in which it occurs, as opposed to recording the entire payout in a single accounting period.

In Nevada, gaming taxes are paid on win, but tax liability is often calculated using the following formula,[20] which differs from the previous win formula.

$$\text{Win} = \text{Drop} - \text{Attendant Pays} - \text{Fills} - \text{Vouchers Issued}$$

Notice that no progressive accrual term is listed in the win formula.[21] For tax purposes, the dollar-value of all progressive jackpots is included in *Attendant Pays*, in the month that the jackpot is won. *Drop* is the dollar-value of all currency and vouchers collected from the game's cash can plus the dollar-value of all coin collected from the game's drop bucket.[22] *Attendant Pays* represents the dollar-value of any payment made by a casino representative (usually a slot attendant). This includes hand paid jackpots and other payments resulting from the game's inability to dispense coin or a voucher.[23] *Fills* does not differ from the previous definition. Again, fills are rare in modern casinos, as most

---

[17] Win divided by coin-in equals the game's actual hold percentage.

[18] Although the dollar-value of a hand pay is set at the game level, $1,200 usually serves as the trigger. Payouts equal to or greater than $1,200 require the completion of IRS Form W-2G/1042-S.

[19] The hopper is the internal storage container that dispenses the coins from the game in the event of a jackpot. As the frequency and/or magnitude of jackpots increases, the hopper may contain an insufficient number of coins to make a payout, resulting in the need for a fill to continue operation.

[20] In Nevada, licensees are afforded two options when reporting win to the NGCB. That is, win can be reported on a cash or accrual basis. This formula represents the cash basis computation.

[21] If management were to compute win from drop, the progressive accrual term would be added to this formula.

[22] For the purpose of computing gaming tax liability, operators are afforded the option of reporting metered drop (i.e., as recorded by the slot operating system), instead of reporting actual/counted drop.

[23] Such events include game malfunctions preventing players from cashing out credit balances.

games are coinless. *Vouchers Issued* represents the total dollar-amount of all vouchers issued by the game.[24]

Participation Games

Participation is an industry term used to describe a particular form of financial agreement between an operator and a game manufacturer. Such agreements represent one way for operators to acquire games from game makers. There are two primary forms of participation agreements: Performance-based agreements and fee-based agreements. In most performance-based agreements, the game maker and casino operator share or split the game's win. For example, the operator would retain 80% of the game's win, and the game maker would receive a payment from the operator for an amount equal to 20% of the game's win. Of course, the agreement would stipulate that the game's win would be computed over a specified length of time, such as a calendar month. In this case, the operator would settle the game maker's account at the end of each month.

The other common form of participation agreement is the fee-based model, whereby the operator pays the game maker a flat fee for a game. For example, the operator may agree to pay the game maker/provider a fee of $15 per day, per game (i.e., unit). Similar to the performance-based agreement, a fee-based agreement would require the fees to be paid to the game maker at the end of a stated time interval (e.g., a calendar month).

In return for a share of the operator's revenue or a daily fee, the game maker provides the game to the casino operator at no charge. The participation model may be attractive to casino operators with little or no capital budget for new games. Despite their impressive returns, slot machines are expensive.

Although participation agreements may be right for some, these deals have damaged relationships between game makers and many casino operators. The operators often wish to purchase games that the game makers will not sell them. That is, game makers will only provide certain games via participation agreements. Many operators feel that game makers have used participation agreements to wrongfully make their way on to their clients' casino floors. Further, many operators argue that game makers created participation agreements to increase the cost of the games to the operators. Operators state that it would be much less expensive for them to pay the going purchase price for the game than to make continued revenue-sharing payments, over the game's tenure on the casino floor.

Questions/Exercises:

1. In *Alternative Configurations*, there is a description of a Las Vegas gaming operator's incorporation of alternative progressive technology. Within the framework described in *Configurations*, which of the three forms of traditional progressive configurations does this example most resemble? Explain your answer.

---

[24] Vouchers Issued includes the dollar-amount of vouchers issued for credits that were never wagered.

2. With respect to winning the top-award, what is the primary difference between the alternative progressive process and the conventional progressive process?

3. Assume a patron inserts a $100-bill into a slot machine's currency acceptor, makes no wagers, hits the cash-out button, collects a $100 voucher, and leaves the game. How much coin-in was generated by this activity?

4. Describe the mapping process as it applies to virtual reels.

5. In terms of the game design, what was the key distinction of the nontraditional game described in the text (i.e., *Deal or No Deal*)?

6. List the factors responsible for the near extinction of coins from the slot floors of contemporary casinos.

7. What is the name of the device that connects peripheral hardware devices on slot machines to the game processor and slot operating system?

8. When weighted mapped virtual reels are employed are slot machine outcomes random? Explain your answer.

9. A game maker has agreed to provide 100 units of a popular game to a casino operator with 11 casino properties in Nevada. The game maker is not selling these games to the operator, so there is no sales price per se. However, in exchange for the games, the operator has agreed to pay the game maker $10 per day for each of the 100 units, for as long as the units reside on the operator's slot floors. How is such an arrangement described in the gaming industry?

10. Use the appropriate data to compute slot win from coin-in. Hint: Precise definitions found in *Win Formulas*.

Hand Paid Jackpots	$22,000
Coin-in	$120,000
Progressive Accrual	$1,200
Drop	$100,000
Vouchers Issued	$75,000
Coin-out	$80,000
Fills	$0

Chapter 10
Slot Operations II

What are the basic calculations that underlie reel slots and video poker games?
Do reel slots and video poker games have a single house advantage?
How does server-based gaming work and what are the (dis)advantages?
How might a game's location on the casino floor influence its performance?
What are game mix variables?
How does a game's volatility affect time on device?
What makes a slot machine loose or tight?

Scope

This chapter is designed to demonstrate basic par sheet calculations for both reel slots and video poker games. The jargon and par sheet metrics common to slot operations shop talk are demystified. Once the basic game mechanics are understood, the reader is ready to review the interaction between a game's volatility and the player's time on device. Next, the determinants of a loose/tight game are discussed, with conclusions that may be surprising. The basic forms of server-based gaming are also defined and discussed in detail. The chapter closes with a discussion of slot floor layout, bank configuration, and game mix issues. It is important to mention that any discussion of slot operations will involve a considerable amount of industry jargon and technical terminology. As this is an introductory text, every effort has been made to explain these terms as they appear in the chapter.

Chapter Goals

- Discuss the various forms, advantages, and disadvantages of server-based gaming
- Review the par sheet contents and calculations for an actual reel slot machine
- Define key terms used to describe the performance and design of slot machines
- Examine a video poker game sheet and address the basic mechanics of the game
- Examine the determinants of loose and tight games
- Introduce important slot floor layout and game configuration issues

Server-based Gaming

Debuting in 1987, Nevada's Megabucks games were most likely the inspiration for server-based gaming technology. The same game maker that wired these wide-area progressive games to an external server led the way in the development and implementation of server-based gaming. Megabucks demonstrated the efficiency and effectiveness by which data could be securely transferred between the individual games and a server. The current commercial forms of server-based gaming may differ from the game maker's original notion, but the basic idea remains intact.

Delivery Models

There are two basic forms of this game delivery system. In both forms, the game server resides in the hotel-casino property. In the true server-based form, the game files reside on the server. In this form, all critical game processing occurs on the server, with only the results transmitted to the gaming terminal for display. For example, when the player hits the spin button, the game is actually played on the server, and the result is sent to the player's screen.

In the server-based model, some operators are concerned with the consequences of power outages and wiring failures. Without power or a connection to the central game server, none of the games can operate. That is, gaming will come to a complete halt. Power outages and system failures do happen. However, with the current configuration, management is able to work around power outages and system failures so that gaming does not completely halt on all units. Proponents of the server-based systems claim that the appropriate redundancies have been built into the game delivery process to avoid such a catastrophe.

The second form of server-based gaming is the downloadable model, in which the game files reside on the games themselves (i.e., the physical games). That is, once a game is downloaded from the server, the game files are recorded on the game's internal memory. In the downloadable model, all critical game processing occurs at the game level, as opposed to the server level. The location of the critical game processing function is the primary difference between these two delivery systems.

Going live in December 2009, the CityCenter project in Las Vegas was Nevada's first large-scale implementation of server-based slot machines. The downloadable model was chosen as a means of game delivery. Only time will tell the extent to which this technology will change the face of slot operations.

Game Processing

What is meant by critical game processing? Consider the following example of a reel slot game. Critical game processing refers to the operation of the game's random number generator and its interface with the game's virtual reels.[1] Once the random number generator produces a number, the game's computer identifies the symbol associated with (or assigned/mapped to) the randomly generated number. This symbol is then displayed. With virtual reels, symbols can be assigned to a range of numbers. For example, if the

---

[1] Most modern reel slots use virtual reels. With virtual reels, the probability of an outcome is determined by the mathematician who designs the game. The probabilities of outcomes are not limited by the number of physical stops on each reel.

random number generator stops on 11, 12, or 13, a Triple-Bar symbol is displayed on Reel #1.

In general, critical game processing refers to the process of sampling (i.e., outcome selection). This could refer to symbol selection, in the case of reel slots, or card selection, in the case of video poker. All of the electronic games discussed in this chapter produce either a random or randomized sample from a population of elements. This action is categorically referred to as critical game processing.

Potential Benefits

The following bullet points describe advantages associated with server-based gaming in general. Selected items will be further described in the subsequent paragraphs.

- Greatly increased flexibility with regard to game mix variables
  - More game choices on each machine
  - Games can be displayed in multiple languages (e.g., Spanish or English)
  - Minimum betting units (i.e., game denominations) can be increased during peak business periods and decreased during low demand periods
  - Par and standard deviation options can be managed
  - Ability to quickly offer the newest and most popular games to the extent demanded by the clientele
- Advent of conversion credits (vs. conversion kits)
- Cross-marketing opportunities via increased connectivity to other operating systems within the property
- Improved service delivery and overall guest experience

Conversion credits would allow operators to download new games from the game maker's server to the casino's server. Once the game is on the casino's server, it can either be downloaded to or accessed from individual games, depending on the game delivery model.

As previously described, casino executives would use the internet to download these games from the game maker's server. However, it is likely that this would not meet the security standards of regulators in all jurisdictions. At worst, the same task could be accomplished by mailing a DVD containing the new game files to the casino. In either case, this is much easier than mailing and installing an entire conversion kit.

Conversion kits for traditional games usually contain new belly glass, top glass, and game files.[2] Once these items have been received they must be physically installed. In contrast, server-based gaming terminals have no glass. The glass is replaced with monitors/screens. New games files obtained by way of conversion credits are readily displayed on the game's top and belly monitors.

---

[2] Game files are usually stored on media such as DVDs and USB flash drives.

Cross-marketing opportunities exist in several forms. These opportunities arise from the increased connectivity offered by the improved system interface capacity of the modern technology included in the server-based games. Management is able to send a variety of messages related to gaming and nongaming activities to the slot machines. For example, daily dining specials and undersold shows can be cross-marketed through the message display panels on the games. Other forms of notices and/or messages can also be disseminated through this technology such as "No waiting in the steak house."

Most of these cross-marketing measures could be achieved without server-based games, but retrofitting the existing games with the necessary hardware and wiring would be cost prohibitive. A project such as CityCenter was afforded the opportunity to install server-based games in mass, as the technology was available at the time the casino was developed and opened. By doing so, management was able to sidestep the expensive retrofits needed to achieve the same level of connectivity on an existing slot floor.

The capacity to cross-market comes with the challenge and responsibility of doing it effectively. That is, it may not be in the best interest of casino operators for players to leave slot machines to take advantage of immediate seating in the steak house. That is, cross-marketing strategies must be carefully planned and monitored to optimize the benefit to the overall resort.

Improved service delivery can also be achieved through the enhanced connectivity of the server-based games. For example, slot players can place drink orders through the games, as opposed to waiting for a waitress to take their order. Players can also request to have their car retrieved by valet and notified when it is has arrived at the door. Players waiting for a table in a restaurant can be notified on the game when their table is ready. In general, the increased connectivity improves the customer experience by decreasing wait times and allowing customers to gamble while waiting.

Potential Challenges

The following bullet points describe challenges associated with server-based gaming in general. Selected items will be further described in the subsequent paragraphs.

- Pricing issues between casinos and game providers
- Perceptions of fleecing resulting from attempts to maximize yield
- Total disruption of play from power outages (as previously described)
- Service delivery glitches common to most forms of new technology
- Alienation and/or loss of mechanical reel players (these games are not provided on server-based games)
- Reluctance of some to accept and maximize the benefits of the new technology

Pricing issues arise, as server-based gaming is content driven once casino executives acquire the initial hardware. That is, physical games (with monitors in place of the glass) are only purchased once. Going forward, all new games are purchased in the form of content downloads. The price of the new content must be both affordable to the casino operators and provide an acceptable return for the content suppliers (i.e., game makers). Given the longstanding objections of casino executives to the participation fees levied upon them by game makers, the price negotiation over server-based content will be fierce.[3]

Perceptions of fleecing may arise from management's new ability to increase pars, standard deviations, and minimum betting units (i.e., denomination) during peak demand periods such as weekends and holidays. Although betting limits are already yield managed in table games, this concept is new to slot players, and no one is sure how they will react. Many players may be offended by such measures and choose to patronize a property with the physical form of their favorite game and pay table. Management must carefully manage the increased product flexibility offered by server-based gaming, giving proper regard to existing and valuable customer relationships.

Par Sheets

Par sheets describe the underlying calculations and game design of a slot machine. Important summary-level performance measures are also listed in par sheets. There is a par sheet for each unique version of a pay table, as game makers are required to provide this information to licensing/regulatory authorities.

Figure 10.1 is a par sheet for a mechanical reel slot machine. As par sheets are not usually easy to decipher or interpret, we have taken the liberty of simplifying the presentation of this one. Further, we have chosen a relatively simple game, as the goal is to interpret and describe the basic computations included in a par sheet. The following paragraphs provide in-depth descriptions of the contents found in Figure 10.1 (parts a, b, and c).

Summary Data

Game summary data, listed in the boxes appearing at the top of the par sheet, include basic information about the game. For example, it is a three-reel, 32-stop game, with a cycle of 32,768 spins. The game's payback and hold percentages along with its hit frequency are also listed at or near the top of the par sheet.

This game's cycle is computed by raising the number of stops per reel to a power equal to the number of reels. For example, $32^3 = 32,768$ spins. The basic computations of the remaining summary measures will be discussed in subsequent paragraphs.

The table listing the symbol inventory by reel tells us that there are only five discrete (or unique) symbols on this game (i.e., $\sim\sim$, 1B, 5B, 7B, & JW). The double-tilde symbol ($\sim\sim$) represents a blank. Notice that the number of blanks increases from Reel 1 to Reel 3, while the number of jackpot symbols either decreases or remains constant, moving from Reel 1 to Reel 3.

---

[3] See Chapter 9 for more on participation fees and the related rift between operators and game makers.

Reel Strip	Pay Table	Max. Coin Hold %	Max. Wager	# of Reels	# of Reel Stops	Cycle
Q-237	QR-14	14.505%	2 coins	3	32	32,768

# of Coins Bet	Payback Percent	Hit Frequency	Total Hits	Total Pays
1	76.080%	14.212%	4,657	24,930
2	85.495%	14.212%	4,657	56,030

Symbol Inventory by Reel			
Symbol	Reel 1	Reel 2	Reel 3
~~	17	19	21
1B	9	7	6
5B	4	4	3
7B	1	1	1
JW	1	1	1

(A)			(B)			(C)	(D) 32,768 / (C)	(E)	(F) (C) x (E)
Pay Combinations			Symbols Per Reel			Hits Per Cycle	Pulls Per Hit	Coins Paid Per Hit	Coins Paid Per Cycle
JW	XX	XX	1	31	31	841	39	2	1,682
XX	JW	XX	31	1	31	821	40	2	1,642
XX	XX	JW	31	31	1	793	41	2	1,586
JW	JW	XX	1	1	31	21	1,560	5	105
JW	XX	JW	1	31	1	19	1,725	5	95
XX	JW	JW	31	1	1	17	1,928	5	85
AB	AB	AB	15	13	11	1,479	22	5	7,395
1J	1J	1J	10	8	7	559	59	10	5,590
							Coin 2 →	**25**	
5J	5J	5J	5	5	4	99	331	50	4,950
							Coin 2 →	**125**	
7J	7J	7J	2	2	2	7	4,681	200	1,400
							Coin 2 →	**500 P**	
JW	JW	JW	1	1	1	1	32,768	400	400
							Coin 2 →	**1,000 P**	
Totals:						4,657			24,930

Symbol Legend:
AB: 1B, 5B, 7B, JW; **1J:** 1B, JW; **5J:** 5B, JW; **7J:** 7B, JW; **XX:** Any symbol other than JW; ~~ : Blank

Figure 10.1. Example of a Reel Slot Machine Par Sheet (a).

Physical Reel Strip Listing			
Pos. #	Reel 1	Reel 2	Reel 3
1	~~	~~	~~
2	1B	1B	1B
3	~~	~~	~~
4	5B	5B	5B
5	~~	~~	~~
6	1B	1B	1B
7	~~	~~	~~
8	7B	7B	7B
9	~~	~~	~~
10	1B	1B	1B
11	~~	~~	~~
12	5B	5B	5B
13	~~	~~	~~
14	1B	1B	1B
15	~~	~~	~~
16	5B	1B	1B
17	~~	~~	~~
18	JW	5B	5B
19	~~	~~	~~
20	1B	1B	1B
21	~~	~~	~~
22	5B	JW	JW

Virtual Reel Strip Listing			
Pos. #	Reel 1	Reel 2	Reel 3
1	~~	~~	~~
2	~~	~~	~~
3	1B	1B	1B
4	1B	~~	~~
5	~~	~~	~~
6	5B	5B	5B
7	~~	5B	~~
8	1B	~~	~~
9	~~	~~	1B
10	~~	1B	~~
11	7B	~~	~~
12	~~	~~	7B
13	~~	7B	~~
14	1B	~~	~~
15	1B	~~	1B
16	~~	1B	~~
17	~~	~~	~~
18	5B	5B	5B
19	~~	~~	~~
20	1B	~~	~~
21	1B	1B	1B
22	~~	1B	~~
23	5B	~~	1B
24	~~	1B	~~
25	~~	~~	~~
26	JW	~~	5B
27	~~	5B	~~
28	~~	~~	~~
29	1B	1B	1B
30	1B	~~	~~
31	~~	~~	~~
32	5B	JW	JW

Figure 10.1. Example of a Reel Slot Machine Par Sheet (b).

215

90% Confidence Intervals: Payback Percentages		
# of Spins	Lower Bound (%)	Upper Bound (%)
1,000	54.11	116.88
10,000	75.57	95.42
100,000	82.36	88.63
1,000,000	84.50	86.49
10,000,000	85.18	85.81
Volatility Index: 9.926 (at maximum coin wager)		

Figure 10.1. Example of a Reel Slot Machine Par Sheet (c).

Pay Table Data

For reference purposes, the column headers of this section of the par sheet are labeled "A" through "E", with the formula for the contents of columns "D" and "F" appearing immediately below the column headers. Column A lists the combinations of symbols that result in a payout or hit. The definitions of these symbols can be found in the Symbol Legend appearing below this section of the par sheet. For example, 1J could be either 1B or JW. Column B lists the number of each symbol (as defined in Column A) found on each of the three reels. For example, there are ten 1J symbols on Reel 1. Referencing the Reel 1 column of the Symbol Inventory by Reel, there are nine 1B symbols and one JW symbol, for a total of ten 1J symbols. Remember, 1J is defined in the Symbol Legend as any 1B or JW symbol.

Column C, Hits Per Cycle, is likely to cause the most confusion, as it is shown net of subordinate jackpots. This expression is best explained by way of example. Consider the first line item: JW, XX, XX. Moving ahead to Column E, this combination pays 2 coins (with a one-coin wager). Per the Symbol Legend, the XX symbol represents any of the 32 stops on Reels 2 and 3, except for the JW stops. There is one JW stop on each reel; hence, XX equals 31 on both Reel 2 and Reel 3. Column B expresses this condition as follows: 1, 31, 31. Here is where it may become a little confusing.

It might appear that the 841 hits per cycle shown in Column C is an error. That is, $(1)(31)(31) = 961$, and not 841. This difference of 120 hits $(961 - 841)$ is reconciled by subtracting the symbols included in the expression of XX that would result in a jackpot greater than 2 coins. Moving to the middle of this section, we see that AB, AB, AB pays 5 coins, which certainly represents a jackpot greater than 2 coins. The AB symbol includes any jackpot symbol, including JW. However, the occurrence of the JW symbols has already been considered, per the definition of XX. That leaves all other jackpot symbols in the AB symbol set, or 1B, 5B, and 7B. Per the Symbol Inventory by Reel, there are 12 such symbols on Reel 2 and ten on Reel 3. These symbols represent the

216

difference of 120 hits (i.e., (12)(10) = 120) Remember, the JW symbols have already been excluded in the definition of XX.

In summary, when JW appears on Reel 1 and any other jackpot symbol that is not JW appears on Reel 2 and on Reel 3, the resulting jackpot will be at least 5 coins. As the definition of XX includes the other jackpot symbols (i.e., 1B, 5B, & 7B), the hits per cycle in Column C must be reduced by the number of hits resulting in the greater jackpot (i.e., 5+ units). Alternatively stated, outcomes such as JW, (1B, 5B, or 7B), (1B, 5B, or 7B) can be expected to occur 120 times. That is, (1)(12)(10) = 120, and 961 − 120 = 841. This general condition occurs throughout this section of the par sheet. That is, the effect of subordinate jackpots is not reflected in Column B (i.e., Symbols Per Reel). This form of presentation can be most confusing to those unfamiliar with par sheets. At a minimum, a footnote advising readers of the presence of subordinate jackpots should be provided.

Column D simply divides the cycle (32,768 spins) by the entry in Column C (Hits Per Cycle) to estimate the frequency of each jackpot, in terms of a spin interval. For example, JW, XX, XX can be expected to produce a 2-coin jackpot once in every 39 spins.

As noted, Column F, Coins Paid Per Cycle, represents the product of Column C and Column E. For example, over the course of the 32,768-spin cycle, the game is expected to produce 841 two-coin jackpots resulting from the outcome of JW, XX, XX. All entries listed in Column F are computed under the assumption of a single-coin wager. To compute comparable payouts for a two-coin wager, one would simply double the payouts listed in Column E, except where bolded entries appear. The bolded entries represent jackpot amounts that are increased at a rate that exceeds the standard doubling. These hyper-increased jackpots are a commonly employed incentive for players to make the maximum wager. The other variable in the Column F calculation, Hits Per Cycle, from Column C, does not change as a result of the two-coin wager. As an aside, the "P" listed after the two top awards indicates that these jackpots could be linked to progressive meters, should the operator wish to offer progressive jackpots on the game.

Hit Frequency

Notice the total of Column C. This sum represents the total number of expected hits per cycle. That is, the game is expected to produce 4,657 outcomes that result in some form of a payout. If 4,657 is divided by 32,768 (i.e., the cycle), the quotient of 0.14212 represents the game's hit frequency. This game metric is included in the summary information appearing at the top of the par sheet. Specifically, Hit Frequency is listed at 14.212%. As this game is a multiplier, only the payouts change from one- to two-coin wagers. The number of hits will not change, holding the hit frequency constant at 14.212%, for both one- and two-coin wagers.

It is important to mention that, in general, a *hit* does not imply a win or a net increase in the player's wealth. For example, if a player wagered 10 coins on a spin that resulted in a 5-coin payout, that spin would constitute a hit. It is considered a hit despite the fact that the player experienced a net loss of five coins on the spin.

Payback Percentages

The payback percentage is computed by dividing the number of coins paid out, over the cycle, by the number of coins wagered over the cycle. The total of Column F indicates that the expected number of coins to be paid out over the cycle is equal to 24,930. Given a one-coin wager and a cycle of 32,768 spins, 32,768 coins are expected to be wagered over the course of the cycle. If 24,930 (coin-out) is divided by 32,768 (coin-in), the quotient of 0.76080 represents the game's payback percentage for one-coin wagers. Notice that the summary information at the top of the par sheet lists the one-coin payback percentage at 76.080%.

Unlike the hit frequency, a multiplier game's payback percentage will change at maximum-coin wagers. The summary information at the top of the par sheet lists the two-coin payback percentage at 85.495%. This is a direct result of the jackpots that are increased at a rate beyond that of two times the one-coin payout. Alternatively stated, this difference results from the bolded entries appearing in Column E (i.e., the hyper-increased jackpots).

The par or house advantage associated with the game can be computed by subtracting the payback percentage from 1.0. For example, 1.0 less 0.85495 equals 0.14505, or 14.505%. Per the game's summary information, the Max. Coin Hold % is listed at 14.505%. By coincidence, this par happens to be very near the game's hit frequency of 14.21%.

Reel Strips

As this game is a mechanical reel slot machine, both the physical and virtual reel strips are illustrated in the par sheet (see Figure 10.1 part b). The physical reel is a proxy for the symbol configuration that is actually attached to the physical reels. The virtual strip represents the symbol population from which the game's computer selects the symbols to be displayed on the pay line.

To highlight the differences in these two reel strips, consider the following example. There are 21 blanks (~~) and 32 possible stops on Reel 3 of the virtual strip. As a result, the probability of selecting a blank for display on the pay line is equal to 65.6% (i.e., 21/32). Let's compare this probability to that of the same outcome produced by randomly selecting a symbol from the physical reel strip. There are 11 blanks (~~) and 22 possible stops on Reel 3 of the physical strip. As a result, the probability of selecting a blank for display on the pay line is equal to 50.0% (i.e., 11/22).

Game Volatility

Only two game metrics are needed to compute the confidence intervals shown in the last table of the par sheet. These metrics are the game's payback percentage (p) and standard deviation (σ). All remaining terms are supplied by the person computing the confidence interval. These terms represent the number of spins (n) and the desired width of the confidence interval (z). The upper and lower bounds of the confidence interval (CI) are constructed using the following formulas:

$$\text{Upper Bound of CI} = p + \sigma z / n^{0.5}$$

$$\text{Lower Bound of CI} = p - \sigma z / n^{0.5}$$

The exponent (0.5) is used in these formulas to produce the square root of the number of spins (n). The confidence interval can be computed for any number of spins (n) or degree of confidence (z). The standard deviation of the game (σ) is computed using information from the game's par sheet. The payback percentage (p) is computed as shown in the previous section (i.e., in Payback Percentages).

Perhaps an example will clarify the computation of a confidence interval. Let's assume the following inputs:

$p = 0.85495$
$\sigma = 6.01504$
$n = 100,000$
$z = 1.65$ (used to construct a 90% confidence interval)[4]

Plugging these values into the formula, the upper and lower bounds of the confidence interval are computed as follows:

Upper bound: $0.85495 + 6.01504 \times 1.65 / 100,000^{0.5} = 0.8863$

Lower bound: $0.85495 - 6.01504 \times 1.65 / 100,000^{0.5} = 0.8236$

When expressed as percentages, the lower bound (82.36%) and the upper bound (88.63%) match those found in the table of confidence intervals included in Figure 10.1 (part c).

What does the game's standard deviation (σ) represent? In short, it is a measure of the game's volatility. More specifically, the game's standard deviation is a function of all possible outcomes,[5] the probability associated with each possible outcome, and the game's house advantage or par. Although manageable, its calculation is beyond the scope of this book. The game's standard deviation is given in some par sheets, although it is not provided in the example shown in this text. It is more important for the reader of an introductory text to understand what it represents. That is, the game's standard deviation represents the average distance of all possible outcomes from the game's mean, or par.

---

[4] Z-scores, a.k.a. standard scores, have a mean of zero and a standard deviation of one. When a variable is normally distributed, 90% of the observations will produce z-scores that fall within 1.65 standard deviations of the mean.
[5] Where *outcomes* are all possible net pays. For example, when a spin produces a payout of ten coins, with one coin wagered, the net pay would be -9, i.e., 1 – 10, from the perspective of the casino.

The standard deviation of a game is always expressed in terms of coins, as opposed to dollars. This is a common misunderstanding.

What does the confidence interval computed in this section tell us? Management can expect this game's payback percentage to range between 82.36% and 88.63%, in 90 out of every 100 samples of 100,000 spins. Although it is possible for the payback percentage to fall outside of the 90% confidence interval, such a result would serve as a caution flag, causing management to watch the game carefully. The further the actual payback percentage falls from the confidence interval endpoints, the greater the concern.

The list of confidence intervals found in the par sheet demonstrates one of the most important tenets of casino games. Specifically, as the number of trials (n) increases, the more likely it becomes that the game will perform as designed. That is, assuming the game provides a house advantage, the more times it is played, the more likely it becomes that it will take the toll it is designed to take. In Figure 10.1 (part c), notice how the upper and lower bounds of the confidence intervals converge on the designed payback percentage (85.495%), as the number of spins (n) increases.

Why is Volatility Important?

Frequent slot players have well-established expectations related to the play time generated by their standard trip bankroll. For example, if a regular player has a trip bankroll of $100, she expects that it will afford her some minimum number of spins. Of course, the choice of game and wagering behavior are assumed to be held constant. Just the same, slot players often complain that their trip bankrolls do not provide them sufficient play time. Management refers to the notion of play time as time on device (TOD). It is very important for management to match the casino's slot product to the TOD expectations of the primary target markets. But what drives TOD?

Determinants of TOD

There have been several simulation studies designed to understand the relationships between specific slot metrics and TOD.[6] The first study examined the relationship between the hit frequency of slot machines and TOD, failing to make a connection between these two variables.[7] The second study examined the relationship between the standard deviations of slot machine pay tables and TOD.[8] This study found increases in standard deviation to produce decreases in TOD. Among other things, the third study examined the relative effects of standard deviation and par on TOD.[9] This study found that a game's standard deviation produced a much stronger influence on a player's TOD

---

[6] Lucas, A.F. & Singh, A.K. (2008). Decreases in a slot machine's coefficient of variation led to increases in customer play time. *Cornell Hospitality Quarterly, 49*(2), 122-133; Lucas, A.F., Singh, A.K., & Gewali, L. (2007). Simulating the effect of pay table standard deviation on pulls per losing player at the single-visit level. *Gaming Research & Review Journal, 11*(1), 41-52; and Kilby, J., Fox, J., & Lucas, A.F. (2004). Casino Operations Management, 2nd ed., New York: Wiley.

[7] Kilby, Fox, & Lucas, op. cit., p. 137-8.

[8] Lucas, Singh, & Gewali, op. cit.

[9] Lucas & Singh, op. cit.

than that of par. All of these simulations included bankroll and exit criteria for the virtual players. For example, under one scenario, virtual players would begin with 200 credits and play until the credits were either doubled or completely lost.

The results of the research discussed here make a clear case for the importance of game volatility (i.e., standard deviation) on TOD. Further, the importance of TOD to the slot players is equally clear. Despite these findings, it is a widely held belief that par has the greatest effect on TOD. While par may be a meaningful long-term and/or aggregate measure, players engage slot machines with limited bankrolls. To clarify, the following paragraphs highlight the limitations of par as a proxy for TOD.

Casino executives have positioned their slot floors with regard to price (i.e., par) for many years, but how does par affect TOD? In the long term, a player will produce more wagers on a game with a 5% par than she will on a game with a 6% par, all else held constant. This is true because the 5% game keeps less of her bankroll each time that it is cycled through the machine. For example, on a 5% game, if she makes 100, one-dollar wagers, on average, she will have $95 of her bankroll remaining for additional wagering. Consider the same scenario for the 6% game. She would expect to have $94 remaining after 100, one-dollar wagers. In the long run, as par increases, the number of pulls or spins per player decreases, all else held constant. At this point, some might conclude that lower pars would provide more TOD. However, there is more to consider when it comes to the effect of par.

Consider the following example of how the effect of par can be misunderstood.[10] Table 10.1 is a summary of a hypothetical reel strip for a three-reel slot machine.

Table 10.1

Symbol Inventory of a Three-reel Slot Machine

Symbols	Reel 1	Reel 2	Reel 3
Blanks	200	200	200
Cherries	1	1	1
Total	201	201	201

Note. Cell contents represent the number of symbols on each reel.

Given this game's configuration, there are 8,120,601 possible outcomes. This is the product of the total number of symbols on each reel (i.e., 201 x 201 x 201). However, assume that only one combination will result in a payout (i.e., 3 cherries). That payout could be 90% of the amount wagered over those 8,120,601 trials, or it could be 95%. That is, the par of this game could be equal to 10%, 5%, or some other percentage. In any case, the game's par is determined by the magnitude of its only payout. Further, almost everyone that plays this game will wager their bankroll only one time, before it is completely lost. This does not look like a game that will produce a desirable experience with regard to TOD. In fact, a player would need an enormous bankroll and an abundance

---

[10] From Lucas, Singh, & Gewali, op. cit.

of time to simply determine whether the game's par was 5% or 10%. Although this is an extreme example, it makes the point that par alone is not the best proxy for TOD.

Loose/Tight Games

Many operators and players use par to determine whether a game is loose or tight. A game is considered loose when it provides generous TOD, by way of relatively frequent and ample payouts. The confusion stems from the notion that games with low pars take their modest toll at an even, steady, or uniform rate. While this may appear to be the case when looking at aggregated data, it is clearly not the case when looking at the individual player's experience. Let's stay with the previous example from Table 10.1 to demonstrate this point.

If three cherries were to payout 99% of the coins wagered over the course of the cycle, the game illustrated in Table 10.1 would have a 1% par, by design. According to many operators and players, this game would be considered loose, with its 1% par. However, over the course of this game's cycle, only one player would ever call this game loose! Aside from the lucky player who hits the jackpot, every other player will have the worst possible gaming experience. That is, every other player will lose their entire wager on every spin, until their bankroll is completely lost. Despite this game's 1% par, it is not likely that these players would describe it as loose. Again, it is the pay table's standard deviation that serves as the best proxy for labeling a game as loose or tight.

Slot Player Satisfaction Model

Figure 10.2 models a critical part of the slot player satisfaction process.[11] The importance of pay table volatility may be more apparent when its role in the gaming experience is framed within the customer satisfaction process. Management knows that most slot players are going to lose, and there is nothing that can be done about that. Also, it is assumed that most winning players will be satisfied with their gaming experience. This brings us to the losing players. How will they measure satisfaction? Given the great number of losing players, understanding their satisfaction process is vital.

Figure 10.2 illustrates the theory that losing players use TOD as proxy for satisfaction with their gaming session. The bottom portion of the model shows the determinants of TOD. As previously noted, when bankroll is held constant, the research suggests that the game's standard deviation produces the greatest effect on TOD.[12] It is important to note that this research measured the effects of par and standard deviation on TOD at the single-session level. The single-session constraint is used to limit the analysis of TOD effects. That is, players do not have infinite gaming budgets. For example, operators catering to a repeater market clientele might expect their average slot player to bring $200 to the casino. This $200-bankroll would define the player's loss limit for the day (i.e., visit or session).

---

[11] Figure 10.2 adapted from Lucas, Singh, & Gewali (2007), op. cit. & Lucas & Singh (2008), op. cit.
[12] Lucas & Singh (2008), op. cit.

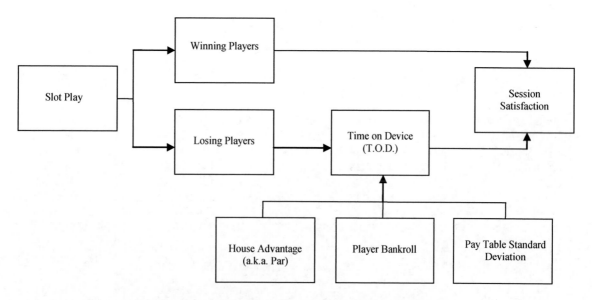

Figure 10.2. Slot Player Satisfaction Model.

Video Poker Game Math

Table 10.2 illustrates a video poker game sheet for a 7/5 pay table. Especially in their infancy, video poker pay tables were often identified by the payouts associated with the full house and flush hands. For example, with a single-coin wagered, the payout for a full house is 7 units, while the payout for a flush is 5 units, hence the 7/5 reference. Other pay tables include the following payouts for the full house and flush hands: 8/5, 9/6, and 10/7.

In Table 10.2, "Dealt" refers to the initial five-card poker hand dealt to the player. These cards are randomly selected by the game's computer. There are 2,598,960 unique five-card hands, assuming a standard 52-card deck. However, in this pay table, any hand less than a pair of jacks pays nothing. There are 2,062,860 of these hands dealt to players.

As this is draw poker, players are permitted to discard any number of the cards dealt to them, in an attempt to improve their hand (i.e., optimize the game's payback percentage). It is the discard-draw decision that makes video poker a game of skill. This brings us to the Built column.

The numbers in the Built column are derived from an algorithm. This algorithm considers factors such as the original five-card hand dealt to the player, all possible outcomes, the probability of each possible outcome, and the game's pay table. Based on these conditions, the algorithm plays the original hand such that the payback percentage to the player is optimized. That is, the algorithm makes the discard-draw decision that optimizes the player's expected value. Computing the numbers in the Built column is the most difficult task in the compilation of a schedule such as that shown in Table 10.2. The column labeled Total contains the sum of the entries in the Dealt and Built columns.

				1 Coin Wagered		5 Coins Wagered	
Hand	Dealt	Built	Total	Pays	Coin-out	Pays	Coin-out
Royal Flush	4	60.71	64.71	250	16,178.53	4,000	258,856.40
Straight Flush	36	244.17	280.17	50	14,008.40	250	70,041.98
4-of-a-Kind	624	5,515.00	6,139.00	25	153,475.09	125	767,375.43
Full House	3,744	26,172.37	29,916.37	7	209,414.58	35	1,047,072.90
Flush	5,108	23,230.28	28,338.28	5	141,691.40	25	708,457.01
Straight	10,200	19,120.94	29,320.95	4	117,283.79	20	586,418.93
3-of-a-Kind	54,912	138,532.49	193,444.49	3	580,333.47	15	2,901,667.37
Two Pair	123,552	211,745.02	335,297.02	2	670,594.03	10	3,352,970.14
Pair: J's - Aces	337,920	221,091.87	559,011.87	1	559,011.87	5	2,795,059.33
< Pair of Jacks	2,062,860			0	0	0	0
Totals	2,598,960				2,461,991.14		12,487,919.50

Table 10.2
7/5 Video Poker Schedule[13]

Coin-in	2,598,960.00	12,994,800.00
Less: Coin-out	2,461,991.14	12,487,919.50
Win	136,968.86	506,880.50
House Advantage	5.27%	3.90%
Payback %	94.73%	96.10%

To the immediate right of the Total column, the Pays column contains the payouts for each hand, assuming a one-coin wager. The adjacent column, Coin-out, contains the product of the entries found in the Total and Pays columns. The sum of the Coin-out column represents the expected number of coins (i.e., credits) dispensed over the course of the cycle. Remember, the cycle for a standard 52-card video poker game is 2,598,960 hands.

Assuming only single-coin wagers are placed, the game can be expected to accept 2,598,960 in coin-in over the cycle. When the sum of the coin-out column (2,461,991.14) is subtracted from the expected coin-in for the cycle, the difference (136,968.86 coins) represents the game's expected win. Remember, this expected win assumes optimal play. That is, it assumes the player makes the optimal decision on every hand.

When the sum of the Coin-out column (2,461,991.14) is divided by the cycle (2,598,960), the quotient (94.73%) represents the game's payback percentage on one-coin wagers. Located just above the one-coin payback percentage, is the game's expected house advantage of 5.27%. The house advantage is computed by subtracting the payback percentage (94.73%) from 100%.

The two columns on the far right of Table 10.2 simply repeat this process for five-coin wagers. The payback percentage and house advantage for five-coin wagers vary from

---

[13] The numbers in the Built column were truncated to two decimal places to fit Table 10.2 on the page. As a result, the products and sums contained in the Coin-out columns will be slightly different from calculations based on data from the Built and/or Total columns. These line-item rounding errors are minimal, with the Royal Flush line contributing the greatest difference. In the original version of Table 10.2, the entry in the Built column was 60.7141 for the Royal Flush, for a Total of 64.7141 (64.7141 x 250 = 16,178.53).

those produced by one-coin wagers. This difference is due to the 4,000-coin payout on a royal flush, with five-coins wagered. Notice that all payouts associated with five-coin wagers are exactly five times greater than the same payout on one-coin wagers, with one exception. That exception is the 4,000-coin payout on the royal flush, which is 16 times greater than the payout on the one-coin royal flush. Because of this enhanced payout (i.e., > 5X the one-coin payout), the game's house advantage is decreased and the payback percentage is increased. These enhanced top-award payouts on maximum-coin wagers are standard practice in video poker pay table designs. Such features are designed to encourage maximum-coin wagers.

Video Poker & Par

Also known as the house advantage, the par of a video poker game is difficult to pinpoint. This is because video poker is a game of skill. Because of the skill condition, video poker par sheets often contain three different pars. Consider the game shown in Table 10.2. The maximum-coin par at optimal play is 3.90%. However, no casino has a clientele comprised of video poker players who make no mistakes. As a result, game makers include two other pars for maximum-coin wagers. These pars are computed under the assumption that players make certain types of mistakes when playing the game. However, the underlying assumptions related to these mistakes are usually not disclosed by the game makers.

The three pars are known as optimal play, high end of the range, and low end of the range. Optimal play is the lowest par, with low end of the range in the middle, and high end of the range representing the greatest par. For example, the par sheet for the game described in Table 10.2 might list the following pars for maximum-coin wagers:

Optimal Play:	3.90%
Low End of the Range:	5.90%
High End of the Range:	7.90%

When management values players in terms of theoretical win, a choice must be made regarding which of these three pars will be entered into the player tracking system. That is, management must decide which of these three pars best describes the skill level of its clientele, in general. While no one would select optimal play, a Las Vegas Strip operator might select the high end of the range, as slot players in Strip casinos are considered less skilled than those who patronize repeater-market casinos. By the same rationale, gaming executives in repeater-market casinos might choose to use the low end of the range, as their players visit more frequently and are considered to be more knowledgeable than players patronizing casinos in tourist markets.

Game Configurations

Most games are arranged in what are known as banks. Figure 10.3 illustrates a 12-unit bank, including chairs. Typically, banks take the form of a single row of games or a back-to-back configuration as shown in Figure 10.3.

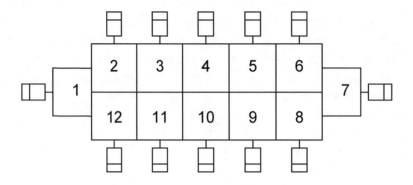

Figure 10.3. Bank of 12 Games with End Caps.

Within Figure 10.3, units 1 and 7 are referred to as end caps, given their perpendicular orientation to the body of the bank. Within the 10-unit body of the bank, units 2, 6, 12, and 8 are referred to as lateral end units (a.k.a. end units). All else held constant, end caps and end units are expected to outperform the remaining units in a bank configured such as that in Figure 10.3. The end caps and end units offer easier access for players and are less given to the crowding sensation, as they are not directly bordered by games on both sides. In one study of unit-level slot machine performance, end units were found to produce 35.5% more coin-in than their interior counterparts.[14] This result was produced from a model that accounted for the impacts of many other game and location characteristics before estimating the effect of the end-unit condition.

Games are also arranged in circular configurations known as pods. While pods offer easier access to the games and increased personal space, the circular arrangement requires more floor space per unit than traditional rectangular bank designs.

As previously noted, banks can be arranged in a single row such as games 2 through 6, taken as a subset of Figure 10.3. Single-row configurations effectively accommodate certain spaces of the slot floor. For example, single-row banks are ideal for wall locations. That is, games located against a wall. Many tall games are forced into wall locations, as they can decrease sight lines when located in the interior sections of the slot floor.

Chevron configurations make games in rectangular banks easier to survey when players are walking down a casino aisle. That is, by angling the games against the line of the aisle, those walking down the aisle are afforded a better view of the game fronts. This technique was borrowed from retailers.[15] Figure 10.4 compares the visual orientation of banks arranged in a chevron formation to that of a standard perpendicular layout.

---

[14] Lucas, A.F., & Dunn, W.T. (2005). Estimating the effects of micro-location variables and game characteristics on slot machine volume: A performance – potential model. *Journal of Hospitality & Tourism Research, 29*(2), 170-193.

[15] Underhill, P. (2000). *Why we buy: The science of shopping*. Simon & Schuster: New York.

However, like pod configurations, the chevron orientation is less space efficient. As shown in Figure 10.4, the chevron formation has reduced the number of banks from 12 to 10. This illustration accurately portrays the decline in space efficiency, as operators can expect to realize somewhere near a 20% decline in units resulting from the arrangement of games in the chevron formation.[16]

Perpendicular Orientation   Chevron Orientation

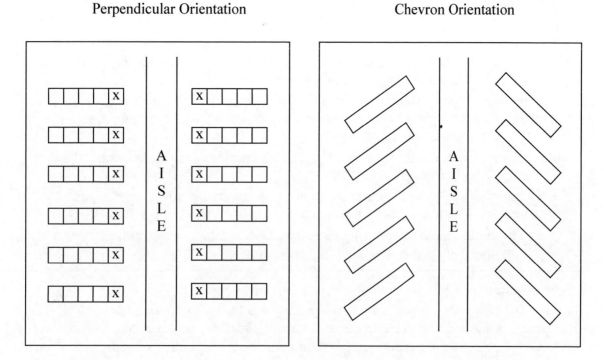

Figure 10.4. Bank-Aisle Orientation: Perpendicular vs. Chevron.

Figure 10.4 can be used to make another interesting point about the effect of a game's location on its performance. Specifically, the units marked with an "x" in the left panel of Figure 10.4 are referred to as aisle units, as they border a major casino walkway (i.e., aisle). One study found such units to produce 22.5% more coin-in than the units that did not border a major walkway.[17] This result was produced after accounting for the fact that many of the aisle units were also end units. The authors theorized that the increased performance of the aisle units may have stemmed from increased visibility and accessibility afforded by their proximity to foot traffic.

Game Mix

Although opinions and theories on the matter of game mix are abundant, very little is actually known about this subject. One of the more widely held views on game mix is based on the notion that properties catering to a clientele characterized by frequent visitation should offer a greater proportion of video poker games than a casino operating in an emerging market. In this case, the demand for video poker games is theorized to

---

[16] General retail estimate from Underhill, op. cit., pp. 79-80.
[17] Lucas & Dunn, op. cit.

increase as players become more familiar and involved with the activity of gaming. Along the same lines, the theory holds that less sophisticated players in newer/emerging markets are drawn to reel slots, as no skill is required to play these games.

Game mix can be described in terms of many different dimensions. The following bullet points describe some of the more common game mix considerations. At this point in the text, the terms used in the bullet points have been previously addressed and/or described.

- Proportions of minimum betting unit denominations (i.e., pennies, nickels, etc.)
- Proportions of reel, video poker, video keno, electronic table games, and nontraditional games (as previously described)
- Proportions of video reels and mechanical reels (within the reel category)
- Proportions of multipliers, line games, buy-a-symbol, and hybrid games
- Proportion of progressive games
- Proportions of WAPs, LAPs, and stand-alone progressive games (within the progressive category)
- Proportions of games featuring high, low, and midrange house advantages
- Proportions of games featuring high, low, and midrange standard deviations
- Proportions of games featuring high, low, and midrange top awards
- Proportions of slant-top, upright, and tall games

As you can see from this abridged list, there are many game mix dimensions to consider. Fortunately, customer demand serves as a guiding light for many of these decisions. However, management must closely monitor the performance of the games, as customer preferences are constantly changing. Game mix management is a never-ending job.

Questions/Exercises:

1. From the information listed in Figure 10.1, how can you tell that the game is a multiplier?
2. What is the cycle length of the physical reel strip (not the virtual reel strip) shown in Figure 10.1?
3. What are the two primary forms of the server-based game delivery system and what is the primary difference between these two processes?
4. For the purposes of evaluating video poker players in terms of theoretical win, which of the three par choices discussed in the text would most likely represent the casino's advantage (i.e., par), assuming the property operates in a destination market and caters to tourists who visit 3 to 4 times a year?
5. Assuming one-coin wagers, compute the hit frequency and par from the following game data: Three-reels with 20 stops per reel; Expected hits per cycle = 2,000; Expected number of coins to be dispensed over the game's cycle = 7,000.
6. Game 12230405 has a designed payback percentage of 89% (i.e., an 11% par) and a standard deviation of 9.55 coins. After 10,000 spins, the game's actual payback percentage is 102%. Management is alarmed and has asked you to compute a 95% confidence interval around the game's designed payback percentage (z = 1.96). What is your conclusion? Is there genuine cause for concern?

7. What is the primary advantage and primary disadvantage of the chevron bank formation?
8. Why does the par of the video poker game shown in Table 10.2 decline from 5.27% on one-coin wagers to 3.90% on five-coin wagers?
9. Describe the general mission of game mix management.
10. Describe the difference between an end cap and an end unit.
11. Which aspect of a game's pay table would provide the best indication of its looseness/tightness?

Chapter 11
Blackjack

How would you describe the objective of Blackjack?
What is an insurance bet? What is basic strategy?
How might a player obtain a soft 20?
What is a surrender option?
What is the primary advantage of dealing the cards face up?
How do casino operators discourage back counters?

Scope

Blackjack is one of the most popular table games in the world. Although many are familiar with the basic structure of the game, this chapter provides a level of coverage well beyond that of an overview. There is far more to this complex game of skill than most would believe. This chapter is designed to provide the reader with a deep understanding of the game and the related management issues. While all the basic game material is covered, an extra effort has been made to explain why specific rules, practices, and procedures are critical to successful management of the game.

Chapter Goals

- Define key terms and operating language central to any discussion of blackjack
- Describe the options available to the blackjack player in various game situations
- Review the process of producing a hand of blackjack
- Explain how the rules of the game affect the casino advantage
- Review basic strategy and the importance of understanding it
- Demonstrate the importance of game speed in the player rating/valuation process
- Describe countermeasures used to deter card counting

History

Little information is available on the origin of blackjack, which is also known as twenty-one. There are those who contend that blackjack is a variation of the Spanish game *veintiuna*,[1] which appears in early 17th century literature.[2] In veintiuna, the object of the

---

[1] From the Spanish word veintiuno, meaning twenty-one.
[2] Lorente, M.J. (1917). *Rinconete and Cortadillo*, translation from Spanish. Boston: The Four Seas Press. Original work: Cervantes, M. (1613). *Rinconete y Cortadillo*, (in *Novelas*). Madrid: Juan de la Cuesta.

game was to obtain a hand value of twenty-one points, without exceeding twenty-one points. The aces were valued at one or eleven, just as they are in the modern version of blackjack. The 1864 edition of *The American Hoyle* describes a game called vingt-un, which is also very similar to modern blackjack.[3] The description read as follows:

"For a little gentle gambling – say for trifling stakes of a dime or ten thousand dollars – there is no more easily acquired game than Vingt-un; certainly few more amusing.

"Vingt-un (twenty-one) may be played by two or more players; about six or eight is the best number. The cards bear the same respective value as Cribbage. The tens and court cards are each reckoned for ten; but the *ace in each suit may be valued as one or eleven*, at the option of the holder, according to the exigencies of his hand."[4]

In vingt-un,[5] a natural was any two-card hand comprised of an ace and *tenth* card. In an 1885 edition of *The American Hoyle*, the definition of a natural was changed to the following: "If a player has an Ace and a court card dealt him, which reckons twenty-one (called a natural Vingt-un), he turns his hand face-upwards on the table and receives double his stake from the dealer."[6] In the modern form of blackjack, a natural is any two-card hand comprised of an ace and a ten-valued card. Ten-valued cards include kings, queens, jacks, and tens.

For a casino game to be commercially viable in today's gaming industry, it must provide the operator with a positive expected value. That is, a casino advantage. All of the well-known casino games were designed to produce a casino advantage, except for blackjack. Even the modern form of blackjack was not designed to produce a casino advantage. Blackjack evolved from other card games, eventually making its way to the casino floor. The casino advantage on wagers found in games such as craps or roulette is easy to calculate. This is not the case for blackjack, where the casino advantage is much more difficult to compute. In fact, prior to the computer age, the casino advantage on blackjack games was not known.

In the late 1950s, a group of mathematicians set out to calculate the casino advantage on the game of blackjack.[7] This was a difficult task, as any attempt would somehow have to incorporate the skill of the player, with regard to the numerous draw and stand decisions. In fact, to calculate the casino advantage, these researchers would have to determine the optimal play for every possible blackjack hand. Initially, their analysis held that the

---

[3] "Trumps" (1864). *The American Hoyle or Gentlemen's Hand-Book of Games*. Dick & Fitzgerald: New York, 212-215.
[4] Ibid, 212.
[5] From the French word for twenty-one, also appearing in the literature as vingt et un and vingt un.
[6] "Trumps" (1885). *The American Hoyle or Gentlemen's Hand-Book of Games,* p. 238. New York: Dick & Fitzgerald.
[7] Baldwin, R., Cantey, W., Maisel, H., & McDermott, J. (1956). The Optimum Strategy of Blackjack. *Journal of the American Statistical Association, 51*, 429-439.

player had a disadvantage of 0.62%, but subsequent calculations would show that the player actually had a slight *advantage* of 0.09%.[8]

These subsequent calculations produced a somewhat alarming result. Specifically, the findings indicated that the casino advantage operators had realized for decades must have been the result of player errors (i.e., misplayed hands). That is, the house edge was not produced by mathematical design. It was these early attempts to compute the game's true expected value that piqued the interest of many talented researchers bent on unlocking the mysteries of blackjack.

Operational Overview

Blackjack is a card game which usually features between one and seven players and a dealer, who represents the casino. Depending on the rules in place (and there are many options), the following numbers of decks (of cards) are used to deal the game: One, two, four, six, or eight. Alternatively, some casino operators use continuously shuffling shoes on their blackjack games. These automatic shufflers usually contain four, six or eight decks of cards.

The players make an initial wager, which must be between the posted table minimum and table maximum bets. The minimum and maximum wagers are determined by management, and they are expressed in terms of dollar amounts (or other forms of currency). Once the bet is placed, the cards are shuffled by the dealer and cut by one of the players. The first card from the shuffled and cut deck or pack is removed from play. This card is known as the *burn* card.[9] The deck is now ready for play. Next, the dealer will deal one card to each player on the game, beginning with the player seated at the far left of the dealer and continuing in a clockwise direction. The dealer will also deal one card to himself. The dealer's initial card is dealt face up (i.e., exposed for all players to see). This is known as the dealer's up card. The dealer then repeats this operation, dealing each player, and himself, a second card. The dealer's second card is dealt face down. This is known as the dealer's hole card. At this point, each player knows the value of his hand and the value of the dealer's up card.

In blackjack, the suit of the card is not recognized, only its rank or value matters. Cards with ranks 2 through 10 are counted at face value. The Jacks, Queens, and Kings all carry a value of ten. The value of the aces is either one or 11, depending on the needs of the player. For example, the ace in a two-card hand comprised of an ace and a 9 would be valued at 11, giving the player a hand total of 20. In a three-card hand consisting of a 9, 7, and an ace, the ace would be valued at one, for a total of 17. If it were valued at 11, the player's hand total would exceed 21, which would certainly not benefit the player.[10]

---

[8] Thorp, E. O. (1966), *Beat the Dealer*, New York: Random House, 16. Baldwin et al. originally computed a casino advantage of 0.62%, which was later revised to 0.32%. Subsequent analysis would prove both calculations incorrect.

[9] In the late 19th century, this was called the *burnt* card. See, "Trumps," 1885, op. cit.

[10] Although players can incorrectly value an ace in certain instances, the dealer will always value the ace such that any hand total is optimized. In this example, the dealer would correct the player's valuation error.

If the player is dealt a natural, he would expose the hand to the dealer.[11] If the dealer also has a natural, the hands tie. That is, there would be no decision (i.e., a winner or loser). If the dealer does not have a natural, the player's wager would be paid at a rate of 1.5 to 1 (or 3 to 2). Unfortunately for players, this is an infrequent event. In most cases, the player must evaluate his two-card hand along with the dealer's up card. Using this information, the player must decide how to play his hand.

Assuming the player is not dealt a natural, he is afforded several options regarding the play of his initial two-card hand. These options vary according to the rules put in place by the casino operator. In general, players are granted the following options: Stand, hit, double down, and split. Some casino operators allow players to surrender their two-card hand, but this is not common. All of these player options will be defined in subsequent sections of this chapter.

Once the players have acted on their two-card hands, if necessary, the dealer then executes his hand according to fixed draw and stand rules. That is, the dealer does not consider the value of the player hands, when executing his hand. The dealer only abides by the posted draw and stand rules for the game he is dealing. These draw and stand rules vary across casinos and even across blackjack games within the same casino. Subsequent sections of this chapter address the draw and stand rules in greater detail.

If neither the player's final hand total, nor the dealer's final hand total exceeds 21, the dealer will compare the hand totals and determine a winner. For example, if a player's hand totaled 20 and the dealer's hand totaled 19, the dealer would recognize that the player won hand. The dealer would then pay the player accordingly. As previously noted, if the player's hand total exceeds 21, he loses his wager. If the dealer's hand total exceeds 21, any remaining player hands with a total less than 22 are declared winners.

In the event that the dealer's up card is an ace, the players at the table will be offered the option to insure their wager against a blackjack. The insurance bet is mentioned in our overview, as the blackjack layout prominently displays the area in which this bet is made. The details of the insurance bet will be discussed in a subsequent section of the chapter.

Objective of Twenty-one

Some would argue that the objective is simple - beat the dealer. However, the player does not know the total value of the dealer's hand (only the up card). Therefore, the player must strive for a hand total as close to 21 as necessary, without exceeding 21. The player would certainly consider the value of the dealer's up card in this process. However, without knowledge of the dealer's hole card, and any additional cards that might be added to the dealer's hand, the player does not know the total he must beat. That is, the dealer's hand total certainly sets the mark to beat, yet it is unknown when the player acts on his hand. Because the hands are not played simultaneously, some would argue that the player is not trying to beat the dealer.

---

[11] A natural is also known as a blackjack, which is any original two-card hand comprised of an ace and any ten-valued card.

Adding to the complexity, the dealer's hand is executed (i.e. formed) with absolutely no regard for the player's hand total. For example, the dealer's hand is formed according to a single rule such as: The dealer must stand on any hand total ranging from 17 to 21. Therefore, the dealer makes no decisions in the formation of his hand. It would be difficult to argue that the dealer is playing *against* the player. For example, on a game where the cards are dealt face up, the dealer would be required to stand on 18, knowing that the player had 20. In the end, the player's objective might be best stated as follows: To obtain a hand total as close to 21 as necessary, without exceeding 21.

Terminology

Blackjack or Natural

Again, any two-card hand comprised of an ace and a ten-valued card is recognized as a blackjack. See Figure 11.1 for examples of blackjacks. After receiving their initial two cards, the players check to see if they have received a blackjack. If the dealer's up card is an ace or a ten-valued card, he will check his hole card to see if he has dealt himself a blackjack. The blackjack beats all other hands, with the exception of another blackjack. Should a player be lucky enough to receive a blackjack, the hand is over for that player. The player would show his cards to the dealer, who would pay the wager, provided the dealer did not have a blackjack as well. When both a player and the dealer are dealt blackjacks, their hands push. That is, the hand results in a tie and no money changes hands. When the dealer receives a blackjack the hand is over for all players. The blackjack is an automatic winner for either the player or the dealer, provided a player and the dealer are not dealt blackjacks on the same hand.

Figure 11.1. Examples of Hands Which Result in a Blackjack (a.k.a. a Natural).

A winning natural is paid at a rate of 3 to 2 (i.e., 1.5 to 1). However, this rate varies, with some games offering a 6 to 5 payoff on winning blackjacks. The 6 to 5 payoff equates to a rate of 1.2 to 1. The variations in the payoffs and their implications will be discussed in a subsequent section of this chapter.

Soft and Hard Hands

A soft hand includes an ace that is counted as 11. A hard hand either contains cards other than aces or includes an ace that is counted as one. A hand containing an ace is considered soft, when the addition of any card would result in a hard hand total less than 22. When totaling player and house hands, the dealer will always value the aces in the way that optimizes the hand total. In hands that contain two aces, at least one ace will be valued at one, but the other ace could be valued at one or 11. Figure 11.2 includes several examples of both soft and hard hands.

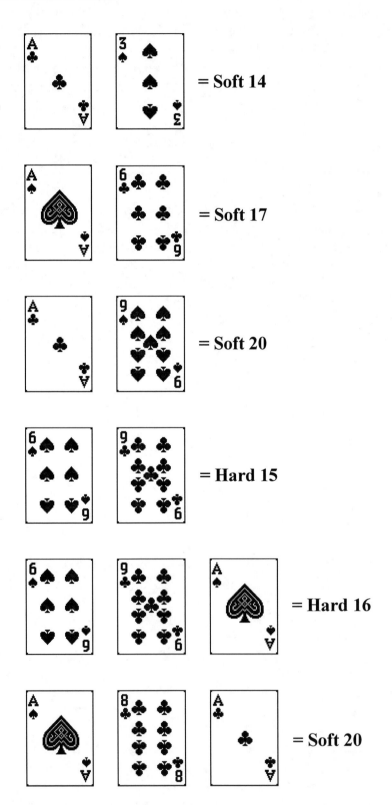

Figure 11.2. Examples of Soft & Hard Hands in the Game of Twenty-one.

Push

When the player's hand and the dealer's hand share the same terminal total, the hand is deemed a tie.[12] In the game of blackjack, a tie hand is referred to as a *push*. When two hands push, neither hand wins nor loses. In fact, the player can remove his bet from the circle and leave the game, following a pushed hand.

Bust

Whenever the player or dealer draws a card that results in a hard hand total greater than 21, the hand is considered a *bust*. Of course, a busted hand results in an immediate loss. If a player's hand is busted before the dealer's hand is eventually busted, the player still loses. That is, if both the player and dealer hands bust, the hand is not considered a tie. The player still loses his wager, because his hand was busted first.

Insurance

When people insure their homes and autos they are actually betting on some form of catastrophe. In the case of fire insurance, they are betting that their home will burn. Hopefully, they will lose the bet (i.e., their house never burns). In principle, the same type of bet is offered in blackjack. In fact, it is known as an insurance wager.

When the dealer's up card is an ace, she will actually have a blackjack in just under ⅓[rd] of those hands. In twenty-one, a player can insure her wager against a dealer blackjack. Before the dealer checks her hole card, the player can make a side bet that the dealer's hole card is a ten-valued card. This side bet is referred to as an insurance wager. If the dealer's hole card is in fact a ten-valued card, she has a blackjack. Of course, her blackjack will beat every player's hand, except for those who were also dealt a blackjack. If a player placed an insurance bet, it would be paid at a rate of 2 to 1. The insurance bet would be paid, because the insurance "policy" covered the loss of the player's wager, resulting from a dealer blackjack.

With home insurance, the home can only be insured to extent of its replacement value. The same principle holds for insurance wagers in the game of blackjack. As previously mentioned, a winning insurance wager is paid at a rate of 2 to 1. Therefore, the maximum insurance wager is equal to ½ of a player's initial wager. For example, let's assume a player's initial wager is $100. When the player sees the dealer's up card is an ace, she decides to make a $50 insurance wager. As it turns out, the dealer did have a blackjack. In this case, the dealer would use the player's original wager of $100 to pay the player's $50 insurance wager.

Let's consider a somewhat rare case. Assume the player insures her blackjack and the dealer also has a blackjack. In this case, the insurance bet is paid, but the original wager

---

[12] In this case, "terminal total" refers to the end result of a hand that has been played to a standing value under 21. That is, any hand with a total greater than 21 cannot result in a push. Additionally, no hand total less than the dealer's minimum allowable standing total (e.g., 17) can result in a push.

results in a push. That is an outcome that would not occur in the conventional insurance world. That is, you could not file a claim on a house or car that was not somehow damaged.

Table Layouts

Blackjack tables can typically accommodate five to seven players. Figures 11.3 and 11.4 illustrate examples of blackjack table layouts. Although both of these layouts accommodate seven *spots* (i.e., gambling positions), many operators are moving toward five-spot tables. Notice that the game depicted in Figure 11.3 requires the dealer to hit a soft 17, while the game shown in Figure 11.4 requires the dealer to stand on all 17s (which includes soft 17s). In Figure 11.3, the boxes at the top of each betting position (i.e., horseshoe) are the areas designated for each player's insurance bet.

Casino Options

Multiple Decks

Gaming was legalized in Nevada in 1931. From that date until the mid-1960s, blackjack was hand-dealt from a single deck of cards. In the mid-1960s, the multiple-deck shoe was introduced in Nevada casinos. Resting on the table's surface, the shoe was a device capable of housing multiple decks of cards. It also allowed dealers to conveniently dispense cards to the players and themselves.

Initially, these shoes contained only 4-decks. Today, casinos have blackjack shoes that can hold as many as 8-decks. Additionally, continuous shuffling equipment is now available, allowing for uninterrupted gaming. That is, after each round, the dealer deposits the cards in the shoe, which automatically combines them with the remainder of cards, creating the equivalent of a never-ending deck.

This technology made some significant contributions to the game. For example, the elimination of shuffling allowed dealers to produce a greater number of hands per hour. Additionally, by using a greater number of decks, the casino advantage was increased. Lastly, the continuous shuffler deters card counting. Both the resulting increase in the casino advantage and the card counting implications are discussed in subsequent sections of this chapter.

Soft 17 Rule

In blackjack, the dealer (on behalf of the casino) is usually required to draw to any hand total under 17. However, some casino operators will require dealers to draw to any hand total under 17 and to any soft 17 total. Figures 11.3 and 11.4 illustrate this difference. In Figure 11.3, the layout reads, "Dealer Must Hit Soft 17," while the layout in Figure 11.4 reads, "Dealer must draw to 16 and stand on all 17's."

Dealer Position

Figure 11.3. Seven-spot Blackjack Table Layout: Must Hit Soft 17.

Dealer Position

Figure 11.4. Seven-spot Blackjack Table Layout: Stand on All 17s.

Face Down vs. Face Up

When cards are dealt from a hand-held deck they are dealt face down. On a face down game, the players pick up the cards dealt to them. To draw an additional card from the dealer, the player gathers the two original cards in her hand and uses them to scratch the table's surface. When the dealer sees this scratching motion she knows the player is requesting an additional card. If the player is content with her original two-card hand, she slides the two cards under her bet.

If permitted by the regulations of the gaming jurisdiction, casino operators can choose whether the games are dealt face down or face up. As previously noted, on a face-down game, the players touch/handle the cards. When players touch cards, the game becomes less secure. For example, some players will use this opportunity to mark cards or slip other cards into the game. Casino operators have learned that some players are quite adept at cheating the game.

From the casino operator's perspective, the game security is greatly increased when the cards are dealt face up. A face-up game prohibits the player from touching the cards. If a player wants to draw additional cards, she motions with her hand or finger instead of scratching the table top with her cards. If the player is content with her hand total, she indicates so by waving her hand.[13]

6 to 5 Payout

Traditionally, when a player received a natural it was paid at a rate of 3 to 2, or 7 ½ to 5. However, casino operators have discovered that they can significantly increase the game's theoretical advantage by paying blackjacks at a rate of 6 to 5. In spite of this considerably unfavorable rule change, there is still demand for the game. It would seem that players either do not understand the effect of this rule variation or they are unable to perceive its negative incremental effect. That is, a 6 to 5 payoff on blackjacks gains the casino operator about 1.36% over the base game. Given the very slim advantage offered by the base game, this equates to an enormous increase for the operators. For example, on a base game with a 0.57% casino advantage, moving to a 6 to 5 payoff would result in a 239% increase in the casino advantage (i.e., an increase from 0.57% to 1.93%).[14]

Player Options

Double Down

Nearly every blackjack game will offer players some sort of double-down option. A double-down option describes the conditions in which the player is permitted to double her initial bet. However, when a player elects to double down, she agrees to draw only one card to her original two-card hand. For example, let's assume the player's original wager is $100 and that she is dealt two cards that total 11. Further, let's assume that the dealer's up card is a 5. These are ideal conditions for the player to double her wager. That is, many cards would give the player a strong hand, and there is a good chance the dealer

---

[13] With her palm facing the felt, the player waves her physical hand, as opposed to her hand of cards.

[14] Stated casino advantage (i.e., 0.57%) assumes basic strategy play against a game with Las Vegas Strip rules, dealt from an 8-deck shoe. These rules will be covered in a subsequent section of this chapter.

would bust, as the dealer would have to draw at least one card. At this point, the player would place another $100 in cheques next to her original wager. The dealer would then deal one additional card to the player's hand. Of course, in this example, the player would be hoping that this additional card has a value of ten, giving her a hand total of 21.

Most casino operators permit the player to "double" for less.[15] That is, to increase her wager by something less than the amount of her original wager. Staying with the previous example, the player might choose to increase her original wager by only $50, rather than the full $100.

Some operators restrict the player's doubling options. From the player's perspective, the ability to double down on any two-card hand total would be the most beneficial option. From the operator's perspective, increases in double-down opportunities lead to decreases in the casino advantage. Some operators do not allow players to double down on soft hands, while others only permit doubling on two-card hand totals of ten and 11.

Split

The player is permitted to split her hand, provided she is dealt an initial two-card hand comprised of any pair or two cards of equal value. Equal value pertains to a card's blackjack value. For example, a player could split a hand comprised of a ten and a jack, because each of these cards is assigned a value of ten in blackjack.

Let's assume a player wagers $100 and receives an initial two-card hand consisting of two 8s. Further, let's assume the dealer's up card is a 5. Given these conditions, the player elects to split the two 8s. At this point, the player is required to wager another $100 to split her two 8s into two separate one-card hands. Next, the player draws cards to the first hand until she is either satisfied with the hand or busts. This process is repeated for the second hand.

Sometimes the first card drawn to a split hand is a card of equal value. In this case, the hand can be split again, forming a third hand. This is sometimes referred to as a *re-split*. Continuing the previous example, if the player splits two 8s and draws another 8 to the first split 8, she is permitted to re-split. That is, she places yet another $100 wager, to form a third one-card hand consisting of an 8. She then draws cards to each of the three hands until she is either satisfied with the hand totals or busts. She first completes the hand located at the dealer's far left, with the order of play continuing to the dealer's right.

Most casino operators will allow the player to form a maximum of four hands via the split option. This is due in large part to the number of possible splits produced from a multiple-deck shoe. For example, if the table is full and several players choose to split their hands, there would not be enough space for the dealer to spread all of their hands. Surveillance must be able see all of the card faces, so the dealer cannot stack cards on top of one another. For these reasons, operators restrict the number of splits to four.

---

[15] The phrase "doubling for less" might be confusing as such an expression is oxymoronic. That is, a wager cannot be *doubled* for *less*. Nevertheless, *doubling for less* is the language used in the industry.

Double After Splitting

Some casino operators will allow players to double down after splitting their hand. When this is permitted, the split hands are afforded the same double-down opportunities as the original two-card hand. Let's revisit our previous example. Assume the player's original two-card hand consists of two 8s, and that the dealer's up card is a 5. After splitting the 8s, the player draws a 3 to the first split. The hand total of the first split is now 11, and, with a 5 showing, the player believes there is a good chance the dealer will bust. At this point, the player would be permitted to double his wager on the first split.[16] Allowing the player to double after splitting is a rule that is advantageous to the player.

Surrender

Some casino operators offer the surrender option to players. When surrender is offered, the player is allowed to surrender his hand, but only if the dealer does not have a natural. That is, the dealer must first verify that his hand is not a natural, before the surrender option is available to the player.[17] Surrender permits the player to forfeit his initial two-card hand and ½ of his wager to avoid playing the hand under what he deems to be very unfavorable conditions. That is, the player is permitted to forfeit 50% of his original wager to avoid playing a hand that he feels is likely to result in the loss of 100% of his original wager. Let's assume a player has wagered $100 on a hand of blackjack. Further, assume this player is dealt a two-card total of 16, with the dealer showing a ten (as an up card). Under these conditions, the player would certainly consider the surrender option. If he elected to do so, he would surrender his cards and forfeit $50 of his initial wager.

When New Jersey legalized gambling, its casino regulations included a surrender option. However, four of the five Casino Control Commission members authorized to write the regulations were very unfamiliar with casino operations. These regulators did not thoroughly understand the mechanics of the surrender option. As a result, the New Jersey regulations allowed the player to surrender his hand *before* the dealer checked for a natural. This option is referred to as *early surrender*. In the traditional form, the surrender option is only available to the player, after the dealer checks her hand for a natural. This traditional form is referred to as *late surrender*. The critical difference between early and late surrender is the effect of each option on the casino advantage. That is, early surrender is very advantageous for the player, whereas late surrender is of minimal value to the player. Although it was several years before this oversight was finally corrected, it is doubtful that early surrender will appear again, in any jurisdiction.

Hit or Stand

Lastly, we come to the most basic of options. Specifically, a player always has the option to draw or stand. Once the player knows the value of his hand and the value of the dealer's up card, she must decide whether to draw or stand. When the player draws a card, the act is referred to as *hitting* the hand. That is, a draw is also called a *hit*. Some

---

[16] It should be noted that the value of the dealer's up card does not effect whether the player would be permitted to double after the split, it was only mentioned here to provide context for the example.
[17] Of course, this verification would only occur if the dealer's up card were a ten-valued card or an ace.

players will say, "hit me," although the dealer must require the player to motion for the card as well. The motion can be seen by surveillance, whereas the verbal request cannot be visually verified.

If a player does not draw, then he is electing to *stand*. In the late 19th century, the dealer would ask the player, "Are you content?" [18] Of course, this was just another way of asking the player if he would like to hit or stand. In today's casino, the dealer is not likely to ask a player whether he would like to stand or hit. This is because all player actions must be signaled by hand motions or physical acts, which are visible to surveillance.

Procedural Review

Now that the key terminology and operational aspects of the game have been covered, let's consolidate the details. The following outline is designed to provide a brief and general review of the game production process.

1. The player places a wager.
2. The dealer shuffles the cards.
3. The shuffled cards are presented to the player to cut.
4. The first card is burned.
5. One card is dealt to each player and the dealer's hand. The first card dealt to the dealer's hand is the up card.
6. A second card is then dealt to each player and the dealer hand. In the dealer's hand, the second is the hole card.
7. Any player dealt a natural will turn his cards face-up and display them to the dealer. Unless the dealer also has a blackjack, the player's hand is a winner. If the dealer's up card is an ace or a ten-valued card, the dealer must view his hole card, before paying the player. However, if the up card is an ace, there are additional procedures.
8. If the dealer's up card is an ace, the players are offered the option to insure their wager (i.e., place an insurance bet), before the dealer views his hole card.
9. Following the insurance offer, the dealer checks his hole card to see if he has a blackjack. In the event of a dealer blackjack:
   a. The dealer exposes his hole card and the hand is over for everyone at the table.
   b. All two-card player hands less than a blackjack lose. Player blackjacks push.
   c. The dealer settles any insurance wagers as the losing bets are collected.
10. If neither the player nor the dealer are dealt a natural, the player completes the hand by choosing from options such as hit, stand, double, or split. The full extent of these options is determined by the cards in the player's hand and the house rules in place.

---

[18] "Trumps" (1864). *The American Hoyle or Gentlemen's Hand-Book of Games*, p. 213. New York: Dick & Fitzgerald.

Basic Strategy

Depending on the rules in place, the player has three mutually exclusive options on every hand:

      1) Draw another card;

      2) Do not draw another card; or

      3) Double the bet and take one additional card (if permitted by the rules).

Respectively, these options are known as hit, stand, and double down. If the player's original two cards are of equal value, the player has one additional option. That is, the player can choose to split his hand, which also requires him to double his original wager.

Since the player makes decisions regarding the play of her hand, the player's disadvantage is contingent upon her knowledge of the game. A player who always makes the decision that either minimizes her disadvantage or maximizes her advantage is someone who plays according to *basic strategy*. A basic strategy player always makes the optimal decision, based only on the knowledge of her own cards and the dealer's up card. In fact, basic strategy assumes the player has no consideration for or knowledge of any other cards.[19] Basic strategy also depends upon the rules in place and the number of decks in use. For example, changes in game rules can lead to changes in basic strategy.

Given the great number of possible hand conditions, Table 11.1 is provided to summarize the decision process of a basic strategy player. The title of the table includes important information regarding the number of decks and game rules. The first column on the left represents the player's hand (i.e., PLR). Rows "8" through "16" represent hand totals, while rows "A,2" through "9,9" represent specific two-card hands. The last row labeled "X,X" represents any two ten-valued cards. The column headers "2" through "A" represent the value of the dealer's up card.

The following example is provided to aid the reader in interpreting the contents of Table 11.1. Assume the player has two 8s and the dealer's up card is a five. Locate the intersection of row "8,8" and column "5." This cell (i.e., intersection) displays a "P," which stands for split. That is, according to basic strategy for the rules in place, the correct way to play the hand is to split the 8s.

Continuing the previous example, let's assume that the rules allow the player to double down after splitting a hand. Further, assume the player draws a 3 to his split 8, giving him a temporary hand total of 11. To determine the correct play, locate the intersection of the row "11" and column "5". Remember, 5 is the dealer's up card. A "D" is displayed in the intersection of row "11" and column "5," indicating a double down as the optimal play for this scenario.

Let's discuss what is missing from Table 11.1. Notice that no hand totals less than eight are listed, aside from the soft hands. This is because they are not played differently from

---

[19] For more on the definition of basic strategy, see Griffin, P. (1988). *The Theory of Blackjack*, 4th ed., Las Vegas: Huntington Press, p. 12.

the listed hand total of eight. That is, basic strategy would require a player to hit these omitted hand totals, against any up card. Hard hand totals ranging from 17 to 19 are also omitted, as is 21. This is because basic strategy would require the player to stand on all of these totals, against any up card.

Table 11.1
Basic Strategy: Four or More Decks
House Stands on Soft 17 & No Doubling After Splits

	Dealer's Up Card: 2 through Ace (A)									
PLR	**2**	**3**	**4**	**5**	**6**	**7**	**8**	**9**	**X**	**A**
8	H	H	H	H	H	H	H	H	H	H
9	H	D	D	D	D	H	H	H	H	H
10	D	D	D	D	D	D	D	D	H	H
11	D	D	D	D	D	D	D	D	D	H
12	H	H	S	S	S	H	H	H	H	H
13	S	S	S	S	S	H	H	H	H	H
14	S	S	S	S	S	H	H	H	H	H
15	S	S	S	S	S	H	H	H	H	H
16	S	S	S	S	S	H	H	H	H	H
A,2	H	H	H	D	D	H	H	H	H	H
A,3	H	H	H	D	D	H	H	H	H	H
A,4	H	H	D	D	D	H	H	H	H	H
A,5	H	H	D	D	D	H	H	H	H	H
A,6	H	D	D	D	D	H	H	H	H	H
A,7	S	D	D	D	D	S	S	H	H	H
A,8	S	S	S	S	S	S	S	S	S	S
A,9	S	S	S	S	S	S	S	S	S	S
A,A	P	P	P	P	P	P	P	P	P	P
2,2	H	H	P	P	P	P	H	H	H	H
3,3	H	H	P	P	P	P	H	H	H	H
4,4	H	H	H	H	H	H	H	H	H	H
6,6	H	P	P	P	P	H	H	H	H	H
7,7	P	P	P	P	P	P	H	H	H	H
8,8	P	P	P	P	P	P	P	P	P	P
9,9	P	P	P	P	P	S	P	P	S	S
X,X	S	S	S	S	S	S	S	S	S	S

Notes: H = Hit; S = Stand; D = Double; P = Split; X = Any 10-value card

As noted previously, basic strategy may change as the rules of the game change. For example, if the casino operator allows a player to double down after splitting his hand, then the correct way to play some of the splits will change from that displayed in Table

11.1. Table 11.2 summarizes these changes. Again, it is important to note the information in the title of Table 11.2, as changes in these conditions can alter the table's contents.

Table 11.2
Basic Strategy for Splitting a Hand: Four or More Decks
House Stands on Soft 17 & Doubling After Splits is Allowed

PLR	Dealer's Up Card: 2 through Ace (A)									
	2	**3**	**4**	**5**	**6**	**7**	**8**	**9**	**X**	**A**
2,2	P	P	P	P	P	P	H	H	H	H
3,3	P	P	P	P	P	P	H	H	H	H
4,4	H	H	H	P	P	H	H	H	H	H
6,6	P	P	P	P	P	H	H	H	H	H
7,7	P	P	P	P	P	P	H	H	H	H

Notes: H = Hit; P = Split; X = Any 10-value card

The Casino Advantage

Although luck is most certainly involved, blackjack is a game of skill. The casino advantage is a function of the game's rules and the skill of the player. That is, player errors are the source of tremendous contributions to the casino advantage. When players adhere to basic strategy, the casino advantage is decreased dramatically from the levels provided by unskilled or less knowledgeable players.

Table 11.3 lists the casino advantage by number of decks, including the incremental effects of many popular rule modifications. All of the content in Table 11.3 was computed based on the assumption that the player was adhering to basic strategy. Because most players do not play this well, the results are conservative. However, the basic strategy assumption is necessary, as specific player errors would have to be identified to compute any other level of casino advantage. The usefulness of any such attempt to identify *specific* errors would produce results with very limited applicability.

Table 11.3 is constructed from the casino operator's perspective. Therefore, positive numbers reflect a casino advantage and/or increases to the casino advantage. When blackjack analysis first began in the mid 1950's, the standard game rules were referred to as *Strip rules.*[20] All rule modifications are deviations from Strip rules, which assume:

- Dealer stands on soft 17
- Player is not permitted to double down after splitting
- Player may double down on any two-card hand
- Player may split any pair (except aces), up to 4 times
- Player may split aces (original two cards only). Split aces draw one card only.
- No surrender

---

[20] In reference to the Las Vegas Strip.

Casino Advantage Against a Basic Strategy Blackjack Player by Number of Decks[1]

Number of Decks	1	2	3	4	5	6	7	8
Casino advantage: Strip rules[2]	-0.01%	0.32%	0.43%	0.49%	0.52%	0.54%	0.56%	0.57%
Add applicable rule variations to Strip rules base:[3]								
No double on a 2-card total of 11	0.78%	0.70%	0.67%	0.65%	0.64%	0.64%	0.63%	0.63%
No double on a 2-card total of 10	0.52%	0.49%	0.48%	0.47%	0.46%	0.46%	0.46%	0.46%
No double on a 2-card total of 9	0.12%	0.09%	0.08%	0.08%	0.08%	0.08%	0.07%	0.07%
No double on a 2-card total of 8	0.01%	0.01%	0.01%	0.01%	0.01%	0.01%	0.01%	0.01%
No soft doubling	0.13%	0.11%	0.10%	0.09%	0.09%	0.09%	0.09%	0.09%
Double on a 2-card total of 11 only	0.78%	0.70%	0.67%	0.65%	0.64%	0.64%	0.63%	0.63%
Double on 2-card totals of 10 & 11 only	0.26%	0.21%	0.19%	0.18%	0.18%	0.18%	0.17%	0.17%
Double on 2-card totals of 9, 10, & 11 only	0.14%	0.12%	0.11%	0.10%	0.10%	0.10%	0.10%	0.10%
Double on 2-card totals of 8, 9, 10, & 11 only	0.13%	0.11%	0.10%	0.09%	0.09%	0.09%	0.09%	0.09%
Dealer hits soft 17	0.19%	0.21%	0.22%	0.22%	0.22%	0.22%	0.22%	0.22%
Player blackjack pays 1 to 1	2.32%	2.29%	2.28%	2.27%	2.27%	2.27%	2.26%	2.26%
Player blackjack pays 6 to 5	1.39%	1.37%	1.37%	1.36%	1.36%	1.36%	1.36%	1.36%
No hole card[4]	0.11%	0.11%	0.11%	0.11%	0.11%	0.11%	0.11%	0.11%
Double on any number of cards	-0.24%	-0.23%	-0.23%	-0.23%	-0.23%	-0.23%	-0.22%	-0.22%
Re-split aces	-0.03%	-0.05%	-0.06%	-0.07%	-0.07%	-0.07%	-0.08%	-0.08%
Double after splitting	-0.12%	-0.13%	-0.14%	-0.14%	-0.14%	-0.14%	-0.14%	-0.14%
Double after splitting, on a total of 11 only	-0.06%	-0.07%	-0.07%	-0.07%	-0.07%	-0.07%	-0.07%	-0.07%
Double after splitting, on totals of 10 & 11 only	-0.11%	-0.12%	-0.12%	-0.12%	-0.12%	-0.12%	-0.12%	-0.12%
Early surrender	-0.62%	-0.63%	-0.63%	-0.63%	-0.63%	-0.63%	-0.63%	-0.63%
Early surrender (dealer hits soft 17)	-0.70%	-0.71%	-0.72%	-0.72%	-0.72%	-0.72%	-0.72%	-0.72%
Late surrender	-0.02%	-0.05%	-0.06%	-0.07%	-0.07%	-0.07%	-0.07%	-0.07%
Late surrender (dealer hits soft 17)	-0.04%	-0.07%	-0.09%	-0.09%	-0.09%	-0.09%	-0.10%	-0.10%
6-card automatic winner	-0.04%	-0.11%	-0.13%	-0.15%	-0.15%	-0.16%	-0.16%	-0.16%
Player blackjack pays 2 to 1	-2.32%	-2.29%	-2.28%	-2.28%	-2.27%	-2.27%	-2.27%	-2.27%
Dealer's blackjack ties with player's built 21	-0.17%	-0.17%	-0.17%	-0.17%	-0.17%	-0.17%	-0.17%	-0.17%

Notes: [1] Table contents calculated using Stanford Wong's *Bledge Software* (1995), available from Pi Yee Press, La Jolla, CA. [2] Strip rules assume: Dealer stands on soft 17, no double after splitting, player may double on any two cards, any pair can be split up to 4 times (except aces), split aces receive only one card, and no surrender. [3] For a given number of decks, sum the effects of all applicable rule variations and add to "Casino advantage: Strip rules" to determine the revised casino advantage (negative sum indicates a casino disadvantage). [4] European version: Player loses all doubles and splits to dealer blackjack.

Table 11.3. Casino Advantage on Blackjack Games by Number of Decks & the Additive Effects of Rule Variations.

Table 11.3 is most helpful in determining the disadvantage of a basic strategy player, given a specific set of game rules. Remember, the player's disadvantage is also the casino operator's advantage. When computing the casino advantage, the Strip rules serve as the starting point. The incremental effects of any rule variations are added to this base advantage. For example, let's use Table 11.3 to compute the casino advantage for an operator offering the following blackjack game: 6-decks; double after splitting; and the dealer hits soft 17. Table 11.4 contains the results of our calculations.

Table 11.4
Casino Advantage Computations

Strip rules: 6 decks	0.54%
Add rule variations:	
Double after splitting	-0.14%
Dealer hits soft 17	0.22%
Casino advantage	0.62%

Note: Assumes basic strategy play.

Remember, aside from the rule variations listed, this operator is offering Strip rules. Also, it is important to note that all advantage data come from the 6-deck column of Table 11.3.

Importance of Understanding Basic Strategy

Casino executives should have a firm understanding of what constitutes a good blackjack player. They should also be able to identify one. Remember, the game's earning power is a function of the player's skill.

The win/loss results of players can be deceiving. That is, management should not use such results to determine who is a good player. Instead, the skill of players should be evaluated based on the quality of the decisions they make. That is, skill judgments should be based on how the player plays - not the results. Basic strategy is a good yardstick for evaluating skill. However, management must be familiar with basic strategy to determine how closely a player is adhering to it. Short of counting cards, basic strategy represents the optimal or correct way to play blackjack.

Player valuation is a critical issue, as it is the basis for all reinvestment decisions. Reinvestment refers to expenses such as room, food, and beverage comps, as well as more costly play incentives. All reinvestment is a function of the player's value. A player's value is expressed in terms of theoretical win. If the casino has an advantage, theoretical win will always be a positive number. In table games, theoretical win associated with a particular player is often computed based on the following formula:

$$\text{Theoretical win} = (AB)\,(TP)\,(GS)\,(HA)$$

AB stands for the player's average bet and TP represents time played. Both of these variables are observed and recorded by a floor person. More specifically, TP is an estimate of how long the player played (i.e., in hours). GS stands for game speed, which is usually expressed in terms of hands per hour. That is, the number of hands the player played per hour. Unfortunately, in most tracking systems the GS term is constant. A constant term ignores changes in the game speed, resulting from differences in the numbers of players on a game.[1] Finally, HA represents the house advantage, which is also known as the casino advantage. The HA term is based on the rules of the game (as described in Table 11.3) and the player's skill level. Again, unfortunately, this term is also often entered as a constant in the system, which ignores the often great differences in player skill levels.

Now that we have briefly reviewed the theoretical win formula used to value table game players, let's take a closer look at the worth of a blackjack player. For our examination, let's use the casino advantage computed in Table 11.4, i.e., 0.62%. This casino advantage was computed under the assumption of basic strategy play. Given this casino advantage, if a player were to wager $1,000 per hand, the casino operator could expect to win $6.20 per hand, on average. This may be surprising, as many would believe a player with a $1,000 average bet would produce a greater per-hand value. However, the margin on basic strategy players is especially thin.

Estimating the Casino Advantage

Luckily for gaming operators, the average blackjack player makes some errors. That is, the average player is not a basic strategy player, providing the operator with a greater casino advantage. Unfortunately, there is very little research on the extent of this difference, or the extent to which the average player deviates from basic strategy.

One gaming company has developed technology that captures and records key table game performance data, at the individual player level.[2] This technology uses empirical data to estimate the individual blackjack player's skill level. That is, the software analyzes the quality of each player's actual decisions. It also produces accurate wagering records for each player. These are monumental contributions. Such data allow casino operators to greatly improve the accuracy of blackjack player valuations.

This technology was installed in an Indian casino located in Southern California. Data from this installation were analyzed to learn more about the actual skill level of blackjack players, and the extent to which players vary from basic strategy. Data were captured on both 6-deck and 2-deck games. The following rules applied to all games:

- Dealer hits soft 17
- Double down after splitting is allowed
- Late surrender is allowed
- Re-splitting of aces is allowed

---

[1] Operators should track game speed by estimating the average number of players on the game, rather than guessing at the actual hands per hour. A constant game speed term will often produce a very inaccurate estimate of a player's theoretical win (i.e., true value). For more on theoretical win see, Lucas, A.F., & Kilby, J. (2008). *Principles of Casino Marketing*, 24, San Diego: Gamma Press.

[2] *TableEye21* was developed by Tangam Gaming. See TangamGaming.com for more information.

Based on these rules, the casino advantage against a basic strategy player was computed for both the 6-deck and 2-deck games. The results of these computations can be found in Table 11.5.

Table 11.5

Casino Advantage Against Basic Strategy Play

	6-deck Game	2-deck Game
Strip rules	0.54%	0.32%
Add:		
Dealer hits soft 17	0.22%	0.21%
Double after splitting allowed	-0.14%	-0.13%
Late surrender	-0.09%	-0.07%
Re-splitting aces allowed	-0.07%	-0.05%
Casino advantage	0.46%	0.29%

Notes. Source: Table 11.3.

From Table 11.5, the two-deck game provided a particularly slim advantage over the basic strategy player (i.e., 0.29%). Table 11.6 contains the casino advantages computed from the observations of blackjack players in the Southern California casino.

Table 11.6

Average Observed Casino Advantage in Blackjack

	Average Casino Advantage	Standard Deviation	Variance from Basic Strategy [a]	
			Amount	%
6-deck game	1.47%	0.94%	1.01%	220.57%
2-deck game	1.25%	1.21%	0.96%	331.03%

Source: Proprietary analysis of observed blackjack play from a Southern California casino.[3] Note: [a] As cited in Table 11.5.

Let's start with the 6-deck game. The observed casino advantage was 1.47%, which was 1.01% greater than the 0.46% produced by basic strategy play. To clarify the significance of this result, the observed casino advantage was 220.57% greater than the casino advantage produced by a basic strategy player. Alternatively stated, the casino advantage on the actual blackjack players was 2.21 times greater than the casino advantage against basic strategy play. In general, these results held for the two-deck games as well. In fact, the average casino advantage on the observed blackjack play was 3.31 times greater than the advantage associated with basic strategy play.

---

[3] Tangam's sample consisted of 1,000 player rating sessions of 45 minutes each, which included a total of 30,799 hands of blackjack. The casino advantage shown here was the average of the individual session results.

Both standard deviations indicated a wide variety of observed skill levels. Such variety in skill level highlights the importance of identifying both the best and worst players. That is, these results suggest that management should definitely not assume all players are of a similar skill level. Moreover, any such assumption would certainly result in both over- and under-valuation of players. Remember, accurate player valuation leads to accurate reinvestment in players.

Of course, the results of any such analysis could vary, as not all operators cater to players of identical skill. Additionally, repeating the same study at the same casino could also produce a different result. Just the same, this study provides valuable insight into the average player's skill level, as compared to the benchmark of basic strategy.

Importance of Game Speed

While the casino advantage is clearly an important component of the earning process, the speed of the game is equally critical. Some blackjack players prefer to play alone. Others prefer more populated tables. This simple preference can dramatically affect both the earning and valuation processes. The data set from the previously reviewed study of player skill also included game speed measurements. That is, game speed was observed and recorded at different levels of blackjack table occupancy.[4]

Before discussing the results of the game speed study, let's define the common game speed metrics. Some casino operators track *hands per hour* (HPH), while others track *rounds per hour* (RPH). To compute HPH, management tracks the number of hands dealt to all players on the game. To calculate RPH, management counts the number of dealer hands produced on the game. So, as the number of players on the game increases, the RPH can be expected to decrease.

When attempting to measure or monitor dealer productivity, tracking HPH can be problematic. For example, high limit blackjack games accommodate the greatest wagers, but they also attract the fewest players. Consider the high limit dealer who deals to a single high roller. This dealer is likely to produce just over 200 HPH. However, with only one player on the game, this dealer's HPH is equal to his RPH. In comparison, a dealer on a lower limit game could produce almost 400 HPH, when dealing to a full table. However, the dealer on the full game would have an RPH under 60. When management tracks dealer productivity by way of HPH, the dealers must hope for high table occupancy.

Now we are ready to discuss the results of the game speed study. Table 11.7 summarizes the key findings. Column headers (A) through (E) are used to clarify the computations in the cells of Table 11.7.

---

[4] *Table occupancy* refers to the number of players on the game, at any given time.

Table 11.7
Results of Game Speed Study[5]
HPH vs. RPH by Table Occupancy Level

(A)	(B)	(C)	(D) 220 ÷ (C)	(E) (C) ÷ 220
# of Players	Total Table HPH	RPH	Head-up Multiple	% of Head-up RPH
1	220	220	1.00	100%
2	282	141	1.56	64%
3	313	104	2.12	47%
4	334	84	2.62	38%
5	350	70	3.14	32%
6	364	61	3.61	27%
7	376	54	4.07	25%

Let's begin by looking at the results in columns (A), (B), and (C). As expected, increases in the table occupancy (i.e., # of players) are followed by increases in Total Table HPH and decreases in the RPH. These results come as no surprise. That is, one would expect the number of dealer hands per hour (or RPH) to decline, as the number of players on the game increases.

The results in columns (D) and (E) reveal the importance of game speed in the player valuation process. For example, "Head-up Multiple" represents the number of hours a player would need to play before equaling the number of hands played by a head-up player. Head-up play occurs on a game occupied by a single player. To clarify, let's take a closer look at the results for games with seven players. On games occupied by seven players, each player received an average of 54 hands per hour. Therefore, such a player would need to play for 4.07 hours on that game, to equal the number of hands received in one hour of head-up play (i.e., 220 hands). That is, 220 RPH ÷ 54 RPH = 4.07 hours.

Column (E), "% of Head-up RPH" expresses the same relationship as column (D), but in different terms. Continuing the previous example, column (E) simply divides the 54 RPH (at seven players) by the 220 RPH (Head-up) to compute the percentage of head-up RPH (i.e., 25%). To clarify, consider the following example. Player A and Player B both play for one hour, both wager $1,000 on each hand, and both play at exactly the same skill level. The only difference is that Player A is on a game occupied by seven players, whereas Player B is on a game occupied by one player – herself. Because Player B will play 220 hands in the hour and Player A will only play 54 hands, the casino operator can expect to win 4.07 times more from Player B. Alternatively stated, for that hour of play, the value of Player A is 25% of the value of Player B. Table 11.8 summarizes the relationships discussed in this example.

---

[5] Proprietary study conducted by Tangam Gaming.

Table 11.8

Reconciliation of Table Occupancy, Game Speed, & Theoretical Win

Player	Table Occ.	Avg. Bet		House Adv.		Hands Per Hr.		Hours		Theo. Win
A	7	$1,000	x	1%	x	54	x	1	=	$540
B	1	$1,000	x	1%	x	220	x	1	=	$2,200

Note: $540 ÷ $2,200 = 25% (per Column E of Table 11.7). Alternatively, $2,200 ÷ $540 = 4.07 (per Column D of Table 11.7).

Player rating systems often default to a fixed game speed, which can produce considerable consequences. For example, let's assume the player tracking system fixed the game speed at 84 rounds per hour. This setting assumes an average occupancy of 4 players, per Table 11.7. Given this setting, players who chose to play head-up would be worth 2.62 times their system-generated value. That is, the results from Table 11.7 estimate head-up play at 220 rounds per hour, which is 2.62 times greater than the fixed speed of 84 rounds per hour. Players who chose to play on full tables would be worth only 64% of their system-generated value, as these players would experience only 54 rounds per hour. Unfortunately for management, these same players would receive credit for 84 rounds per hour.

The consequences associated with a fixed game speed are considerable, as many operators will return as much as 50% of the system-generated value (i.e., theoretical win). That is, management will reinvest in players by way of comps and other monetary play incentives. A 50% reinvestment rate on a theoretical win that is only 64% of the system estimate does not leave much for the company. To the contrary, the reinvestment rate in the head-up players will be too low. In fact, any tracked play that occurs on a game with less than four players will be undervalued. At some point, players who prefer these low-occupancy games are likely to feel underappreciated and may choose to gamble elsewhere.

Side Bets

Side bets on blackjack games have become common. While most casinos offer some form of side bet on their blackjack games, the variety of these bets is extensive.[6] Perhaps the best way to describe a side bet is to discuss one. Let's take a look at an actual side bet known as buster blackjack. In this case, the player makes a separate wager, which is independent of his blackjack hand. The player is betting that the dealer will bust. The more cards it takes to bust the dealer hand, the greater the payout. Of course, if the dealer does not bust, the player loses the wager. Table 11.9 summarizes the various payouts, probabilities, and player disadvantage associated with this side bet.

---

[6] As of July 1, 2011, over 40 different side bets were listed on http://wizardofodds.com. This listing is abridged, as many more side bets exist.

Table 11.9
Buster Blackjack Side Bet
Computation of Player Disadvantage

Outcome	Gain or Loss (-)	Probability of Outcome	Player Disadvantage
Dealer busts with 8+ cards	250	0.000012	0.002986
Dealer busts with 7 cards	50	0.000214	0.010722
Dealer busts with 6 cards	12	0.002638	0.031651
Dealer busts with 5 cards	4	0.020473	0.081890
Dealer busts with 4 cards	2	0.089392	0.178784
Dealer busts with 3 cards	2	0.173032	0.346064
Dealer does not bust	-1	0.714241	-0.714241
			-0.062143

Notes: Assumes a six-deck shoe and the dealer hits on soft 17.

From Table 11.9, the buster blackjack side bet has a player disadvantage of 6.21%. Alternatively stated, the casino operator can expect to earn $6.21 of every $100 wagered on this side bet, in long run. A closer look at the content in Table 11.9 reveals a parallel structure to that of a one-coin slot machine. That is, the most the casino operator can win is the coin the player wagers (i.e., "-1"). Additionally, as the outcomes become less frequent the payouts become greater, just an in a slot machine pay table.

Card Counting

In blackjack, is it possible for the player to have an advantage over the casino operator? The answer is yes. The game of blackjack is governed by a dependent-trial process. That is, the chance of winning the next hand depends upon which cards were removed in the previous hand/s. In sampling theory, this is referred to as selection without replacement.

In 1962, Edward O. Thorp wrote *Beat the Dealer*.[7] In his book, Thorp demonstrated that tracking the cards removed from play allows the player to gain an advantage over the house. Thorp's book was the first of many to address the practice of what came to be known as card counting. While card counting remains a threat, casino operators have become increasingly aware of the mechanics and are now able to employ measures to discourage would-be counters.

For a card counter to be successful, he must do two things. First, he must identify when he has an advantage. Second, he must increase his wager when he has an advantage. However, casino personnel are keenly aware of the second criterion. That is, they pay close attention to players who vary their bets. Card counters must wager small sums in unfavorable conditions and much greater sums in favorable conditions. This oscillating betting behavior often alerts management to their presence on a game. To avoid

[7] Thorp, E.O. (1962). *Beat the Dealer.* New York: Random House.

detection, counters needed a way to conceal the sometimes great differences in their wagers. *Back counting* provided a temporary solution to their problem. In fact, it became quite popular.

When back counting, the card counter observes the game from a distance. Once he recognizes that the deck is advantageous (i.e., his opportunity), he enters the game and places a bet. He will leave the game once the deck is no longer advantageous. It appears as though a back counter never varies his bet, making it difficult for management to identify him. In fact, by design, a back counter will appear to make the same wager on each hand - his maximum bet. However, in reality, the back counter is actually *increasing* the variation in his wagering behavior, by either making no wager or his maximum wager. That is, his wager ranges from *zero* to his maximum wager, which is a variation that is even more advantageous to a card counter. Remember, in the traditional approach to card counting, the counter would at least make token wagers until recognizing his opportunity to place a maximum wager.

At this point, it must seem as though back counting had solved the problem of detection, by eliminating any visible variation in wagering behavior. However, casino operators thwarted the practice of back counting by preventing any player from making a *mid-shoe entry*. That is, no player is permitted to make a wager on a game, unless that player began wagering on the first hand of a freshly shuffled shoe. Now the counter must revert to the practice of varying his wager, making it easier for management to detect his presence on the game.

Continuous shuffling devices provide even greater protection against card counters, as each hand is in effect the first hand of the shoe. By reintroducing the cards from the previous hand, no cards are ever removed from the deck. Remember, the premise of card counting is to gain an advantage by tracking the cards removed from the deck(s) on previous hands. Therefore, card counters are not able to gain an advantage on a game with a continuous shuffler, as each hand is dealt from a full complement of the cards. The same holds true for most online blackjack games. That is, each hand is the first hand of a new deck.

Questions/Exercises:

1. What is the definition of basic strategy?
2. When an operator increases the number of decks, how does it affect the game's house advantage?
3. Why might a casino operator choose to deal the cards face up?
4. Define/describe Strip rules in detail.
5. Who would benefit from the following rule change (i.e., the player or the casino operator)? Dealers will no longer stand on soft 17, i.e., going forward, dealers will hit soft 17.
6. Assuming Strip rules on a game with 4+ decks, when would a basic strategy player split an original two-card hand consisting of two 6s?

7. Assuming Strip rules on a game with 4+ decks, when would a basic strategy player hit an original two-card hand consisting of two 7s?

8. Assuming Strip rules on a game with 4+ decks, when would a basic strategy player stand on a hard hand total of 13?

9. Assuming Strip rules on a game with 4+ decks, when would a basic strategy player stand on an original two-card hand consisting of an ace and a 6 (i.e., a soft 17)?

10. Assuming Strip rules on a game with 4+ decks, when would a basic strategy player hit a hard hand total of 15?

11. Assuming Strip rules on a game with 4+ decks, when would a basic strategy player double down on an original, two-card, hard, hand total of 9?

12. Assuming Strip rules on a game with 4+ decks, when would a basic strategy player double down on an original two-card hand consisting of an ace and an 8?

13. Assuming Strip rules on a game with 4+ decks, when would a basic strategy player stand on a hard hand total of 12?

14. Assuming Strip rules on a game with 4+ decks, when would a basic strategy player split an original two-card hand consisting of two 9s?

15. Use Table 11.3 to compute a basic strategy player's disadvantage, based on the following game rules? Assume there are no additional adjustments to Strip rules.
    - 8-decks
    - Dealer hits soft 17
    - Late surrender permitted
    - Aces can be re-split
    - Double after splitting permitted

16. Based on your answer to the previous question, a basic strategy player could be expected to lose _____, per $1,000 in wagers.

17. Per the text, would a player be permitted to split an original two-card hand consisting of the king of clubs and the queen of hearts?

18. Per the text, when a player elects to double down, is she permitted to draw cards to her hand until she is either satisfied with her hand total or busts?

19. List the items or rules put in place to discourage card counters and those intending to cheat the game.

20. In terms of procedure, what is the critical difference between early and late surrender?

21. Summarize the concerns related to the use of a fixed game speed in the casino's player tracking system?

22. When playing a hand of blackjack, how does the general approach of a basic strategy player differ from that of a card counter?

Chapter 12
Chemin de Fer & Baccarat

What is chemin de fer? How is it played?
What is a punter? What are pips?
What is the critical difference between chemin de fer and baccarat?
What are the sources of the casino's advantage on baccarat wagers?
How is a casino advantage created in no commission baccarat?
What is a differential betting policy? How is this policy related to chemin de fer?

Scope

This chapter begins with rare and detailed coverage of chemin de fer, the game that inspired modern baccarat. Next, baccarat is covered to the extent that the reader could follow betting action on a live game. This thorough and comprehensive coverage of baccarat addresses all of the following items: Key terminology, draw and stand rules for each hand, commission structures, the casino advantage, dealing and operating procedures, side bets, and more.

Chapter Goals

- Provide a detailed review of the precursor to modern baccarat: Chemin de fer
- Describe the necessary evolution of baccarat from chemin de fer
- Review the betting layout of full-sized and midi-baccarat games
- Examine the specific basic betting propositions offered on baccarat games
- Review the basic game procedures, including how the baccarat game is called by the dealer (i.e., the caller)
- Describe the draw and stand protocol for both the player and banker hands
- Explain the various commission procedures, including no commission baccarat
- Examine baccarat side bets and differential betting policy

Overview

The game known as baccarat in the United States and Asia is known as punto banco in Europe and South America. Differences in name aside, it would be difficult to find a table game that wins more money worldwide than baccarat. Baccarat has established itself as the game of choice for most of the world's premium table game players. To illustrate this point, let's consider Nevada's gaming market. In 2011, Baccarat (all forms) represented a mere 6% of the total number of table and card games, yet it generated 32%

of the annual gross gaming win produced by these sources.[1] In fact, no card or table game produced a greater percentage of Nevada's annual gross gaming win than baccarat.

In Asia, baccarat is clearly the most popular table game in the mega-casinos, which combine to form some of the world's greatest gaming markets. Baccarat games dominate the floors of these properties, making unmatched contributions to gross gaming win. For example, in Macau, baccarat games produced 90% of the gross gaming revenue in 2010.[2]

Baccarat's current global gaming volume is nothing short of staggering. However, today's game owes much of its modern success to chemin de fer, a game popularized in Europe centuries ago. That is, baccarat is nothing more than an evolved version of chemin de fer.

Chemin de Fer

This game takes its name from the French word for railway, referring to the fast tempo of the game.[3] However, it could be said that the name refers to the speed at which fortunes change hands. Once played almost exclusively by royalty and members of the aristocracy, the 1966 film *Casino Royale* introduced chemin de fer to the world as the preferred game of secret agent James Bond. Today, the game of chemin de fer has all but disappeared from the casino landscape. Our research revealed only a few active games in European and South American casinos.[4] Regardless of its declining popularity, this game's rich history and clear connection to baccarat make it worthy of discussion.

Although the exact origin of chemin de fer is not known, the game has been played for centuries in Europe. Charles VIII brought chemin de fer to France in 1490, where it gained popularity among members of the French court.[5] In 1958, the Stardust Casino in Las Vegas was the first of several Las Vegas casinos to introduce chemin de fer.[6] Unfortunately, chemin de fer requires players to bet on opposite sides of a proposition (i.e., to oppose one another), instead of betting against the house. It is this requirement that made the game difficult to offer, leading to its demise in the U.S.

---

[1] Nevada Gaming Control Board (2011). *Gaming Revenue Report, April 2011*. Retrieved on June 10, 2011 from http://gaming.nv.gov/documents/pdf/1g_11apr.pdf. Annual gross gaming revenues were comprised of the 12-month period ended April 30, 2011.

[2] Gaming Inspection and Coordination Bureau, Macao SAR (2011). *Quarterly Gaming Statistics*. Retrieved on July 1, 2011 from http://www.dicj.gov.mo/web/en/information/DadosEstat/2011/content.html #n1.

[3] Chemin de fer. *Collins English Dictionary – Complete & Unabridged 10th ed., 2009*. New York: HarperCollins.

[4] As of December 2011.

[5] Chemin de fer. *The Columbia Electronic Encyclopedia, 6th ed., 2007*. New York: Columbia University Press.

[6] Scarne, John (1974). *Scarne's New Complete Guide to Gambling*, 459-460. Simon and Schuster: New York.

Chemin de fer was played in Great Britain long before gaming was legalized.[7] The game was extremely popular with their European clientele and remained so throughout the 1970s. In 1976, New Jersey's Casino Control Commission authorized the operation of both baccarat and chemin de fer in Atlantic City casinos. Although the current New Jersey gaming regulations specify how chemin de fer is to be operated, the game has never been offered by a licensed Atlantic City casino operator.

Objective of the Game

In chemin de fer, also known as chemmy, participants are often referred to as *punters*. As for the game itself, there are two hands dealt in chemmy. One hand is referred to as the *player hand* and the other is called the *banker hand* (a.k.a. bank hand). Both are community hands. That is, the fate of all punters who choose to bet on the proposition known as the player hand is determined by the outcome of a single player hand (i.e., dealt for the table). Likewise, everyone who wagers on the proposition known as the banker hand is wagering on the outcome of a single hand that is dealt for the table. The goal of the punter is to wager on the hand (i.e., player hand or banker hand) that he thinks will produce a hand total closest to nine. A two-card hand total of nine represents the best possible hand, which guarantees an outcome no worse than a tie. Chemmy hands consist of at least two, but not more than three cards. Of course, the hand with a total closest to nine wins. The specific rules governing the formation of hands will be covered in a subsequent section.

Chemmy is similar to blackjack in that the punter has the option to draw or stand on certain two-card totals, introducing a skill component to the game. Chemmy also has similarities to poker in that the casino is not at risk of loss. That is, the wagers lost on the losing hand are used to pay the wagers placed on the winning hand. Like poker, chemin de fer is not a house-backed game. While poker games charge a rake to create revenue for the casino, chemmy games require five percent of winning banker-hand wagers to be paid to the house.[8] This payment or commission is the only source of revenue on a chemmy game. Because neither poker nor chemmy are house-backed games, management will never incur a loss on these games.[9]

Personnel Requirements

The game of chemin de fer is operated by one dealer, called a croupier, one changeur, and one supervisor or inspector.[10] The changeur operates much like a cashier and assists the croupier and punters. The game begins once the table is *complete*, which requires between 9 and 11 willing punters. Figure 12.1 illustrates the table layout, including the nine numbered punter stations and the dealer position.

---

[7] That is, chemin de fer was played in Great Britain prior to the 1968 Gaming Act, i.e., Gaming Act (1968, October 25), c. 65, UK Public General Acts.

[8] Rake: A percentage of the pot won by the player(s), which is remitted to the casino as a fee for providing the game.

[9] *Loss* refers to a net loss to the game, resulting from a dollar-amount of payouts to players that exceeds the dollar-amount of wagers won by the casino, for a given accounting period.

[10] The croupier also serves as the caller, i.e., the dealer who announces the operation of the game.

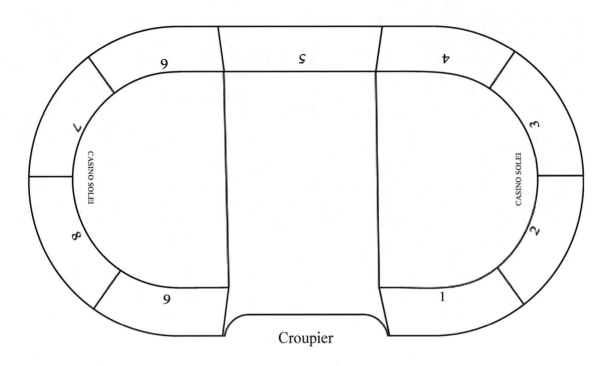

Figure 12.1. Chemin de Fer Table.

Chemin de Fer Cards

The game is played with six decks of cards. The cards have no indices. That is, only the pips are shown on the cards (See Figure 12.2). The backs of the cards used in a chemmy deck are also different from those used in other casino games. The chemin de fer cards have solid-colored backs, which feature no printed pattern. Typically, casino operators will use decks of cards with an identical pattern printed on the back of each card. These traditional decks are used on popular games such as baccarat, blackjack, and poker.

Figure 12.2. Chemin de Fer Card: Pips Only – No Rank Indicated (e.g., 3).

Card Values and Hand Totals

In Chemmy, the Ace is counted as one, the 2 through 9 cards are counted at face value, and the 10, Jack, Queen, and King are all counted as zero. The cards in both the player hand and the banker hand are totaled. If the total exceeds 9, the first digit is dropped. For example, in blackjack, the hand total of a 5, 3, and 9 is 17, but in Chemmy, this hand total is expressed as 7 (See Figure 12.3).

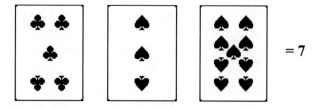

Figure 12.3. Example of a Double-digit Hand Total in Chemin de Fer.

Naturals

In Chemmy, any two-card total of eight or nine is referred to as a *natural* (See Figure 12.4). If either the player hand or banker hand shows a natural, the hand is over. If both the banker hand and the player hand are dealt naturals, then the greatest natural wins. If both naturals have the same value (e.g., 9 & 9), then the hand ends in a tie. Tie hands result in a push, for those who bet on either the player hand or the banker hand. That is, neither hand wins nor loses.

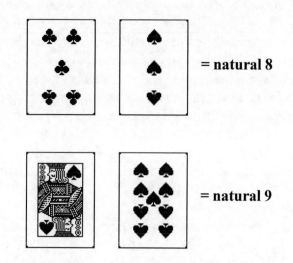

Figure 12.4. Examples of Naturals in Chemin de Fer.

Shuffle and Cut Procedures

Prior to play, the dealer chemmy-shuffles the cards.[11] The players at the game are also given the opportunity to chemmy-shuffle the cards. If any player chooses to do so, which is rare, the cards are returned to the dealer who then performs one last riffle shuffle.[12]

---

[11] This rather imprecise process involves the croupier spreading all six decks of cards face down and sliding or stirring them around with his hands, while keeping his fingers open and the palm of his hand flat against the table's surface. The chemmy-shuffled cards are then assembled into two single stacks from which they are riffle shuffled.

[12] A riffle shuffle is the standard shuffling procedure, such as that produced on a blackjack game.

Once the cards are shuffled, the players are afforded the opportunity to cut the pack (i.e., the multiple decks of cards). The shuffled pack is first offered to the player on the immediate left of the dealer. If that player refuses to cut, the cut is offered to the other players at the table, moving in a counterclockwise direction. This process continues until a player is found who is willing to cut the cards. If no punter wishes to cut the cards, the pack will be cut by the croupier. The shuffled and cut pack is then inserted into the shoe. The game is now ready for play.

Selecting the Banker

Prior to play, the croupier must find a punter willing to act as the banker. The shoe, or bank, is first offered to the punter sitting to the croupier's immediate right.[13] If this punter refuses the bank, the croupier will offer the bank to the next punter, moving in a counterclockwise direction, until a punter agrees to act as the bank.[14] The banker must wager an amount on the banker hand that is at least as great as the table minimum. During the last years of chemin de fer at Monaco's Casino de Monte-Carlo, the minimum wager was set at 500 Euros (about $685).[15]

Although the house is never at risk in Chemin de Fer, management will often enforce a table maximum as well (i.e., a maximum allowable wager). Table maximums help management keep the game alive by restricting wagers. Without restrictions, a single hand could end the game for the night. Additionally, maximum betting limits sometimes protect players from themselves and each other. For example, this restriction might prevent a punter from making an excessive wager, in the heat of the moment. That is, players are capable of provoking one another into producing excessive wagers in chemmy, as the game pits them against each other. When the game was offered at the Casino de Monte-Carlo, the maximum allowable wager was 300,000 francs (about $63,700).[16] Aside from the posted minimum and maximum wagers, the banker establishes the table stakes.[17] Of course, this assumes that a punter or group of punters is willing and able to match the banker wager.

Casino de Monte-Carlo's management offered a *garage* feature to the banker. After winning three consecutive hands, the banker was permitted to put aside (or park) half of his winnings, while continuing to bank with the remaining half. New Jersey's regulations state that each banker's wager must be at least as great as his previous wager and no more than twice the amount of his immediately preceding wager.[18] For example, if a banker

---

[13] In some jurisdictions, the bank is auctioned to the highest bidder, before the first hand is dealt. Thereafter, the bank is rotated counterclockwise from punter to punter. See N.J. Casino Control Commission Regulations, Chapter 47, 19:47-4.5; and Scarne, J. (1965). *Scarne on Cards*, 202. New York: Signet.

[14] In some jurisdictions, punters were required to take their turn as banker. If the punter refused, he was required to leave the game.

[15] Given the currency exchange rates as of May 2011.

[16] Given the currency exchange rates as of May 2011.

[17] In some jurisdictions, bettors (sitting or standing) were permitted to place a bet in the same amount as the banker, in an "association," but these bettors were not allowed to see the cards or influence play.

[18] N.J. Casino Control Commission Regulations, Chapter 47, 19:47-4.5.

placed a wager of $10,000 and won, that banker would have to wager at least $10,000 on the following hand, but no more than $20,000. These policies and regulations were designed to manage the volatility of the game, as players could be wiped-out by well financed banker runs or streaks of luck. Given that chemmy requires punters who are willing to place opposing wagers, managing the maximum wager becomes an important part of keeping the game alive.

Player Hand Wagering

As previously mentioned, the amount wagered on the banker hand must be matched by an equal amount wagered on the player hand. Once the banker has made his wager, the croupier will "animate" the party by announcing, "Place your bets please" or "Are there no more bets?" The croupier will encourage the players to wager against the banker, until the banker wager is covered.

There are three ways to cover the bank (i.e., the banker-hand wager):

1. A single punter can cover the bank in full, by announcing, "*Banco*" or "*Banco seul*." These two terms mean the same thing. It is possible for more than one punter to announce banco, on a given hand. In this case, the banco announcement of the first punter to the right of the banker takes precedence.[19] This right is referred to as *banco prime*. Should this happen, all of the other punters at the table become nothing more than spectators. Anyone who calls and executes banco, has the right of *banco suivi* (following banco), should he lose the hand, regardless of his position at the table.[20] That is, his right to call banco on the next dealt hand is recognized over all others who call banco on that hand. Bystanders are also permitted to call banco. In fact, this is the only time a non-seated player is permitted to touch the cards;

2. *Avec la table* (with the table), which means one punter elects to cover half of the bank. In this case, the remaining half of the bank wager must be covered by the other players; and

3. If no punter announces banco or avec la table, then the croupier will encourage the punters to wager partial sums until the bank is covered. In this case, the offer to place partial wagers begins with the first eligible punter to the right of the banker, continuing in a counterclockwise rotation until the bank is covered. Once the bank is covered, all remaining punters become spectators.

Should the amount wagered on the player hand exceed the amount wagered on the banker hand, the banker is permitted to increase his wager to match the full amount wagered on the player hand. Alternatively, the banker can refuse to increase his wager above his initial bet, resulting in a withdrawal of player hand wagers, until the balance of the player hand is equal to the initial bank wager. Should the total amount wagered on the player hand fall short of the initial bank wager, the banker must reduce his wager to match the

---

[19] In the 1800s, it was a gentleman's rule for the player to the immediate right of the banker to call banco seul, during the first bank's (i.e., shoe's) rotation around the table.
[20] Scarne, J. (1965) *Scarne on Cards*, 203. New York: Signet.

amount wagered on the player hand.[21] If the bank is not covered by players seated at the table, bystanders may place wagers to cover the shortfall. However, these bystanders are not permitted to see the cards or influence play.

Bystanders

In its day, chemin de fer was a very popular game. It was often difficult to obtain a seat at a chemmy game. Because of this popularity and limited seating, standing players, i.e. bystanders, were often allowed to play. In fact, bystanders were permitted to call banco seul and actually take the cards off the table. This would be difficult for today's gaming managers to imagine, given the contemporary concern for game protection, especially in markets such as Macau.

General Procedures & Rules

The banker will control the shoe, and act as banker, for as long as he continues to win. The cards are actually drawn from the shoe by the banker, as opposed to the croupier (i.e., dealer). The croupier manages/calls the game, collects losing bets, and pays winning bets.

The banker will make all draw/stand decisions related to the play of the banker hand. The punter with the greatest wager on the player hand becomes the *active* player, and he will make all draw/stand decisions for the player hand. Those punters betting with the active player are subject to the decisions made by the active player. Only the active player knows the value of the player hand and only the banker knows the value of the banker hand.

Once the amount wagered on the player hand is equal to the amount wagered on the banker hand, the dealer announces, "no more bets." Next, the croupier will announce, "cards" and the punter acting as the banker will initially draw four cards from the shoe. The first card drawn from the shoe is the first card of the player hand. The second card from the shoe is the first card of the banker hand. The third and fourth cards drawn from the shoe become the second card of player hand and the second card of the banker hand, respectively. The croupier uses a wooden spatula to distribute the cards to the active player. This spatula is also known as a *pala* or *palette* (See Figure 12.5).

Figure 12.5. Chemin de Fer Pala (or Palette).

---

[21] If a punter were to bet in "association" with the banker, and the amount wagered on the player hand did not cover the bank, the bets placed by the associate would be the first to be withdrawn (i.e., returned).

Once the initial four cards have been drawn, the active player and the banker evaluate their respective two-card hands. They are obligated to show (i.e., turn face-up) any natural. Showing a natural ends the hand. If no natural is shown, play continues according to the draw/stand options outlined in the next two sections.

Player Hand Draw/Stand Rules[22]

- The active player is obligated to stand on any two-card total of 6 or 7.
- The active player must draw on any two-card total less than 5.
- The active player has the option to draw or stand on a two-card total of 5.

When a card is drawn to the player hand it is placed face-up on the table, providing information to the banker regarding the possible totals of the player hand. Once the player hand has been completed, the banker hand is played according to the draw/stand rules outlined in the next section.

Banker Hand Draw/Stand Rules[23]

- Banker hand draws on any two-card total less 3.
- Banker hand draws on any two-card total less than 6, when a 3rd card is *not* drawn for the player hand.
- See Table 12.1 for all other banker-hand draw/stand rules.

Table 12.1
Banker Hand Draw & Stand Protocol: Chemin de Fer
Two-Card Banker Hand Totals of 3, 4, 5, & 6
Assuming a Third Card is Drawn for the Player Hand

Banker Hand's Two-Card Total	Banker Hand Draws if Player Hand's 3rd Card is:	Banker Hand Stands if Player Hand's 3rd Card is:	Option if Player Hand's 3rd Card is:
3	A-7, 10, J, Q, K	8	9
4	2-7	A, 8, 9, 10, J, Q, K	
5	5-7	A, 2, 3, 8, 9, 10, J, Q, K	4
6[24]	6-7	A, 2, 3, 4, 5, 8, 9, 10, J, Q, K	

In both France and Monaco, casino operators referred to these rules as the *tableau*. In London casinos, the tableau was also known as *Crockford's Drawing Card*.[25]

[22] Some rule variations allow a banco seul player (i.e., a single punter covering the bank) to draw or stand on *any* two-card total. In fact, players would occasionally stand on a natural 8 or 9, in the hopes of changing the order of the cards and/or rhythm of the game. However, when a player elected to do so, his two-card natural would be treated as a three-card 8 or 9. That is, instead of having an automatic winner, the banker could tie or even beat what would have been a player natural.
[23] Some variations allow the banker to draw/stand on any total short of a natural or zero.
[24] Crockford's Drawing Card also gave the banker the option to draw or stand on 6 when the active player did not call for a 3rd card.
[25] Kendall, M.G. and Murchland, J.D. (1964), Statistical Aspects of the Legality of Gambling, *Journal of the Royal Statistical Society*, 365.

The Single Source of Casino Win

To some extent, the punter's disadvantage is dependent upon his skill. That is, punters can misplay hands. Skill level aside, the banker hand has a slight advantage over the player hand, because the player hand is completed first. Winning player hand wagers are paid even-money (i.e., at a rate of 1 to 1). If a punter wagers $10,000 on the player hand, and he wins, he is paid $10,000. Of course, the source of this $10,000 payoff is the losing wagers that were placed on the banker hand. However, the casino earns no revenue when the player hand wins. The single source of casino revenue is a commission charged on winning bank wagers. The casino charges a commission equal to 5% of the amount won by the banker, which is paid only when the bank hand wins. For example, if the banker wagers $10,000, and he wins, the casino will charge a 5% commission, or $500, resulting in a net gain of $9,500 for the punter (i.e., the punter acting as the banker).

The Challenge of Making a Market for Chemmy

While chemin de fer is an elegant game with a rich and long history, like any game, it has its strengths and weaknesses. That is, there is no risk of loss to the chemmy game, which is very attractive to casino operators. Specifically, in chemmy, the money wagered on the losing hand is used to pay the bettors who wagered on the winning hand. The casino operators simply charge a 5% toll every time the banker hand wins. However, chemin de fer also comes with some challenges for casino operators and casino marketers. Like so many things, the feature that makes chemmy attractive is also its greatest weakness.

In the golden era of chemin de fer, the games were scheduled and everyone knew the likely participants. Steady demand for the game was not an issue. While it is nice to have a steady supply of bettors who are willing to wager amounts that directly offset one another, this balance can be difficult to achieve in the modern casino. Specifically, it is not always easy for operators to attract or recruit groups of punters who are willing to bet against each other. In chemmy, a player cannot simply walk up to the game and place a wager, as an opposing wager is required. If such a player were to approach the game, he would not be able to place any wagers until the requisite number of players were assembled. He would have to wait for other players to arrive, just as poker players must often do.

Another challenge for chemmy is the independent nature of the modern gambler and modern casino games. For example, the draw/stand decisions made by a single punter can affect the outcome of wagers placed by other punters. If Player A loses, following a decision made by Player B, Player A may question the wisdom of that decision. When gamblers lose, even wise decisions are sometimes challenged.

The primary challenges associated with chemin de fer can be overcome by a single adjustment. This adjustment represents the critical difference between chemin de fer and baccarat. That is, in baccarat, the casino has a built-in advantage on any wager. Therefore, opposing wagers (i.e., from additional punters) are not required. This was achieved by a slight modification of the chemin de fer rules.

While the advent of baccarat's independent house advantages made the game much easier for casino operators to offer, it also introduced considerable volatility. By eliminating chemmy's requirement for opposing wagers, baccarat games became vulnerable to substantial swings in the house win, as well as occasional losses to the game. Baccarat results are far from the smooth and always-positive outcomes produced by chemin de fer.

Baccarat

The modern version of baccarat originated in Argentina, migrating to Cuba in the 1950's.[26] In 1959, the Las Vegas Sands recruited personnel from Cuba and opened the first baccarat game in the United States.[27]

In review, baccarat punters are wagering against the casino rather than against each other. Therefore, baccarat can accommodate wagering activity from both a single player and multiple players. Multiple players can all bet on the same side (i.e., player or banker) or they can bet on opposite sides. However, by allowing unbalanced wagering, baccarat games can experience losses. Further, because baccarat often attracts betters who wager great sums, the losses to the game can be extreme. Baccarat wins and losses can be great enough to affect the quarterly results of the entire casino.[28] In fact, history has shown us that the results of a single baccarat player's wagering activity can severely damage a casino's earnings.[29]

While chemmy is dealt from a 6-deck shoe, baccarat is typically dealt from an 8-deck shoe. Baccarat tables appear in multiple forms. The full-sized table is capable of accommodating between 12 and 14 punters (See Figure 12.6). Operation of a full-sized table requires 3 dealers: One caller and two base dealers. Figure 12.6 illustrates the conspicuous absence of the betting positions numbered 4, 13, and 14. This is due to the superstitious nature of gamblers. The numbers 4 and 14 are considered unlucky in some Asian cultures, while many regard 13 as an unlucky number in the U.S.A.[30]

Baccarat is also offered on a smaller table, requiring only a single dealer. This increasingly popular version of the game is known as midi-baccarat. Figure 12.7 illustrates the layout and dealer position of a midi-baccarat table. As depicted, a midi-baccarat table usually seats seven players. Although it seats seven, notice that there is no betting station numbered four. Again, four is considered an unlucky number in many parts of Asia. Different from the full-sized baccarat layout shown in Figure 12.6, the betting positions on the midi-baccarat layout illustrated in Figure 12.7 are not expressly numbered. The absence of the number four on the midi-baccarat layout can only be

---

[26] Renzoni, T. (1973), *Renzoni on Baccarat*. Secaucus, NJ: Lyle Stuart, 11.

[27] Ibid, 460

[28] Lucas, A.F., Kilby, J. & Santos, J. (2002). Assessing the profitability of the premium player segment. *Cornell Hotel & Restaurant Administration Quarterly, 43*(4), 65-78.

[29] Eadington, W.R. & Kent-Lemon, N. (1992). Dealing to the premium player: Casino marketing and management strategies to cope with high-risk situations. In *Gambling and Commercial Gaming: Essays in Business, Economics, Philosophy and Science*, ed. W.R. Eadington & J.A. Cornelius, Reno: Institute for the Study of Gambling and Commercial Gaming, University of Nevada, Reno.

[30] The numbers four and 14 are associated with the word for death in multiple Asian languages/dialects.

detected by referring to the numbered commission box, located in front of the dealer position. The betting station numbers range from one to eight, with no number four. The operation of the commission box will be discussed in a subsequent section.

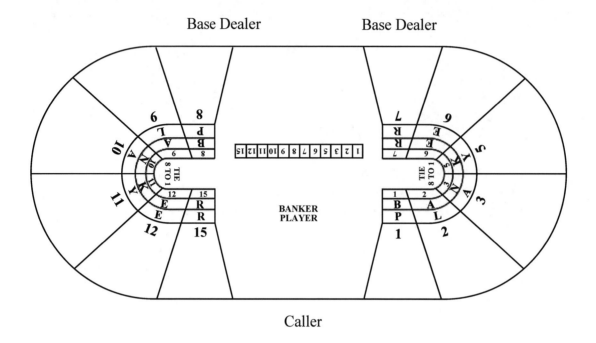

Figure 12.6. Full-sized Baccarat Table.

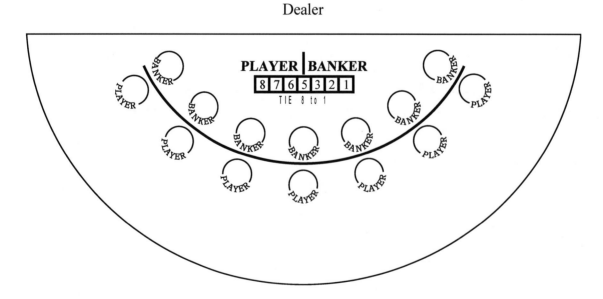

Figure 12.7. Midi-Baccarat Table.

Regardless of the layout, baccarat punters make only two choices in the wagering process: Which bet to make and how much to bet. For example, a punter may choose to wager $100 on the banker. Unlike chemmy punters, baccarat punters make no decisions on the actual play of the hands. The rules governing how the baccarat hands are played are established by the casino. These rules are fixed, removing the need for any decisions regarding the play of the hands.

Like chemmy, there are only two hands dealt per round of baccarat: A banker hand and a player hand. Both hands are community hands. The punter can bet on either the banker hand or the player hand. Every punter wagering on the player is betting on the community player hand and every punter wagering on the banker is betting on the community banker hand. Also, because baccarat is banked by the house, punters are permitted to wager on the tie proposition. This bet wins if the ending totals of the two community hands are equal. The tie bet loses if the ending totals of the two community hands are not equal.

The cards can be dealt either face down or face up. When dealt face down, selected punters will expose the card values for all to see. When dealt face up, the punters do not handle the cards. In the face-up version of the game, the dealers arrange the dealt cards to form both the player and banker hands. A face-up game provides more game protection for the casino, as it affords no opportunity for the players to touch the cards. The face-down game is often referred to as a *squeeze game*, in casino parlance. The term squeeze is used to describe the very slow and seemingly strenuous manner in which many players choose to expose the faces of the cards. In fact, the amount of force the players apply to the cards in a squeeze game is so great that the cards are used only one time. That is, the cards are bent to the extent that they cannot be shuffled. Squeeze games are very popular in Asia.

Because the draw/stand rules are predetermined and fixed, knowing the value of the community player or banker hand cannot affect the outcome of the hand. Therefore, there is no operational reason for the players to touch the cards. That is, there is no reason to ever conceal the two-card total of either community hand. The squeeze games are most likely a nostalgic remnant of chemin de fer, where the handling and concealment of the cards was necessary. At best, the squeeze games are popular with the punters, playing to the ceremonial and superstitious nature of gamblers. That said, many casino operators in Asia have fallen victim to punters with the ability to substitute cards into squeeze games. Of course, the effects of card substitution scams can be devastating, leading to tremendous casino losses.

Producing the Game

Prior to play, the eight decks are shuffled by the dealer/s and then cut by one of the punters. Following the cut, the cards are inserted into the shoe and the punters place their bets. The amount of the wagers must be within the table's posted minimum and maximum bets. Once the wagers are placed, the dealer will slide and expose the first card from the freshly shuffled shoe. The value of that first card determines how many subsequent cards will be burned (i.e., discarded) before dealing the first hand. For example, if the exposed card is an 8 of spades, then the dealer will slide eight additional cards from the shoe. These eight additional cards will remain face down, as they are known as the burn cards. Once these burn cards have been placed in the discard rack, the first hand can be dealt.

On a full-sized face-down baccarat game, a punter will handle the shoe, just as in chemin de fer. To handle the shoe, the punter must have a wager on the banker hand. Like chemin de fer, the shoe stays with the punter until the banker hand loses to the player hand. Such a loss results in the counterclockwise rotation of the shoe to the next punter with a banker hand wager.

Play begins when the caller announces, "cards please." The punter in control of the shoe will slide one card to the caller, then one card to himself, a second card to the caller, and then a second card to himself. We will assume the cards are dealt face down. The two cards that were slid to the caller represent the player hand. Without exposing the faces of the cards, the caller will toss the cards to the punter with the largest wager on the player hand. When the caller announces, "player hand please," that punter will then expose the faces of the cards and toss them back to the caller. The caller will then announce the value of the player hand. For example, "player shows 3." The caller will then say, "bank hand please." The punter with the shoe will then expose the faces of the two cards comprising the banker hand, before tossing them to the caller. The caller will then announce the banker hand. For example, "bank has 5." From this point onward, all draw and stand actions are governed by a prescribed set of rules. That is, neither the dealers nor the punters are actually making any decisions. The outcomes of the hands are determined by the hit and stand rules of the game, much like that of the dealer hand in twenty-one.

In midi-baccarat, if the cards are dealt face down, the dealer will handle the shoe. After sliding the cards from the shoe, the dealer will toss the banker-hand cards to the punter representing the bank and the player-hand cards to the punter with the greatest player-hand wager. On a face-up midi-baccarat game, all cards are dealt and exposed by the dealer. The players do not touch the cards on this type of game.

Draw/Stand Rules: Player Hand

In chemin de fer, the active player has the option to draw or stand on a two-card total of five, while baccarat rules dictate that the player hand must draw to any total less than six. That's it. In baccarat, the player hand must draw to any two-card total less than six. Alternatively stated, the player hand will stand on the following two-card totals: Six, seven, eight, and nine. There are no more draw/stand rules for the player hand. The draw/stand rules for the banker hand are a little more complex.

Draw/Stand Rules: Banker Hand

A complete description of the draw/stand protocol for the banker hand is provided next.

- The banker hand stands on two-card totals of 7, 8, and 9.
- A third card is drawn to any banker-hand total less than 3. Specifically, a third card is drawn to a two-card total of 0, 1, or 2.
- A third card is drawn to a banker-hand total less than 6, when a third card is *not* drawn for the player hand.
- If the banker hand totals 3, 4, 5, or 6, the rule governing whether a third card is drawn for the banker hand is determined by the value of the player hand's third card. Table 12.2 summarizes these various contingencies.

Table 12.2
Baccarat Draw & Stand Protocol: Banker Hand
Rules for Banker-Hand Totals 3, 4, 5, & 6
Assuming a Third Card is Drawn for the Player Hand

Banker Hand's Two-Card Total	Banker Hand Draws if Player Hand's 3rd Card is:	Banker Hand Stands if Player Hand's 3rd Card is:
3	A-7, 9, 10, J, Q, K	8
4	2-7	A, 8, 9, 10, J, Q, K
5	4-7	A, 2, 3, 8, 9, 10, J, Q, K
6	6-7	A, 2, 3, 4, 5, 8, 9, 10, J, Q, K

The draw/stand rules covered here are common to the traditional form of baccarat. Using these fixed and specific draw/stand rules, the win frequency of each proposition (i.e., bet) in baccarat can be computed. Table 12.3 summarizes these win frequencies, the payoffs on winning wagers, and the resulting punter disadvantages.

Table 12.3
Win Frequency, Payoff, & Punter Disadvantage by Wager
Baccarat (with 5% commission)

Outcome	Probability	Payoff Rate	Punter Disadvantage
Banker Hand Winning	0.458597	0.95 to 1	-1.06%
Player Hand Winning	0.446247	1 to 1	-1.24%
Both Hands Tie	0.095156	8 to 1	-14.36%

Because the banker hand's probability of winning exceeds that of the player hand, the casino must pay winning banker-hand wagers at a rate that is something less than 1 to 1. Such a payoff creates a house advantage on banker-hand wagers.

Typically, casinos charge a 5% commission.[31] As shown in Table 12.3, winning banker-hand wagers are paid at a rate of 0.95 to 1, which creates a player disadvantage of 1.06%. Of course, the player disadvantage translates to a house or casino advantage. That is, the casino enjoys a 1.06% advantage on all banker-hand wagers. The following formula uses the contents of Table 12.3 to express the punter's disadvantage, when wagering on the banker hand.

$$(0.458597)(0.95) + (0.446247)(-1) = -0.015799 \text{ or } -1.06\% \text{ (rounded)} \text{ }^{[32]}$$

The player-hand wagers can be paid at a rate of 1 to 1, because the player-hand win frequency is less than that of the banker hand. Therefore, the casino will win a greater number of player-hand wagers than it will lose. Alternatively stated, the casino will collect or win more units wagered on the player hand than it will pay out, assuming the amount wagered on the player hand remains constant.

Commission

As previously stated, winning banker-hand bets are paid at a rate of 0.95 to 1. For example, if a bettor wagers $100 on the banker hand and wins, the bettor is paid $95. This bettor most likely wagered a single $100 cheque. However, the $95 payoff would be comprised of three $25 cheques and four $5 cheques. This is a cumbersome and time consuming payoff for such a simple wager. To speed-up the game, winning banker-hand bets are often paid at a rate of 1 to 1. The 5% commission owed to the casino is tracked in a *commission box* (See Figure 12.8).

Figure 12.8. Commission Box on a 7-Spot Midi-Baccarat Game.

Baccarat games are stocked with an inventory of small plastic buttons called *lammers*. These lammers have numbers printed on their faces, which represent their monetary value. The lammers are used to mark the amount of the commission owed by punters who have won one or more wagers on the banker hand. Returning to the previous example, let's assume the bettor is seated in position 3 (on the baccarat table) when he wins his $100 wager on the banker hand. This bettor would be paid $100 for his winning banker-hand wager, but the dealer would also place a $5 lammer in position 3 of the commission box. This lammer indicates the bettor's commission liability to the casino. In most casinos, any outstanding commission is collected from the bettors at the completion of each shoe.

---

[31] In the late 1980s, the Horseshoe in downtown Las Vegas charged a 4% baccarat commission. In effect, this reduced the casino advantage on the banker wagers by about 50%. Not to be outdone, the Sahara later offered a no commission game, which resulted in a 1.06% advantage for punters wagering on the banker hand. This game did not last long, nor did the manager who decided to offer it.

[32] Minor differences due to rounding will occur. This is caused by differences in the precision of the terms.

Prepaid Commission

Many casinos do not mark the commission, eliminating the need for a commission box. In these casinos, the pace of the game is increased by requiring the bettors to prepay the commission on banker-hand wagers. For example, if a bettor wishes to place a $100 wager on the banker hand, he must also place a $5 cheque next to his wager. If the bet is won, the dealer would pay the bettor $100 and collect the $5 cheque as commission. If the bet is lost, the dealer would collect the $100 wager and leave the $5 cheque in the circle. So, although the commission is prepaid, it is only collected when the bettor wins the banker-hand wager.

The Game in Operation

The following bullet points provide an overview of the operation of a baccarat game.

- The 8-deck shoe is shuffled, cut, and made ready for play.
- Punters place a wager on the player hand or the banker hand, and/or the tie.
- The caller locates a punter willing to place a wager on the banker hand. He will first look to his immediate right, moving counterclockwise until such a punter is located. This player is asked to serve as banker and handle the shoe.
- The caller then announces, "place your bets." Once all bets are placed the caller announces, "cards please," and the punter with the shoe (hereafter referred to as banker) deals four cards.
- The caller tosses the cards comprising the player hand to the punter with the largest player-hand wager.
- The caller asks for the player-hand cards. The punter exposes the cards and tosses them back to the caller, who announces the value of the hand. For example, the caller would announce, "player shows 5."
- The caller asks for the banker hand by announcing, "bank hand please." The banker exposes the banker-hand cards and tosses them to the caller. Let's assume the banker hand is comprised of a 6 and a 4. The caller would announce, "bank has nothing" or "bank has baccarat." These two announcements indicate the same hand total (i.e., zero).
- The caller evaluates both the player hand and the banker hand, according to the draw/stand rules covered in this chapter.
- If the hand requires a bank draw, the caller will announce, "draw bank, five to beat," assuming the total of the player hand was five.[33] The banker then draws a card, exposes it, and tosses it to the caller.
- The caller evaluates the hand and announces the results. For example, the caller would announce, "Player wins 5 over 3."
- The two base dealers collect the losing bets and pay all winning bets.
- The punter serving as the banker continues to handle the shoe until the player hand wins. Tie hands do not result in banker-hand losses (or player-hand losses) and therefore, have no bearing on the rotation of the shoe. Following a banker-

---

[33] In the case of a bank draw, the caller would substitute the appropriate player-hand total, when calling the number for the bank to beat.

hand loss, the bank (i.e., shoe) rotates in a counterclockwise direction to the next punter wagering on the bank.

Calling the Hands

In baccarat, etiquette governs the manner in which the hands are called. Of course, there are a great number of circumstances, including rule and game delivery variations, which could potentially alter the language used to call a baccarat game. The goal here is to provide the reader with examples of the language used by the caller in a traditional baccarat game. All quotes denote announcements made by the caller on the game.

Opening stages of the hand:
"Place your bets please." A prompt to open betting.
"No more bets please." An announcement to close betting.
"Cards please." A request for the banker to produce the first four cards.
"Player hand please." Asking the active player for the player-hand cards.
"Bank hand please." Asking the banker for the banker-hand cards.

Announcing the player hand (all 2-card totals):
"Player shows nothing."
"Player shows 1." Same call for 2, 3, 4, & 5.
"Player shows 6 and must stand." Same call for 7.
"Player shows a Natural 9. There will be no draws." Same call for a natural 8.

Announcing the banker hand (all 2-card totals):
"Bank has nothing." or "Bank has baccarat." Both announcements indicate a banker-hand total of zero.
"Bank has 1." Same call for 2, 3, 4, 5, and 6.
"Bank has 7 and must stand."
"Bank wins with a Natural 8." Same call for a natural 9.
"Bank ties it up, 8 – 8." Same call for hand totals of 9 – 9.

Announcing third card draws:
"Card for the player." Request to draw a third card to the player hand.
"Draw Bank, 6 to beat." Request to draw a third card to the banker hand. Assumes the terminal value of the player hand is 6. Caller would announce any of several possible hand totals in place of 6.

Decision Announcements:
"Player wins 5 over 4." Announcement of terminal hand totals in favor of the player hand.
"Bank wins 7 over 2." Announcement of terminal hand totals in favor of the banker hand.
"We have a tie hand, 6 - 6" or *"Bank ties it up, 6 - 6."* Announcement of terminal hand totals that end in a tie.

No Commission Baccarat

No commission baccarat is a version of the traditional game that is gaining popularity, especially in Asia. In traditional baccarat, winning banker bets are paid 0.95 to 1, which equates to a 5% commission. As noted previously, this payoff (i.e., 0.95 to 1) results in an awkward and time consuming process. In Sri Lanka, in 1987, a slightly modified version of baccarat was introduced by Rakesh Wadhwa, Vice Chairman & Managing Director of the Nepal Recreation Centre Pvt. Ltd. Mr. Wadhwa changed the rules governing his baccarat games to eliminate the awkward commission process. He decided to pay winning bank wagers at a rate of 1 to 1, except when the bank won with a total of six. When the banker hand won with a total of six, the punters were paid at a rate of 0.5 to 1 or ½ to 1.

As the no commission game proved popular with his clientele in Sri Lanka, Mr. Wadhwa decided to introduce the game in another of his own casinos located in Nepal. While on a visit to Nepal, David Packer, a South American casino operator saw the game and liked it. Mr. Packer then brought no commission baccarat to Casino Iguazu, his own casino located in Iguazu, Argentina.

In baccarat, the banker hand wins with a total of six about 5.386% of the time. If the bank is paid 0.5 to 1 in those instances, the punter's disadvantage on a banker-hand wager is computed as follows:

$$(0.404733)(1) + (0.053864)(0.5) + (0.446247)(-1) = -0.014581, \text{ or } -1.4581\%$$

In the previous equation, the 0.404733 term represents the probability of a banker-hand win, with a hand total other than six, and the 0.053864 term represents the probability of a banker-hand win, with a total of six. The 0.446247 term represents the probability of a banker-hand loss, just as it does in the traditional form of baccarat. This term is multiplied by -1, because it represents a loss of one betting unit for the punter. To the contrary, "1" and "0.5" both represent payments to the punter resulting from banker-hand wins. It is important to note here that a player *disadvantage*, results in a casino *advantage*. That is, management can expect to win 1.4581% of the dollar-amount wagered on the banker hand, in the long run. This is a significant improvement over the traditional form of baccarat, which offers a 1.0579% casino advantage on banker-hand wagers.

Differential Betting

Some casino operators impose differential betting limits on their baccarat games. These limits establish the maximum exposure (or risk) the casino operator is willing to endure. For example, let's assume the casino operator imposes a $300,000 differential betting limit. This means that the difference between the dollar-amount of the wagers on the banker hand and the dollar-amount of the wagers on the player hand cannot exceed $300,000. For example, if a punter wishes to bet $1,000,000 on either the player hand or the banker hand, the wagers on the opposite proposition must total between $700,000 and $1,300,000. While the idea of differential betting limits may sound attractive, enforcing the limits can be somewhat difficult to manage. For instance, when there are multiple punters who wish to place wagers, management must sometimes determine who is permitted to play. In these cases, management will often apply a right-to-wager protocol similar to that employed in chemin de fer. These rules determine who is allowed to wager in a given situation, along with the amount each punter is permitted to wager.

Any Pair Side Bets

Many Las Vegas baccarat games feature any-pair side bets on both the full-sized and midi-baccarat tables. Specifically, punters can wager on whether the player hand or the banker hand will be dealt a pair. For example, let's assume a punter wagers $10 on the proposition known as the *player-hand pair*. If the two-card player hand results in *any* pair, the punter is paid $110. Winning bets are paid at a rate of 11 to 1, which is the same as 12 for 1. In fact, "12 FOR 1" is printed on most layouts, in the hope that some punters will believe it is a more generous payout than the 11 to 1 equivalent. Of course, punters can wager on any banker-hand pair as well. Winning wagers on the banker-hand pair are also paid at a rate of 11 to 1. Third cards have no bearing on the outcome of the any-pair wagers. Only the first two cards of each hand are used to determine the outcome of this popular side bet. The player's disadvantage on the any-pair side bet is computed in Table 12.4.

Table 12.4
Player Disadvantage on the Any-Pair Side Bet

Outcome	Probability	Gain or Loss (-)	Player Disadvantage
Any pair[34]	0.074699	11	0.821687
No pair[35]	0.925301	-1	-0.925301
			-0.103614

Note: Assumes game is dealt on an 8-deck shoe.

While the 10.36% player disadvantage is well beyond those associated with wagers on both the player and banker hands, it is actually less than that associated with a bet on the tie (-14.35%, from Table 12.3). Still, for a table game wager, 10.36% represents a considerable player disadvantage. The casino operator benefits greatly from those willing to bet on the tie or a proposition such as any pair.

[34] Probability computed from the following equation: [(13)(32)(31) / 2] / [(416)(415) / 2] = 0.074699, where 416 represents the number of cards in an 8-deck shoe (i.e., (8)(52))
[35] Probability computed from the following equation: 1 − 0.074699 = 0.925301

Questions/Exercises:

1. Use the following probabilities to compute the player disadvantage on banker bets, on a baccarat game that charges a 4% commission. Assume all other aspects of the game are consistent with the traditional form of baccarat, as described in the text.

Tie	9.5156%
Banker Win	45.8597%
Player Win	44.6247%

2. What is a punter?

In the following baccarat questions, a third card will be drawn to both the player hand and the banker hand, in spite of whether it is appropriate. Per the rules of traditional baccarat, you must ignore the third card if it should not have been drawn, evaluate the hand totals (per the correct draw & stand rules), and select the winning hand.

Example:

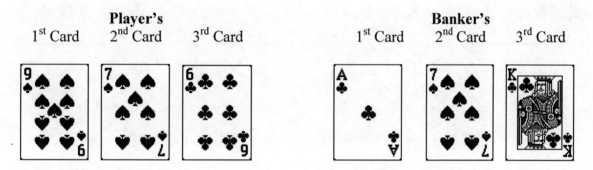

| | **Player's** | | | | **Banker's** | |
| 1st Card | 2nd Card | 3rd Card | | 1st Card | 2nd Card | 3rd Card |

Answer: If the hand were played correctly, the banker would have had a natural 8 and the player would have had a hand total of 6 (i.e., 9 + 7). The banker hand would have won 8 to 6. Neither the player hand nor the banker hand would have drawn a third card. That is, both of the third cards should have been ignored in the evaluation of the hands.

3. Select the winning hand, assuming both hands were played correctly.

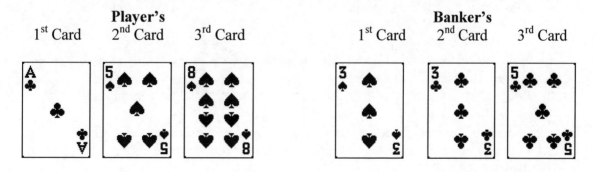

| | **Player's** | | | | **Banker's** | |
| 1st Card | 2nd Card | 3rd Card | | 1st Card | 2nd Card | 3rd Card |

4. Select the winning hand, assuming both hands were played correctly.

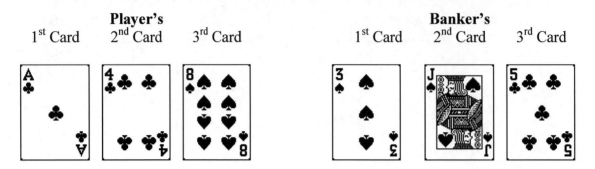

Player's
1st Card   2nd Card   3rd Card

Banker's
1st Card   2nd Card   3rd Card

5. Select the winning hand, assuming both hands were played correctly.

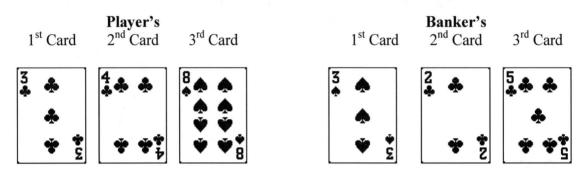

Player's
1st Card   2nd Card   3rd Card

Banker's
1st Card   2nd Card   3rd Card

6. Select the winning hand, assuming both hands were played correctly.

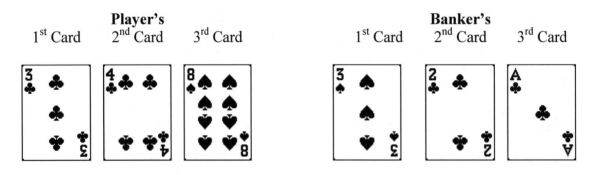

Player's
1st Card   2nd Card   3rd Card

Banker's
1st Card   2nd Card   3rd Card

7. What is it about chemin de fer that makes it difficult for casino operators to offer the game in today's casinos?

8. Regarding baccarat, what is the primary advantage of the no commission modification that was first advanced in Sri Lanka?

9. What is the source of the casino advantage in no commission baccarat?

10. In the game known as _____, the punters are required to make draw and stand decisions.

11. What is the primary purpose of the commission box?

12. In chemin de fer, the punter who places the greatest wager on the player hand is known as the _____.
13. What is the chief advantage of differential betting?
14. What is the primary challenge associated with differential betting?
15. How does prepaid commission affect the use of the commission box?
16. In baccarat, which hand is completed first (i.e., player or banker)?
17. In baccarat, when a punter places a wager on the player hand and the hand (i.e., round) ends in a tie, is the bet lost?
18. Describe the any-pair side bet, including the payoff on a winning wager?

Chapter 13
Craps

What are the duties of the boxman?
What is the source of the casino advantage on don't pass wagers?
Are all throws of the dice either a come-out throw or a point throw?
How do come bets differ from place bets?
How is the maximum wager determined for don't pass odds bettors?
What are true odds and why are they so important in the game of craps?
What is a lay bet and how does the casino operator gain an advantage on these wagers?

Scope

While craps may be the most intimidating of all table games, after carefully reading this chapter, this will no longer be the case. No familiarity with the craps is required to navigate the material presented here. Although the game appears utterly chaotic, craps is actually one of the most organized of casino games. This is achieved through many tricks of the trade, which will all be revealed. A careful study of this material will provide you with sufficient knowledge to follow betting action on a live game. Moreover, the depth of coverage offers an opportunity to understand why specific rules, policies, and procedures are in effect.

Chapter Goals

- Describe the equipment and personnel needed to operate a craps table, including the specific job duties of the dealing and supervisory positions
- Define key terms and operating language central to any discussion of the game
- Review the outcome distribution of two, six-sided, fair dice
- Examine the craps layout and each of the many betting propositions, including the odds wagering process
- Explain how each bet is won and lost
- Describe how dealers are able to know which bets belong to whom
- Explain the basis of the all-important casino advantage on dice wagers
- Examine the folly of marketing by way of rule modifications

A Brief History of Craps

Craps also known as dice is played with two six-sided cubes, which comprise a pair of dice. That said, gamblers have been betting on the outcome of tossed cube-like objects for a very long time. The ancient Greeks actually cast six-sided heel bones salvaged from dead animals.[1] These early "dice" were known as astragali. The astragali were used for both gambling and religious purposes.[2] For example, the outcomes produced by tossing the astragli were interpreted as answers to questions put before the oracle.

Modern craps evolved from a dice game known as hazard, which dates to at least the 13th century.[3] While hazard became wildly popular in medieval Europe, it is thought to be of Arabic origin. In fact, the word hazard comes from the Arabic *al-zahr*, which means die (as in cube).[4] The rules of craps are similar in many ways to those of hazard. Craps may have taken its name from "crabs," a name for a throw/outcome in the game of hazard.[5] In fact, crabs described a throw resulting in 1-1 or 1-2, which form two of the three results known as *craps* in the modern version of the game (i.e., 2, 3, & 12).

From the early 1900s until the mid-1970s, craps was the most popular game of chance in the USA. In 1974, John Scarne wrote, "Craps, history's biggest and fastest-action gambling game, is undoubtedly the most widely played game of chance in the United States today; more money is won and lost at Craps every day than at any other form of gambling, with the exception of sports betting and betting on horse races."[6]

It is likely that both WWI and WWII fueled the popularity of craps in the 20th century. Craps provided an easy and exciting way for soldiers to entertain themselves during their downtime in the base camps. A pair of dice was easily transported in a soldier's pocket, and there were always plenty of willing bettors looking for a distraction from the war. After WWII, the USA was flooded with craps-savvy veterans.

Although gambling became legal in Nevada in 1931, records of the type and number of games in each casino were not maintained until decades later.[7] During this reporting void, only photographs served as records of game popularity. Photos from the 1930s and 1940s support the notion that craps was the dominant casino game of that era. Taken in the 1940s, Photograph 13.1 is a picture of the Last Frontier Casino on the Las Vegas Strip. The casino boasts three craps games, one roulette wheel, and one blackjack game.

---

[1] Mlodinov, L. (2009). *The drunkard's walk: How randomness rules our lives*, p. 27. New York: Random House.
[2] Ibid.
[3] hazard. (2011). In *Encyclopædia Britannica*. Retrieved from http://www.britannica.com/EBchecked/topic/257915/hazard.
[4] Ibid.
[5] Ibid.
[6] Scarne, J. (1974). *Scarne's New Complete Guide to Gambling*, p. 259. New York: Simon & Schuster.
[7] Assembly Bill 98 was the enabling legislation that legalized gambling in Nevada. It was signed into law on March 19, 1931, signaling the birth of modern casino gambling.

Photograph 13.1. Interior of the Last Frontier on the Las Vegas Strip (circa 1945).

As with all games, the popularity eventually wanes. Craps is no exception. Although still a significant source of table game revenue in US casinos, the number of craps games has fallen well behind the number of blackjack tables. Craps games are virtually non-existent in the balance of the world's casinos. Hopefully, craps will survive, as there is nothing quite like the excitement of a hot roll on a craps game. Moreover, this excitement is broadcast throughout the casino, making undeniable contributions to the overall atmosphere.

The Intimidation Factor

The nature of the game itself may have contributed to its decline in popularity. Craps is not the most approachable game, especially for a new player. Typically, you have several people, mostly men, huddled over a table, with some cheering and others cursing the outcome of each toss of the dice. All an approaching player would see is the backs of the players. There are no smiling dealers to greet new players. This is not an environment conducive to questions such as how do you play? Even for those brave enough to ask such a question would be met with little satisfaction. That is, on a busy craps game, there is precious little time for the dealers to explain the game to a novice.

Gamblers interested in learning how to play craps are left with options such as asking for instruction from a friend who is familiar with the game. For this approach to work, an interested player must know someone who is familiar with craps, willing to instruct him, and available to accompany him to the game. Alternatively, some casinos do offer free craps lessons along with low-stakes craps games. The low-stakes games allow novice players a chance to become familiar with craps, before risking any substantial sums of money. Most people are not comfortable risking money on unfamiliar and confusing propositions of any kind.

While craps can certainly intimidate a novice player, the game can be just as daunting to casino executives who have never dealt the game. Whether you are a gaming industry executive, aspiring executive, or simply an interested reader, this chapter will provide you with in-depth knowledge of how the game is played, produced, and managed. Although it is certainly fast-paced and confusing at first blush, it is also a fascinating and surprisingly organized game.

Equipment

Dice tables typically measure 10-, 12- and 14-feet in length. There is also a one-man 6½-foot table that is occasionally found in the smaller casinos in Northern Nevada. The dice are ordered from a manufacturer and usually come in sets of five or six. The casino operator will specify the number of dice per set and whether each set is assigned a common serial number.[8] If so, all dice in a given set will have the same serial number stamped on one face of each die. A player who tosses the dice is known as a shooter. Prior to her first toss, the shooter will select two dice from the set of five or six. A rubber dice bowl is used to store the remaining dice, keeping them separated from the dice in action.

The felt layout and payoff odds will vary by both casino and jurisdiction. The most common differences in payoff odds occur on the number 12 in the *field* wager and the proposition bets on the numbers 2, 3, 11, and 12. These differences in payoff odds are most often due to competitive pressures or marketing philosophies. This topic will be discussed further in a subsequent section of this chapter.

Personnel

The group of dealers required to operate a craps game is known as a crew, which is usually comprised of four dealers. One of these four dealers is always on a 20-minute break. That is, a crew of four allows each dealer to work on the game for one hour, before taking a 20-minute break. When a dealer returns from a break he will usually relieve the *stickman*, who will then relieve the *base dealer* who is due for his break. Figure 13.1 provides an illustration of a craps table and the location of each dealing position. Additionally, an individual craps game will often be assigned a supervisor known as a *boxman*. Although the title of the position would imply otherwise, there are certainly female boxmen. The same is true for stickman. These are both job titles which were created in a less-inclusive era, yet they remain as terms of the trade.

---

[8] Other forms of dice security include (1) having a letter engraved on the back of one spot, which can be verified by looking through the die from the opposite side of the keyed spot. (2) ultraviolet marking; and (3) pit managers who intentionally scratch the surface of the dice with an identifying marks of their own.

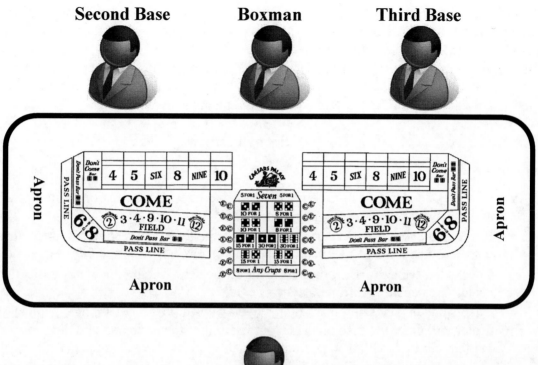

Figure 13.1. Craps Table Personnel: Dealer & Boxman Locations.

In the never-ending quest to reduce labor costs, many casino operators have eliminated the boxman position. However, this decision is not without consequences. The boxman plays an important role in the operation of a craps game. Cost savings from the elimination of this position should be weighed against the costs incurred from the loss in supervision provided by the boxman. This argument will become clear when the specific duties of the boxman are described in a subsequent section of this chapter.

In some cases, a fifth dealer is added to the crew in lieu of the boxman. This new position is referred to as "sitting bank," as this dealer is not officially a boxman and has no supervisorial duties. When sitting bank, the dealer is responsible for counting buy-ins received from players, game protection, and oversight of payouts. A dealer sitting bank is not responsible for oversight of dealing procedures, but will assist dealers in the calculation of difficult payoffs. They wear a dealer uniform and receive a full share of the dealers' tips (a.k.a. tokes). To accommodate the fifth dealer, all dealers on the crew work 80 minutes, before taking a 20-minute break.

As labeled in Figure 13.1, each dealing position is referred to by a specific name. The dealer who handles the dice and proposition box wagers is known as the stickman.[9] The boxman sits facing the stickman on the opposite side of the table. The dealer position to the boxman's right is referred to as 2nd base. The dealing position to the boxman's left is called 3rd base. The area between the pass line and the edge of the table is known the Apron, although "Apron" is not printed on an actual craps layout.

Job Duties by Position

Boxman

- Observes all actions on the game. Responsible for game protection matters, such as identifying past-posters and dice scooters.[10]
- Responsible for customer service, usually in the form of assisting players with questions about the game or correct betting increments for a specific wager.
- Checks the accuracy of all payoffs made by dealers. The boxman may assist the dealer in calculating difficult payoffs.
- Counts and deposits buy-ins. When players buy-in (i.e., buy gaming cheques), the dealer will place the cash on the layout in front of the boxman, who then counts it in plain view. He will then instruct the dealer to give the player cheques in the amount of the buy-in. Finally, the boxman will deposit the player's cash buy-in in the game's drop box (hence the name *box*man).
- Mediate and resolve disputes. The boxman may request assistance from a supervisor such as a dice floorman or a pit manager, if the dispute involves a significant amount of money.
- Responsible for dice integrity.
  - Ensures that the dice used in the game are the same dice that were verified at the beginning of the shift.
  - Observes whether the shooter's hand is open or closed before the shooter picks up the dice. It should be open.
  - Observes whether the shooter's hands are open or closed after she throws the dice. They should be open. The boxman must verify that shooters are not somehow introducing their own dice into the game. For example, when a shooter selects the dice, her hand obscures them from view, affording her an opportunity to substitute her own dice. It is the boxman's responsibility to ensure that the shooter throws the casino's dice.
  - Verify dice that have tumbled off of the game, before the dice are reintroduced into the game. For example, when dice fly off the game and on to the casino floor, they are first handed to the boxman for verification before they are thrown again. At a minimum, the serial number on the die/dice would be verified.

---

[9] Although the stickman is depicted facing the reader in Figure 13.1, he would be facing the game when dealing.

[10] Past-posting describes a cheating technique whereby a wager is placed after an outcome has occurred. For example, placing a Don't Pass wager after the come-out throw. Such a wager would have a positive expected value for the player, and represents a clear violation of the rules. *Dice scooters* refers to players accomplished at tossing the dice in a way that limits the possible outcomes. This is also not permitted.

- Shares responsibility with the base dealer for all occurrences on what is referred to as "his end" of the game. In terms of accountability, each end of a dice game has double coverage. The stickman is responsible for the end opposite of the shooter. The boxman is accountable for the end from which the dice are thrown. For example, referencing Figure 13.1., if a player to the immediate right of the stickman is the shooter, the dice must be thrown to the opposite or furthest end of the table. That is, the shooter will be throwing the dice in the direction of the second base dealer. In this case, the second base dealer and the stickman would be responsible for the same end of the game, while the boxman and the third base dealer would be responsible for the third base end of the game.

Stickman

- Runs the game and controls the speed of the game. Ensures the base dealers have completed the tasks of paying winning wagers and collecting losing bets before allowing the game to continue.
- Responsible for all events on the end of the game opposite of the shooter.
- Announces the outcome of the shooter's throw for all to hear.
- Responsible for all proposition box wagers. These wagers will be explained in detail in a subsequent section of this chapter.

Base Dealers

- Collect losing bets and pay winning bets on their respective ends of the table. Base dealers are instructed to keep their eyes on their end of the layout. They *listen* for the call of the outcome from the stickman, to determine which bets to pay and which bets to take. Therefore, they do not need to *look* at the stickman or the dice to perform their pay, take, and game protection duties. Because of this protocol, numbers which can be mistaken for one another are announced in a particular way. This is done to avoid misunderstandings by the base dealers. For example, a throw of 11 is announced by the stickman as "yo-leven," to clearly differentiate it from "seven." "Five, fever five" and "nine, nina" are also used by the stickman to differentiate throws of five and nine.

Overview of the Game

At first glance, a busy dice game is likely to appear impossibly chaotic, confusing, and disorganized. While this take on the game is understandable, the operation of craps actually relies on organization. This will become clear with additional knowledge of how the game is played and dealt.

Players can oppose one another on most wagers in craps. For example, an outcome of seven can result in a win for a *pass line* bettor, while simultaneously resulting in a loss for a *don't pass* bettor. These nearly opposite wagers represent the most basic bets, which will be described in subsequent sections of the chapter.

In dice, every outcome or number that can be thrown has a name. That is, 7 and 11 are known as *naturals*; 2, 3, & 12 are called *craps*; with the remainder of the possibilities known as *points* (i.e., 4, 5, 6, 8, 9, & 10). Additionally, every throw has a name. Each throw is either a *come-out* throw or a *point throw*. These terms will be described in a subsequent section of this chapter.

Before going any further into the terminology-heavy game of craps, let's review the outcome distribution of two dice. A basic understanding of this outcome distribution will be most helpful in gaining an overall understanding of the game. Every bet in craps was created by way of the outcome distribution. Table 13.1 lists all possible outcomes resulting from a toss of two fair dice.

Table 13.1
Outcome Distribution Associated with a
Toss of Two, Fair, Six-sided Dice

#s	Permutations of Outcomes						# of Ways
2	1,1						1
3	1,2	2,1					2
4	1,3	3,1	2,2				3
5	1,4	4,1	2,3	3,2			4
6	1,5	5,1	2,4	4,2	3,3		5
7	1,6	6,1	2,5	5,2	3,4	4,3	6
8	2,6	6,2	3,5	5,3	4,4		5
9	3,6	6,3	4,5	5,4			4
10	4,6	6,4	5,5				3
11	5,6	6,5					2
12	6,6						1
							36

When reviewing the permutations listed in Table 13.1, it may be helpful to imagine that one die is red and one die is blue. For example, the outcome of "2,4" is different from "4,2", because in "2,4", the red die is "2", while in "4,2", the red die is "4". Also, notice that the outcome of 7 lies at the center of the distribution. This number is all-important to the game of craps. While there are six ways to throw a 7, there is only one way to throw either a 2 or a 12.

In total, there are 36 possible outcomes. Therefore, the probability of throwing any outcome is computed by dividing the number of ways to make it by the total number of possible outcomes. For example, the probability of throwing a 7 is 0.167 (i.e., 6 ÷ 36). Next, we will describe how each bet works.

The Pass Line Wager

At the heart of the game is the pass line bet. It represents the basis of all dice bets. All other bets are essentially side bets made possible by a pass line bettor throwing the dice in pursuit of a decision.[11]

When a pass line wager is made, the bettor is an instant winner, if the first throw of the dice (i.e., the come-out throw) results in either a 7 or an 11. A pass line wager is an instant loser if the come-out throw results in a 2, 3, or 12. If neither a natural (7 or 11) nor craps (2, 3, or 12) is tossed on the come-out throw, then the throw must have resulted in a point (4, 5, 6, 8, 9, or 10). If in fact the come-out throw results in a point, the pass line bettor wins if that same point is thrown a second time, before the shooter throws a 7. Conversely, the pass line bettor loses if the shooter throws a 7 before throwing the point number a second time. All winning pass line wagers are paid at a rate of one to one.

Whether a pass line bet wins or loses, the outcome is known as a *decision*. A pass line decision is analogous to a reset button on a video game. That is, the craps game is reset for the pass line bettor, and a new game begins. The throw following a pass line decision is known as the come-out throw, with "come-out" signifying the beginning of a new game.

The following bullet points provide a review of the pass line decision criteria.

- The pass line bet **wins** if: (1) the come-out throw results in a natural, or (2) the come-out throw results in a point, which is thrown a second time before the shooter throws a 7.

- The pass line bet **loses** if: (1) the come-out throw results in craps, or (2) the come-out throw results in a point, which is *not* thrown a second time before the shooter throws a 7. That is, the shooter throws a 7, before throwing the point a second time.

These fairly simple decision criteria can be expressed mathematically. It is helpful to review these calculations, as they will provide a much deeper understanding of the game. Table 13.2 is provided to summarize the calculation of the player's disadvantage on pass line wagers.

As shown in Table 13.2, the player disadvantage on a pass line wager is expressed as -0.0141414, or -1.414% (rounded). Remember from Table 13.1, when two fair dice are tossed, there are 36 discrete outcomes. Assuming a player makes 36 one-unit wagers, the player would expect to lose only 0.509 of one unit, on average.[12] That is, 36 x -1.414% = -0.509. This is a slim margin.

---

[11] *Decision* refers to an outcome, i.e., a win or a loss.
[12] When discussing gaming math, *unit* is a term used to represent any constant-value wager.

Table 13.2
Computation of the Player Disadvantage on Pass Line Wagers

Come-out Throws	Contribution of Each Outcome to Player Disadvantage	
Instant Win/Loss:		
2	.... 1/36 x -1 =	-0.0277778
3	.... 2/36 x -1 =	-0.0555556
7	.... 6/36 x 1 =	+0.1666667
11	.... 2/36 x 1 =	+0.0555556
12	.... 1/36 x -1 =	-0.0277778
Points:		
4	(3/36 x (1/3 x 1)) + (3/36 x (2/3 x -1)) =	-0.0277778
5	(4/36 x (4/10 x 1)) + (4/36 x (6/10 x -1)) =	-0.0222222
6	(5/36 x (5/11 x 1)) + (5/36 x (6/11 x -1)) =	-0.0126263
8	(5/36 x (5/11 x 1)) + (5/36 x (6/11 x -1)) =	-0.0126263
9	(4/36 x (4/10 x 1)) + (4/36 x (6/10 x -1)) =	-0.0222222
10	(3/36 x (1/3 x 1)) + (3/36 x (2/3 x -1)) =	-0.0277778
	Player Disadvantage =	-0.0141414

The contents of Table 13.2 might be a little confusing, at first glance. Let's work through a couple of examples to clarify these computations. Assume the come-out throw is a 2. There is a 1 in 36 chance of throwing a 2, hence the "1/36" term. If a 2 is thrown on the come-out throw, the pass line bettor loses the unit he wagered, hence the "-1" term. All of the calculations related to the come-out throws which result in an instant win or loss are interpreted this way. For example, there is a 6 in 36 chance that a 7 will be thrown. If it is, then the player will win one unit.

Hopefully, that wasn't too bad. Now let's tackle a point. The calculation is a little more complicated, when the come-out throw is a point. If the come-out throw is a point number, then only two numbers matter to the pass line bettor; the point number that was thrown and 7. Let's assume the shooter throws a 4 on the come-out throw. There is a 3 in 36 chance of throwing a 4, hence the "3/36" term. On the throws that follow, only the 4 or 7 will produce a decision. From Table 13.1, there are three ways to throw a 4 and there are six ways to throw a 7. So, in total, there are nine ways in which a decision can occur. Of these nine ways, three, or 3/9[ths] of the ways, represent wins for the pass line bettor, while six, or 6/9[ths] of the ways, represent losses for the pass line bettor. Of course, 3/9[ths] can be reduced to 1/3rd and 6/9[ths] can be reduced to 2/3[rds]. Consider Table 13.3 for a breakdown of the line from Table 13.2, representing a come-out throw of 4.

Table 13.3
Breakout of Table 13.2 Content: Come-out Throw of 4

Chance of Throwing a 4 on Come-out Throw & Winning		Chance of Throwing a 4 on Come-out Throw & Losing		Contribution to Player Disadvantage
(3/36 x (1/3 x 1))	+	(3/36 x (2/3 x -1))	=	-0.0277778

Expression of the Casino Advantage

Notice form Table 13.3, the unit (i.e., "1") is expressed as a positive number in the part of the calculation representing a player win. The unit is expressed as "-1" in the middle column of Table 13.3, as this part of the calculation expresses a player loss. As you can see from Table 13.2, if a point is thrown on the come-out throw, the player's chances of losing the pass line wager will always be greater than her chances of winning it.

On most games, the casino advantage is earned on a per-hand basis, as in blackjack or baccarat. That is, a decision occurs after the hand. In roulette, a decision occurs after each spin, so the casino advantage is earned on a per-spin basis. Craps is a little different.

If the come-out throw results in a point, throws will continue until either a 7 or the established point is thrown. One of these numbers must be thrown to reach a decision (i.e., settle the wager). However, a shooter may throw several numbers before a decision occurs. Consequently, when discussing craps, the casino advantage is usually referred to on a per-decision basis, as opposed to a per-hand basis.

To highlight the implications of this difference, consider the following decision intervals. A pass line bet will span an average of 3.38 throws before a decision is reached. Some bets in dice will always produce a decision in a single throw, while others require an average of 5.68 throws to produce a decision. This can cause considerable confusion when deciding on a casino advantage for use in the player tracking system. It makes more sense to express the casino advantage on a per-throw basis. For example, the pass line wager has a casino advantage per throw of 0.419%, or 0.00419 (i.e., 0.01414 ÷ 3.376 throws = 0.00419).[13]

The Don't Pass Wager

As previously stated, most craps wagers have what is referred to as an opposing wager. For example, the pass line and don't pass bets would be considered opposing wagers. However, "opposing" is used in the general sense. If the don't pass bettor were to win whenever the pass line bettor lost, the don't pass bettor would in effect be in the same position as the casino. That is, the don't pass bettor would have an advantage. To create a casino advantage on don't pass wagers, the 12 is "barred." This means that when a 12 is thrown, the pass line bettor loses, but the don't pass bettor ties (i.e., pushes). To clarify, Table 13.4 summarizes the decisions for each of the two bets, in all possible scenarios.

Table 13.4
Decisions by Event: Pass Line Bet vs. Don't Pass Bet

Event	Pass Line Bet	Don't Pass Bet
7 or 11 tossed on the come-out throw	Wins	Loses
2 or 3 tossed on the come-out throw	Loses	Wins
12 tossed on the come-out throw	Loses	**Pushes**
Established point is thrown before a 7	Wins	Loses
7 is thrown before the established point	Loses	Wins

---

[13] "0.01414" comes from Table 13.2; however, in this example it represents the *casino* advantage, hence the sign reversal (i.e., from "-0.01414").

Terminology

To this point, a few terms central to the game of craps have been defined within the limited context of examples. This section further defines these terms along with other key terms, several of which are used extensively in subsequent sections of this chapter.

- **Throw:** A single toss of the dice.
- **Roll:** (1) Includes all throws between pass line decisions. A roll could contain any number of throws. (2) Sometimes used in lieu of *throw*.
- **Decision:** The outcome of bet, i.e., a win, loss, or tie. A pass line decision can occur after one throw when the come-out throw is a natural or craps number, or it can occur after multiple throws when a point is established on the come-out throw.
- **Hand:** (1) Includes all throws from a shooter before she loses the dice to the next shooter. For example, given an established point, a pass line bettor would lose the dice after throwing a seven. A hand could be as brief as two throws or it could include multiple throws or rolls/decisions. For example, a shooter could make several points before losing the dice. (2) Hand is also sometimes referred to as a roll.
- **Sequence:** (1) The rolls within a hand. (2) The throws between decisions.
- **Seven-out:** The act of throwing a seven before throwing an established point. For a pass line bettor, this would result in a loss.
- **Come-Out Throw (or Roll):** The throw immediately following a pass line decision.
- **Right bettors:** One of two classifications of bettors, i.e., *right bettors* and *wrong bettors*. Right bettors are those who bet on the pass line and make wagers such as come bets, buy bets, put bets, and place bets.[14] With the exception of the come-out throw, a seven will cause the right bettor's wagers to lose.
- **Wrong bettors:** One of two classifications of bettors, i.e., *right bettors* and *wrong bettors*. Wrong bettors are those who bet on the don't pass and make wagers such as don't come bets, place bets to lose, and lay bets.[15] With the exception of the come-out throw, a seven will cause the wrong bettor's wagers to win.
- **Off on the Come-Out:** A default option that prevents bets surviving a pass line decision to be classified as ineligible for a decision on the next come-out throw. For example, players might have come bets with odds or place bets that remain in play after a point is made. If these bets were to remain in play and a seven were tossed on the ensuing come-out throw, the bets would lose. However, the same seven would cause a pass line bet to win. On a dice game, it is assumed that place bets, buy bets, and the odds portion of come bets are off on the come-out throw, unless the bettor requests otherwise. This rule allows all right bettors on the game to cheer/hope for the same result. That is, if these bets are off, tossing a seven (or any other number) on the come-out throw will have no effect on them.

---

[14] Come bets, buy bets, put bets, and place bets will all be defined in subsequent sections of the chapter.
[15] Both *place bets to lose* and *lay bets* will be defined in subsequent sections of this chapter.

Who Shoots the Dice?

When a game opens, the player on the stickman's immediate left is offered the dice, as the first shooter of the new game. In order to shoot the dice, the player must have an interest in the outcome of the roll. That is, the shooter is required to place a bet on either the pass line or the don't pass. In some casinos, players who only place a don't pass wager are not permitted to shoot. However, this is not the typical case.

The shooter controls the dice until she fails to make a point. This is called a seven-out. Once this occurs, the dice are passed in a clockwise direction to the next eligible player. This player would have the option to shoot or pass the dice to the next eligible player on the game. Not all players wish to shoot.

While the dice shooting etiquette we have described here is well established, some players choose not to follow all aspects of it. For example, some shooters choose not to continue until they seven-out, and the casino operators cannot force them to do so. The following bullet points describe problematic situations that arise when a shooter quits before a seven-out:

- **A don't pass shooter who makes his point**. For example, consider the shooter who makes a wager on the don't pass and tosses an eight on the come-out throw. If this shooter throws a second eight before throwing a seven, he would make the point, but lose his bet. Because he made the point (i.e., eight), he would retain control of the dice. That is, he lost his bet, but did not seven-out. This shooter cannot be forced to make another wager and continue to shoot until producing a seven-out. He can choose to leave the game or pass the dice to the next player. However, according to etiquette, it is still his roll. Other players on the game may not wish to finish the existing/previous shooter's roll. Many gamblers are superstitious. This is why some operators do not allow don't pass bettors to shoot.
- **A pass line shooter who makes his point and leaves the game.** For example, consider the shooter who tosses a six on the come-out throw and throws a second six before throwing a seven. This shooter has made his point (i.e., 6) and won his pass line bet. Choosing not to place another wager, he leaves the game. According to etiquette, this shooter still controls the dice. Although, he cannot be forced to continue, his mid-roll departure from the game may not be appreciated by the remaining players.
- **A pass line shooter who establishes a point, surrenders his bet, and leaves the game.** Although it is rare for a shooter to leave the game prior to a decision on his wager, it does occur. When this happens, of course, the shooter's roll is not completed.

When shooters fail to complete a roll, bets are often left on the game in need of a decision. One remedy is to let the next eligible shooter finish the roll. This player would shoot the dice until a seven-out occurs. In this case, the fill-in shooter would be permitted to shoot their own hand, before the dice rotate to the next eligible shooter. Although other issues can arise from incomplete rolls, we must limit our coverage to the listed items.

Come-Out Throw

Remember, in craps, every throw is either a point throw or a come-out throw. Anyone who walks up to a live game would be able to tell which type of throw is coming next, by looking at the *dice puck*. The dice puck is a double-sided marker with "OFF" printed on one side and "ON" printed on the other side. "OFF" is printed in white capital letters on a black background, and "ON" is printed in black capital letters against a white background (See Figure 13.2).

Figure 13.2. Both Sides of a Dice Puck (a.k.a. a Button or Marker).

When the upcoming throw is a come-out throw, the base dealers will display the off-side of the puck and place it in the betting box labeled, "Don't Come" (See Figure 13.3). Anyone looking at the snapshot illustrated in Figure 13.3 would be able to conclude that the next throw is a come-out throw. Therefore, the pass line bet "A" would win if the shooter were to throw a natural and it would lose if she were to throw craps. The don't pass bet "B" would win if the next throw were a 2 or 3, and lose if the next roll were a 7 or 11. Of course, bet "B" would push if the next roll were a 12.

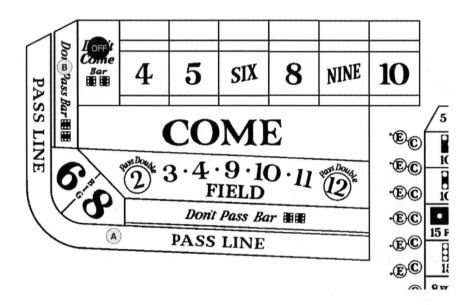

Figure 13.3. Dice Puck Placed to Indicate an Upcoming Come-Out Throw.

In Figure 13.4, the come-out throw was a six. Consequently, the base dealer has displayed the puck such that "ON" is facing up and placed it in the six betting box. This puck placement indicates the win-loss rules for bets "A" and "B," on the next throw.

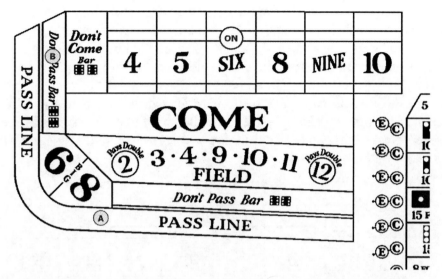

Figure 13.4. Dice Puck Placed to Indicate an Upcoming Point Throw.

Come and Don't Come Bets

If craps only allowed players to bet on the pass line, bettors would have to wait an average of 3.376 throws for a decision. To provide additional betting opportunities, the come and don't come wagers were created. A come bet operates exactly like a pass line bet. That is, it wins if the next throw is a 7 or 11, and it loses if the next throw is a 2, 3, or 12. If a point is thrown, the come bet is moved to that number. It wins if that number is thrown before the shooter throws a seven and it loses if the converse occurs.

In Figure 13.5, the bet labeled "C" is a come bet. This bet will only reside in this location for one throw. If a natural is thrown, the bet will be paid at a rate of one to one. If craps is thrown, the bet will lose. If a point is thrown, the bet will be moved by the dealer to the corresponding point box.

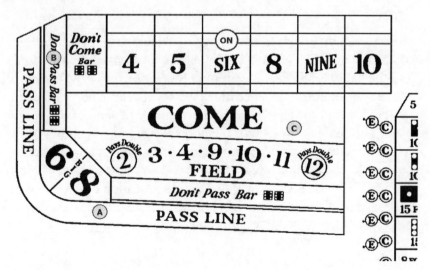

Figure 13.5. Illustration of the Initial Location of a Come Bet.

Let's work through an example in which come bet "C" makes its way to a point box. Working from the snapshot in Figure 13.5, assume the next throw is a nine. Figure 13.6 illustrates the new location of bet "C," resulting from the throw of nine. Notice that the puck resides on the point number six, which indicates the throw required for pass line bettors to win. However, the point number to which come bet "C" was moved (i.e., nine) indicates the throw required for that bet to win. The snapshot depicted in Figure 13.6 indicates the following conditions: A six must be thrown before a seven for bet "A" to win; a seven must be thrown before a six for bet "B" to win; and a nine must be thrown before a seven for bet "C" to win.

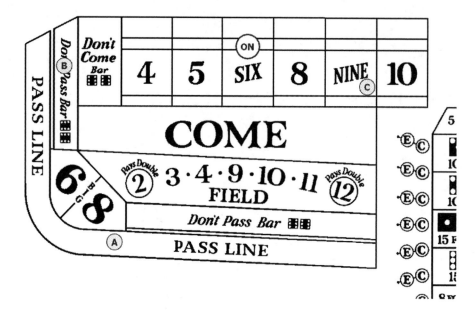

Figure 13.6. Final Location of Come Bet "C".

Bet Placement

Dealers use a bet location system to keep track of which come bets belong to individual players. Dealers arrange the come bets such that the location of the bets in the betting box corresponds to the bettor's physical location on the perimeter of the game. That is, the location of the player on the game determines where his come bet is placed in the box. A full-sized crap table can accommodate eight players at each end of the game. On the second-base end, the dealer will number the players from one to eight, in a clockwise direction. On the third-base end, the positions of the players are numbered in a counterclockwise direction. Figure 13.7 illustrates the relationship between the location of bettor "1" on the 2nd-base end of the game and the location of his come bet within the *NINE* point box. Notice that the come bet is placed inside the box, as opposed to on the lines. This placement identifies the wager as a come bet.

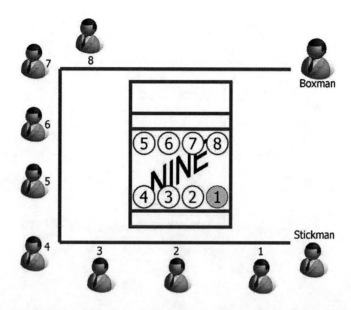

Figure 13.7. The Relationship Between Come Bet Location & Player Location.

Don't Come Bet

Just as the don't pass opposes the pass line, the don't come opposes the come. In Figure 13.8, bet "D" is a don't come bet belonging to the player standing to the immediate right of the second base dealer. It will reside in that spot for only one throw. If that throw is a two or three, the bet wins. If the throw is a 12, the bet will push. If the throw is a point, the dealer will move the bet to the area behind the point. The dealer will place the bet in a location that corresponds to the bettor's position at the table. For example, let's assume a five is thrown. Figure 13.9 illustrates where the dealer would locate the bettor's don't come wager within the betting box.

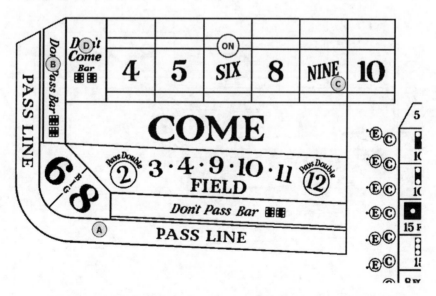

Figure 13.8. Initial Location of Don't Come Bet "D".

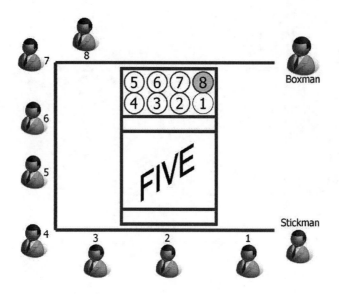

Figure 13.9. Final Location of Don't Come Bet "D".

From Figure 13.10, we know the following:

- Bet "A" is a pass line bet belonging to the player standing at position 3. It wins if a six is thrown before a seven.
- Bet "B" is a don't pass bet belonging to the player standing at position 8. It wins if a seven is thrown before a six.
- Bet "C" is a come bet belonging to the player standing at position 1. It wins if a nine is thrown before a seven.
- Bet "D" is a don't come bet belonging to the player standing in position 8. It will win is a seven in thrown before a five.

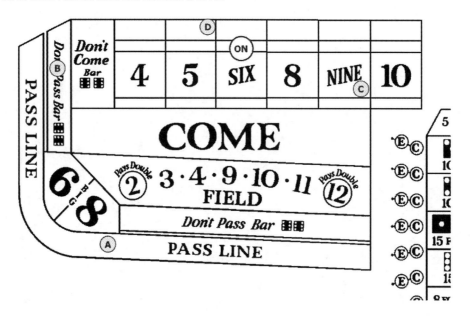

Figure 13.10. Illustration of Various Bet Locations: Point of Six.

Odds on Pass Line Bets

The odds bet is one of the earliest examples of table game marketing by way of price. It is the only dice bet with no casino advantage. Before explaining how the odds bet works, we must first explain what those in gaming refer to as true odds. [16]

True odds represent the payoff on a winning wager that would result in neither a casino advantage nor a casino disadvantage. For example, let's assume a player wagers that a four will be thrown before a seven. The only outcomes capable of producing a decision are the four and the seven. A four can be thrown thee different ways, while a seven can be thrown six different ways. Consequently, there are nine outcomes (i.e., 3 + 6) capable of producing a decision on this wager. If this wager were placed nine times, we would expect the bettor to win three times and lose six times. Of course, we can reduce 3/9 to 1/3, and 6/9 to 2/3. Therefore, we would expect the bettor to win one of every three wagers. Assuming this bet is paid at a rate of one to one, how much would the bettor be paid, if there were no casino advantage on this wager? The answer is two units.

Continuing the previous example, every time the bettor wins one wager, he can expect to lose two others. Therefore, the bettor would have to be paid at a rate of two to one to break even on the bet (in the long-run). That is, when he wins, his wealth is increased by two units, but every time he wins he must cover two losses of one unit each. Table 13.5 lists the true odds for each point number on the craps game.

Table 13.5
True Odds Schedule for All Point Numbers

Points	# of Ways for the Player to Lose	# of Ways for the Player to Win	Total # of Ways to Produce a Decision	Probability of Loss	Probability of Win	True Odds[a]
4	6	3	9	6/9	3/9	2:1
5	6	4	10	6/10	4/10	3:2
6	6	5	11	6/11	5/11	6:5
8	6	5	11	6/11	5/11	6:5
9	6	4	10	6/10	4/10	3:2
10	6	3	9	6/9	3/9	2:1

Note: [a] True odds represent the payoff odds on a winning odds wager. True odds are the odds against throwing the point before throwing a seven.

At this point, you may be wondering why the casino operator would offer a bet with no house advantage. The catch is that the player must first make a pass line bet, before making an odds wager. That is, players are not permitted to make an odds wager without making a pass line bet

---

[16] In craps, "true odds" represent the odds against an event occurring. Therefore, true odds represent the payoff odds on winning wagers.

When a casino operator offers double odds (i.e., 2x odds) its means that the player is permitted to make an odds wager that is two times as great as his pass line wager. Originally, the odds bet was designed to encourage greater pass line wagers; however, it is not likely to have achieved the intended effect. In fact, a knowledgeable player would bet less of his available funds on the pass line, in order to maximize his odds wager. That is, there is no incentive for a player to wager his bankroll on a bet that carries a casino advantage, especially when he can wager it on a bet that has none. In spite of its failure to achieve its stated objective, the odds bet remains. Players expect casino operators to offer odds bets. In fact, operators are often pressured to increase the allowable odds bet multiple, to keep pace with their competitors.

It is important to note that the odds bet can only be made after a point is established. From the layout illustrated in Figure 13.11, we can determine the following information related to the odds wager:

- The come-out throw was a six.
- Bet "E" is an odds bet. The amount of bet "E" is equal to or greater than that of "A." "E" is most likely some multiple of "A." For example, "E" might be two times that of "A" (i.e., 2x odds).
- If the point (i.e., six) is thrown before a seven, bet "A" will be paid 1 to 1, but bet "E" will be paid 6 to 5. Per Table 13.5, a winning odds bet with a point of six pays 6 to 5.
- Both bets "A" and "E" will lose if the shooter throws a seven before throwing a six.

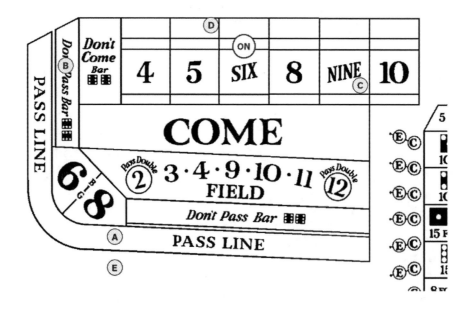

Figure 13.11. Illustration of Odds Bet "E" behind Pass Line Wager "A".

Since there is no casino advantage on the odds bet, the casino operators frequently allow players to increase their odds wagers such that winning bets can be paid with one denomination of cheques. This prevents dealers from awkward and slow payoffs. Operators do not want to the slow the game down for a bet with no house edge.

On a craps game offering double odds, players are permitted to make an odds wager up to two times that of their pass line bet. However, when the point is six or eight, players are permitted to take up to 2.5x odds, on a double-odds game. This is permitted in order to maintain the pace of the game. Otherwise, dealers would have to make cumbersome payoffs on certain odds wagers. For example, a player wagering $10 on the pass line with six as the point would be permitted to make a maximum odds wager of $20 (assuming 2x odds). If the shooter were to make the point, the odds bet would be paid $24. In this case, operators allow players to wager $25 in odds (i.e., 2.5x the pass line bet). This makes the payoff on a winning odds bet equal to $30, which is both easier and faster for the dealer.

The amount that can be wagered in the odds position is determined by casino policy. The payoff on a winning odds bet is based on the probability of making the point. The chance of making a point of six is considerably greater than making a point of four. Consequently, a winning odds bet with a point of four pays 2:1, but if the point were six, it would only pay 6:5 (i.e., 1.2:1). In both cases, the payoffs reflect what is known as true odds.

Many operators now offer 3/4/5x odds. That is, when the point is four or ten, the bettor can take 3x odds. When the point is five or nine, the bettor can take 4x odds. If the point is six or eight, the bettor can take 5x odds. A player taking maximum odds will always be paid six units when the bet wins. Use the content of Table 13.5 to test this claim of a constant six-unit payoff. Assume a pass line bet of $100.

The following bullet points provide a review of the rules governing odds bets for pass line bettors:

- To place an odds wager, the player must have a pass line wager.
- A point must be established before placing an odds bet.
- The odds multiple offered to the players is determined by management (i.e., 2x, 3x, 3/4/5x, etc.).
- The odds bet payoff is based on the probability of making the established point.
    - For a point of 4 or 10, the odds bet payoff is 2 to 1.
    - For a point of 5 or 9, the odds bet payoff is 3 to 2.
    - For a point of 6 or 8, the odds bet payoff is 6 to 5.
- Because there is no casino advantage on an odds bet, and it is placed after a point has been established, the odds bet can be increased, decreased, or removed from the game at any time prior to a decision (i.e., on the established point).

Laying Odds

When the odds of losing the bet are greater than the odds of winning it, anyone wagering on such a bet is said to be *taking* odds.[17] For example, when a player makes a pass line

---

[17] When the odds *against* an event occurring are greater than the odds *for* the event occurring, a bettor is said to be *taking* odds.

bet and follows it with an odds bet, the player is said to be *taking odds*. When the odds of the bet winning are greater than the odds of the bet losing, the bettor is said to be *laying odds*. For example, don't pass bettors lay odds. Let's assume a player has made a don't pass bet and the point is four. At this point, the player lays an odds bet. The player can expect to win this bet two out of three times. Because the bet is more likely to win than lose, a winning odds bet paid at a rate of one to two (i.e, 1:2). This payoff rate is such that neither the casino nor the player has an advantage on the bet. This 1:2 rate is the opposite of the pass line bettor's payoff rate on a winning odds bet (i.e., 2:1). The reason for this it that the pass line bettor can expect to lose two of every three odds bets, with a point of four.

Don't pass bettors are permitted to lay odds for an amount equal to the payoff on an odds bet made by a pass line bettor (i.e., someone who is taking odds). For example, let's assume the point is four on a game that offers 2x odds. A player with a $100 pass line wager decides to take full odds for $200. If the bet wins, the odds portion of the wager would be paid 2 to 1, or $400. Therefore, in this situation, a don't pass odds bettor with a $100 don't pass bet would be permitted to lay $400 to win $200.

Don't pass bettors who lay odds will "heel" the odds bet as depicted in Figure 13.12. Assuming single odds, Figure 13.12 illustrates odds laid against a point of six or eight. The dealer would know this because the bettor has laid six units to win five. Alternatively, with a point of four or 10 and a bettor laying 2 to 1 would "bridge" the odds bet. This technique is depicted in Figure 13.13.

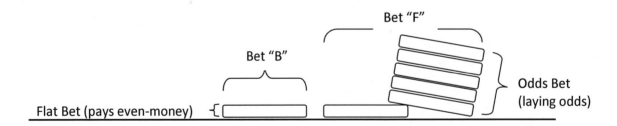

Figure 13.12. Don't Pass Bet "B" with Heeled Odds Bet "F".

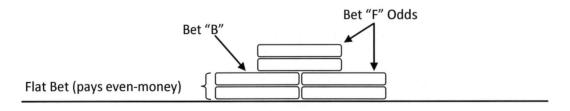

Figure 13.13. Illustration of Don't Pass Bet with Bridged Odds Bet.

Among other bets, Figure 13.14 illustrates the placement/location of a don't pass odds bet (see bet "F"). From the layout illustrated in Figure 13.14, we can determine the following information related to the odds wagers:

- The next throw is a point throw. We know this from the position of the puck. Remember, there must be a point before players can take or lay odds.
- Bets "A" and "E" belong to the player standing at position 3. Bet "A" is a pass line wager and bet "E" is the associated odds wager. The player has taken odds. For these bets to win, a six must be thrown before a seven. If this occurs, bet "A" will be paid even-money (i.e., 1:1), and odds bet "E" will be paid at a rate of 6 to 5.
- Bets "B" and "F" belong to the bettor standing to the second base dealer's immediate right (i.e., position 8). Bet "B" is a don't pass wager and bet "F" is the associated odds wager. This player has laid odds. Both bets "B" & "F" win if a seven is thrown before a six. Bet "B" will be paid even-money and bet "F" will be paid at a rate of 5 to 6.

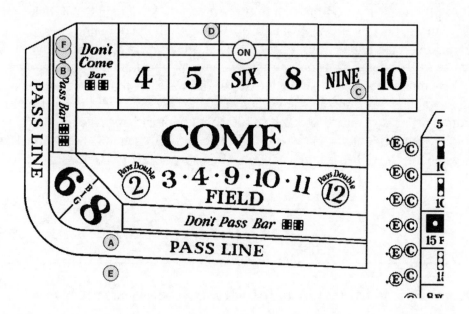

Figure 13.14. Illustration of Don't Pass Odds Bet "F".

The following bullets provide a review of the rules governing don't pass odds bets:

- To lay an odds wager, the player must have a don't pass wager.
- A point must be established before laying an odds bet.
- The odds multiple offered to the players is determined by management (i.e., 2x, 3x, 3/4/5x, etc.). In most cases, don't pass bettors are permitted to lay odds for an amount equal to the payoff on an odds bet made by a pass line bettor (i.e., someone who is taking odds).

- The don't pass odds bet payoff is based on the probability of making the established point.

  o For a point of 4 or 10, the odds bet payoff is 1 to 2.
  o For a point of 5 or 9, the odds bet payoff is 2 to 3.
  o For a point of 6 or 8, the odds bet payoff is 5 to 6.

- Because there is no casino advantage on an odds bet, and it is placed after a point has been established, the odds bet can be increased, decreased, or removed from the game at any time prior to a decision (i.e., on the established point).

Odds Bets on Come & Don't Come Wagers

Players can take or lay odds on come and don't come bets just as they can on pass line and don't pass bets. As previously stated, the come and don't come bets operate like the pass line and don't pass bets. The only difference is that the puck marks the number that must be thrown for the pass line bet to win, whereas the number on which the come bet resides marks the throw required for the come bet to win. Of course, throwing a seven will also produce a decision for both of these of bets. This all applies to don't pass and don't come wagers as well, subject to the differences in the outcomes/decisions. When making a pass line or don't pass odds bet, the players place the bet without the assistance of a dealer. This is not the case when making a come or don't come odds bet. These bets must be placed or set by the dealer. In this case, the player will place her odds bet on the table, in the amount she wishes to take or lay. She will then instruct the dealer accordingly. For example, if she has a $100 come bet that has made its way to the four, she might say, "$200 Odds on my four." The dealer will then take her cheques and stack the odds bet on top of her original come bet in a staggered or offset fashion (See Figure 13.15).

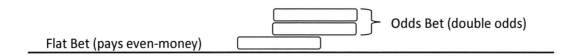

Figure 13.15. Illustration of an Offset Odds Bet Stacked on Top of a Come Bet.

A bettor who wishes to lay odds on a don't come bet will place the appropriate cheques on the table and instruct the dealer accordingly. The dealer will gather the cheques and move the odds bet next to the associated don't come bet, as depicted in Figure 13.16. The dealer will position the cheques comprising the don't pass odds bet as described in Figures 13.12 and 13.13.

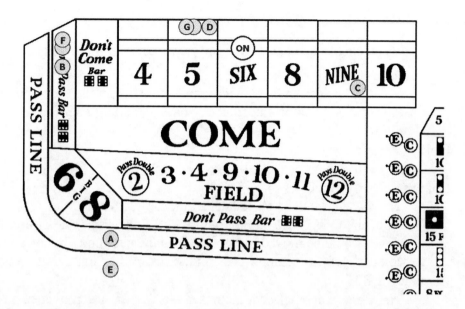

Figure 13.16. Depiction of Don't Come Odds Bet "G" Next to Don't Come Bet "D".

Self-Service Bets

Figure 13.17 illustrates the areas of the layout dedicated to self-service bets. Self-service bets are those that can be placed and positioned on the layout by the bettor, without assistance from a dealer. However, there are some important rules related to self-service bets. As an example, let's consider the following circumstances. Once a point is established, there is a greater chance that a seven will be thrown before the point. This holds for any of the point numbers. Consequently, after a point is established, a bet on the don't pass is more likely to win, while a pass line bet is more likely to lose. Given this reality, a bettor is certainly not permitted to remove a pass line wager or to place a don't pass wager after the point has been established. However, the bettor may increase a pass line wager or remove a don't pass wager at any time.

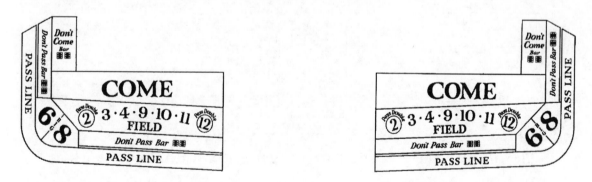

Figure 13.17. Areas of the Craps Layout Dedicated to Self-Service Bets.

Summary of Self-Service Bet Rules

All of the following bets can be placed by a player, without a dealer's assistance.

- Pass Line and Don't Pass
    - Don't pass bets can be placed immediately before the come-out throw.
    - Pass line bets can be placed at any time, including after the come-out throw.[18]
- Field[19]
    - A one-throw bet that can be placed at any time.
- Come and Don't Come
    - These wagers can be placed at any time. However, if wagered immediately before a come-out throw, the player's come or don't come wager would be moved by the dealer to the pass line (in the case of the come wager) or the don't pass (in the case of the don't come wager).
- Big 6 & Big 8[20]
    - These bets can be placed, increased, decreased, or removed at any time.

Bets Requiring Dealer Assistance

Unlike self-service wagers, dealer assisted wagers are placed in an area of the layout controlled entirely by the dealers. For these bets, players typically call the bet and toss the appropriate cheques to the dealer. The actual placement of the wager on the layout may only be executed by a dealer. Figure 13.18 illustrates all areas of the layout in which dealer assisted bets are placed. Any bet placed in the areas shown in Figure 13.18 must be put there by the hand of a dealer. This includes all come and don't come bets. While all come and don't come wagers are initially placed by the bettor, they are moved to point numbers by the dealer (i.e., should a point be thrown). This area of the layout is often referred to as "the boss's cash register."[21]

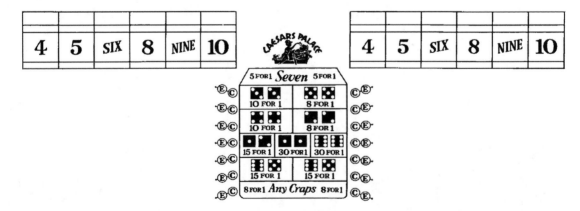

Figure 13.18. The Boss's Cash Register: Dealer Assisted Wagering Areas.

---

[18] However, it is in the player's best interest to place a pass line bet before the come-out throw, as placing it after the come-out throw greatly increases the casino advantage.

[19] This bet will be explained in a subsequent section of this chapter.

[20] This bet will be explained in a subsequent section of this chapter.

[21] Cutolo, R. & Taucer, V. (1993). *Craps: Dealing and Supervision*, p. 5. Las Vegas: Casino Creations, Inc.

Place Bets

Bettors who place pass line bets and come bets are not betting on specific numbers. While these bettors would certainly like to see a seven or an 11 on the come-out throw, they are equally happy if the shooter eventually makes the point. Place bets differ from pass line and come bets in that players can select and wager on a specific number. With a place bet, a player is betting that the selected point number will be thrown before a seven. Therefore, the only throws affecting the outcome of a place bet are seven and the point number the bettor selected.

Place bets require the assistance of the dealer. They are not self-service bets. However, place bets can be increased, decreased, or removed at any time before the next throw. Unlike other wagers in craps, the probability of the casino winning or losing a place bet does not change. That is, it is the same on every throw.

Casino Advantage

To fully understand place bets, it is most helpful to review the source of the casino advantage. From Table 13.5, we know how the true odds are computed for each of the point numbers. Place bets are wagers on these same point numbers. However, we also know from our discussion on odds wagers that a bet which pays true odds offers no casino advantage. Table 13.6 contains all the information needed to demonstrate the source of the casino advantage on each of the place bets.

Table 13.6
Place Bet Odds Schedule

(A) Point	(B) True Odds[a]	(C) True Odds Equivalent	(D) Place Bet Payoff Odds
4	2:1	10:5	9:5
5	3:2	7.5:5	7:5
6	6:5	7.2:6	7:6
8	6:5	7.2:6	7:6
9	3:2	7.5:5	7:5
10	2:1	10:5	9:5

Note. [a] Odds against throwing each point before throwing a seven (from Table 13.5).

To produce a casino advantage, the payoff odds on the place bets must be something less than true odds. Let's start with Column C, which is titled "True Odds Equivalent." Column C is nothing more than a restatement of Column B. For example, 2:1 = 10:5. Column C is included in Table 13.6 because the restated odds ratios are in terms of the amounts wagered on a craps game. For example, a bettor would place a $6 six, indicating a place bet for $6 on the point number six. This brings us to Column D, which is entitled "Place Bet Payoff Odds." Keeping with the example of the $6 six, we see from Column D that the true odds equivalent for the six is 7.2 to 6; however, a winning place bet on the six pays only 7 to 6. This difference represents the source of the house advantage. When comparing Columns C and D, it becomes clear that the winning place bet is always paid an amount less than the true odds equivalent.

Using the data from Table 13.6, let's compute the casino advantage on a $5 place bet on the four. The difference between the true odds equivalent (10:5) and the payoff odds of (9:5) is 1 unit. We know from Column B that the player can expect to win one of every three wagers. Given this ratio, on average, if the player makes three wagers of $5 each, he can expect to win one of them. He will be paid $9 on the winning $5 wager (per Column D). However, he can expect to lose a total of $10 on the other two $5 place bets, resulting in a $1 loss for the three-bet series (i.e., $9 won - $10 lost). To sum it up, the player can expect to lose $1 of every $15 dollars wagered, resulting in a house advantage of 6.67% ($1 ÷ $15). This same basic process produces a casino advantage for each of the place bets.

Changes in Status

On come-out throws, the default status of a place bet is off, or not working. In the industry vernacular, place bets are said to be "off on the come-out." However, a bettor can request for her place bet to be *working* on the come-out.[22] If a place bet is working on the come-out and a seven is thrown, the bet will lose. Of course, if the place bet point is thrown on the come-out, the bet will win.

Dealer Placement of Bets

The simplest way to explain how the dealers keep track of place bets is to provide an example with an illustration. Let's assume a player standing at the #2 position were to make a place bet on the eight for $600. The dealer would take this player's cheques and place them in the position illustrated in Figure 13.19. Note that place bets are set on the lines within the betting box. This is different from come bets, which are placed inside the lines (See Figure 13.7). Figure 13.19 illustrates the dealer's placement of the place bet belonging to the player standing at position 2.

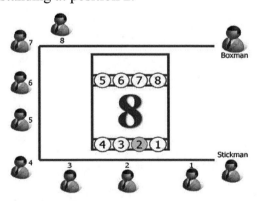

Figure 13.19. The Relationship Between Place Bet Location & Bettor Location.

---

[22] "On" is sometimes used in place of "working." For example, the place bet was "on" on the come-out. Both terms are used to communicate that the place bet is subject to the outcome of the come-out throw.

Figure 13.20 illustrates the location of the place bet within the broader perspective of the game's layout. This figure also provides examples of several of the bets discussed thus far.

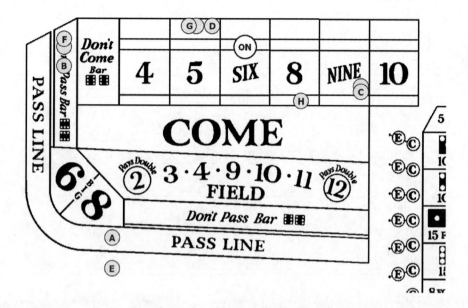

Figure 13.20. Illustration of the Location of Place Bet "H".

The following bullet points summarize what can be inferred from the layout shown in Figure 13.20. That is, by observing the placement of the bets depicted in Figure 13.20, we know the following:

- The come-out throw was a six (i.e., the point is six).
- Bet "A" is a pass line bet with odds (bet "E"). These bets were made by a player standing at position three. If these bets win, bet "A" will be paid at a rate of 1 to 1, while bet "E" will be paid at a rate of 6 to 5.
- Bet "B" is a don't pass bet, with odds (bet "F"). These bets were made by a player standing at position eight. If these bets win, bet "B" will be paid at a rate of 1 to 1, while bet "F" will be paid at a rate of 5 to 6.
- Bet "C" is a come bet, with odds (see offset odds cheques). These bets were made by a player standing at position one. If these bets win, bet "C" will be paid at a rate of 1 to 1, while the affiliated odds bet will be paid at a rate of 3 to 2.
- Bet "D" is a don't come bet, with odds (bet "G"). These bets were made by a player standing at position eight. If these bets win, bet "D" will be paid at a rate of 1 to 1, while bet "G" will be paid at a rate of 2 to 3.
- Bet "H" is a place bet on the eight. This bet was made by a player standing position two. If it wins, bet "H" will be paid at a rate of 7 to 6.

Place Bets to Lose

New Jersey gaming regulations permit players to make wagers known as *place bets to lose*. These bets are available in other jurisdictions as well, but they are not common. Place bets to lose are a form of lay bet. That is, the bettor is wagering that seven will be thrown before a selected point number. Of course, this will always be more likely than not, which requires the bettor to wager more than she will win. Table 13.7 compares the payoff odds to the true odds equivalent for each point number.

Table 13.7
Odds Schedule: Place Bets to Lose

Point to Lose	True Odds	True Odds Equivalent	Payoff Odds on Place Bet to Lose
4	1:2	5:10	5:11
5	2:3	5:7.5	5:8
6	5:6	4:4.8	4:5
8	5:6	4:4.8	4:5
9	2:3	5:7.5	5:8
10	1:2	5:10	5:11

To understand the origin of the casino advantage, consider a player who wagers against the four. If there were no casino advantage, the bettor would lay ten dollars to win five dollars (See "True Odds Equivalent" column). However, the payoff odds in the far-right column of Table 13.7 indicate that a bettor would have to lay eleven dollars to win five dollars. Once again, the casino advantage is derived from paying the wager at something less than true odds.

Buy and Lay Bets

There are other ways for players to make a wager on a specific point. For example, the bettor can *buy* a number. When a player buys a number, she wins if that specific number is thrown before a seven is thrown. Of course, she loses if a seven is thrown first. Winning wagers are paid at what we defined as true odds; however, players who make buy bets must pay a wagering commission (i.e., fee). This commission represents the casino advantage. Specifically, buy bettors are charged a commission equal to 5% of the amount wagered. Consequently, in effect, the casino operator pays winning wagers at something less than true odds.

To clarify the origin of the casino advantage on buy bets, consider the following example. A bettor buys the four for $100. If her bet wins, she will be paid true odds (i.e., 2 to 1, or $200). However, she will be charged a $5 commission when placing her wager (i.e., 5% of her $100 bet). In effect, she has wagered $105 ($100 wager + $5 commission). If her bet wins, the $5 commission is not refunded to her. Consequently, a winning wager nets her $195 ($200 payoff - $5 commission). Fully disclosed, she is betting $105 to win $195. This structure results in a casino advantage of 4.76% on all buy bets.[23]

---

[23] The house advantage is the same on all buy bets, when the commission is paid on the amount wagered.

Due to competition for dice players among the Las Vegas Strip resorts, many casino operators have modified the commission rules on buy bets. That is, they have instituted a "free buy" modification, to increase the attractiveness of the buy bet. With free buy, the bettor is only charged the 5% commission when his buy bet wins. In most cases, operators only offer free buy to players who buy the four or the ten. This results in a significant decrease in the casino advantage, as the commission is only charged when the bet wins (i.e., on $1/3^{rd}$ of the bets). In fact, free buy on the four and ten reduces the casino advantage on these wagers from 4.76% to 1.67%. For the casino to win the same amount of money on these buy bets, the players must either increase the amount wagered by 2.85 times or increase the number of bets placed by 2.85 times. That is, when operators offer free buy, wagering volume must increase dramatically to maintain the win levels, prior to the free buy modification.

Lay bets are the opposite of buy bets. Lay bets are wagers against the number. For example, if a player lays the four, she is betting that a seven will be thrown before a four. Winning lay bets are paid true odds. That is, if a player lays the four for $200, she is paid 1 to 2 (i.e., $100), if the bet wins. Traditionally, the commission on lay bets is equal to 5% of the payoff on a winning wager. For instance, if the bettor lays the four for $200, a winning wager would be paid $100. Therefore, the bettor would be charged $5 (i.e., 5% of the potential $100 payoff). This structure results in a casino advantage of 2.439% on lay bets on the four and ten. If the operator were to charge the commission only when the lay bet wins, the casino advantage on the four and ten would be reduced to 1.67%.

Buy bets are positioned in the same location as come bets, and lay bets are positioned in the same location as don't come bets. When two bets reside in the same location, but carry different payoffs, the dealers must have some way of differentiating the wagers. The solution is a plastic button, which is placed on top of the buy and lay bets (see Figure 13.21). Either "BUY" or "LAY" appears on the face on the button, signaling the dealer to pay winning wagers at true odds.

Figure 13.21. Plastic Buttons Used to Identify Buy & Lay Bets.

Figure 13.22 illustrates the use of buttons to mark both a buy bet and a lay bet. You can see that buy and lay bets occupy the same locations as come and don't come bets, respectively. Figure 13.22 depicts a buy bet on the four, placed by a player standing at position four, and a lay bet on the ten, placed by a player standing at position eight.

Unlike don't pass and don't come wagers, the chances of the casino winning a buy bet or lay bet are constant across all throws. Consequently, the bettor can increase, decrease, or remove these wagers at any time before the next throw. On come-out throws, the default status of buy bets is off. That is, the come-out throw will not produce a decision on a buy bet. However, bettors can request to have their buy bets *on* or *working* on the come-out throw. Lay bets are always working, unless called "off" by the bettor.

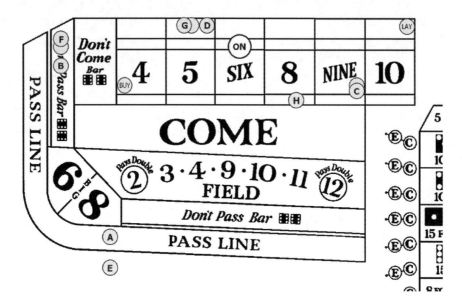

Figure 13.22. Illustration of Buttons Marking a Buy Bet and a Lay Bet.

Field, Big 6, and Big 8 Bets

The field is the simplest of dice bets. It is a one-throw self-service bet. The bettor wins if any of the field numbers are thrown (i.e., 2, 3, 4, 9, 10, 11, 12) and loses if any other number is thrown (i.e., 5, 6, 7, 8). A winning field bet pays 1 to 1, unless a 2 or 12 are thrown. Figure 13.22 illustrates a game on which both the 2 and 12 are paid at a rate of 2 to 1. On some games, the field bet is paid 2 to 1 on the 2, and 3 to 1 on the 12. This increased payoff rate on the 12 is yet another example of a price modification to make a wager more appealing to the bettors.

A wager on the big 6 wins if a six is thrown before a seven. The big 8 bet wins if an eight is thrown before a seven. Traditionally, winning bets are paid at a rate of 1:1. However, when New Jersey legalized gambling, its regulators felt that the big 6 and big 8 took advantage of less informed gamblers. That is, it seemed unfair to pay winning bets on the big 6 and big 8 at 1:1, when a place bet on the six or eight pays 7:6. On the other hand, the big 6 and big 8 allow bettors to make smaller wagers (e.g., $1). Most operators would not be able to accommodate a place bet of $1 on the six, while paying winning wagers at 7:6.

In any case, the New Jersey regulators require casino operators to pay winning big 6 and big 8 bets at a rate of 7 to 6, which is equal to the place bet payoff rate on those points. This regulation can be troublesome when Atlantic City gamblers visit a Las Vegas casino, where winning wagers on the big 6 and big 8 bets are paid 1:1. Consequently, many Las Vegas operators have removed the big 6 and big 8 bets from their craps layouts.

From Figure 13.23, bets "I," "J," and "K" are placed on the field, big 6, and big 8, respectively. The field is a one-throw bet, but the big 6 and big 8 bets can span multiple throws. However, the odds of the casino winning either wager remain constant across throws. Consequently, the bettor can increase, decrease, or remove the big 6 and big 8 bets at any time before the next throw.

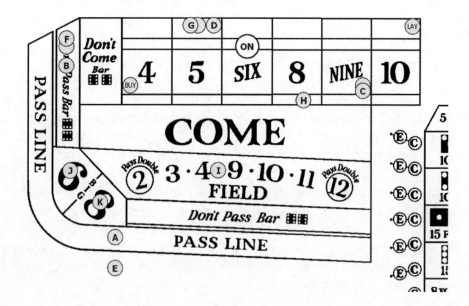

Figure 13.23. Illustration of Field Bet "I", Big 6 Bet "J," & Big 8 Bet "K".

Proposition Bets

In the area of the layout known as the proposition box, the payoffs are often expressed in terms of *for 1* (e.g., 30 FOR 1).[24] This is simply a marketing ploy. When payouts are expressed in this manner, the winning bet is exchanged for the payout, just as in a slot machine. For example, let's assume a player wagers $1 on a bet that pays 5 for 1. If the player wins, her $1 bet would be *exchanged* for the $5 payoff. Therefore, she has *won* $4, not $5. In effect, a 5 *for* 1 payout is equivalent to a 4 *to* 1 payout. The "for 1" wording allows management to post greater payout numbers, which is nothing more than an attempt to increase the attractiveness of the proposition box wagers.

Regardless of the payoff printed on the layout, the dealers always pay winning wagers in terms of *x to 1*, where *x* is either the posted payoff or a *for 1*-equivalent. This allows the dealer to leave the bettor *up* for the same wager.[25] For example, if a proposition box bet on the 11 pays 15 for 1, per the layout, the dealer would pay this bet 14 to 1. That is, the dealer would leave the player's bet on the 11 in place, and pay the player 14 units. This payoff allows the dealer to assume the player would like to make the same bet again. If

---

[24] See Figure 13.18 for examples.

[25] *Leaving the bettor up* is industry jargon describing the practice of paying a winning wager such that the dealer leaves the player's winning wager in action for the next throw (i.e., the same bet). This practice is not limited to payoffs on proposition bets.

the dealer were to pay the winning wager 15 *for* 1, the 15-unit payoff would be *exchanged* for the player's one-unit wager.

Of course, when a dealer leaves a player up, the player can request to have this bet removed. However, operators capitalize on the reality that some players will not know that the remaining bet (left by the dealer) can actually be removed.

Hard Way Bets

Bettors require a dealer's assistance to place these proposition bets. The four, six, eight, and ten are all numbers that can be thrown one of two ways: The *easy* way or the *hard* way. "Hard way" simply refers to a specific way to throw a number. For example, a six can be thrown five different ways: 2,4; 4,2; 1,5; 5,1; or 3,3. Notice that there is only one way to throw a 3,3, making it the *hardest* (or most difficult) way to throw a six. The remaining four outcomes represent the *easy* ways to throw a six.

When a bettor makes a hard 6 wager, he wins if 3,3 is thrown before any easy six or a seven. There are six ways a seven can be thrown and five ways a six can be thrown. Of those 11 ways (i.e., possible outcomes), only one way produces a win for the bettor. The remaining ways result in a loss for the bettor. If a winning wager were paid at 10 to 1, the casino operator would have no advantage. However, a winning hard 6 bet is paid at 9 to 1, creating a casino advantage of 9.09%.

Although hard way bets can be decided in a single throw, they can also span several throws before a decision is produced. Hard way bets are the only wagers in the proposition box that can require multiple throws to settle. That is, all other proposition box wagers are settled after a single throw.

One-Throw Bets

The following bullet points provide terse descriptions of the one-throw bets in the proposition box:[26]

- **Seven:** A bet that the next throw will be a seven. A winning wager is paid 4 to 1.
- **Individual craps numbers:** A bet that the next throw will be one of the specific craps numbers (i.e., a 2, 3, or 12). Some casino operators pay 30 *for* 1 on the 2 and 12, and 15 *for* 1 on the 3 and 11. Other operators pay 30 *to* 1 on the 2 and 12, and 15 *to* 1 on the 3 and 11, to make the bets more enticing.
- **Any craps**: Instead of specifying a particular craps number, the bettor wagers that the next throw will be any of the craps numbers. The bet wins if a 2, 3, or 12 is thrown. A winning bet is paid 7 to 1.
- **Eleven:** A bet that the next throw will be an 11. Some operators pay winning wagers at 15 *for* 1, while others try to entice bettors with a 15 *to* 1 payoff.
- **Hop:** A bet that is made verbally, often while the dice are in the air. Specifically, the bettor is calling the outcome of the current throw. Consequently, there is no time or place on the layout to mark a hop bet. For example, if a bettor believes the

---

[26] Placing any of these bets requires assistance from a dealer.

upcoming throw of the dice will result in a 6, he must call exactly how it will appear, i.e., 4-2, 3-3, or 5-1. In this example, a *6 hop bet* can be thrown the easy way or the hard way. An *easy way hop 6* could be called as 4-2 or 5-1. For example, the bettor could call, "four-two on the hop." The 3-3 outcome represents the hardest (i.e., most difficult) way to throw a 6. *Hard way hop bets* carry the same payoff and player disadvantage as proposition bets on the 2 or 12. *Easy way hop bets* carry the same payoff and player disadvantage as proposition bets on the 3 or 11. Any of the eleven numbers that can be thrown can be called on the hop (i.e., 2, 3, 4…12).

- **Horn:** A combination bet on the 2, 3, 11, and 12. A horn bet is equivalent to individual bets on the 2, 3, 11, and 12. Of course, only one of these bets can win. Casino cheques are often minted in denominations that are multiples of five, such as $5 and $25. Consequently, bettors will throw one of these cheques toward the proposition box and call-out a bet such as *horn high 3*. This instructs the dealer that the bettor wants $1/5^{th}$ of the cheque's value wagered on the 2, $1/5^{th}$ on the 11, $1/5^{th}$ on the 12, and $2/5^{ths}$ on the 3. The bet on the 3 would be twice as great as the bets on the other horn numbers, because of the bettor's request (i.e., horn *high 3*). If the bettor were to call, "horn high 12," the 12 would receive $2/5^{ths}$ of the cheque's value, assuming its denomination was a multiple of five.
- **World:** A combination bet on the 2, 3, 7, 11, and 12. A world bet is equivalent to a bettor making individual bets on each of the five numbers.

Stickman's Responsibilities

The stickman is responsible for all proposition bets. This includes computing all payoffs on winning wagers and keeping track of which bets belong to specific players. The graphic shown in Figure 13.24 is added to most layouts to facilitate the tracking process for bets placed on the eleven and/or any craps. The "E" stands for eleven and the "C" stands for any craps. When bettors place a simultaneous wager on both bets it is referred to as a C & E bet. For example, a player might throw the dealer two $1 cheques and verbally request a C & E. The dealer would then place one cheque on each of the two circles depicted in Figure 13.24.

Figure 13.24. Layout Graphic Used to Track Ownership of Proposition Bets.

The stickman must also track the ownership of the remaining proposition bets. This is achieved by positioning each bet within the betting box in a manner that corresponds to the bettor's location on the game.[27] Figure 13.25 provides an example of the tracking system employed on the game. Each cheque in Figure 13.25 contains a number that identifies a specific bettor's position (i.e., location) at the table.

---

[27] Where "bettor" refers to the player who made the specific wager.

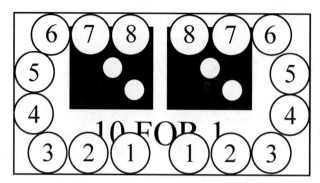

Figure 13.25. Tracking Scheme Used to Match Bets to Specific Players.

Let's review the bet placement protocol for the proposition box by examining Figure 13.26. The following bullet points identify the betting position of the player who made each of the bets shown in Figure 13.26.

- Bet "M" was made by the player in position #1 (i.e., to the stickman's immediate left).
- Bet "N" was made by the player in position #1 (i.e, to the stickman's immediate right).
- Bet "O" was made by the player in position #8 (i.e., to the immediate right of the second base dealer).
- Bet "P" was made by the player in position #7 (i.e., the second player to the right of the second base dealer).
- Bet "Q" was made by the player in position #8 (i.e., to the stickman's right).
- Bet "R" was also made by the player in position #8 (i.e., to the stickman's right).
- Bet "S" was made by the player in position #3 (i.e., to the stickman's left).

Marketing via Rule Modifications

Operators who are trying to increase their profits from craps games, often turn to rule modifications. These operators have great expectations, regarding the impact of these changes on the games. Typically, increasing the odds multiple is the operator's first modification. Operators will offer multiples of 2x, 5x, 10x, 50x, and even 100x odds, in an attempt to attract players to the games. The hope is that players will perceive the value of this modification, resulting in increased play.

In general, for a rule-change strategy to be effective, players must be knowledgeable enough to see the value in the modification(s). For example, a 10x odds offer will do little to attract a potential player who is interested in craps, but new to the game. That is, such a player is not likely to appreciate the value of something as nuanced as an increase in the odds multiple. Additionally, a modification must also change the player's behavior in a way that benefits the casino operator. For example, how likely is it that a craps player would bring a greater bankroll to the game, just to take advantage of a 10x odds offer? Is it more likely that the player would simply bet less of his bankroll on the pass line, and more of it in the odds position? These are important questions to consider.

Figure 13.26. Bet Placement within the Proposition Box.

Let's assume an operator decides to increase the allowable odds multiple from 2x to 10x. Further, let's assume a craps player enters the casino with his usual $500 bankroll. In the past, this player has bet $25 on the pass line and taken $50 in odds. The operator would expect to earn 1.414% of this player's $25 pass line bet, but nothing on the player's odd bet. Let's further assume that this established player is fully aware of the value in the increased odds multiple (i.e., from 2x to 10x). Given these assumptions, the operator must decide which of the following scenarios is more likely.

(a) The player will continue to make his customary $25 pass line, but now wager $250 in odds (i.e., 10x odds); or

(b) The player will decrease his pass line wager so that he can use his bankroll to make more bets in the odds position (e.g., a $5 pass line bet, with $50 in odds).

The fact is that neither outcome is beneficial to the operator. Let's assume the player continues to bet $25 on the pass line and takes $250 in odds. All players have what is known as exit criteria. That is, a player will leave the game once he loses an amount in the neighborhood of *x,* or wins an amount near *y.*[28] Regardless of the amounts, the general notion of exit criteria is firmly established in a great majority of players. On the

---

[28] A third exit criterion would be time available to play the game. That is, at some point, players have to leave the game/casino for any of several possible reasons.

loss side, players can only play for as long as their trip bankroll survives. With an odds wager of $250, a player with a $500 bankroll could not survive two consecutive losses. As the maximum odds bet increases so too does the volatility of the outcome. That is, increases in the odds multiple will decrease a player's average play time and result in less win for the casino.

Taking it a step further, let's assume the increased odds offer shows signs of clear success. How long will it be before a competitor matches the offer? What happens when a competitor not only matches the odds offer, but exceeds it? In most cases, rule modifications only benefit the players, at the expense of the operators. Nevertheless, new casino management teams are often expected to improve profits. Rule modifications often represent their first attempt to do so, in spite of the remarkably low success rate.

Limiting the payment of commissions to winning buy bets, increased payouts on proposition bets, and increases in odds multiples are all examples of price discounting. Such gimmicks are easily imitated and do not result in sustainable competitive advantages. More times than not, these kinds of price discounts result in a permanent loss of profits. Before deciding to implement one of these rule modifications, it is a good idea to compute the increase in wagers needed to sustain the existing level of win (i.e., before the rule change). The results of this calculation are likely to deter some from moving forward with the proposed change.

Put Bets

Gimmickry such as a 100x odds multiple will entice some players to make put bets. Put bettors will make a nominal pass line bet, after a point is established, for the right to make an odds wager. This is done in spite of the fact that the player's disadvantage on a pass line wager increases significantly when it is made *after* a point is established. For example, let's assume the point is 6. If a bettor were to place a pass line wager after this point was established, the casino operator would have a 9.09% advantage on the bet (vs. 1.414%, if the same bet were placed prior to the come-out throw). This is clearly not an optimal strategy, but what if the casino operator offered 100x odds?

Let's assume a player makes a pass line bet of $10, on a game with 100x odds. If the player were to make this bet before the come-out throw, his disadvantage would be 1.414%. That is, he would expect to lose 14¢ of his $10 wager, on average. But what if he could bet $1,000 in odds? Keeping with the previous example, if the point were 6, the bettor would be facing an expected value of -14¢ on the conventional pass line bet of $10, and -90.1¢ on a $10 put bet (i.e., $10 x 9.09%). For some, this difference of 76¢ is a small price to pay for a chance to make a $1,000 bet with no player disadvantage. Players most often make put bets against a point of 6 or 8, when the operator offers at least 10x odds. Of course, as the odds multiple increases, so too does the prevalence of put bets.

Casino Advantage by Wager

Table 13.8 provides a schedule of all the craps bets discussed in this chapter along with the casino advantage on each wager.

Table 13.8 (Part A)
Schedule of Casino Advantage by Wager

Wager	Additional Wager Information	Casino Advantage per Decision	Avg. Throws per Decision	Advantage per Throw
Pass/Come:		1.414%	3.376	0.419%
	1x Odds	0.848%	3.376	0.251%
	2x Odds	0.606%	3.376	0.180%
	3x Odds	0.471%	3.376	0.140%
	3/4/5x Odds	0.374%	3.376	0.111%
	10x Odds	0.184%	3.376	0.055%
	50x Odds	0.041%	3.376	0.012%
	100x Odds	0.021%	3.376	0.006%
Don't Pass/Don't Come:		1.360%	3.472	0.392%
	1x Odds	0.680%	3.472	0.196%
	2x Odds	0.453%	3.472	0.131%
	3x Odds	0.340%	3.472	0.098%
	3/4/5x Odds	0.272%	3.472	0.078%
	10x Odds	0.124%	3.472	0.036%
	50x Odds	0.027%	3.472	0.008%
	100x Odds	0.013%	3.472	0.004%
Big 6 & Big 8		9.090%	3.270	2.780%
Field (2, 3, 4, 9, 10, 11, 12):				
	2 & 12 Pay Double	5.560%	1.000	5.560%
	2 Pays Double 12 Pays Triple	2.778%	1.000	2.778%
Place Bets:				
	4 & 10	6.660%	5.680	1.173%
	5 & 9	4.000%	5.115	0.782%
	6 & 8	1.515%	4.650	0.326%
Place Bets to Lose:				
	4 & 10	1.818%	4.000	0.455%
	5 & 9	2.500%	3.600	0.694%
	6 & 8	3.030%	3.270	0.927%
Buy Bets (commission paid at buy):				
	4 & 10	4.760%	5.680	0.838%
	5 & 9	4.760%	5.115	0.931%
	6 & 8	4.760%	4.650	1.024%

Table 13.8 (Part B)
Schedule of Casino Advantage by Wager

Wager	Additional Wager Information	Casino Advantage per Decision	Avg. Throws per Decision	Advantage per Throw
Buy Bets (commission paid if won):				
	4 & 10	1.670%	5.680	0.294%
	5 & 9	2.000%	5.115	0.391%
	6 & 8	2.270%	4.650	0.488%
Lay Bets (commission paid at buy):				
	4 & 10	2.439%	4.000	0.610%
	5 & 9	3.225%	3.600	0.896%
	6 & 8	4.000%	3.270	1.223%
Lay Bets (commission paid if won):				
	4 & 10	1.667%	4.000	0.417%
	5 & 9	2.000%	3.600	0.556%
	6 & 8	2.273%	3.270	0.695%
Proposition Bets				
Hard Ways:				
	4 & 10	11.110%	4.000	2.778%
	6 & 8	9.090%	3.270	2.780%
Ace-Deuce & Eleven:				
	Pays 15 for 1 (14 to 1)	16.667%	1.000	16.667%
	Pays 16 for 1 (15 to 1)	11.111%	1.000	11.111%
Aces:				
	Pays 30 for 1 (29 to 1)	16.667%	1.000	16.667%
	Pays 31 for 1 (30 to 1)	13.889%	1.000	13.889%
Twelve:				
	Pays 30 for 1 (29 to 1)	16.667%	1.000	16.667%
	Pays 31 for 1 (30 to 1)	13.889%	1.000	13.889%
Any Craps		11.111%	1.000	11.111%
Any Seven		16.670%	1.000	16.670%

Questions/Exercises:

Use the following figure to answer questions 1 through 11.

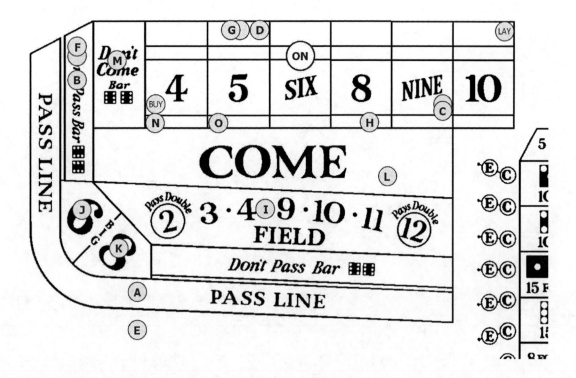

1. What type of throw is the next throw of the dice?
2. If the next throw were a 7, which bets would win and which bets would lose?
3. If $120 were bet at "H," and the bet were to win, how much would the bet pay?
4. If a player were to buy the 4 for $200, how much would he pay in commission?
5. If a player were to lay the 10 for $200, how much would she pay in commission?
6. If the next throw were a 6, how much would a $200 bet at "E" pay?
7. If the point were *NINE,* and a player had wagered $200 at "E", how much would "E" pay, if the bet were to win?
8. If the point were 4, and a player had wagered $200 at "E", how much would "E" pay, if the bet were to win?
9. Would it be permissible for the bettor to remove bets "A" and/or "E"? Explain your answer.
10. Would it be permissible for the bettor to remove bet "B"? Explain your answer.
11. If a player had bet $200 at "D," what is the maximum dollar-amount he could lay in odds? Assume the casino is offering 2x odds.
12. Can a bettor make a don't pass wager after the point is established? Explain your answer.
13. Are all proposition box bets always decided by a single throw of the dice?
14. List the self-service bets.
15. List the odds against throwing each of the points before a seven (i.e., the true odds).
16. On the come-out throw, place bets are _____, while lay bets are _____.

Chapter 14
Roulette, Three Card Poker, & Fan Tan

Is roulette the only game in the casino that uses chips?
How are the hands ranked in three card poker?
What is fan tan and how is it played?
What are the primary differences between American, English, & French Roulette?
Why does the house advantage in three card poker vary by casino?
What is a nga tan bet?

Scope

This chapter is designed to introduce readers to the games of roulette, three card poker, and fan tan. These games are all very different. One produces an outcome with a ball and a wheel, another with cards, and the third with buttons – that's right, buttons. The chapter includes a full description of betting layouts, wagers, and more. After reading this chapter, you should be able to follow and understand wagering action on a live version of each of these games.

Chapter Goals

- Identify the important differences between the three versions of roulette
- Describe how the roulette bets win and lose
- Explain the formula used to compute the casino advantage on roulette wagers
- Describe the game of three card poker and its primary wagers
- Review the hierarchy of the three card poker hands and the game's various pay tables
- Identify the five fan tan wagers, and explain how each one wins and loses
- Provide an overview of how the fan tan game is produced

Roulette

Roulette is found in nearly every casino gaming jurisdiction in the world. Like most casino games its origin is difficult to pinpoint. Roulette most likely evolved from a game called hoca, which was played in Europe in the 17th century.[1] A hoca wheel featured up to 40 numbered pockets, including three pockets marked zero. The wheel had a center

---

[1] Shelley, R.(1987), *Roulette Wheel Study*, p. 2. Las Vegas: Gambler's Book Club.

spindle with six spokes. To produce an outcome, a ball was placed between the spokes and the wheel was spun. This resulted in the ball being thrown to the outside edge of the wheel, where it eventually came to rest in one of the numbered pockets. This should sound familiar, as it is quite similar to the modern game of roulette.

Because of its broad appeal and long history, the roulette wheel has achieved an iconic status in the modern casino industry. When the ball spins around the wooden wheel and skips over the frets, it produces some of the unmistakable sounds of gaming. For centuries this elegant game has maintained a faithful following of gamblers.

There are three different versions of roulette: American, English, and European (a.k.a. French). However, the different versions of the game are certainly not restricted to the boundaries of their geopolitical namesakes. For example, there are English roulette wheels in American casinos and vice versa. The important differences between these three versions are related to the wheel itself, the layout, and the bets.

The American Wheel

American roulette is usually played on what is known as a double-zero wheel, which contains numbered pockets ranging from 1 to 36, plus pockets numbered zero and double zero (i.e., 38 pockets in total). In the industry, "American roulette" is used to describe a game featuring a double-zero wheel. Figure 14.1 depicts a double-zero wheel, while Figure 14.2 illustrates the layout that would accompany a double-zero wheel.

Chips are only used on roulette games. That is, no other casino game uses chips. The typical roulette game will have between six and eight different colored chips. There are 15 stacks of 20 chips, for each different color. The term chips is used to imply an absence of permanent monetary value. Unlike casino cheques, which feature a value printed on each face, chips have no monetary value printed on them. For example, when a player buys into the game, he will ask for chips of a certain denomination. The dealer will assign this player a unique color of chips. No other player on the game will have chips of this color. At the time of issue, the dealer will mark the value of the player's chips so that they can be purchased from the player, once he has finished gambling.

To clarify, consider the following example. Assume a player named Tony places a $100 bill on the table and requests to purchase $5 chips. The dealer will select a color that no other player on the game is using and mark that color as $5 chips. The dealer will then hand Tony a stack of 20 roulette chips. Only Tony will be wagering with that color of chip. Before Tony leaves the game, he will sell his remaining chips to the dealer at $5 per chip. This returns the color assigned to Tony to the game, making it available for another player. By assigning a unique color of chips to each player, several players can make the same wager without the dealer having to remember which bet belongs to whom.

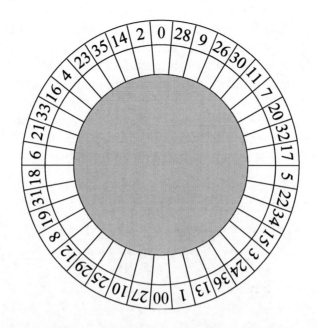

Figure 14.1. Double-Zero Roulette Wheel (a.k.a. an American Wheel).

		0	00	
1 to 18	1st 12	1	2	3
		4	5	6
EVEN		7	8	9
		10	11	12
RED	2nd 12	13	14	15
		16	17	18
BLACK		19	20	21
		22	23	24
ODD	3rd 12	25	26	27
		28	29	30
19 to 36		31	32	33
		34	35	36
		2 to 1	2 to 1	2 to 1

Figure 14.2. Double-Zero Roulette Layout.

There are several bets a player can make on a roulette game. American roulette offers the least number of bets. In fact, both English and French roulette offer many bets that are not available on the American version of the game. This is to due to differences in the layout. These bets will be covered in subsequent sections of this chapter, but for now, let's start with a review of the bets featured on an American roulette game. Table 14.1 summarizes these bets. The column entitled "Example" contains letters representing illustrations of each bet, which are subsequently illustrated in Figure 14.3. Most of the bets appearing in Table 14.1 can also be made on both English and French roulette tables.

Table 14.1
Summary of Roulette Bets:
American Version

Type of Bet	#s Bet	Payoff	Example
Straight-up	1	35:1	A
Split	2	17:1	B
Street or 3 #s	3	11:1	C
Corner	4	8:1	D
Top 5	5	6:1	E
Alley	6	5:1	F
Column/Dozen	12	2:1	G
Odd/Even	18	1:1	I
Red/Black	18	1:1	J
1 to 18 / 19 to 36	18	1:1	H
0/00 Split	2	17:1	X
Basket	3	11:1	Y

Outside and Inside Bets

In roulette, the bets that pay 1 to 1 and 2 to 1 are known as outside bets. These bets are marked H & G in Figure 14.3. All other bets are referred to as inside bets. These are the bets placed on the number grid ranging from zero to 36 (i.e., bets A through F). Although it holds no practical significance, it is interesting to note that the sum of all the inside numbers on a roulette layout is 666. Bet X in Figure 14.3 is also interesting. This is a convenience for players at the far end of the table who would like to bet the ever-popular 0/00 split. The dealer will interpret a bet placed on the line between the 2nd dozen and 3rd dozen as a bet placed on the line separating zero from double-zero (i.e., 0/00 split).

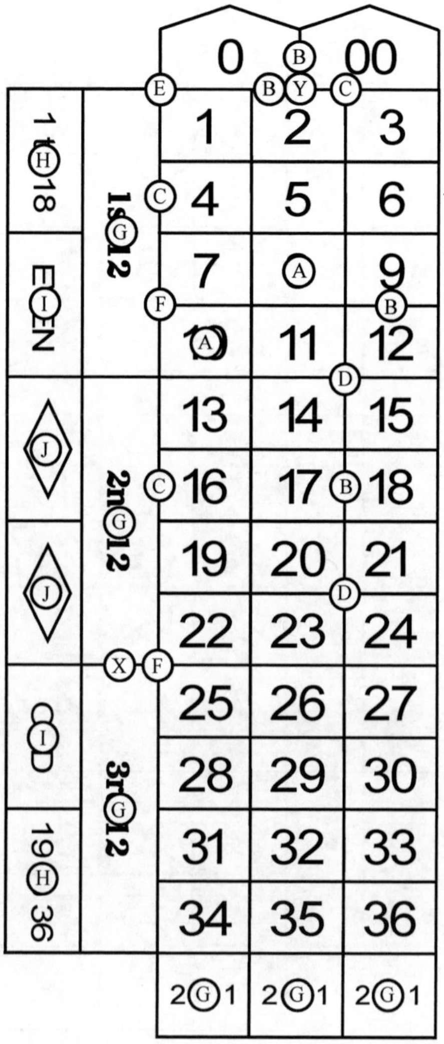

Figure 14.3. Illustrations of Bet Placement for the Wagers Listed in Table 14.1.

Snake or Crisscross Red

The snake bet also known as the crisscross red is available to players on some games, but not others. This bet covers 12 numbers. It is known as a crisscross red because each of the 12 numbers is a red number. In Figure 14.4, the chip marked "S" designates where this bet is placed on the layout. The line drawn on the layout indicates the numbers comprising the snake bet. If the ball settles in any numbered pocket corresponding to a number on the line, the snake bet wins. A winning snake bet is paid 2 to 1.

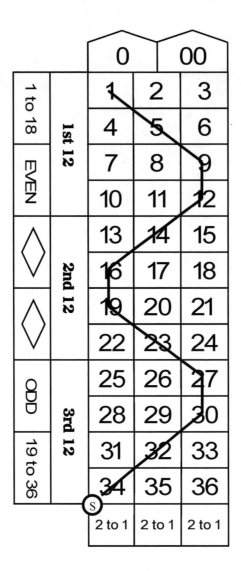

Figure 14.4. Illustration of the Snake Bet or Crisscross Red

Player Disadvantage

With the exception of the top 5 bet, all bets on a double-zero wheel carry a player disadvantage of 5.26%. The top 5 wager has a player disadvantage of 7.89%. Equations 14.1 and 14.2 demonstrate the simplicity of these calculations for roulette wagers.

$$(20/38)\ (-1) + (18/38)\ (1) = -0.0526, \text{ or } -5.26\%$$

Equation 14.1. Player Disadvantage: Outside Wager on Red.

$$(33/38)\ (-1) + (5/38)\ (6) = -0.0789, \text{ or } -7.89\%$$

Equation 14.2. Player Disadvantage: Top 5 Wager.

In Equation 14.1, "(20/38)" represents the probability of losing the bet on red. There are 38 numbers on the American wheel, and 20 of those numbers are not red (i.e., 18 are black and both 0 and 00 are green). When the ball settles in a black or green pocket, the player loses his bet, hence the "(-1)" appearing next to "(20/38)." As always, it is assumed that the bettor has wagered one unit. The product of "(20/38)" and "(-1)" is added to the product of the next two terms. The "(18/38)" represents the probability of the ball settling in a red pocket and "(1)" represents the payoff on a winning wager (from Table 14.1). The sum of the two products in Equation 14.1 is -0.0526, or -5.26%.

Equation 14.2 differs only in the numbers of ways to win and lose the bets, along with the payoff on a winning wager (i.e., 6 units). Using this basic approach, try to compute the player disadvantage on some of the remaining roulette wagers. Table 14.1 provides all the information you will need.

Personnel

The standard American and English roulette games are administered by a single dealer. If the game incurs unusually heavy betting action, a *mucker* might be assigned to the game. A mucker assists the dealer by sorting and stacking the chips won by the casino. A mechanical device known as a chipper is also available to aid dealers in the time-intensive task of separating and sorting the roulette chips. However, not all operators have a chipper.

English Roulette

The English version is played on a table similar in size to that of its American counterpart. While the American version uses a double-zero wheel with 38 possibilities (36 numbers plus 0 & 00), the English version typically employs a single-zero wheel with only 37 possibilities (36 numbers plus 0). The sequence of the numbers on the English wheel is completely different from that of the double-zero wheel.

For the most part, the English game operates like the American version. That is, aside from the top 5 bet, all of the same wagers and payoff rates are offered on the English game. The top 5 bet is not available on the English version because there is no 00 pocket on the wheel. A bet placed in the same location on an English layout covers the top four numbers (0, 1, 2, & 3), which is paid like a corner bet, i.e., 8 to 1. That is, a bet placed in the location of "E" in Figure 14.3 would cover the top 4 numbers on an English roulette layout. See Figure 14.5 for an illustration of the English game. Notice the oval track on the right side of Figure 14.5. Often referred to as the race track, this feature of the English game is enlarged in Figure 14.6. The race track facilitates several wagers that are not expressly offered on the American version of roulette.

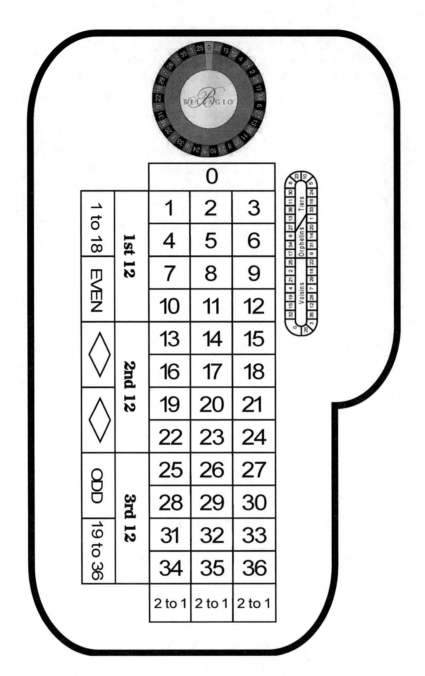

Figure 14.5. English Roulette Table and Wheel.

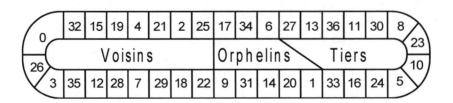

Figure 14.6. English Roulette Race Track

Both English and European roulette games allow bettors to play sections of the physical wheel. The following three sections are labeled in Figure 14.7: Grands voisins du zero (neighbors of zero), tiers du culindre (third of the wheel), and orphelins (orphans).

Figure 14.7. Bet Section Diagram of a Single-Zero Roulette Wheel.

As previously noted, the race track feature facilitates betting on areas of the physical wheel. For example, assume Tony wants to bet voisins du zero. This is a nine-chip wager that covers 17 numbers.[2] A nine-chip voisins du zero wager is equivalent to the following bets: A two-chip bet on 0/2/3, a two-chip corner bet on 25/26/28/29, and one-chip bets on each of the following splits 4/7, 12/15, 18/21, 19/22, and 32/35. Clearly, it is much easier for the player to simply announce "voisins du zero" and hand the dealer a stack of nine chips. The dealer would then place Tony's nine chips in the area of the racetrack labeled "Voisins." These types of bets are called *announce* or *call bets*. Table 14.2 lists and describes call bets made by way of the race track.

Table 14.2
Schedule of Call Bets on a Single-Zero Roulette Game

Name of Bet	Chips Required[a]	Wagering Unit Breakdown & Numbers Covered
Voisins du Zero	9	2 units on 0/2/3 & 2 units on 25/26/28/29 corner
		1 unit each on: 4/7, 12/15, 18/21, 19/22, 32/35
Jeu de Zero	4	1 unit each on: 26, 0/3, 12/15, 32/35
Tiers du Culindre	6	1 unit each on: 5/8, 10/11, 13/16, 23/24, 27/30, 33/36
Orphelin Cheval	5	1 unit each on: 1, 6/9, 14/17, 17/20, 31/34 split
Orphelin Plein	8	1 unit each on: 0, 6, 9, 14, 17, 20, 31, 34

Notes. [a] Multiples of this minimum requirement are also acceptable. "25/26/28/29" indicates a corner bet. "4/7" indicates a single bet covering both numbers, a.k.a. a split.

---

[2] Nine chips would be the minimum wager, as any multiple of 9 chips could be wagered on voisins du zero.

Although not shown in Table 14.2, the race track facilitates another five-chip[3] call bet known as voisins du nombre (i.e., the neighbors bet). To make this bet, the player must choose a number (any number) on the wheel. Once he chooses a number and announces the bet, the dealer knows to place one unit on the announced number, one unit on each of the two numbers immediately preceding the announced number (on the track), and one unit on each of the two numbers immediately following the announced number (on the track). For example, assume a player calls "voisins du nombre 23" and hands the dealer five chips. The dealer would know that these five chips represent one-chip bets on the following numbers: 23, 30, 8, 10, and 5. For further clarification, locate these five numbers on the race track, and you will quickly see why it is known as the neighbors bet.

When announcing this bet, getting the language right is important. For example, if a player were to announce "23 and its neighbors *by* $25," she would have requested to place five wagers of $25 each, for a total bet of $125. If she were to call "neighbors of 23 *for* $100," she would have requested to wager four units of $25 to be equally divided among the neighbors of 23, with no bet on 23 itself. That is, a $25 bet would be placed on each of the following numbers: 30, 8, 10, and 15.

European Roulette

This version of the game is also known as French roulette. While nearly all of the previously described bets and payoff rates are offered in European roulette, there are some distinct differences in the way it is played. For example, all players wager with cheques or cash chips called *jetons*. As each player on the game is *not* issued a unique color of chips, the dealers must know which bets belong to whom. Casino operators who cater to the premium player market sometimes use *plaques* in lieu of cheques or jetons. Because of the considerable monetary value of these plaques, they usually contain anti-counterfeiting features and unique serial numbers.

There are three dealers on a European roulette table, two *croupiers* and one *bout de table*.[4] There is also one *table chef* (supervisor) on the game. Figure 14.8 illustrates the European roulette table, personnel stations, and betting layout. Both the table and layout are designed to accommodate bettors on both sides of the game, hence the additional personnel. American and English tables do not allow betting on the lateral side of the layout nearest the dealer. Additionally, on a European roulette table, all dealing and supervisory personnel are seated. On the American and English games, a single dealer deals the game from a standing position.

There are other differences related to the dealing procedures. For example, the European roulette dealers use a long stick with a paddle on the end, which is known as *le rateau* (i.e., the rake). This device is used to mark winning numbers, clear the layout of all losing bets, and assist players in placing difficult-to-reach bets. While it is clearly a roulette game, the size and appearance of the table, the seated dealers, and the use of le rateau come together to form a very unique and elegant roulette experience.

---

[3] Multiples of 5 chips would also be acceptable, within the posted minimum and maximum wagers.
[4] *Croupier* is the French term for dealer. *Bout de table* means at the end of the table, describing this dealer's location on the game.

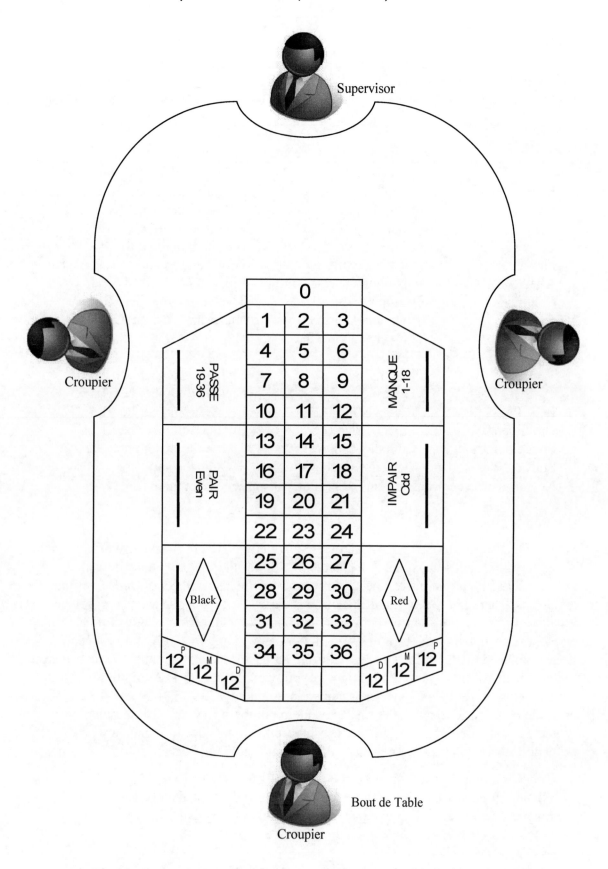

Figure 14.8. European Roulette Table, Betting Layout, & Personnel Stations.

Basic Bets

While most of the basic bets in European roulette are not different from those offered on the English and American versions, the names of the wagers are distinctly different. Table 14.3 provides a schedule which matches the bet names to their French equivalents.

Table 14.3

Bet Schedule: European/French Roulette

Wager	French Equivalent	Bet & Payoff Ratio
Straight-up	Plein	Single-number bet; 35:1
Split	Cheval	Two-number bet; 17:1
Street	Transversale plein	Three-number bet; 11:1
Corner	Carre	Four-number bet; 8:1
First Four	Quatre Premiers	Four-number bet (0, 1, 2, 3); 8:1
Alley/Line	Sixain/transversal simple	Six-number bet; 5:1
Column	Colonne	Twelve-number bet; 2:1
1st 12	Premiere Douzaine	Numbers 1-12; 2:1
2nd 12	Moyenne Douzaine	Numbers 13-24; 2:1
3rd 12	Derniere Douzaine	Numbers 25-36; 2:1
1 to 18	Manque	Eighteen-number bet; 1:1
19 to 36	Passe	Eighteen-number bet; 1:1
Red/Black	Rouge/Noir	Eighteen-number bet; 1:1
Odd/Even	Impair/Pair	Eighteen-number bet; 1:1
Split Column	Colonne `a cheval	Two-column split bet; 1:2
Split 1st, 2nd, 3rd dzn.	Douzaine `a cheval	Two-dozen split; 1:2

Notes. "dzn." represents dozen (i.e., set of 12 consecutive numbers).

Les Finales Bets

Some of the wagers in European roulette are distinctly different from those offered in the American and English versions of the game. In addition to the previously described voisins, tiers, and orphelins call bets, European roulette also offers *les finales,* or final-digits bets. There are two types of finales bets: *Finales en plein* and *finales a cheval.* Finales en plein is a straight-up bet keyed to a common single digit. For example, "finales en plein zero" entails straight-up bets on all numbers ending in zero. That is, an equal wager is placed on 0, 10, 20, and 30, requiring at least four betting units.[5] If the ball were to land on any of these four numbers, the payout would be 35 to 1. A minimum of four units is required for bets on the finales en plein numbers 0, 1, 2, 3, 4, 5, and 6. Only three units are required for bets on the finales en plein numbers 7, 8, and 9, with winning wagers paid at a rate of 35 to 1. These are three-unit wagers because there are no 37, 38, or 39 pockets on the wheel. The details of les finales en plein bets are summarized next.

Finales en plein 0 is a four-unit bet covering 0, 10, 20, and 30, paid at 35:1.
Finales en plein 1 is a four-unit bet on 1, 11, 21, and 31, paid at 35:1.
Finales en plein 2, 3, 4, 5, and 6 are all four-unit bets, paid at 35:1.
Finales en plein 7, 8, and 9 are all three-unit bets, paid at 35:1.

---

[5] "Unit" represents a wagering quantity of constant or equal monetary value. A unit can be equal to any of many different monetary values (e.g., $2, $5, or $100), provided its value remains constant.

Finales a cheval is a wager on pairs of numbers that end in the same digits. For example, a wager on finales a cheval 0 & 1 requires five units. This wager covers all numbers ending in 0 and 1. Split bets are made where possible. If a split wager is not possible, one unit is bet on the number (i.e., the number is bet straight-up). For example, finales a cheval 0 & 1 would require one unit on the 0/1 split, one unit on the 10/11 split, one unit on the 20/21 split, one unit on 30, and one unit on 31. Figure 14.8 illustrates why the numbers 30 and 31 cannot be split, i.e., they are not adjacent to one another on the layout.

Referencing Figure 14.4, it is evident that six units are required for finales a cheval 3 & 4. That is, one unit is bet on the 3; one unit is bet on the 4; one unit is bet on 13/14 split; one unit is bet on the 23/24 split; one unit is bet on 33; and one unit is bet on 34. Five units are required for bets on the following pairs: 0 & 1, 1 & 2, 2 & 3, 4 & 5, and 5 & 6. Four units are required for bets on the following pairs: 0 & 3, 1 & 4, 2 & 5, 3 & 6, 7 & 8, and 8 & 9. Three units are required for bets on the following pairs: 4 & 7, 5 & 8, 6 & 9, 7 & 10, 8 & 11, and 9 & 12. Try to verify one bet from each of the previous lists. For example, select a pair from each of the lists and verify the number of units required to make the wager. Remember, a split bet is always made when possible. The remaining finales a cheval pairings are summarized next.

Finales a cheval 0 & 1 is a five-unit bet on 0/1, 10/11, 20/21, 30, & 31.
Finales a cheval 2 & 3 is a five-unit bet on 2/3, 12, 13, 22/23, & 32/33.
Finales a cheval 3 & 4 is a six-unit bet on 3, 4, 13/14, 23/24, 33, & 34.
Finales a cheval 4 & 5 is a five-unit bet on 4/5, 14/15, 24, 25, & 34/35.
Finales a cheval 5 & 6 is a five-unit bet on 5/6, 15, 16, 25/26, & 35/36.
Finales a cheval 6 & 7 is a five-unit bet on 6, 7, 16/17, 26/27, & 36.
Finales a cheval 7 & 10 is a three-unit bet on 7/10, 17/20, & 27/30.
Finales a cheval 8 & 11 is a three-unit bet on 8/11, 18/21, & 28/31.
Finales a cheval 9 & 12 is a three-unit bet on 9/12, 19/22, & 29/32.
Finales a cheval 7 & 8, 8 & 9, 9 & 10, 0 & 3, 1 & 4, 2 & 5, and 3 & 6 are all four-unit bets.

Why isn't finales a cheval 4 & 7 a four-unit bet, with one unit on 4/7, one on 14/17, one on 24/27, and one on 34? Give up? The answer is because all sequences of the pairing cannot be completed. That is, the 34/37 split does not exist because there is no number 37. Therefore, no bet is placed on the number 34, making the finales a cheval 4 & 7 a three-unit bet. The same condition holds for finales a cheval 5 & 8, as there is no number 38.

Bet Placement

Due to differences in the layout, the bet placement is somewhat different in European roulette. Figure 14.9 is provided to illustrate these differences. For example, in addition to betting a column (i.e., a 12-number bet), players can place a split bet on two adjacent columns (i.e., a 24-number bet). Because the chances of winning a split column bet are greater than the chances of losing it, winning wagers are paid 1 to 2.

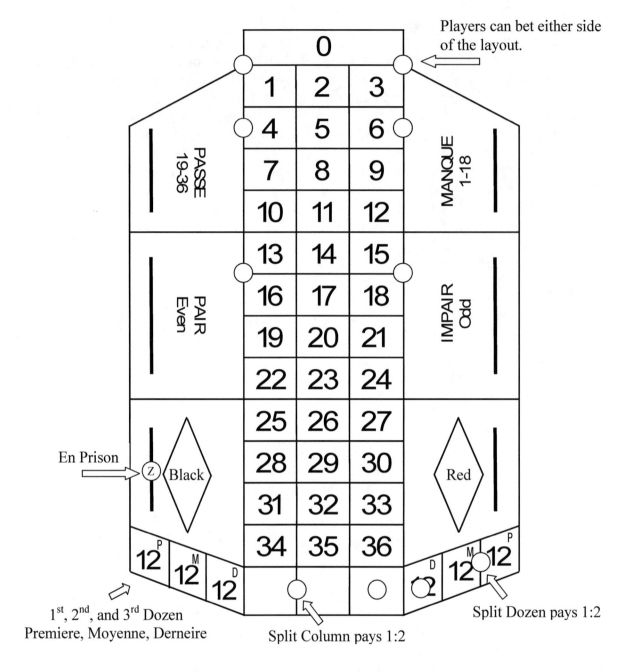

Figure 14.9. Bet Placement on a European Roulette Layout.

En Prison

This feature is available on the French and English versions, but not on the American game. In Figure 14.9 you will see bold lines next to the outside wagers that are paid 1 to 1. When a player makes a wager in one of these areas and the ball settles in the zero pocket, his bet is moved to the bold line next to the original area of his wager. For example, let's assume Tony places a $100 bet on black, but the ball settles in the zero pocket (which is green). In American roulette, Tony would lose his wager. In European and English roulette, his bet is moved to the bold line in Figure 14.9 labeled *en prison* (see bet Z). If the ball were to settle in a black pocket on the next spin, Tony would keep his bet. However, if the ball were to settle in a red pocket on the next spin, Tony would lose his wager. If the ball were to settle in the green pocket, i.e., zero on the next spin, Tony's bet would remain en prison. That is, only a black or red number can settle his wager. This applies to all the even-money bets (i.e., bets that pay 1:1). That is, if Tony were to place a bet on even and the ball were to land in the zero pocket, his bet would be moved to the en prison position and would remain there until the ball settled in an even or odd numbered pocket. This rule variation reduces the casino advantage on all even-money wagers by 51%, from the level of 2.703%. Equation 14.3 computes the casino advantage on even-money wagers, with the en prison rule in effect.

$$(18/37)(-1) + (18/37)(1) + (1/37)(18/37)(-1) = -0.01315, \text{ or } -1.315\%$$

Equation 14.3. Casino Advantage on Even-Money Wagers with the En Prison Rule.

Equation 14.3 applies to any outside wager that pays winning bets at a rate of 1 to 1. For example, let's assume Tony bets one unit (of any amount) on red. The first "(18/37)" term of Equation 14.3 represents the probability of the ball settling in a black pocket, while "(-1)" represents Tony's loss of one unit. The next "(18/37)" represents the probability of the ball settling in a red pocket, while the "(1)" represents Tony's gain of one unit. Lastly, the "(1/37)" represents the probably of the ball settling in the zero pocket. The adjacent "(18/37)" represents the probability of the ball settling in a black pocket on a subsequent spin, and, of course, the last "(-1)" represents Tony's loss of one unit. That is, Tony would lose the bet if the ball settled in the zero pocket on the first spin *and* in a black pocket on the second spin. Alternatively, if the ball were to settle in a red pocket on the second spin, Tony's bet would push.

La Partage

This is another feature offered on European roulette which has roughly the same effect on the casino advantage as the en prison rule. When a bet is en prison, it must remain on the layout until it wins or loses. When *la partage* is the house rule, the bettor will surrender ½ of his even-money outside wager if the ball settles in the green pocket. For example, let's assume Tony wagers $100 and la partage is in effect. If the ball settles in the green pocket on the ensuing spin, the dealer will collect half of Tony's wager (i.e., $50). However, Tony can remove the remaining half of his wager, as la partage does not require him to leave the bet in action until it pushes or loses. Although double-zero roulette is the standard in Atlantic City, the gaming regulations provide operators the option to offer la partage. Specifically, New Jersey Casino Control Commission regulations state:

> "When roulette is played on a double zero wheel and the roulette ball comes to rest in a compartment marked zero (0) or double zero (00), a player shall lose, at the casino licensee's option, either one-half of each wager on red, black, odd, even, 1 to 18, and 19 to 36 or the entire wager." [6]

---

[6] New Jersey Casino Control Commission Regulations 19:47-5.2 b

Three Card Poker

There are several hundred licensed games and variations of existing games available to casino operators. Like products, these games experience a life cycle, which eventually ends in declining popularity. For example, in 1986, there were over 300 red dog games in Nevada casinos.[7] In December 1990, the number of games had decreased to 49, and by December 1996 there were only three.[8] Similarly, in 1995, there were 150 Caribbean stud games and 214 let-it-ride games in Nevada casinos.[9] By December 2010, only 106 let-it-ride games and eight Caribbean stud games remained in operation.[10] In 2011, the most popular carnival game in Nevada was three card poker.[11] In fact, as of March 2011, three card poker was the 4th most popular table game in Nevada casinos, based on number of units in operation.[12]

Figure 14.10 provides a top-down view of a three card poker layout, while Figure 14.11 offers a tighter shot of the information displayed at the player's betting station. Both of these figures should be helpful references, as the subsequent sections of this chapter describe how the game is played.

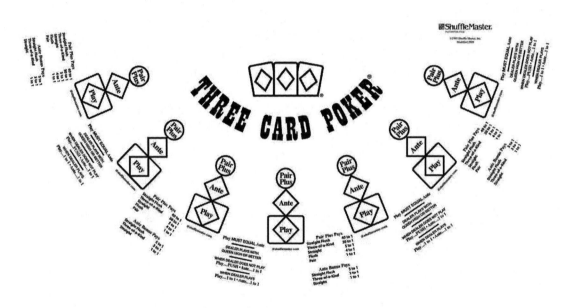

Figure 14.10. Three Card Poker Layout.

---

[7] Nevada Gaming Control Board. (1986, June). *State revenue analysis*. Carson City: Author. Red dog is the casino version of acey/duecy.

[8] Nevada Gaming Control Board. (1990 & 1996, December). *State revenue analysis*. Carson City: Author.

[9] Nevada Gaming Control Board. (1995, June). *State revenue analysis*. Carson City: Author.

[10] Nevada Gaming Control Board. (2010, December). *State revenue analysis*. Carson City: Author.

[11] Carnival games are table games other than blackjack, baccarat, craps, and roulette. Live poker is not considered to be a table game, nor is it a carnival game.

[12] Nevada Gaming Control Board. (2011, March). *State revenue analysis*. Carson City: Author.

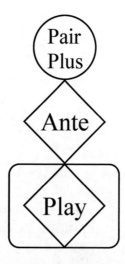

Play MUST EQUAL Ante

**DEALER PLAYS WITH
QUEEN HIGH OR BETTER**

**WHEN DEALER DOES NOT PLAY
Play…PUSH • Ante…1 to 1**

**WHEN DEALER PLAYS
Play…1 to 1 • Ante…1 to 1**

<u>**Pair Plus Payouts**</u>

Straight Flush	**40 to 1**
Three-of-a-Kind	**30 to 1**
Straight	**5 to 1**
Flush	**4 to 1**
Pair	**1 to 1**

<u>**Ante Bet Bonus Payouts**</u>

Straight Flush	**5 to 1**
Three-of-a-Kind	**3 to 1**
Straight	**1 to 1**

Figure 14.11. Three Card Poker Betting Area, Conditions of Play, & Pay Tables.

Overview

Three card poker is a fairly simple game. The game begins with the player placing a bet in the ante area, the pair plus area, or both areas (see Figure 14.11). Next, three cards are dealt to each player and the dealer. All cards are dealt face down from a single deck. The game then proceeds as follows:

- The players examine their hands. The dealer's three cards remain concealed.
- Each player must then act upon their hand. This process begins with the player at the extreme left of the dealer and moves in a clockwise direction.
- If the player made an ante wager, he must then decide to fold or raise, based only on the perceived strength of his hand. The dealer's cards are not exposed.
    - If the player folds, he surrenders his ante wager.
    - If he elects to raise, he must place an additional wager in the area of Figure 14.11 marked "Play." The play bet must be equal to his ante wager. For example, if a player were to place a $10 ante bet, and after reviewing his hand decided to raise, his play bet (i.e., raise) must also be $10.
    - The player cannot stand. That is, he must either fold or raise.
- After all players have acted upon their hands, the dealer then exposes his cards.
- The dealer's hand must be queen high or better to "qualify." This means the hand must have at least a queen, pair, flush, or straight, to stay in the game. For the dealer's hand, failing to qualify is similar to the act of folding.
    - If the dealer's hand does not qualify, then each player will win his ante wager and tie, or push, on the play wager. The ante wagers are paid even money (i.e., a rate of 1 to 1).
- If the dealer's hand qualifies, then each player's hand will be compared to the hand of the dealer. Of course, the highest hand wins, based on the rank order of poker hands shown in Table 14.4.

Table 14.4
Three Card Poker Hand Rankings
(From Highest to Lowest)

1. Straight flush
2. Three of a kind
3. Straight
4. Flush
5. Pair
6. Ace high or less

- If the player's hand beats the dealer's hand, the ante and play wagers are each paid even money.
- If the dealer's hand beats the player's hand, both the ante and play wagers lose.
- If the dealer and player hands tie, both the ante and play wagers push.
- If the player makes the ante bet and holds a straight or higher, he will receive an ante bonus, regardless of the dealer's hand. This bonus will vary by casino. Table 14.5 lists four popular ante bonus schedules.[13]

---

[13] Some casino operators will include a bonus payout for a mini royal flush, which serves as the top award.

Table 14.5
Ante Bet Bonus Schedules

	Schedule A	Schedule B	Schedule C	Schedule D
Straight Flush	5 to 1	4 to 1	3 to 1	5 to 1
3 of a Kind	4 to 1	3 to 1	2 to 1	3 to 1
Straight	1 to 1	1 to 1	1 to 1	1 to 1

Player Disadvantage

With regard to the ante bet, the player disadvantage is a function of skill and the bonus schedule offered by the operator. Assuming the player adheres to the optimal strategy (i.e., plays perfectly), Table 14.6 lists the player disadvantage on the ante bet with each of four bonus schedules in effect.[14]

Table 14.6
Player Disadvantage by Bonus Schedule: Ante Bet

	Bonus Schedule A	Bonus Schedule B	Bonus Schedule C	Bonus Schedule D
Straight Flush	5 to 1	4 to 1	3 to 1	5 to 1
3 of a Kind	4 to 1	3 to 1	2 to 1	3 to 1
Straight	1 to 1	1 to 1	1 to 1	1 to 1
Disadvantage	-3.37%	-3.83%	-4.28%	-3.61%

As previously noted, the pair plus bet is a separate wager, which is not related to the ante bet. When a player makes a pair plus bet, he is simply wagering that his hand will consist of a pair or better. The player disadvantage on the pair plus bet varies by pay table. Table 14.7 lists several pay tables offered by casino operators.[15]

Table 14.7
Player Disadvantage by Pay Table: Pair Plus Bet

Player Hand	Prob. of Hand	Pay Table A	Pay Table B	Pay Table C	Pay Table D	Pay Table E	Pay Table F
Straight Flush	0.0022	40	35	40	35	50	40
3 of a Kind	0.0024	30	33	25	25	30	30
Straight	0.0326	6	6	6	6	6	6
Flush	0.0496	4	4	4	4	3	3
Pair	0.1694	1	1	1	1	1	1
Nothing	0.7439	-1	-1	-1	-1	-1	-1
Disadvantage	....	-2.32%	-2.70%	-3.49%	-4.58%	-5.10%	-7.28%

---

[14] Where optimal strategy consists of making the play bet (i.e., raise) with all hands comprised of a queen/6/4 or better, regardless of the bonus schedule in effect. By adhering to this strategy, the player can expect to lose 8.66% of the ante bet and win 5.29% of the play bet. Retrieved on August 14, 2011, from http://wizardofodds.com/threecardpoker. Table 14.6 was adapted from the same source.

[15] Adapted from content retrieved on December 31, 2010, from http://wizardofodds.com/threecardpoker.

Mini Royal Flush

Some casino operators have added excitement to their pair plus bet by including a payout for a mini royal flush. That is, any three card hand comprised of a suited ace, king, and queen. Table 14.8 lists several pay tables used by casino operators offering payouts on mini royal flush hands.[16]

		Table 14.8				
Player Disadvantage by Pay Table (w/ Mini Royal Flush): Pair Plus Bet						
Player Hand	Prob. of Hand	Pay Table 1	Pay Table 2	Pay Table 3	Pay Table 4	Pay Table 5
Mini Royal	0.0002	50	50	200	100	50
Straight Flush	0.0020	40	40	40	50	40
3 of a Kind	0.0024	30	30	30	30	30
Straight	0.0326	6	5	6	6	6
Flush	0.0496	3	4	3	3	4
Pair	0.1694	1	1	1	1	1
Nothing	0.7439	-1	-1	-1	-1	-1
Disadvantage	…………	-7.10%	-5.39%	-4.38%	-4.20%	-2.14%

As you can see, there are many variations of the three card poker pay tables. Therefore, there is no universal casino advantage for this game. With regard to the ante bet, the house edge is a function of the pay table and the player's skill level.

Fan Tan

Although it is found in very few gaming jurisdictions around the world, Fan Tan is still played in the table game-heavy casinos of Macau. While many readers will never see this game in operation, it has most certainly stood the test of time. It is a beautifully simple game, which offers a surprising number of wagering propositions.

Fan Tan is a game of Chinese origin, which dates back to at least the 1st century A.D.[17] In the second half of the 19th century, Chinese immigrant workers introduced the game in the Western United States.[18] When gambling was legalized in Nevada in 1931, the popularity of fan tan was made evident when it appeared on the list of approved casinos games.[19] Fan Tan could still be found in Northern Nevada until the mid-1970s.

In 1901, an article was published in *Timely Topics* that read, "I write this in the Monte Carlo of Asia, in the great gambling hell of Macao, where fan tan runs riot. The chief gambling is in fan tan in which thousands of dollars are won and lost every night by betting on the number of copper cash under the bowls."[20]

---

[16] Ibid

[17] fan-tan. (2011). In *Encyclopaedia Britannica*. Retrieved from http://www.britannica.com/EBchecked/topic/201455/fan-tan.

[18] Ibid.

[19] Kilby, J., Fox, J., & Lucas, A.F. (2004). *Casino Operations Management* (2nd ed.). New York: Wiley.

[20] Carpenter, F. G. (1901, Feb. 8). Something for everybody. *Timely Topics, 5*(23), Whole No. 168, 363.

In 1931, the following passage was authored by former San Francisco Police Chief, Jesse B. Cook, appearing in an article published in the *San Francisco Police and Peace Officers' Journal*:

> "In regard to the gambling games in Chinatown—my first trip to Chinatown was in 1889 as a patrolman in a squad. At that time there were about 62 lottery agents, 50 fan tan games and eight lottery drawings in Chinatown. In the 50 fan tan gambling houses the tables numbered from one to 24, according to the size of the room.

> "The game was played around a table about 10 feet long, 4 feet high and 4 feet wide. On this table was a mat covering the whole top. In the center of the mat was a diagram of a 12-inch square, each corner being numbered in Chinese characters, 1, 2, 3 and 4. At the head of the table sat a lookout or gamekeeper. At the side was the dealer. This man had a Chinese bowl and a long bamboo stick with a curve at the end, like a hook. In front of him, fastened to the table, was a bag containing black and white buttons. He would scoop down into the sack with his bowl and raise it, turning it upside down on the table. The betting would then start."[21]

From both of these historical accounts, it would appear that fan tan was well established in both the Macau and Western U.S., by the late 19th century, if not before. Due to the underground nature of these fan tan games in the U.S., the true extent of the game's popularity is difficult to quantify. Nevertheless, it would appear that there was considerable demand for the game, based on the available anecdotal evidence.

Overview

It would be difficult to find a more simple game to play. Visualize using a cup to scoop into a bag or pile of buttons, coins, or pebbles. Once you have a cupful of objects, imagine dumping them onto a table and counting them, by carefully arranging the objects in rows of four. That is the essence of the game. The bettors are wagering on the remainder of buttons, coins or pebbles in the last row. Specifically, there can be only one, two, three, or four objects in the last row. The game provides considerable suspense, while the objects are counted. Additionally, the odds of specific outcomes can be precisely computed. Finally, there is an element of perceived skill, i.e., one's ability to visually estimate the number of buttons captured under the cup. These basic conditions are all necessary ingredients in the recipe for a successful and exciting casino game.

Figure 14.12 is a drawing of a dealer (far left) and fan tan players huddled around what appears to be something of a makeshift table/layout. Photograph 14.1 depicts an assortment fan tan equipment. The metal (usually copper) bowls shown in Photograph 14.1 can also be seen in Figure 14.12, directly in front of the dealer. Also shown in Photograph 14.1 are the objects (i.e., buttons) and the sorting sticks used to arrange the buttons into rows of four.

---

[21] Cook, J.B. (1931, June). San Francisco's old Chinatown. San Francisco Police and Peace Officers' Journal. Retrieved on January 7, 2011, from http://www.sfmuseum.org/hist9/cook.html.

Figure 14.12. Drawing of a Fan Tan Game in Victoria, British Columbia (c. 1900).

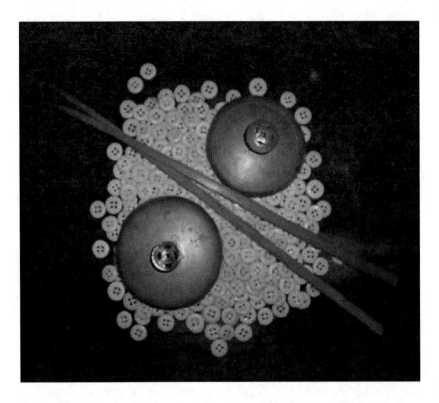

Photograph 14.1. Fan Tan Buttons, Sorting Sticks, & Metal Covers.

Macau casino operators use approximately 500 buttons to deal fan tan. These buttons are no different from those found on a dress shirt. Like roulette, each player is assigned a unique color of chip, allowing dealers to identify which bets belong to whom. The fan tan table is slightly larger than a full-sized dice table.

The layout depicted in Figure 14.13 is featured in the Sands Macau. The surface of the layout consists of a hard plastic material, which can be illuminated by section. Similar to Sic Bo, the betting areas that correspond to the winning outcome(s) are illuminated, once the dealer announces the result. This eases the burden of the dealer on crowded games, with respect to sorting out which wagers are to be paid and which ones are to be collected.

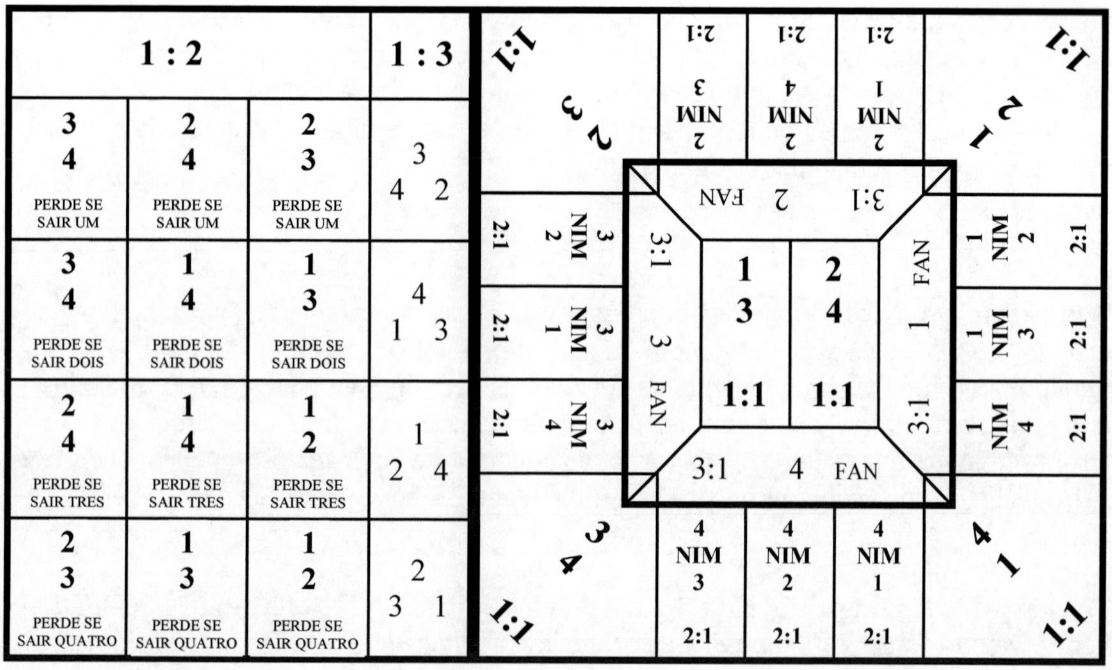

Figure 14.13. Fan Tan Layout: Center Section & One End Section.

Personnel

Operating a fan tan game requires three dealers and one supervisor. One of the three dealers is referred to as the "Counter." This dealer is responsible for handling the buttons and the sorting stick, as well as announcing the results of the count. The counter is positioned at the middle of the table, where the counting of the buttons takes place. A full-sized fan tan table looks much like a craps game, in that both ends of the game feature an identical layout. Like craps, each base dealer is responsible for all activities on his end of the game.

The Game Process

The game or round begins with all of the buttons in a single pile. Again, there are about 500 buttons on the game. The dealer serving as the counter will "shuffle" the buttons by simply running his fingers through the pile at least three times. The counter will then place one of the covers on the pile to separate some of the buttons from the single mass. In Macau, if the counter does not separate and cover at least 40 buttons, the hand/round is considered a misdeal. The second cover is placed on top of the remaining buttons, removing them from play and concealing them from view. Next, the counter will announce "place your bets." Once all wagers have been placed, the counter will announce "no more bets," and the cover concealing the buttons in play is removed.[22] The counter will use the sorting stick to arrange the revealed buttons into rows of four. In Macau, the counter must have enough buttons to form at least ten rows of four.

Once the sorting and arranging of buttons is completed, the counter will announce the result. For example, he might announce "forty-three, winner three." This announcement would indicate that there are at least 40 buttons, with the last row or final group consisting of three buttons. In this case, the winning number would be three. The counter would then push a button on the table that illuminates all betting areas on the layout that would win with a remainder of three buttons.

Fan Wager

While there are five different bets in fan tan, we will start our coverage with the fan wager. The fan wager is nothing more than a bet on the exact number of buttons remaining in the final row. As with all fan tan bets, winning fan bets are paid true odds, less a 5% commission. In the case of the fan wager, true odds are 3 to 1. True odds is a term used in gaming to describe payoff odds equal to the odds against an event occurring. A true odds payoff would provide no casino advantage, hence the 5% commission charge.

To clarify the fan wager and payoff odds structure, consider the following example. If a bettor were to wager $100 on the area of the layout labeled "2 FAN," she would win only if there were two buttons remaining in the final row. Should she win her 2 fan bet, she would be paid $300 (i.e., 3:1), less 5% commission, for a net win of $285. Of course, she would also retain her $100 bet. Figure 14.14 depicts the fan betting area. Notice the 3:1 payoff odds printed next to each of the four fan bets.

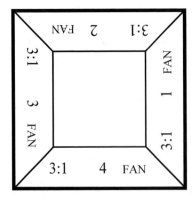

Figure 14.14. The Fan Betting Area

---

[22] Some operators will ring a bell to signify the end of the betting window, instead of only announcing "no more bets."

Kwok Wager

This is a two-number bet that the remainder of buttons will be one of two selected numbers. With four possible outcomes, there are six sets of distinct two-number combinations. That is, there are six different kwok bets. Figure 14.15 illustrates two of these six bets. A bet on the left box would win if the remainder were equal to one or three buttons, while a bet on the right box would win if the remainder were equal to two or four. With kwok bets, there are always two ways to win and two ways to lose. Consequently, the true odds are 1 to 1. Therefore, winning bets are paid 1 to 1, less a 5% commission (i.e., 0.95:1). Figure 14.13 shows all six kwok bets. See if you can locate them on the layout.

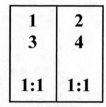

Figure 14.15. Center Kwok Betting Area

Nim Wager

Like the kwok wager, the nim wager is also a two-number bet (see Figure 14.16). However, the nim wager is a little more complicated. The nim bettor wins if the final group contains the top number, ties, if the final group contains the bottom number, and loses, if the final group contains either of the two remaining numbers. For example, if a bettor were to wager on "4 nim 3," the bet would win if the final group contained four buttons, tie if it contained three buttons, and lose if it contained either one or two buttons. Because there is only one way to win a nim bet and there are two ways to lose it, winning wagers are paid 2 to 1, less a 5% commission. One of the four nim betting areas is illustrated in Figure 14.16.

4 NIM 3	4 NIM 2	4 NIM 1
2:1	2:1	2:1

Figure 14.16. "4 Nim" Betting Area

Shen-Sam-Hong Wager

A bet on shen-sam-hong covers three of the four possible numbers of buttons in the final group. Specifically, the shen-sam-hong bettor wins if the final group contains a number of buttons equal to any of the three numbers specified in his wager. The bettor loses if the final group contains the number absent from his selected three-number suite. For example, if a bettor were to place a shen-sam-hong bet in the box labeled "4 3 2," she would win if the final group contained two, three, or four buttons and lose if the final group contained one button. Because there are three ways to win a shen-sam-hong bet and there is only one way to lose it, a winning wager is paid 1 to 3, less a 5% commission. All four of the shen-sam-hong betting areas are depicted in Figure 14.17.

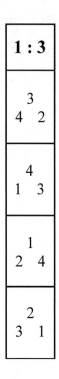

Figure 14.17. Shen-Sam-Hong Betting Areas

Nga Tan Wager

The final section of the fan tan layout is home to the two-number nga tan bets. The nga tan may be the most abstract of the five fan tan wagers. Figure 14.18 depicts the nga tan section of the layout, providing a helpful reference for our explanation of these bets. Referencing Figure 14.18, if a bettor were to place a wager in any of the three boxes in the first row, the bet would lose if the final group contained one button, win if it contained either of the two numbers listed in the selected box, and push if it contained the number omitted from the selected box. As "1" is missing from all the boxes in the first row, the "omitted number" refers to the other number missing from the selected box.

To clarify, let's consider a more definitive example. Assume a bet is placed in the 3-4 box of the first row of Figure 14.18. This bet would win if the final group contained either three or four buttons. The bet would lose if the final group contained one button and it would tie if the final group contained two buttons (i.e., the missing number in the 3-4 box, besides 1). Because "1" is missing from all the boxes in the first row and causes a bet on any of these boxes to lose, any bet in this row is known as an *um wager*. An um bet on the 2-4 box would win if the final group contained two or four buttons and lose if it contained one button. The bet would tie if the final group contained three buttons.

Moving through the second, third, and fourth rows of Figure 14.18, the number omitted from *all* of the cells in each of these rows is the number that causes a bet on any box in that row to lose. Because of this condition, the rows of nga tan bets are named after the number that causes them to lose (i.e., Um (1), Dois (2), Tres (3), & Quatro (4)). Although fan tan is of Chinese origin, these bets have Portuguese names. The language inside the nga tan betting boxes is also Portuguese (e.g., perde se sair dois). The layout examined in this chapter comes from a casino in Macau, which is a former Portuguese city state.

Because there are two ways to win any nga tan bet and only way to lose it, a winning wager is paid 1 to 2, less a 5% commission. All of the possible nga tan bets are shown in Figure 14.18.

An "Um" bet loses on 1, wins on the listed numbers in the selected box, and ties on the remaining number.

A "Dois" bet loses on 2, wins on the listed numbers in the selected box, and ties on the remaining number.

A "Tres" bet loses on 3, wins on the listed numbers in the selected box, and ties on the remaining number.

A "Quatro" bet loses on 4, wins on the listed numbers in the selected box, and ties on the remaining number.

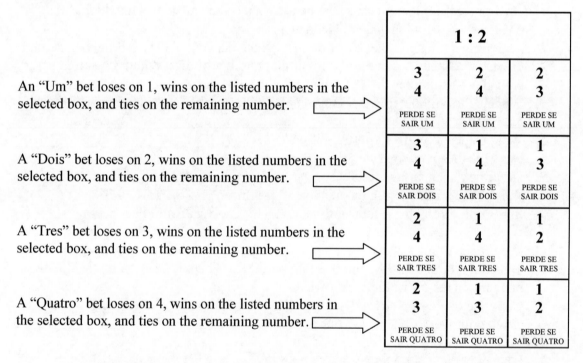

Figure 14.18. Nga Tan Betting Areas: Um, Dois, Tres, & Quatro.

Player Disadvantages

Historically, fan tan has featured some egregious player disadvantages, such as 25% on fan wagers.[23] However, market and competitive pressures have a way of eliminating such margins. As you can see from Table 14.9, the player disadvantages on the fan tan wagers are very much in line with those found on North American core games such as blackjack, craps, roulette, and baccarat.

---

[23] fan-tan. (2011). In *Encyclopaedia Britannica*. Retrieved on May 16, 2011, from http://www.britannica.com/EBchecked/topic/201455/fan-tan.

Table 14.9
Fan Tan
Player Disadvantage by Bet

Wager	Player Disadvantage
Fan	-3.75%
Nim	-2.50%
Kwok	-2.50%
Nga Tan	-1.25%
Shen-Sam-Hong	-1.25%

Questions/Exercises:

1. On a finales en plein 4 wager, the bettor wins if the ball settles in which pocket(s)? A winning wager is paid at a rate of _____.
2. Assuming a finales a cheval bet of 8 & 11, the bettor would win if the ball settled in which pocket(s)? What is the minimum number of units required for this bet?
3. How does a street bet differ from an alley bet?
4. What is the only bet in American roulette with a casino advantage greater than 5.25%?
5. What is meant by the term straight-up?
6. Describe the en prison rule.
7. Describe the la partage rule.
8. What do the following numbers have in common? 17, 34, 6, 1, 20, 14, 31, & 9.
9. In European roulette, a four-unit bet on 2, 12, 22, & 32 would be known as

    _____.
10. In European roulette, a six-unit bet comprised of one unit on the 3, one unit on the 4, one unit on the 13/14 split, one unit on the 23/24 split, one unit on the 33, and one unit on the 34 would be known as _____.
11. Compute the *casino advantage* on a single-number wager in American roulette. Show your work (i.e., show your equation).
12. What are outside wagers?
13. On a hypothetical roulette wheel with 50 pockets, what is the casino advantage on a straight-up wager on 25 (i.e., a single-number bet on 25)? Assume a winning bet is paid at a rate of 47 to 1.
14. With respect to the ante bet, what is the highest hand in three card poker?
15. In three card poker, when a player makes an ante wager, the casino advantage is a function of the bonus schedule in place and _____.
16. In three card poker, when the dealer fails to _____, it is equivalent to folding the hand.
17. Assume a $10 nga tan bet is placed in the "3-4" box of the dois section. Given a remainder of three buttons in the last row, what is the appropriate payout on this wager?
18. List the casino advantage on each wager in fan tan.

Chapter 15
Race and Sports Book Operations

How are money lines established?
What is the difference between a bookmaker and an oddsmaker?
How do bookmakers determine the ideal balance on a money line?
What is a limit in the sports book?
How are payoff odds computed in pari-mutuel horse racing pools?
What is a board track?

Scope

In an area of casino management rife with industry jargon, this chapter explains the race and sports book operation from the perspective of those with little or no exposure to this part of the gaming business. Beginning with the sports book, the following topics are covered: Creation and management of money lines, achieving the ideal balance on a money line, point spread betting, managing the future book, parlay cards, and more. The race book material addresses the following topics: Types of bets and races, pari-mutuel betting, interpreting race results, rebates, off-shore books, and more. After reading this chapter, you will have been exposed to the activities, techniques, and practices critical to the operation of a casino's race and sports book.

Chapter Goals

- Define the key terms central to a discussion about race & sports book operations
- Demonstrate how to create a money line from probable odds
- Explain how bookmakers compute the ideal balance on a money line
- Describe how and why operators move money lines
- Describe point spread betting and line management practices
- Explain the formula used to compute the casino advantage on a future book
- Define the different horse racing bets and types of races
- Explain the mechanics of pari-mutuel wagering
- Describe rebates and the issues that surround this practice

History

The history of race and sports book betting is a fascinating tale, involving some infamous characters. In 1931, Assembly Bill 98 was passed, establishing legal gaming in Nevada and introducing the modern era of casino operations.[1] However, this act did not legalize race or sports betting. Nevertheless, at that time, race and sports wagering was remarkably popular across the United States. Horse and dog tracks provided a legal means of satisfying this demand, while the off-track race books provided an illegal means of satisfaction.

It was not until 1941 that Nevada's chief regulatory body legalized race and sports betting.[2] In 1941, there was no internet, cable television, or even wide-spread telephone service. If Nevada casino operators were to offer wagering on horse races occurring at the legal tracks, they would have to find a way to obtain the results of the races. Specifically, the operators needed to know which horses won and the payoff odds on the winning bets. Unfortunately, the only source of race results was provided by wire services, which were largely controlled by organized crime. These wire services provided results via telegraph. The three major players in the wire service business were Nationwide News Service, Continental Wire Service, and Trans-American Wire Service. The latter was controlled by none other than Al Capone, the notorious mobster.

Bugsy Siegel owned the equivalent of the West coast franchise of the Trans-American Wire Service. Bugsy came to Las Vegas in 1941 to promote his wire service to the casino operators, who could now legally offer race and sports betting. However, if the casino operators were to offer race book betting, they would most likely be forced to make a deal with the devil. That is, mobster-controlled wire services typically demanded a piece of the operator's action in return for providing the results. Nevada's gaming regulators came to realize that any form of partnership with organized crime was not good for the casino operators or the industry in general.

At the national level, there was similar concern regarding the role of organized crime in gaming. In the early 1950s, U.S. Senator, Estes Kefauver, chaired a series of committee hearings conducted in several cities. The focus of these hearings was organized crime activity in the U.S. In particular, Kefauver's committee found evidence of extensive illegal gambling, with organized crime at the center of it. It was estimated that in the late 1930s, Nationwide News Service provided results to over 15,000 illegal bookmakers throughout the U.S.[3]

From the Kefauver committee's findings came laws the government hoped would curtail if not eliminate illegal gambling. One of those laws was the Federal Excise Wagering Tax (FET) of 1951. This law stipulated that any wager not settled immediately after the event was subject to the FET tax. While bets on casino games are settled immediately after the completion of a hand or round, winning race and sports tickets can be redeemed hours or days after the end of the contest/event. The new FET tax was equal to 10% of the dollar-amount wagered. The tax increased the cost of the bet by 10%, and was collected at the time the wager was placed. The FET was paid by the bettor, regardless of

---

[1] Nevada's Assembly Bill 98 was signed into law by Governor Balzar on March 19, 1931.
[2] Nevada Senate Bill 57 amended Chapter CCX of the Laws of Nevada, which specifically prohibited race book wagering and sports pools.
[3] Schwartz, D. G. (2006), *Roll the Bones*, New York: Gotham Books, 366.

the outcome (i.e., win, lose, or tie). That is, even if the game resulted in a tie and the bet was refunded by the operator, the bettor still had to pay the 10% tax.

The FET allowed law enforcement to go after illegal race and sports book operators for tax evasion, when they failed to collect and submit the new wagering tax. Tax evasion was much easier to prove in a court of law. This legislation also required any person who accepted wagers subject to the FET to pay an occupational tax and registration fee of $500. For those who did not comply, law enforcement could levy a second charge for failing to register.

A concerted effort was initiated within Nevada to free casino operators from the undesirable alliance with nefarious wire service operators. In 1952, the Nevada Tax Commission passed a regulation that read as follows:

> "Race Horse Betting is hereby declared to be a form of gambling materially different from other types of gambling. In the interest of public welfare therefore, race book operations shall be conducted only in a building wherein no other types of gaming are operated or liquor dispensed, and no other operations shall be permitted at any time in the room where race book operations are carried on."[4]

In other words, race and sports books had to be segregated from casinos and operate in stand-alone facilities. In 1974, there were only nine legal race and sports books in the entire state of Nevada and, therefore, the U.S. That same year brought significant changes to the operation of race and sports books. Specifically, the Federal Excise Wagering Tax was reduced from 10% to 2%.

By 1975, the Nevada Gaming Commission felt the condition of the industry was such that the books could safely re-enter the casinos. A few months later, the Union Plaza Casino became the first casino in Nevada since 1952 to offer race and sports betting to their patrons. In 1983, the Federal Excise Wagering Tax was reduced further to 0.25%, where it stands today. Interestingly enough, if the wager is illegal, the FET is 2% of the wager.[5] Similarly, for a legal operation, the Occupational Tax and Registration currently stands at $50 per person, per year, and $500 per person, per year, if the operation is illegal within the state.[6] It would be interesting to know if anyone has actually paid these elevated rates, which in effect would be an admission of guilt.

In spite of their checkered past, race and sports books have gained respectability through the decades. As of May 2011, there were 159 race books and 182 sports pools operating in Nevada.[7] Although many states now allow off-track race betting, sports wagering remains restricted to only a few states. The Professional and Amateur Sports Protection Act of 1992 prohibited sports betting in the U.S.; however, a grandfather clause allowed previously legal sports wagering to continue in the following states: Delaware, Montana,

---

[4] Nevada Tax Commission Regulations, adopted April 8, 1952.
[5] Retrieved on July 1, 2011 from http://www.irs.gov/govt/tribes/article/0,,id=181207,00.html.
[6] Ibid.
[7] Nevada Gaming Control Board (2011, May). *Gaming Revenue Report*. Carson City: Author.

Nevada, and Oregon.[8] In spite of its exemption from the act, Oregon subsequently halted sports wagering in 2007.

Sports Book Operations

Prohibited Wagers

Before covering the multitude of available wagers in the sports book, let's establish the types of wagers that cannot be placed. Unlike Great Britain and many off-shore sports books, Nevada does prohibit certain types of wagers.[9] In fact, the following restrictions come from Nevada's gaming regulations.[10]

No wagers may be accepted or paid by any book on:
- Any amateur non collegiate sport or athletic event;
- Any collegiate sport or athletic event which the licensee knows, or reasonably should know, is being placed by, or on behalf of a coach or participant in that collegiate event;
- The outcome of any election for any public office both within and outside the State of Nevada;
- Any event, regardless of where it is held, involving a professional team whose home field, court, or base is in Nevada, or any event played in Nevada involving a professional team, if the team's governing body requests that wagers on the event or series of events be prohibited, and the commission approves the request; and
- Any event other than a horse race, greyhound race, or an athletic sports event, unless such event is administratively approved by the chairman in writing.

In general, for a sports book operator to legally book a wager on an event, the winner must be decided on the field of play (i.e., at the event location) such that the public learns of the outcome at the same time. To the contrary, sports book operators could not book a wager on an event if the person(s) counting the votes knew the winner before the betting public. Therefore, betting lines on events such as the academy awards are for purposes of entertainment only, as no wagers can be legally accepted on such events in the U.S.

Terminology

While the casino industry is somewhat notorious for its confusing vernacular, the sports book is one of the most jargon-heavy areas in gaming. Therefore, much can be clarified by defining some key terms. The next few pages define terms necessary for a deeper discussion of sports book operations.

---

[8] Retrieved on March 2, 2011 from http://www.gambling-law-us.com/Federal-Laws/sports-protection.htm.
[9] Regulations of the Nevada Gaming Commission and State Gaming Control Board as adopted July 1, 1959, and current as of May 2011. Regulation 22, §120, Prohibited wagers.
[10] Ibid.

Line

The line is an amount by which one team or contestant is perceived to be favored over an opposing team or contestant. This line can be expressed in terms of (1) points that are added or subtracted from the final score of one team/contestant or (2) the payoff on a team/contestant relative to the amount wagered. The former is called point spread betting, while the latter is known as money line betting. Both forms will be defined and discussed in subsequent sections of this chapter.

Linemaking Theory

The purpose of the betting line is to create wagering activity such that the bookmaker (i.e., sports book operator) realizes a profit regardless of the outcome of the event. While this is not always the case, it is always the goal. The line is determined by the oddsmaker, the bookmaker, and the bettors. The role of each of these contributors is described in the following paragraphs.

The goal of the oddsmaker is not to predict the outcome of the event, it is to predict how the betting public views the event. That is, the oddsmaker strives to create a line that reflects the sentiment of the betting public. For example, if bettors think that one team is twice as likely to win a particular game, then the oddsmaker would express this opinion in the form of a betting line. The oddsmaker would express the public's view in his line, even if his research suggested the public's view was inaccurate.

There was a time when the bookmaker and the oddsmaker were one and the same. Today, oddsmaking is often provided by third-party specialists with a team of employees who are sports betting enthusiasts. Some sports book operators also use lines vetted in off-shore or online books. For example, online books often post the point spread of an upcoming football game before land-based books. By using the online book's point spread, the land-based operator can feel better about the accuracy of the line. That is, the off-shore line reflects the public's view of the game, to the extent that the wagers that have been *placed* on the game are representative of the public's view.

Once the opening line is received from the oddsmaker, the bookmaker books/accepts wagers on the event, pays winning bets, and, if necessary, adjusts the initial line. For example, let's assume a bookmaker posts a line on a football game that was provided by an oddsmaker. Unfortunately, the early bettors are only interested in betting on one side of the line (i.e., on Team A). In an effort to minimize his risk of loss, the bookmaker will move/adjust the initial line, to attract wagers on the other side (i.e., on Team B).

The bettors greatly affect the line, as they represent the demand for bets on both sides of the line. Remember, the oddsmaker is attempting to provide a line that in effect splits the betting public into two equal camps. If the public were to bet the ideal amount on each side of the initial line, the bookmaker would be very happy with the oddsmaker's line. However, for a variety of reasons, this does not happen. That is, it is not uncommon for bettors to wager disproportionately on one side of a line, which creates great wins and great losses for the book. Fortunately for bookmakers, when this happens across many lines, and it does, the big wins and losses often offset one another, at least to some extent.

Types of Bets

Aside from futures bets, which will be defined later, there are three primary forms of wagering in the sports book. The following bullet points define each type of bet.

- **Straight bet**: A wager that one *side* will win the event. A side could be a team or a contestant. Straight bets are often referred to as a bet on a side (or simply *a side*).
- **Total bet** (a.k.a. *over/under*): This is a wager on the total number of points scored by both teams over the course an entire game. For example, a total score for a game will be posted in the book. Let's assume the posted total for the Packers vs. Steelers is 44 points. Bettors wagering on this total must choose to bet on the over or the under. A bet on the over would win if more than 44 total points were scored in the game, while a bet on the under would win if less than 44 points were scored. If the final score were Packers 31 and Steelers 25, the bets on the over would win, as 56 points were scored. When a bettor wagers on a total, the side (e.g., team) that wins the event has no bearing on the outcome of her wager.
- **Proposition bet**: This type of bet is best explained by way of example. Consider the following proposition bets:
  - The fight will last more than "x" rounds;
  - Team "A" will score first; and
  - Team "B" will win the coin toss.

  Of course, a bettor could wager on the opposite side of each of these proposition bets as well. For example, Team A will win the coin toss.

While parlays and round-robin bets are also offered in the sports book, these wagers are nothing more than combinations of straight bets, totals, and proposition bets. Parlay card wagering will be covered in a subsequent section of this chapter.

Probability and Odds

Probabilities are often used to express the likelihood of specific events occurring. For example, there is a one in six chance (i.e., 0.167) of throwing a 2, given a single, six-sided, fair die. In sports wagering, the precise probability of an event is usually not known. Odds are related to probabilities. Continuing the previous example, the odds *for* throwing a 2 would be expressed as 1 to 5, while the odds *against* throwing a 2 would be expressed as 5 to 1.

Let's assume Team A were playing Team B, and Team A paid 3 to 2 odds on a straight bet to win. Assuming no casino advantage in the payoff odds, this odds ratio would indicate that the betting public believed Team A would lose three of five times (i.e., if the two teams were to play five times). If the odds against a team winning a game were 7 to 1, the betting public would view the team to have a 1 in 8 chance of winning.

Money Lines

On money line wagers, any perceived inequality in opponents is adjusted by changes in the wager to win ratio. Money lines are most often used in sports such as boxing, baseball, golf, tennis, hockey, soccer, and football. For example, Vladimir Klitschko was scheduled to fight David Haye on July 2, 2011. Line 14.1 provides an example of a money line on this fight.

Klitschko   -195
Haye   +170

Line 14.1. Example of a Money Line on a Bet to Win a Boxing Match.

The negative number (i.e., -195) represents the dollar-amount a bettor must wager to win $1. For example, if the bettor believed Klitschko would win, he would have to bet $1.95 to win $1.00. If the bet were to win, the wager would be paid $1.00, plus the $1.95 he wagered, for a total payoff of $2.95.

The positive amount (i.e., +170) represents how much a $1.00 wager would be paid, should Haye win the fight. If a bettor wagered $1.00 on Haye, a winning bet would be paid $2.70, which would include $1.70 of win and a $1.00 refund of his wager.

Money lines are also used to book action on proposition bets. An example of one such bet from the Klitscho-Haye fight is provided in Line 14.2.

Fight will end under 9.5 rounds   -160
Fight will last over 9.5 rounds   +135

Line 14.2. Example of a Money Line on a Proposition Bet.

Favorites and Dogs

In the language of the sports book, when a team is perceived to be the likely winner of a game, it is referred to as the *favorite*. The other team is referred to as the *dog*, which is short for underdog. In Lines 14.1 and 14.2, the favorites are "Klitschko" and "Fight will end under 9.5 rounds," respectively.[11] A favorite will always be a negative number in a money line.

Point Spread Betting

Point spreads are most often used for wagering on football, basketball, hockey, and baseball run lines. For example, the University of Oklahoma played a football game against Florida State University on September 17, 2011, in Tallahassee, Florida. Line 14.3 provides an example of a point spread line on this game.

Oklahoma University   -14 -110
Florida State University   -110

Line 14.3. Example of a Point Spread Line on a College Football Game.

---

[11] For what it's worth, the bout actually went 12 rounds (i.e., the scheduled distance), with Klitschko winning by a unanimous decision. Therefore, a bet on Klitschko was a winner, as was a bet on Over 9.5 rounds.

By looking at Line 14.3, the bettor knows that Florida State University is the home team, as it is listed below Oklahoma University. When games are played on a neutral field, the designated home team will appear as the bottom team in the line. The "-14" is the point spread. In effect, when the game begins, Florida State is ahead by 14 points. Therefore, Oklahoma must score at least 15 points more than Florida State, for those betting on the favorite to win. For example, let's assume the final score of the actual game was Oklahoma 21 and Florida State 14. While this score means everything to the teams that play the game, it is not the score used to settle wagers on the game. That is, for those who bet on Oklahoma, this final score would be interpreted as Oklahoma 7 and Florida State 14. For those who bet on Florida State, the same final score would be interpreted as Florida State 28 and Oklahoma 21. Although Florida State actually lost the game, those betting on Florida State would have won their bets, as the final score per Line 14.3 would have been Oklahoma 21 and Florida State 28. If a bet wins after the point adjustment (from the point spread line), the team is said to have *covered the spread*. In this example, Florida State would have covered the point spread.

The "-110" appearing in Line 14.3 represents the amount the bettor must wager to win $1.00. For example, bettors on either side of the line would have to wager $1.10 to win $1.00. Under ideal conditions, the 14-point line would attract an equal amount of wagers on both teams. That is, for every $1.10 wagered on Oklahoma at -14, the operator would book $1.10 on Florida State at +14. To clarify, consider the following conditions:

Amount Wagered on Oklahoma	$110
Amount Wagered on Florida State	110
Total Amount Wagered	$220

Unless Oklahoma wins the game by exactly 14 points, only one side of the bet will win. No matter which team wins, the bookmaker will return the $110 wager plus $100 in win, for a total payout of $210. However, the bookmaker received $220 in wagers, resulting in a net gain of $10, or 4.5% (i.e., $10 ÷ $220). Under these conditions the bookmaker cannot lose, regardless of which team wins the game. If Oklahoma were to win by exactly 14 points, all bets would push. That is, the bookmaker would simply refund the wagers to the bettors.

Point Spread and Money Line Combinations

It is not uncommon for bookmakers to post a line on a game which features some form of a point spread (e.g., a run line) and a money line. Line 14.4 provides an example of what is known as a combination line.

Teams	Run Line	Money	Over/Under
Philadelphia Phillies (Kendrick)[12]	-1 ½ +155	-106	Over 8 -105
New York Mets (Pelfrey)[13]	+1 ½ -175	-104	Under 8 -115

Line 14.4. Example of a Combination Line on a Baseball Game.

---

[12] Kendrick is the scheduled pitcher for the Phillies. Baseball lines are dependent upon the scheduled or "listed" starting pitchers. That is, if Kendrick fails to start the game, the line(s) will change.
[13] Pelfrey is the listed pitcher for the Mets.

Looking at Line 14.4, you will see that the bettor can wager on the run line, which is baseball's equivalent of points. For example, assume Sarah wagers on the Phillies. She would have to give 1½ runs to the Mets, but she would be paid $1.55 for every $1.00 she bets, i.e., should the Phillies win by at least 2 runs. Alternatively, Sarah could wager on the money line, where she would be betting on one team to win, with no concern for the score. For example, if Sarah believed the Mets were going to win the game (by any number of runs), she would bet $1.04 to win $1.00. Finally, Sarah could bet the over or under run total. If she liked "Over 8" total runs, Sarah would bet $1.05 to win $1.00. Conversely, if she preferred "Under 8" total runs, Sarah would bet $1.15 to win $1.00.

Of course, Sarah could bet any dollar-amount the book would accept on these wagers. The amounts cited in these examples are for explanatory purposes only. That is, it is not likely that anyone would actually bet only $1.55 on a game.

Bettor's Disadvantage on Money Lines

On a money line wager, the bettor's disadvantage is determined by the size of the line. The size of the line is defined as the difference between what the bettor risks on the favorite and how much the book risks on the dog. To clarify, consider Line 14.5.

-145
+135

Line 14.5. Example of a Money Line.

Per Line 14.5, the bettor risks 145 on the favorite and the bookmaker risks 135 on the dog. The difference is 10 (i.e., 145 − 135). Because the difference is 10, Line 14.5 would be considered a 10¢ line (or dime line). Table 15.1 provides supporting calculations. Be sure to read the notes in Table 15.1.

Table 15.1
Computing the Size or Price of the Money Line Shown in Line 14.5

		Amt. Kept by Book if Side Wins	
Cost to Bet the Favorite	145	0	(245 collected − 245 paid-out[a])
Cost to Bet the Dog	100	10	(245 collected − 235 paid-out[b])
Total Amt. Collected	245	10	Sum = Size of Line

Notes. [a] 245 payout = 145 in wager + 100 in win. [b] 235 payout = 100 in wager + 135 in win. All payouts by the book are comprised of one part refunded wager and one part bettor win. Because the book retains 10, Line 14.5 is a 10¢ line.

While it may be easy to see why Line 14.5 would be considered a dime line, the size of the money line shown in Line 14.6 may not be so easy to see.

-110
-110

Line 14.6. Example of a Money Line on Evenly Matched Sides.

Table 15.2 shows the computations necessary to calculate the size of the money line shown in Line 14.6. Again, be sure to read the notes.

Table 15.2
Computing the Size or Price of the Money Line Shown in Line 14.6

		Amt. Kept by Book if Side Wins	
Cost to Bet Side A[a]	110	10	(220 collected – 210 paid-out[b])
Cost to Bet Side B[a]	110	10	(220 collected – 210 paid-out[b])
Total Amt. Collected	220	20	Sum = Size of Line

Notes. [a] As the public perceives both sides to be evenly-matched, there is no favorite or dog, at least in relative terms. [b] 210 payout = 110 in wager + 100 in win. All payouts by the book are comprised of one part refunded wager and one part bettor win. Because the book retains 20, Line 14.6 is a 20¢ line.

While Line 14.6 might appear to be a 10¢ line, it is in fact a 20¢ line. By working through the calculations in Tables 15.1 & 15.2, a deeper understanding of line size can be gained.

From Creating the Odds to Setting the Line

Remember, the oddsmaker seeks to create a line that is attractive to bettors on both sides of it, regardless of its accuracy. Let's assume that the oddsmaker has studied the betting public's view of an upcoming football game and estimates that the bettors view one team as a 7 to 5 favorite. This means that the bettors believe the favorite would win seven times, if the two teams were to play 12 games. Once the odds have been provided by the oddsmaker, the bookmaker would use them to create a money line. The process of creating such a money line is described in the following three-steps.

1. Convert the 7 to 5 odds ratio into a money line with no casino advantage. To do this, the odds ratio provided by the oddsmaker is converted into a "to 1" equivalent. The following process is one way to achieve this task.

$$
\begin{array}{ccc}
7 & to & 5 \\
\div 5 & & \div 5 \\
\hline
1.4 & to & 1 \\
\times 100 & & \times 100 \\
\hline
140 & to & 100 \\
\end{array}
$$

The odds ratio of 1.4 to 1 is multiplied by 100 to express it in terms common to the sports book. Although 140 to 100 is equivalent to 7 to 5, there is still no casino advantage in this line.

2. Convert the restated odds ratio into a money line with no casino advantage. Given a money line with no casino advantage, a winning bet on the favorite would pay an amount equal to the cost of the wager plus the cost of a wager on the dog. In the current example, the cost of betting on the favorite is 140, while the cost of betting on the dog is 100. Therefore, the bookmaker must create a line whereby bettors who wager 140 on the favorite and win are paid 140 + 100. A line of -140

on the favorite satisfies this constraint. Next, a line must be created that pays winning dog bettors an amount equal to the cost of their wager (100) plus the cost of a wager on the favorite (i.e., 140). The line that accomplishes this task is +140. At this point, the line would stand as follows:

-140

+140

3. Build a casino advantage into the money line. Let's assume the bookmaker wishes to create a 10¢ line. In sports wagering, a casino advantage is produced by paying winning bettors something less than the *probable odds* (i.e., 7 to 5). In this example, the bookmaker would post the favorite at -145, which is 5¢ beyond the public's view of the odds. On the dog side, the bookmaker will also pay winning bets 5¢ less than the public's view of the odds. The following 10¢ money line is based on the original 7 to 5 odds provided by the oddsmaker.

-145

+135

Computing the Casino Advantage

Continuing the previous example, let's estimate the disadvantage of a bet on the favorite, given 7 to 5 probable odds and a 10¢ line. With 7 to 5 odds, there are 12 possible outcomes. As previously stated, the betting public believes the favorite would win seven times and the dog would win five times. Assuming these odds are correct and a 10¢ line is in place, the book's net win can be estimated. The formula for this estimate is shown in Equation 15.1.

Estimated Book Win on Favorite = (Total # of Outcomes) (Cost to Bet the Favorite) –
(# of Times Favorite is Expected to Win) (Total Amount Returned to the Bettor)

Equation 15.1. Formula for Estimating the Book's Net Win on a Bet on the Favorite.

From Equation 15.1, it is important to remember that the Total Amount Returned to the Bettor includes the amount won (100) plus the amount wagered (145). Now let's plug the numbers from the current example into Equation 15.1. This is shown in Equation 15.2, where the bets on the favorite are equal to $1.45 each.

$$(12) (\$1.45) - (7) (\$2.45) = \$0.25$$

Equation 15.2. Book's Net Win: -145 Bet on the Favorite at 7:5 Probable Odds.

Once the book's estimated net win is computed, the book's advantage on the wager can be estimated. However, it is important to remind readers that the casino advantage is the quotient of the expected win (i.e., $0.25) and the total amount wagered on the bet(s). For the total wagered on the favorite we look to a portion of Equation 15.2. That is, "(12) ($1.45)" or $17.40 represents the totaled amount wagered on the favorite. Now that we have everything that we need, the book's estimated advantage on a bet on the favorite is computed in Equation 15.3.

$$\$0.25 \div \$17.40 = 1.437\%$$

Equation 15.3. Book Advantage: -145 Bet on the Favorite at 7:5 Probable Odds.

Let's put this result in perspective. For every $100 bet on the favorite the bookmaker can expect to win $1.44. This might be surprising, given the individual bettor's extreme perspective, i.e., he either wins or loses. Neither of those outcomes even remotely resembles a loss of 1.437%. Of course, the bookmaker's perspective is very different, as his reality is comprised of many results, which offset one another. In the end, the bookmaker can expect to win somewhere near 1.437% of the dollar-amount bet on the favorite, given the assumptions of the current example.

Now let's turn our attention to computing the dog bettor's disadvantage against 7 to 5 probable odds on the favorite and a 10¢ line.[14] Before we begin, do you think it will be the same as the favorite bettor's disadvantage? Equation 15.4 is the formula for estimating the book's net win on underdog wagers.

Estimated Book Win on Dog = (Total # of Outcomes) (Cost to Bet the Dog) –
(# of Times Dog is Expected to Win) (Total Amount Returned to the Bettor)

Equation 15.4. Formula for Estimating the Book's Net Win on a Dog Bet.

Next let's enter the numbers from the current example into Equation 15.4. This is shown in Equation 15.5, where the bets on the dog are equal to $1.00 each.

$$(12) (\$1.00) - (5) (\$2.35) = \$0.25$$

Equation 15.5. Book's Net Win: +135 Bet on the Dog at 7:5 Probable Odds.

Before computing the book's advantage, the total amount wagered on the dog must be computed from Equation 15.5. This amount is equal to $12, i.e., "(12) ($1.00)." Now we have everything that we need. Equation 15.6 computes the book's edge on the dog wager.

$$\$0.25 \div \$12.00 = 2.083\%$$

Equation 15.6. Book Advantage: +135 Bet on the Dog at 7:5 Probable Odds.

Although the book's expected win remains the same, at $0.25, the amount wagered on the dog bets ($12.00) is less than that wagered on the favorite ($17.40). This results in a greater book advantage on the dog bet. In fact, given the assumptions of the current example, the bookmaker can expect to win 2.083% of every dollar wagered on the underdog and only 1.437% of every dollar wagered on the favorite.

Line Price Effect

The size (i.e., price) of the line will affect the casino advantage on both favorite and underdog bets. Staying with the previous example of a line based on 7 to 5 probable odds, let's create a 20¢ money line (see Line 14.7).

$$-140 \quad -10¢ \quad = \quad -150$$
$$+140 \quad -10¢ \quad = \quad +130$$

Line 14.7. A 20¢ Money Line Based on 7:5 Probable Odds.

---

[14] Probable odds represent the ratio of "expected # of successes" to "expected # of failures." However, in gaming, probable odds are stated in terms of a bet on/for the favorite (e.g., 7:5 vs. 5:7).

Using Equations 15.1 through 15.6, the casino advantages on the favorite and dog bets are 2.778% and 4.167%, respectively. With a 10¢ line, the casino advantages on these same bets were 1.437% and 2.083%, respectively. As you can see, by doubling the price of the line, the casino advantage is doubled on the dog wager and nearly doubled on the favorite bet. Of course, this is no coincidence. As the price of the line increases, the casino advantage increases, assuming all other conditions are held constant. Table 15.3 demonstrates this effect.

Table 15.3

Relationship Between Price of Line & Book Advantage at 7:5 Odds

Probable Odds	Price of Line	Favorite	Dog	Book Advantage Favorite	Dog
7 to 5	10¢ line	-145	+135	1.437%	2.083%
	20¢ line	-150	+130	2.778%	4.167%
	30¢ line	-155	+125	4.032%	6.250%

Note. While this table only reflects the changes in the book advantages at 7:5 probable odds, the relationship shown here holds for any fixed rate of probable odds.

Probable Odds Effect

As the probable odds of the favorite winning are increased, the casino advantages on both favorite and dog wagers are decreased. This is best explained by way of example. Let's assume the probable odds of a team winning a game were 8 to 5, instead of 7 to 5. An 8 to 5 money line with no casino advantage would be computed as follows:

$$
\begin{array}{ccc}
8 & \text{to} & 5 \\
\div 5 & & \div 5 \\
\hline
1.6 & \text{to} & 1 \\
\times 100 & & \times 100 \\
\hline
160 & \text{to} & 100
\end{array}
$$

Assuming this money line were converted to a dime line, it would be expressed as follows:

$$-165$$
$$+155$$

Line 14.8. A 10¢ Money Line Based on 8:5 Probable Odds.

Again, using Equations 15.1 through 15.6, the casino advantages on both the favorite and dog wagers were calculated at 1.166% and 1.923%, respectively. The same casino advantages on a dime line at 7 to 5 probable odds were 1.437% and 2.083%, respectively. As you can see, an increase in the probable odds of the favorite winning the game leads to a decline in the casino advantage, even with the price of the line held constant at 10¢.

Table 15.4 illustrates this point nicely. Notice how increases in the probable odds are met with declines in the casino advantages on both favorite and dog wagers.[15]

Probable			Book Advantage	
Odds	Dime Line		Favorite	Dog
5 to 5	-105	-105	2.381%	2.381%
5.25 to 5	-110	+100	2.217%	2.439%
5.50 to 5	-115	+105	2.070%	2.381%
5.75 to 5	-120	+110	1.938%	2.326%
6.00 to 5	-125	+115	1.818%	2.273%
6.25 to 5	-130	+120	1.709%	2.222%
6.50 to 5	-135	+125	1.610%	2.174%
6.75 to 5	-140	+130	1.520%	2.128%
7.00 to 5	-145	+135	1.437%	2.083%
7.25 to 5	-150	+140	1.361%	2.041%
7.50 to 5	-155	+145	1.290%	2.000%
7.75 to 5	-160	+150	1.225%	1.961%
8.00 to 5	-165	+155	1.166%	1.923%
8.25 to 5	-170	+160	1.110%	1.887%
8.50 to 5	-175	+165	1.058%	1.852%
8.75 to 5	-180	+170	1.010%	1.818%
9.00 to 5	-185	+175	0.965%	1.786%
9.25 to 5	-190	+180	0.923%	1.754%
9.50 to 5	-195	+185	0.884%	1.724%
9.75 to 5	-200	+190	0.847%	1.695%
10.00 to 5	-205	+195	0.813%	1.667%

Table 15.4
Relationship Between Odds of Favorite
Winning & Book Advantages

In summary, the bookmaker can increase the casino advantage by increasing the price of the line (i.e., from 10¢ to 20¢). In fact, this is the only way to increase the house edge. Unfortunately, such an act might be met with protest from the clientele, as changes in the price of lines will not go unnoticed. Additionally, competitors may lure away bettors with better-priced lines.[16] However, as the odds of the favorite winning the event are increased, the bookmaker *must* increase the price of the line in order to maintain/protect the casino advantage.

---

[15] There is one exception. The second line of Table 15.4 shows an increase in the casino advantage on the dog wager from Line 1 (i.e., instead of a decrease from Line 1). This is caused by the inability of a dime line to adapt to the fractional change in the probable odds, i.e., from 5:5 to 5.25:5.

[16] Over the years, baseball money lines have dropped precipitously, as a result of competitive pressures.

Ideal Balance

Probable odds merely represent the public opinion. The accuracy of probable odds depends on the public's ability to consider all variables capable of influencing the result of an event. As shown in Table 15.1, if every $1.45 bet on the favorite is matched by a $1.00 wager on the dog, the book can only realize a profit if the dog wins.

The content of Table 15.1 is based on 7 to 5 probable odds against a 10¢ line. Of course, 7 to 5 probable odds offer no guarantee that the dog will win five times in 12. Consequently, the bookmaker strives to achieve what is known as ideal balance.

Ideal balance guarantees the book will make a profit, regardless of the odds. For example, let's assume for some unimaginable reason, the public thought that Jim Kilby was an 8.25 to 5 favorite in a prize fight against Wladimir Klitchshko, making a case for the possible inaccuracy of public opinion. Further, let's assume the book posts the 70¢ money line shown in Line 14.9.

$$\begin{array}{ll} \text{Kilby} & -200 \\ \text{Klitschko} & +130 \end{array}$$

Line 14.9. A 70¢ Money Line Based on 8.25 to 5 Probable Odds.

Regardless of the "possible" inaccuracy of this line, the book could still be guaranteed to profit from it, by achieving the ideal balance. The formula for ideal balance is shown in Equation 15.7.

$$\cfrac{\cfrac{CF}{CF + WF}}{\cfrac{CF}{CF + WF} + \cfrac{CD}{CD + WD}}$$

Equation 15.7. Ideal Balance Formula for Money Line Wagering.

In Equation 15.7, "CF" represents the cost to bet the favorite and "WF" represents the bettor's win on a favorite bet, which does not include the amount of the wager. On the dog side, "CD" represents the cost to bet the dog and "WD" represents the bettor's win on a dog bet, which also does not include the amount of the dog wager. Equation 15.8 plugs in numbers from the current example, which may clarify the ideal balance formula.

$$\cfrac{\cfrac{200}{200 + 100}}{\cfrac{200}{200 + 100} + \cfrac{100}{100 + 130}} = 60.526\%$$

Equation 15.8. Ideal Balance for Money Line Wagering on Kilby vs. Klitschko.

In spite of the public's questionable view of this fight, if 60.526% of the amount wagered were bet on the favorite, Kilby, with the balance (i.e., 39.474%) wagered on the dog,

Klitschko, the book would be guaranteed a profit. To further demonstrate this somewhat amazing phenomenon, let's assume that a total of $10,000 was wagered on the money line, with $6,053 bet on Kilby and $3,947 bet on Klitschko. Table 15.5 shows how the ideal balance would guarantee a profit.

Table 15.5
Demonstrating Ideal Balance on Line 14.9: Kilby vs. Klitschko

	(A)	(B)	(C) (A) x (B)	(D) (A) + (C)	(E) $10k – (D)	(F) (E) ÷ 10k
Potential Winner	Amount Wagered	Win/Wager	Bettors' Win	Total Returned	Sports Book Profit Amt.	%
Kilby	$6,053	100/200	$3,026	$9,079	$921	9.2%
Klitschko	$3,947	130/100	$5,132	$9,079	$921	9.2%
	$10,000					

Bettor's Break-even Rate

Given any money line, the bettor can compute the win percentage required to break-even against the terms of the line. For example, let's assume Sarah is considering betting the favorite at -145. Equation 15.9 provides a simple way to calculate the percentage of identical wagers Sarah would have to win to break-even, in the long term.

$$\frac{\text{Cost to Bet}}{\text{Cost to Bet} + \text{Potential Win}}$$

or

$$\frac{145}{145+100} = 59.184\%$$

Equation 15.9. Bettor's Break-even Rate Against -145 Money Line Bets.

In this example, Sarah would have to win 59.184% of her bets to break-even. However, if she were to bet the dog against this same money line (i.e., +135), she would only need to win 42.553% of her bets (See equation 15.10).

$$\frac{100}{100+135} = 42.553\%$$

Equation 15.10. Bettor's Break-even Rate Against +135 Money Line Bets.

Defining Limits

In the sports book, there are three definitions of a *limit*. Each of these uses are described in the following paragraphs.

1. When betting the favorite or laying a price, a limit is the maximum amount the bookmaker is willing to lose on that bet.[17] For example, let's assume a money line bet is made on the favorite at -140. If the book's posted limit is $10,000, then the maximum wager allowed would be $14,000. That is, if the bettor must lay 1.4 to 1 (i.e., -140), then she would be permitted to make a maximum wager of 1.4 times the posted limit (i.e., 1.4 x 10,000 = $14,000). The $14,000 bet would be referred to as a limit wager because the bettor could win $10,000, i.e., the posted limit.

2. Typically, more bettors wager on the favorite than on the dog. To compensate, dog bettors or those taking a price are permitted to wager an amount equal to the posted limit.[18] This is permitted in spite of the fact that the amount won would exceed the posted limit. That is, a book with a posted limit of $10,000 would accept a $10,000 bet, even if the potential win were $14,000. In this case, the $10,000 bet would be referred to as a limit wager.

3. A limit is the dollar-amount the book is willing to be out of balance, before adjusting the line. For example, when the dollar-value of wagers on one side of a line causes it to become dangerously out of balance, the bookmaker will often adjust the line. Of course, this adjustment will discourage additional bets on the overloaded side of the line, while simultaneously encouraging bets on the other side of the line.

Betting Limits by Sport

In general, as the number of unsophisticated bettors increases, so too will the book's limits. For example, the Super Bowl attracts a great number of casual bettors, whom the bookmaker's usually classify as less knowledgeable about sports wagering. That is, less knowledgeable than their typical clientele. Consequently, bets on the Super Bowl will always be afforded the highest limits. By comparison, hockey bettors are generally very involved and well-versed in the key match-ups in the games. Because of their prowess as bettors, betting limits on hockey games are often conservative. Table 15.6 provides a meaningful comparison of betting limits by sport. The limits in Table 15.6 might be found in one of the larger Las Vegas sports books.

Table 15.6
Betting Limits by Sport & Bet Type: Large LV Book

	Side	Over/Under
NFL – Pro Football	$20,000	$2,000
College Football	$10,000	$1,000
NBA – Pro Basketball	$5,000	$500
College Basketball	$3,000	$500
MLB – Pro Baseball	$5,000	$1,000
NHL – Pro Hockey	$2,000	$500

Note. Limits for all sports are not shown here.

---

[17] *Laying* a price means wagering an amount that exceeds the amount of the potential win. For example, wagering an amount greater than one dollar to win one dollar.

[18] If the potential win exceeds the amount wagered, the bettor is said to be *taking* a price. For example betting one dollar on a line that would produce a win greater than one dollar (e.g., +130).

Moving Money Lines

The money line will be moved/adjusted when a specific outcome would cause the book to lose an amount equal to or greater than the established limit. As previously noted, an adjustment to the line is intended to discourage betting on one side, while encouraging betting on the other side. It is important to remember that lines are moved in an effort to limit the book's exposure to great losses and to work toward the ultimate goal of ideal balance. That said, the general rules governing the movement of lines are as follows:

(1) Line prices < 40¢ are moved in increments equal to ½ the price of the line; and
(2) Line prices ≥ 40¢ are moved in increments equal to ¼ the price of the line.

The simplest way to explain the line movement process is by way of example. Let's assume the book has established a $5,000 loss limit. Further let's assume the current line on a game is as follows:

-190
+170

Finally, assume that the bookmaker is facing each of the three following scenarios, labeled "A," "B", & "C":

	A	B	C
Amount wagered on the favorite	$13,000	$13,000	$13,300
Amount wagered on the underdog	$2,000	$10,600	$2,000

By analyzing the amounts wagered within the context of the assumed limit of $5,000 and the line itself, the bookmaker must determine the following:

(1) Whether the line should be moved under each of the three scenarios; and
(2) The appropriate adjustment, if a move is required.

Again, if the amounts wagered in each of the scenarios expose the book to a loss that is equal to or greater than the established limit (i.e., $5,000), the bookmaker must adjust the line accordingly. Now we are ready to examine each of the three scenarios.

Scenario A – Cases 1 & 2

Case 1: If the underdog were to win, the favorite would lose. In this case, the $2,000 wagered on the underdog would be paid at a rate of $1.70 for every dollar wagered, or $3,400 (i.e., $2,000 x 1.70/1.00). The bookmaker would have no trouble making this payment, as he has collected $13,000 in wagers on the favorite. In conclusion, the amount wagered on the underdog would not require an adjustment to the existing line.

Case 2: If the favorite were to win, the dog bets would lose. In this case, the favorite bettors would be paid at a rate of $1.00 for every $1.90 wagered, or $6,842 (i.e., $13,000 x 1.00/1.90). While the bookmaker has only collected $2,000 in dog bets, the difference of $4,842 (i.e., $6,842 - $2,000) is still less than $5,000. Therefore, no adjustment to the line would be required.

Scenario B – Cases 1 & 2

Case 1: If the favorite were to win, the dog would lose. In this case, the favorite bettors would be paid at a rate of $1.00 for every $1.90 wagered, or $6,842 (i.e., $13,000 x 1.00/1.90). Given that the book has collected $10,600 in dog wagers, there is certainly no need to move this line.

Case 2: If the underdog were to win, the favorite would lose. With $10,600 wagered on the dog, winning bettors would be paid at a rate of $1.70 for every $1.00 wagered, or $18,020 (i.e., $10,600 x 1.70/1.00). As the book has only collected $13,000 in wagers on the favorite, a loss of $5,020 would be incurred. This potential loss exceeds the established loss limit in our example (i.e., $5,000), and, therefore, would warrant an adjustment to the line.

Because it is a 20¢ line, it would be moved in ½-price or 10¢ increments. As too much money has been wagered on the underdog, the bookmaker would adjust the line to discourage further wagering on the underdog, while simultaneously encouraging wagers on the favorite. This would be accomplished by decreasing the payout on winning dog wagers by 10¢ and decreasing the amount favorite bettors must lay by 10¢. The adjusted line would be offered as follows:

-180
+160

Scenario C – Cases 1 & 2

Case 1: If the favorite were to win, bettors would be paid $7,000 ($13,300 x 1.00/1.90). As the bookmaker has only collected $2,000 in underdog wagers, such an event would trigger a loss of $5,000. In this case, the line would be moved to discourage additional wagers on the favorite and encourage additional wagers on the underdog. Given that it is a 20¢ line, each side would be moved by 10¢, resulting in the following line:

-200
+180

Case 2: If the dog were to win, bettors would be paid $3,400 (i.e., $2,000 x 1.70/1.00). Given that the bookmaker has collected $13,300 in wagers on the favorite, paying the winning dog bettors would not be an issue. No adjustment to the line would be required.

Penny Lines

Some books post what are known as penny lines. The name is somewhat deceiving, as it suggests a money line that features a very small spread. Penny lines take their name from the degree to which the line is moved, as opposed to the price or spread. That is, penny lines are moved in increments of 1¢. For example, let's assume a bookmaker posts the following penny line in a book operating with a $10,000 limit.

-122
+112

If the line became out of balance by $2,000 (i.e., 20% of the limit), it would be moved by 2¢ (i.e., 20% of 10¢). While this is a dime line with respect to the spread, it is a penny line with respect to how it is moved. The 2¢ adjustment is shown in the following line.

-124

+114

Moving Over/Under Totals

Just like money line bets on sides, when the bookmaker risks losing the established limit on a game total, he will move the line. In baseball, there are far fewer possible total scores and the totals are much more tightly distributed. For example, not many games end with totals less than three runs or more than 15 runs. Because of these conditions, over/under totals are not usually moved. When a line does become out of balance, the bookmaker will move the money line associated with the run total. For example, let's assume the dollar-amount of wagers on "Over 8" drives a line out of balance. Rather than moving the run total off of 8, the bookmaker would make future Over 8 bets less attractive by moving the money line. Line 14.10 provides an example of a 20¢ line on a total of eight runs, which features an adjustment by way of the associated money line.

Initial Line		Adjusted Line
-110 ov		-120 ov
8		8
-110 un		+100 un

Line 14.10. Baseball Over/Under Line Adjusted via the Money Line.

Point Spread Betting

History

Prior to the early 1940s, the only option available to sports bettors was the money line.[19] It was then, in the early 1940s, that the gambling world experienced the watershed known as point spread betting. Charles K. McNeil was the man credited with its invention.[20] A former math teacher, securities analyst, and maverick gambler, McNeil had changed sports betting forever. Although largely unknown and certainly unsung throughout his gambling career, he was eventually recognized as one of the most influential figures in the evolution of sports betting.

A well-known adage holds that necessity is the mother of invention. And it was certainly necessity that brought McNeil to invent the point spread. The bulk of his early working life spanned the great depression of the 1930s. These lean economic times may have

---

[19] That is, if Notre Dame and USC were to play a football game, an example of the betting line would be as follows: Notre Dame -200 and USC +170. With point spread betting, the line on the same game would be stated as Notre Dame -6 points (or USC +6 points).

[20] Boyle, R.H. (1986, March 10). The brain that gave us the point spread. Sports Illustrated. Retrieved on July 24, 2011, from http://sportsillustrated.cnn.com/vault/article/magazine/MAG1064575/ index.htm.

steered him toward his true ambition – gambling. McNeil's success as a gambler was so prolific it became difficult for him to find wagering outlets. That is, no one wanted to take his bets! It was this reality that drove him to bookmaking.

The notion of the point spread as a bookmaking device, came from McNeil's own system of picking winners as a gambler. For many years, football was his game of choice, both as a fan and as a gambler. His system was predicated in part by estimating the margin of victory, which eventually became known as the point spread. As a bookmaker, he began offering point spreads on football games, which was an instant success. He immediately expanded his business by offering point spreads on college basketball. It was not long before his bookmaking operation became the biggest game in town.

McNeil quit bookmaking in 1950, but remained an avid sports bettor. By his own account, he went on to enjoy staggering success as a professional gambler, and there is no reason to doubt him. Charles McNeil once said, "There are three things a gambler needs: money, guts, and brains. If you don't have one, you're dead. I've got all three." [21]

Point Spread Betting in Football

Like money lines, point spreads provide bookmakers with a way to make two teams equally attractive to the betting public. At least, that is the goal. While most baseball wagers are made by way of the money line, point spread betting is central to football wagering. In baseball wagering, the money line is created and adjusted in an attempt to even the match-up. In football, the point spread is used to achieve the same result. Consider the following line.

> Saints
> Packers -3   41

As previously stated, the bottom team is the home team or designated home team. The Packers are a three point favorite, hence the "-3" next to the team name. Therefore, for a bet on the Packers to win, the Packers must win the game by at least four points. The bet will lose if the Packers win by less than three points, or lose the game outright. Conversely, the opposite conditions hold for a bet on the Saints. If the Packers win by exactly three points, all bets would push. This result would be considered a tie against the spread. The "41" is the over/under total for the game's final score. Typically, over/under wagers are bet at -110 on both the over and the under. That is, regardless of the bettor's selection (over or under), she must lay $1.10 to win $1.00.

Moving Point Spreads

When the bookmaker risks losing the limit at a given point spread, he will consider moving the line (i.e., point spread). This is done to discourage additional wagering on the overloaded side, while simultaneously encouraging betting on the other side. In general, point spreads are moved according to the following rules:

>   (1) Single digit point spreads are moved in ½-point increments; and

---

[21] Ibid.

(2) Double digit point spreads are moved in 1-point increments.

Again, the purpose of moving the spread is to influence future betting behavior. Consequently, the bookmaker may increase the point spread in excess of the guidelines provided here. For instance, if a college football team were a 24-point favorite, it is doubtful that a 1 point adjustment to the line would influence the public's betting behavior. In this case, the bookmaker would move the line by an increment that accomplished his objective. Nevertheless, the previously stated rules apply to most cases and provide a basis for understanding point spread management from the bookmaker's perspective.

Managing Lines on Common Margins of Victory

Certain point spreads coincide with common margins of victory. These spreads are often referred to as *magic numbers*. Bookmakers are reluctant to move the spread off of a magic number. In pro football, victory margins of 3, 6, 7, and 10 are common. Usually, the bookmaker will not move the spread off of 6, 7, and 10, until they risk losing 150% of the limit. Three points is the most common margin of victory in pro football. Most bookmakers will not move the spread off of three, under any circumstances. Rather than moving the spread off of three, most bookmakers will move the money line. For example, let's assume the Tampa Bay Buccaneers are a 3-point favorite, and the book has received too much action on the Buccaneers. Instead of moving the point spread from -3 to -3½, the bookmaker would move the money line on the Buccaneers from -110 to -120. This move would accomplish the objective of discouraging additional bets on the favorite. Of course, the money line on the dog would also be moved from -110 to even, to encourage additional wagering.[22]

Although football was the focus of this explanation of magic number management, other sports have magic numbers as well. For example, the magic number in college basketball is 2.

Moving Totals

In football and basketball totals, the line itself is moved. For example, if betting caused the book to exceed the loss limit on "Over 42," the bookmaker would move the total to "Over 43." In baseball, as previously stated, the money associated line is moved instead of the total itself.

Buying a Half-Point

The option to buy a half-point was once available in most sports books. Today, this option is far less common and usually restricted. In fact, some books no longer allow bettors to buy half-points.

When buying a half-point, the bettor pays a higher price to make a bet against a more favorable point spread. For example, let's assume the San Diego Chargers are an 8-point

---

[22] "Even" is the same as -100 or +100. In both cases, the bettor is wagering a $1.00 to win $1.00. "Ev" is also used to convey these terms.

favorite over the Kansas City Chiefs. A Charger bettor who is willing to buy a half-point could wager on his team at -7½ instead of -8. However, the Charger bettor would have to bet 120 to win 100. If the same bettor took the Chargers at -8, he would only have to bet 110 to win 100. The same terms would be available to a Chiefs bettor, but in this case, buying a half-point would move the spread from +8 to +8½.

The sports books that still sell half-points have heavily restricted the terms of the offer. Seldom, if ever, can a bettor buy off of or on to a 3-point spread. For example, the bookmaker would not sell a half-point to a better who wished to move a spread from 3 to 2½ or from 2½ to 3. The same restrictions are often applied to half-point buys off of, or on to, a 7- point spread.

In general, the online books are more liberal regarding the sale of half-points. Some online books allow the bettor to buy up to three half-points, with each half-point costing 10¢. Continuing the previous example, a Chargers bettor could buy the line down to -7 from -8½, but she would have to bet 140 to win 100. That is, bettors who buy the first half-point must lay 120 to win 100, buying the second half-point requires a bet of 130 to win 100, and buying the third half-point requires a bet of 140 to win 100.

Protection

There is a growing number of individuals and teams who make a science of sports betting. These professional bettors can do serious damage to a book's profitability. Therefore, books have adopted various techniques to minimize their exposure to these bettors. The first of these methods is the limit itself. As previously noted, the limit varies by sport. This occurs because some mainstream sports such as pro football attract a greater number of casual bettors. In general, as the percentage of wagering volume from casual gamblers increases, so too does the betting limit. Table 15.6 supports this argument, as pro football (i.e., the NFL) carries the greatest betting limits of any sport listed.

Another technique is known as *circling* a game. This term comes from the days when race and sports books used chalkboards or whiteboards to post the lines. When a posted line/game was circled, it indicated that the bookmaker had cut the limits in half. Therefore, it took less action to move the line. Games were circled whenever events occurred that added considerable uncertainly to the outcome. Most modern books use electronic boards to post the lines, many of which are capable of illuminating a circle around a line to indicate that lower limits are in effect. Some electronic boards "circle" games by displaying the line within a red betting box.

Finally, bookmakers can take a game *off the board*. This expression is used to describe a game on which no further bets will be booked. If there is a great amount of uncertainty surrounding a contest, the bookmaker may decide to limit his exposure by taking the game off the board. This is the most drastic form of protection, as the book must post lines and take bets to produce a profit. Therefore, the bookmaker must have a strong case for taking a game off the board. To the contrary, failure to take a game down can be damaging to profits as well.

Parlay Cards

On the parlay card shown in Figure 15.1, the bettor can wager on between two and 11 lines. That is, the bettor can choose from point spread bets and over/under totals on each game of the current week. It is presumed that the bettor has an equal chance to win or lose each individual selection on the parlay card. For example, if Sarah selects three teams, her chances of winning all three selections would be expressed as $1 \div 2^3$ or $(0.5)(0.5)(0.5)$. That is, Sarah could expect to win a three-team parlay one time in every eight attempts, or on 12.5% of her attempts. Of course, these probabilities assume each team has an equal chance of winning against the point spread.

From Figure 15.1, a closer look at the column labeled "Line" reveals that this is an example of what is known as a half-point parlay card. With this form of parlay card, no game can end in a tie against the spread. That is, all the point spreads end in half-points (e.g., -3.5), which creates a winner and loser for every game. Using the pay rates from the "Odds" columns of Figure 15.1, Table 15.7 lists the computed book advantages on the half-point parlay card.

Table 15.7
Book Advantage on Half-Point Parlay Card

Parlay	Payoff to 1	Book Advantage
2-teams	2.6	10%
3-teams	5	25%
4-teams	9	38%
5-teams	16	47%
6-teams	30	52%
7-teams	50	60%
8-teams	90	64%

Note. Book advantages on parlays in excess of eight teams are not shown here.

		NFL			12/2/1X
TV Air Time		**Favorite**	**Line**		**Underdog**
8:20 PM	1	NYJ	-3.5	2	**BUF**
	3	Over	37.5	4	Under
1:00 PM	5	DEN	-4.5	6	**KAN**
	7	Over	38.5	8	Under
1:00 PM	9	**PIT**	-14.5	10	OAK
	11	Over	37.5	12	Under
1:00 PM	13	**JAC**	-.5	14	HOU
	15	Over	46.5	16	Under
1:00 PM	17	**IND**	-6.5	18	TEN
	19	Over	47.5	20	Under
1:00 PM	21	PHI	-5.5	22	**ATL**
	23	Over	44.5	24	Under
1:00 PM	25	**CIN**	-13.5	26	DET
	27	Over	42.5	28	Under
1:00 PM	29	NOS	-9.5	30	**WAS**
	31	Over	47.5	32	Under
1:00 PM	33	**CAR**	-6.5	34	TAM
	35	Over	40.5	36	Under
1:00 PM	37	**CHI**	-9.5	38	STL
	39	Over	41.5	40	Under
4:05 PM	41	SDC	-13.5	42	**CLE**
	43	Over	42.5	44	Under
4:15 PM	45	**SEA**	-.5	46	SFX
	47	Over	41.5	48	Under
8:20 PM	49	MIN	-4.5	50	**ARI**
	51	Over	48.5	52	Under
4:15 PM	53	DAL	-2.5	54	**NYG**
	55	Over	45.5	56	Under
1:00 PM	57	NEP	-5.5	58	**MIA**
	59	Over	46.5	60	Under
8:30 PM	61	**GBP**	-3.5	62	BAL
	63	Over	43.5	64	Under

		Home teams in **BOLD**			
Parlay	**Odds**		**Parlay**	**Odds**	**1-Loss Odds**
2-teamer	2.6X		7-teamer	50X	N/A
3-teamer	5X		8-teamer	90X	N/A
4-teamer	9X		9-teamer	160X	5X
5-teamer	16X		10-teamer	300X	10X
6-teamer	30X		11-teamer	500X	15X

Figure 15.1. Example of an NFL Parlay Card.

Computing the book advantage is not difficult on half-point parlay cards, as each selection either wins or loses. However, other parlay cards post full-point lines, which allow games to tie against the spread. Calculating the book advantage on a full-point card is more difficult, because the probability of a tie against the spread must be considered. Table 15.8 shows the frequency with which football games end in a tie against the spread.

Table 15.8
Probability of Game Ending
in a Tie Against the Spread

	Probability of Tie Against Spread[23]	
Spread	NFL	College Football
1	2.50%	2.48%
2	1.98%	1.77%
3	9.79%	6.39%
4	2.99%	2.51%
5	1.68%	1.99%
6	3.40%	2.57%
7	5.72%	5.28%
8	2.14%	1.66%
9	0.90%	0.82%
10	4.91%	3.78%

Teaser Cards

A teaser card is a form of parlay card with point spreads adjusted to benefit the bettors. Typically, bettors will select one side of between three and ten lines. Teasers cards are most often offered on pro football games. To explain the teaser card process, consider the games listed in Figure 15.2, which were excerpted from Figure 15.1.

TV Air Time	Favorite	Line	Underdog
8:20 PM	NYJ	-3.5	**BUF**
1:00 PM	DEN	-4.5	**KAN**

Figure 15.2. Selected Lines from the NFL Parlay Card Depicted in Figure 15.1.

From Figure 15.2, the standard parlay card offers the New York Jets (NYJ) at -3.5. The six-point teaser card would offer the New York Jets at +2.5. That is, on this teaser card, six points would be added to both sides of every line. For example, the standard parlay card offers the Buffalo Bills (BUF) at +3.5, while the six-point teaser card would offer the Bills at +9.5. As you might have guessed, the trade-off for these bettor-friendly point spreads is lower payoff odds. Table 15.9 compares the payoff odds offered on the standard parlay card to several versions of teaser cards. Notice that increases in the number of points added to the spread results in steadily decreasing payoff odds.

---

[23] Retrieved on July 31, 2011 from http://www.sbrforum.com/betting-tools/half-point-calculator/. Note: Google Chrome may be required to view the calculator.

Table 15.9
Comparison of Payoffs Odds: Standard vs. Teaser Parlay Cards

# of Selections		No Add'l Points[a]	6 Add'l Points	6½ Add'l Points	7 Add'l Points
2	pays	2.6 to 1	1 to 1	10 to 11	5 to 6
3	pays	5 to 1	9 to 5	8 to 5	3 to 2
4	pays	9 to 1	3 to 1	5 to 2	2 to 1
5	pays	16 to 1	9 to 2	4 to 1	7 to 2

Note. [a] Payoffs in this column represent those offered on the standard parlay card.

Future Book

A future book is based on a set of odds related to the eventual outcome of a series of events. For example, at the end of the pro football season, bookmakers will post a future book (or futures) on which team will win the next Super Bowl. Futures are also posted for the World Series, Winston Cup, Wimbledon, and several other premier sporting events. Table 15.10 provides an example of the payoff odds associated with futures bets on Super Bowl 46 winners.

Table 15.10
Payoff Odds on Futures Bets to Win Super Bowl XLVI

Team	Open	Current
Pittsburgh	8/1	9/1
Chicago	15/1	14/1
Green Bay	7/1	
New England	7/1	
.		
.		
.		
Carolina	125/1	

A bet on a future book can be placed at any time prior to the event that settles the wager. In Table 15.10, Pittsburgh opened at 8 to 1, but is currently paying 9 to 1, while Chicago opened at 15 to 1, but is currently paying 14 to 1. A future book is managed just like a money line. Whenever the book stands to lose a specified amount on a given team, the payoff odds will be moved. From the payoff data in Table 15.10, we know the bookmaker wants more money wagered on Pittsburgh and less money wagered on Chicago. Consequently, the payoff odds on Pittsburgh were moved to 9 to 1, from 8 to 1, and the payoff odds on Chicago were moved to 14 to 1, from 15 to 1. After the moves, Pittsburgh looks better to prospective bettors while Chicago looks worse.

Computing the Book Advantage

To demonstrate how the book's advantage is computed, let's assume we only have four teams in a future book to win the World Series. These four teams and their associated payoff odds are listed in Table 15.11.

Team	Payoff Odds
Royals	8/5
Astros	2/1
Yankees	5/2
Reds	5/1

Table 15.11
Future Book on
World Series Winners

The formula shown in Equation 15.11 would be used to compute the future book's overall expected advantage for a bet on a team to win the World Series.

Expected Book Advantage = (Sum of Win Probabilities - 1) ÷ Sum of Win Probabilities

Equation 15.11. Expected Advantage Formula for a Future Book.

The "probability" of each of the four teams winning the World Series can be computed from the payoff odds. Of course, these probabilities are derived from the booked wagering volume, and, therefore, do not represent actual probabilities. Table 15.12 lists the odds against each team winning, the odds for each team winning, and the related probability of each team winning.

Table 15.12
Future Book Wagering Data: Bets on World Series Winners

Team	Odds Against Team Winning	Odds For Team Winning	Probability of Team Winning	
Royals	8:5	5:8	5:13	0.3846
Astros	2:1	1:2	1:3	0.3333
Yankees	5:2	2:5	2:7	0.2857
Reds	5:1	1:5	1:6	0.1667
			Sum of Probabilities	1.1703

From Table 15.12, we see that the payoff odds on the Royals are at 8 to 5, which indicates that the betting public feels this team is more likely to lose than win. In fact, this is the case for all the teams in the betting field. Staying with the Royals, the bettors believe that if the season were to be completed 13 times, the Royals would win the World Series in 5 of those seasons and fail to do so in the other 8 seasons. Therefore, the "probability" of the Royals winning the World Series is said to be 0.3846 (i.e., 5/13). It is the sum of each team's probability that is needed to compute the book's advantage (i.e.,

1.1703 in our example). Using Equation 15.11, our future book's overall advantage on bets to win the World Series is expressed as follows:

$$(1.1703 - 1) \div 1.1703 = 0.1455, \text{ or } 14.55\%$$

Proposition Bets

Now that the necessary components and various structures of sports betting have been covered, the variety of proposition bets should come as no surprise. That is, a betting line can be created and offered for many different types of events. The following is a list of somewhat unusual bets offered on the Super Bowl that was played on February 6, 2011.

- How long will it take Carrie Underwood to sing the national anthem?
  - Over/Under 1 minute 42 seconds.

- Will there be a successful 2-point conversion?
  - Yes +400; No -600

- The first end zone celebration will be:
  (Payoff odds appear in parentheses)
  - Ball spike (2 to 1)
  - Flex bicep (4 to 1)
  - Slam dunk football (5 to 1)
  - Punch goalpost (15 to 1)
  - Take out Sharpie and sign ball (20 to 1)
  - Group celebration (20 to 1)
  - Heisman trophy pose (25 to 1)
  - "Ickey" shuffle (100 to 1)

- Color of Gatorade/liquid dumped on the winning coach:
  (Payoff odds appear in parentheses)
  - Yellow (1 to 1)
  - Clear water (7 to 5)
  - Red (25 to 2)

Race Book Overview

Most race books in the modern casino are merely extensions of the race tracks. That is, the money wagered at the casino is combined with the money wagered at the tracks. A *pari-mutuel* system is employed in horse racing, whereby the bettors are wagering amongst themselves as opposed to against the casino or the track. For example, all bets on a horse to win a particular race are funneled into a single *pool* of money. This pool funds payouts on winning wagers and the track's *total takeout*, which covers operating expenses, *breakage*, and serves as the primary source of track profits. Breakage is nothing more than a rounding process that is applied to the computation of payouts on winning bets. Of course, this rounding process benefits the track, adding to amount of the total takeout and ultimately operating profits.

There is a separate wagering pool for every type of bet, including, but not limited to win, place, and show pools. With pari-mutuel wagering the casino's book is very unlikely to lose money on a race, as the chance of the payouts exceeding the amount of money in the pools is slim at best.[24] Therefore, the race book operators simply want to encourage wagering, because it is all profitable business for them. In a subsequent section of the chapter, all of the terms defined thus far along with the general pari-mutuel wagering process will be further explained by way of example.

Types of Race Bets

Win, Place, and Show (WPS) Bets

Collectively, these wagers are referred to as *straight* bets. A win bet is a wager on a particular horse to finish first in a specific race. A place bet is a wager on a particular horse to finish either first or second in a specific race. A show bet is a wager on a particular horse to finish either first, second, or third in a specific race. Bettors can also place what is known as an *across the board* or *combination bet* on a horse. In this case, the bettor is placing three equal win, place, and show bets on a single horse. That is, a $2 across the board bet would cost the bettor $6. The following bullet points describe the different ways to collect on this bet.

- If the selected horse finishes first, the bettor collects on all three wagers (i.e., the win, place, and show bets)
- If the selected horse finishes 2nd, the bettor collects on the place and show bets
- If the selected horse finishes 3rd, the bettor collects on the show bet only

Feature Bets

More commonly known as *QEDs*, these bets consist of the quinella (Q), exacta (E), and daily double (D). The quinella is a bet that two particular horses will finish first and second in a specific race. For the bet to win, either horse can finish first as long as the other horse finishes second. An exacta is a bet on two particular horses to finish first and second in a specific race. In this case, the bettor must specify the order of finish as well, making it more difficult to win than the quinella. The daily double is a bet that spans two different races. Here the bettor must select the winning horse in both races. The track operator will designate the two races that comprise the daily double. Of course, all daily double wagers must be placed prior to the start of the first of the two designated races.

Exotic Wagers

All bets other than straight bets (i.e., WPS bets) and QED bets are often referred to as exotic bets. Exotic wagers win less often but offer greater payouts. For example, to win a *trifecta* (a.k.a. *perfecta*), the bettor must pick the first three finishers of a race, in the precise order. That is, the bettor must specify which horse will finish first, which horse will finish second, and which horse will finish third. The *superfecta* bet is essentially the same wager as the trifecta, with the added challenge of picking the fourth place horse. As you might imagine, these are difficult bets to win.

---

[24] Most states now require a winning wager to pay a minimum of $2.10 ($2.20 in some). Therefore, it is theoretically possible for a track and, consequently, a casino's race book to lose money on a particular race. However, such a loss would be a rare event.

The *pick 3* (a.k.a. *daily triple*) is similar to a daily double, but extends the concept to three races. That is, to win this bet, the bettor must pick the winners of three designated races. All wagers must be placed prior to the beginning of the first designated race. *Pick 4* is the same bet extended to four designated races. There is also a *pick six* bet, which is more of the same applied to six designated races. The win frequency of these bets is low. In fact, at California's Hollywood Park, if no one picks all six winners, those who pick five out of six winners split 30% of the total pick six pool. The remaining 70% of the money in the pool is carried over to the next racing day. This process continues, until someone correctly picks all six winners of the designated races.

Types of Races

This section defines the following five types of races: Claiming, maiden, allowance, handicap, and stakes. A *claiming race* is comprised of horses that are for sale for a designated amount. Claiming races represent the bulk of horse races, across all U.S. tracks. Any horse in the race can be claimed (i.e., purchased) by a horseman, prior to the start of the race. Some tracks even allow spectators to purchase the horses. This keeps all horses in the race relatively equal in quality and price. That is, no one would dare enter a superior horse to pick-up an easy win, for fear that another party would claim it for a price well below the horse's true value.

A *maiden race* is comprised of horses that have never won a race. Once they win a maiden race, they are said to have *broken their maiden*. An *allowance race* is a step up from a claiming race. That is, the horses are not for sale and the purses are usually greater. The "allowance" in an allowance race is set forth in a condition book, which is issued by the track's racing secretary. The condition book specifies the eligibility criteria for the horses in the race, the maximum weight to be carried by each horse, and weight reductions for meeting specific conditions. Figure 15.3 provides an example of a condition book for a claiming race. The conditions for an allowance race would be set forth in very similar terms.

SIX FURLONGS
Claiming Race
Purse $25,300
For Fillies and Mares Three Years Old & Upward
Three-year-olds (120 lbs.); Older (124 lbs.)
Non-winners of two races in 2011: -2 lbs.
Non-winner of a race in 2011: -4 lbs.
CLAIMING PRICE: $12,500, if for $10,500, allowed -2 lbs.
(Maiden and claiming races for $10,000 or less not considered)

Figure 15.3. Example of Condition Book Content.

As you can see from Figure 15.3, the racing secretary uses weight to make the races more competitive. Along with the quality of the horse, the amount of weight it carries is a chief determinant of its speed. In fact, the total weight carried by the horse, including the jockey, gear, and any added weight is prominently displayed in the racing forms and wall charts. Both racing forms and wall charts contain information about the horses scheduled to run in upcoming races. Wall charts are defined in a subsequent section of this chapter.

In a *handicap race,* the racing secretary assigns weights based on his objective opinion of each horse's potential. In theory, these weights put all horses on an equal basis. Some of the major stakes races are run under handicap conditions. A *stakes race* offers the greatest purses, and features the highest profile and quality of horses. The Kentucky Derby, the Belmont, and the Preakness are all stakes races, in which all male horses carry 126 pounds and all female horses carry 121 pounds. Stakes races can be run as allowance or handicap races.

Convenience of Off-track Betting

In Nevada casinos and many Indian casinos, patrons are allowed to bet on horse and greyhound races conducted at tracks across the U.S. These casino books televise the races by way of live satellite feeds from the tracks. The convenience of off-track betting is considerable, as many race bettors live closer to a casino than a horse racing track.[25] Additionally, bettors are able to conveniently place wagers on races at exclusive venues such as the Kentucky Derby or the opening day at Del Mar. Many track operators object to the convenience offered by off-track betting parlors (OTBs), citing a marked decline in track revenues following the legalization of OTBs.

The OTB experience is made possible by what is known as a simulcast, which is provided by a licensed disseminator. The simulcast is nothing more than a live audio/video feed from the track. The disseminator is a licensed entity that provides the casino's race book with verified results/information used to determine winners and/or payoffs on wagers accepted at the book. The casino race book operators pay fees for access to each track's broadcast signal and the verified race results provided by the disseminator. With regard to the simulcasts, most books pay a flat signal decoder fee to each track. These fees range from $100 to $300 per month per track.

Board Track

The interior walls of the race book are covered with *wall charts*, displaying wagering information for each race scheduled for the current day. Most modern books feature electronic wall charts. Each track usually offers between nine and 12 races per day. Again, each of these races would have an associated wall chart. Figure 15.4 provides an example of a wall chart for the 5th race at a board track by the name of Del Mar.

As you may have guessed, the tracks for which racing information is displayed are referred to as *board tracks*. That is, racing information for all tracks running that day will not be displayed on wall charts. Race book operators must select and display the racing information for the tracks they believe will generate the greatest wagering interest (i.e.,

---

[25] In fact, federal law places restrictions on the operation of off-track betting parlors (OTBs) within 60 miles of existing tracks within the same state or, if none, the nearest track in a neighboring state. Subject to the previous criterion, OTBs must seek approval from the existing tracks before commencing operations (See 15 U.S.C. CHAPTER 57 § 3004, Subchapter (b), Part 1, Subparts A & B).

the board tracks). There is not enough room on the walls of the book to post all of the races, at all of the tracks.

DEL MAR
5th

Approx. Post 4:05PM
MAIDEN CLAIMING $20,000-$18,000. PURSE $24,000. FOR MAIDENS, THREE YEARS OLD AND UPWARD. Six Furlongs. (All Weather Turf)

1 Red	Laskie	124	V. Espinoza	3
2 White	Coqui	124	J. Rosario	7/2
3 Blue	Baby Girl	120	M. Pedroza	8
4 Yellow	Peaches	124	J. Talamo	8
5 Green	Newbie	120	D. Flores	12
6 Black	Speedy Gonzales	120	G. Gomez	9/2
7 Orange	Speckles	120	J. Scott	50
8 Pink	Kit Kat	120	D. Rojas	20
9 Turquoise	Lazy	120	T. Baze	5
10 Purple	Not Forgotten	122	A. Castanon	20

Pk3	This is the final race in a Pick 3.
DD	This is the second race in a Daily Double.
TRI	Trifecta bets are permitted on this race.
TQ	Quinella bets are permitted on this race.
X	Exacta bets are permitted on this race.

Figure 15.4. Example of a Wall Chart for a Race at a Board Track.

From Figure 15.4, the approximate post time is 4:05 pm. This is the time that the horse assigned to gate one is expected to enter the starting gate. It is a maiden claiming race for 3-year-olds and up. The distance is 6 furlongs and the racing surface is a synthetic turf (i.e., an all-weather turf). The distance of a horse race is described in terms of furlongs. A furlong is equal to 1/8th of a mile or 220 yards. In this race, Laskie will have a red saddle cloth sporting the number 1. She will be carrying 124 pounds and be ridden by jockey V. Espinoza. The "3" at the top of the far right column represents the morning line on Laskie, which is interpreted as 3 to 1. The morning line is the track handicapper's best guess at the odds against Laskie winning the race, at post time. Of course, the betting public will ultimately determine these odds.

Pari-mutuel Wagering

Nevada gaming regulations permit both pari-mutuel and bookmaking operations in the race book. Until the 1980s, all Nevada race books engaged in bookmaking. That is, the bettors wagered against the casino's race book. Further, these books paid track odds on all winning tickets. Although the race books were profitable, the practice of bookmaking introduced substantial earnings volatility. When bookmaking, the race book operators expose themselves to the possibility of big wins and big losses. Even in the case of a positive outcome, the volatility of this process was often at odds with the emerging corporate culture of the gaming industry.

In the 1980s, Nevada race book operators entered into agreements with various race tracks across the U.S. to allow their wagers to be included in the track pools. These agreements allowed the casinos to book as many race wagers as possible, with virtually no risk of loss. That is, bookmaking was replaced by pari-mutuel wagering.

Mechanics of Pari-mutuel Wagering

As defined, pari-mutuel wagering is a system of betting wherein the bettors wager among themselves rather than against the bookmaker. The payouts are a function of the total amount wagered (a.k.a. handle), less a fee for the track operator. Further, all payouts are expressed in terms of "for a $2 wager." This will all be demonstrated by way of example. Let's begin with the data shown in Table 15.13, which represent wagers booked on a race featuring three horses.

Table 15.13
Sample Wagering Pool Data

Horse Name	Amount Wagered
Laskie	$1,000
Speckles	800
Speedy Gonzales	200
Total Wagered	$2,000

Table 15.13 shows nothing more than the dollar-amount wagered on each horse and the totaled amount wagered in the pool (i.e., $2,000). Next, we will express the wagering activity on each horse in terms of its proportion of the pool total. As you will see from Table 15.14, this relationship can be expressed in two ways: The percentage of total wagers *against* each horse and the percentage of total wagers on (*for*) each horse.

Table 15.14
Proportion of Pool Wagered Against & For Each Horse

Horse Name	Amount Wagered	Proportion of Pool Wagered Against	Proportion of Pool Wagered For
Laskie	$1,000	1/2	1/2
Speckles	800	3/5	2/5
Speedy Gonzales	200	9/10	1/10
Total Wagered	$2,000		

Let's first examine the wagering activity on the favorite, Laskie. The bettors have wagered $1,000 on this horse. As the book has only received a total of $2,000 in wagers for this race, ½ of the money in the pool is wagered on (or for) Laskie. Therefore, ½ of the money in the pool is wagered against Laskie. Speckles is another case. The bettors have wagered $800 for Speckles and $1,200 against her (i.e., $2,000 - $800). Alternatively stated, 2/5ths ($800/$2,000) of the money in the pool is for Speckles and 3/5ths ($1,200/$2,000) is bet against her. Next, these proportions will be converted into payoff odds. However, initially, these payoff odds will include no book advantage. Table 15.15 contains the results of this exercise.

Table 15.15
Transformation of Pool Data into Odds Ratios With No Book Advantage

Horse Name	Wagered	Proportion of Pool Wagered Against	Proportion of Pool Wagered For	Pool Odds to 1 (w/ no adv.)
Laskie	$1,000	1/2	1/2	1:1
Speckles	800	3/5	2/5	1.5:1
Speedy Gonzales	200	9/10	1/10	9:1
Total Wagered	$2,000			

Looking at the far right column of Table 15.15, if the book were to pay winning wagers at these rates, all of the money wagered on the race would be refunded to the bettors, regardless of the winning horse. For example, if Laskie were to win the race, the Laskie bettors would be paid $2,000, in aggregate. That is, this group of bettors would be paid $1,000 in winnings plus a refund of their $1,000 in wagers, for a total payout of $2,000. If Speckles were to win the race, the Speckles bettors would win $1,200. Of course this group of bettors would also receive a refund of their wagers equal to a total of $800, resulting in a total book payout of $2,000 to the Speckles bettors.

At this point, no profit has been engineered into the wagers on this race. Before this is accomplished, the payoff odds will be transformed into terms of "for a $2 wager." This is the standard expression of payoff odds in the horse racing industry.[26] For example, a

---

[26] Some exacta bets are expressed in terms of "for $5." For example, 35 for 5.

payoff of 1 *to* 1 is equal to 2 *to* 2, which is equal to 4 *for* 2. Regardless of the pool odds against the horse winning, the "for $2" transformation maintains the win to wager proportion for all bets. Table 15.16 shows the "for $2" payoff transformation for a $2.00 bet on each of the horses.

Table 15.16

Expression of Payoff Odds in Terms of "For $2"

Horse Name	Wagered	Proportion of Pool Wagered Against	Proportion of Pool Wagered For	Pool Odds to 1	Pool Odds for $2
Laskie	$1,000	1/2	1/2	1:1	$4
Speckles	800	3/5	2/5	1.5:1	$5
Speedy Gonzales	200	9/10	1/10	9:1	$20
Total Wagered	$2,000				

Let's consider the case of Speedy Gonzales. His pool odds are 9 to 1, which is a ratio that is equivalent to 18 to 2, which is equivalent to 20 for 2.

Takeout

Horse racing tracks and casino race books cannot survive by refunding the entire pool to winning bettors. To realize a profit, these operators must pay something less than the total amount wagered on the race. In fact, track owners do withhold an amount from the pool to cover track expenses, taxes, and profits. This amount is known as the official takeout. While the official takeout varies by state, Table 15.17 offers an example of the items covered by the official takeout.

Table 15.17

Example of the Claims Against the Official Takeout

All Items Expressed as a Percentage of the Total Pool

5.7%	State taxes
5.1%	To cover expenses and provide a profit
4.2%	Prize money for winning horses (i.e., purses)
15.0%	Official track takeout

Keeping with the previous example, if the official takeout were 15%, then 85% would be returned to the bettors in the form of payouts on winning wagers. Using the data from the column labeled "Pool Odds for $2" in Table 15.16, the payouts on each horse would be computed, after deducting the official takeout. The results of these calculations are shown in Table 15.18.

From Table 15.18, we know that a winning $2 bet on Laskie would pay $3.40. This payoff would include a profit for the book. As you can see, the book retains $0.60 of this wager by way of the official takeout (i.e., $4.00 – $3.40 = $0.60). Of course, only part of this $0.60 would be profit, as purses, track expenses, and state taxes would claim the majority of this official takeout. This brings us to the payoff on Speckles, which introduces the final step in this process – breakage.

Table 15.18
Payoff by Horse After Deducting the Official Takeout

Horse Name	Pool Odds For $2		1 – Official Takeout		Payoff For $2 After Takeout
Laskie	$4.00	x	0.85	=	$3.40
Speckles	$5.00	x	0.85	=	$4.25
Speedy Gonzales	$20.00	x	0.85	=	$17.40

Breakage

Track operators do not refund exactly 85% of the pool as payouts on winning wagers. For example, if Speckles were to win the race, a winning wager would pay $4.20 for every $2.00 wagered, as opposed to the $4.25 shown in Table 15.18. This difference is known as *breakage*. Track operators will usually round the payoffs down to the nearest 20¢ increment. Even if a horse were scheduled to pay $5.15 after the official takeout, breakage would reduce the payoff to $5.00, for every $2.00 wagered. This form of breakage usually adds about 1% to the official takeout. For example, if the official takeout were equal to 15% and the breakage policy added another 1%, the *total takeout* would equal 16%.

Takeout Variation

As previously noted, the official takeout varies by state. It also varies by type of bet. The takeout on straight bet pools ranges from 15% to 17% and QED takeouts vary from 17% to 20%. The greatest takeout is applied to the exotic wager pools, ranging from 20% to 28%. Overall, across all types of bets, most casino race books realize a takeout near 20%. Over the years, the official takeout percentages have slowly but steadily increased. This trend is not likely to reverse itself in the near future.

Bet Mix

While most people are familiar with the simple concept of the straight bet, this type of wager only comprises about 25% of the wagering activity in a casino race book. The QEDs will account for another 25%, with the exotic bets representing about 50% of the dollar-amount wagered in casino race books. This tendency toward exotic wagering benefits the operators, as the takeout percentage on exotic wagers is the greatest.

Race Book Revenues & Track Fees

Casino race books contract with individual tracks throughout the U.S., in order to participate in track wagering pools. By way of these contracts, the bets accepted at the casino's race book are comingled with the bets made at the track. Of course, the casino's race book claims a proportional share of the profits from this cooperative pari-mutuel wagering process.

The casino books are nothing more than satellite wagering outposts, serving the same function as off-track betting parlors. We should also mention that the casino books do not keep their full share of the total track takeout. That is, the track operators contractually require the casino books to pay track fees, which are expressed as a percentage of the total amount wagered at the casino's book. Track fees for most books are usually near 4%. Off-shore books typically pay more in track fees (i.e., near 6%).

There are a couple theories as to why off-shore books pay greater track fees. First, track operators feel that off-shore outlets book wagers from bettors who would otherwise bet at the track. Second, the casino books taken together have more negotiating leverage with the race tracks. That is, casino book operators have been able to collectively bargain a better rate on track fees.

Race Results

After a race has been run, the results are posted in the race book. These results are usually displayed as follows:

Finish	Win	Place	Show
1st #2	9^{60}	6^{00}	3^{40}
2nd #4		8^{80}	4^{60}
3rd #6			2^{60}
$2 Q 38^{00}		$2 EX 70^{60}	
Off 2:03		Time 01:12.5	

Let's review these results. The horse with saddle cloth #2 won the race, horse #4 finished second, and horse #6 finished third. For every $2.00 bet on horse #2 to win, the bettor was paid $9.60. A bet on horse #2 to place paid $6.00 for every $2.00 wagered, and so forth. A $2.00 quinella (on #2 & #4) paid $38.00 and a $2.00 exacta paid $70.60 for every $2.00 wagered. The race started at 2:03 and the winning horse time was 01:12.5. That is, the winning horse ran the race in 1 minute 12½ seconds. The time that a race starts is known as the *off time* (not the post time).

Rebates

There is a multitude of online race books. To entice bettors, many of these operators offer horse bettors a partial refund of the dollar-amount wagered. These partial refunds are expressed as a percentage of the dollar-amount wagered. When race tracks first started beaming their simulcast racing signal to off-shore betting parlors and including off-shore bets in their pools, it looked like a great deal for the track operators. The tracks charged the off-shore betting parlor about 3% of the total amount wagered (in track fees), leaving the off-shore operator with about 14% to 15% of the total amount wagered.[27] That is, the track operators picked up an additional 3% of what they thought was incremental handle and the off-shore books kept the balance of the takeout. It seemed like a good deal for both sides. However, the off-shore operators were not burdened by the considerable expenses of operating a race track. Because of this cost advantage, offshore operators were able to refund a sizeable percentage of their net takeout, in the form of a gambling incentive. This incentive is known as a *rebate*. As a result of the rebate incentives,

---

[27] Track fees of 3% represented the standard at the time off-shore books became available in mass. This fee has since increased considerably for off-shore operators.

virtually all premium horse bettors patronized off-shore books. The track operators only received 3% of this action, in the form of track fees. If these same wagers were placed at the track, the operator would receive 20% of the action, via the total takeout. This is considerable difference.

Many track operators view these rebate shops as pariahs, claiming that a significant share of their track handle is being diverted to off-shore books that offer rebates.[28] As previously noted, this sentiment may be the driving force behind the increased track fees paid by off-shore books (i.e., near 6%). The rebate shops claim that the volume of wagers they are able to book would not occur without the rebates. Therefore, it is unfair for the track operators to claim that the entire amount of these wagers has been "diverted" from the track.

As of the writing of this text, one popular online book offers a 3% rebate on all straight wagers placed online and a 2% rebate on all straight bets placed over the phone. This operator also rebates 5% on all QEDs and exotic wagers placed online and a 3% rebate on the same wagers placed over the phone. A fully committed rebate shop can afford to offer rebates in the neighborhood of 10%.[29] There are some operators that exceed this mark. However, such generous offers are only extended to the bettors who wager the greatest sums of money.

Questions/Exercises:

1. What must happen for a bettor to win each of the following bets on a particular race: Win, place, and show?
2. Use the following information to compute the total payout for a winning $2.00 wager on each listed horse. Assume you are looking at win pool data from a horse racing track with a 17% takeout. Also assume all payouts are rounded down to the nearest $0.20 (after deducting the takeout).

Horse Name	Amount Wagered on Each Horse to Win
Junior El Gato	$1,000
Benji Boy	$2,000
Spirit of Hercules	$3,000

3. If you were a bookmaker, which type of $10 wager would you least prefer to book? Explain your answer.
4. Describe the outcomes required for the bettor to win each of the following wagers: Quinella, exacta, and daily double.
5. With regard to the bet mix in the race book, describe how the total dollar-amount wagered is divided among the following types of bets: Straight bets, QEDs, and exotic wagers.
6. What are the different types of races discussed in the text? See how many you can list without referencing the text.

---

[28] Finley, B. (2011). Rebate shops give back plenty to sport. Retrieved on February 28, 2011, from http://espn.go.com/horse/columns/misc/1980579.html.
[29] Ibid.

Refer to the following information when answering the next two questions.
- Line prices < 40¢ are moved in increments equal to ½ the price of the line;
- Line prices ≥ 40¢ are moved in increments equal to ¼ the price of the line;
- The sports book's loss limit on a line is equal to $5,000; and
- The line on the game is as follows:

$$\text{Mets} \quad -130$$
$$\text{Padres} \quad +110$$

7. With $39,000 wagered on the favorite and $33,000 wagered on the dog, should the bookmaker move the line? If so, what is the appropriate line after the adjustment is made?

8. With $49,500 wagered on the favorite and $33,000 wagered on the dog, should the bookmaker move the line? If so, what is the appropriate line after the adjustment is made?

9. How is the bookmaker likely to respond to betting activity that causes the book to exceed its loss limit on an over/under total?

10. To achieve ideal balance on the following line, what percentage of the dollar-amount wagered must be bet on the favorite?

$$\text{Floyd ``Money'' Mayweather, Jr.} \quad -650$$
$$\text{``Vicious'' Victor Ortiz} \quad +450$$

11. Compute the expected casino advantage for the following Super Bowl future book.

Future Book Data on Bets to Win Super Bowl		
Team	Odds Against Team Winning	"Probability" of Team Winning
Packers	5:3	3/8 0.375
Steelers	2:1	1/3 0.333
Patriots	7:2	2/9 0.222
Eagles	4:1	1/5 0.200

12. Given the following line on a college football game, compute (a) the book's total payout on a $220 wager on Harvard and (b) the book's total payout on a $110 wager on Princeton. Assume the final score of the game was Princeton 21, Harvard 20.

$$\text{Princeton} \quad -3 \quad -110$$
$$\text{Harvard} \quad \qquad -110$$

13. Per the oddsmaker, the betting public believes that FC Barcelona would win 5 of every 9 soccer matches against Real Madrid. Use this information to create a 20¢ money line for the match.

14. Is a ½-point parlay card likely to offer a greater payout than a 6-point teaser card, assuming the bettor selects four teams and places a $10 wager on both cards? Explain your answer.

15. Per the text, how do bookmakers protect themselves against exposure to excessive risk on games?

Chapter 16
Introduction to Casino Marketing

How do casino marketers pursue premium players?
Which types of activities are used to entice unassigned players?
How do casino marketers pursue slot players?
Which promotions are aimed at entry-level, mid-market, and premium segments?
How does Pareto's Rule apply to casino marketing?
What is an *a priori* discount?

Scope

This chapter provides a general survey of casino marketing activities directed at both hosted and unassigned players (i.e., players without hosts). Because hosted players generate the bulk of gaming revenues, a greater number and variety of activities target this group of players. Additionally, while certain casino marketing activities are reserved for hosted players, few if any preclude them from participation. Therefore, most of the activities described in this chapter would be available to hosted players, while only a subset would be offered to unassigned players. Some distinctions between slot and table game marketing activities are also covered.

Chapter Goals

- Provide a general survey of modern casino marketing practices
- Provide an overview of the special event process
- Describe the casino marketing activities aimed at hosted players
- Describe the casino marketing activities aimed at unassigned players
- Differentiate promotion-based activities from price-based offers

Hosted and Unassigned Players

The gaming industry is similar to many other businesses in that most of the profits are produced by a select group of customers. This general phenomenon is often referred to as the 80/20 rule or Pareto's Rule. As a result of this condition, most of the casino marketing activity is aimed at this small group of players. Casino executives generally refer to this group as premium players or high rollers. However, the definition of a premium player varies across casinos. That is, smaller properties have much less stringent requirements for the premium player distinction. Regardless of the size of the property, premium players are usually assigned to a casino host who accommodates these players during their stay, and recruits them for future visits. Players who are not hosted are referred to as unassigned players.

Special Events

Special events often target the property's best players. The format of the special event is limited only by the imagination of the casino marketers, but the ultimate goal remains constant. That is, casino marketers hope to create events that produce revenues in excess of the costs. To improve the chances of creating a profitable event, all projected revenues and expenses are estimated and listed in a pro forma analysis.

No one knows how many customers will attend the event or how much they will gamble. Given this considerable uncertainty, working through the pro forma process is a crucial step in special event planning. It is equally critical to advance a means by which the results/outcome of the event will be measured. Both successes and failures provide valuable feedback for use in planning future events. However, without a standard for measurement, it is difficult to learn anything from the results.

The following list provides examples of activities which fall under the general classification of special events: Golf tournaments, marquee title fights, New Year's Eve parties, wine tasting events, and cigar smoking events. If there is a common element among these events, it would most likely be an invited guest list produced from the casino's database. As a result, these types of special events usually target rated/known players.

The Event Planning Process

The first step taken by casino marketers is the identification of the target market(s). That is, which customers the event is intended to attract. Once the target market has been declared, casino marketers must consider the event activities and estimate the associated costs. Finally, the number of eligible customers must be estimated from a database query function. Eligible customers are those with sufficient average daily theoretical (ADT) win results or average trip theoretical (ATT) win results. The event's projected response rate and event costs determine what is sufficient, with respect to theoretical win requirements.

Both ADT and ATT are valuation measures that represent the historical rated play of individual players. In the case of special events, these measures are used to estimate future gaming activity. Repeater market operators typically employ ADT as the primary valuation measure, as the mode trip length of their players is one day. Destination market operators, such as Las Vegas Strip properties, rely on ATT, as their players may average three days of play per trip.

Once the number of eligible customers is established, the response rate must be estimated. For example, if 1,000 invitations are mailed to players, casino marketers realize that most of them will not attend the event. That is, the event may garner only a 10% response rate. Estimating the response rate improves with event planning experience. To this end, planners must consider the time of year in which the event will occur, competitor events, the length of time from the last event that targeted the current player base, and more. For most events, it is easier to estimate the cost structure than the response rate. Ideally, events with a predominantly variable cost structure offer some degree of insurance against a poor turnout. That is, the costs are function of the number of guests that attend. If the ADT is greater than the variable cost per guest, the effects of a low turnout are minimized. Unfortunately, it is not always easy to avoid fixed event costs.

For some events, such as New Year's Eve Parties, the demand exceeds the resort's available space. While this is a desirable condition in some obvious ways, it also presents some optimization challenges. That is, when space is limited, casino marketers want to accommodate the best players first. This strategy will maximize profits. However, when event invitations are sent to players from multiple tiers of the database, the lower tier players will often commit to attending the event first. It is for this reason that casino marketers should stagger the invitations. This allows the top tier players a chance to respond before inviting players from the tiers below them.

Separation of Duties

Of course management hopes the events are successful, but casino marketers are responsible for the success of the events. Because of this condition, it is recommended that a list of the invitees is provided to those responsible for analyzing the success of the events. Clearly, event analysis should not be performed by the Casino Marketing Department. Usually, someone from the Accounting Department or an operations analyst will be assigned the task of measuring event results. By providing a list of invitees to the operations analyst, she can cross-reference the members of the event group formed by the casino marketers against the pre-event list of invitees. If there are names in the event group that do not appear in the pre-event list of invitees, the play associated with those names is excluded from the event group. Pressure to perform well has led to the occasional recruitment of in-house premium players for membership in event groups, in order to make the events appear more successful. Of course, the names of these in-house players do not appear on the original list of invitees, hence the recommended separation of duties with regard to the planning and analysis of the special events.

Boosting Attendance

For increased response/attendance rates, casino marketers must insist that hosts follow-up mailed invitations with personal phone calls to the invitees. Automated phone calls and e-mail blasts are other follow-up options. Without these follow-up efforts, the events are likely to attract only those who were planning or considering a trip to the casino during or near the event period. That is, the goal of the event should be to generate incremental profits. Simply mailing invitations and waiting for responses increases the chances of buying existing revenues, by way of events costs, resulting in reduced profits.

External Venues

Special event venues can be within the resort (internal) or outside of the property (external). Some events, such as marquee title fights, might be held at a competitor casino. In this case, casino marketers face the challenge of transporting their players to another casino's event and returning them to their casino, without losing any play. Too often, players are simply told where the driver will be waiting for them after the event. This provides the players an opportunity to explore the host casino, and possibly gamble there. While casino marketers cannot prevent their players from gambling at the property hosting the event, there are some tactics that limit these opportunities. For example, station hosts to receive the players after the event. In this case, the job of the hosts is to keep the group together, take care of any pressing needs (e.g., food or drinks), and steer the players to the waiting driver. It may also be helpful to plan post-event activities, so the hosts have a compelling reason to transport the players back to the resort. That is, the host can remind the players that a post-event party or reception has been prepared for them at their hotel-casino and that a driver is waiting to transport them.

Hybrid Events

Although events such as title fights (e.g., boxing) and concerts are used to lure premium players to casinos, these events also attract other players and the general public. That is, this type of event may attract premium players but it also attracts customers who would not be invited to a special event, hence the name hybrid event. Although hybrid events are capable of generating a substantial amount of on-property excitement and often carry a public relations benefit, it is difficult to determine the indirect effect of these activities on other profit centers. For example, it is difficult to determine the effect of a title fight on gaming revenues. From a measurement perspective, it is difficult to determine the value of these events, as the costs are known but the incremental profits are not clear.[1]

Monetary Offers for Premium Players

This section provides an overview of common programs and practices aimed at premium players. When reading this section, it is important to remember that all casino marketing expenses should be thought of as a function of theoretical win (t-win). Casino marketers must be careful to not give more than they receive. That is, the sum of the player acquisition costs should certainly not exceed the t-win. In fact, t-win should exceed the sum of the acquisition costs by an amount great enough to provide an acceptable profit margin. This basic principle is often violated.

The following equation is used by casino marketers to compute a player's t-win in table games:

T-win = (Average Bet) x (Hours Played) x (Hands Per Hour) x (House Advantage)

T-win for slot players is computed by the online tracking system, according to the following formula:

T-win = (Dollar Amount Wagered) x (Game Advantage on the Wagers)

---

[1] For more on the measurement of hybrid events see Lucas, A.F. & Kilby, J. (2008). *Principles of Casino Marketing*. San Diego: Gamma Press. See also: principlesofcasinomarketing.com

If the cost of a play incentive is divided by the house advantage, the quotient (i.e., result) represents the dollar-amount of wagers needed to break-even on the cost of the play incentive. What's more, this quotient represents the pre-gaming tax wagers needed to break-even. If one considers gaming taxes, an even greater amount of wagers is required to break-even. Of course, other variable costs could be considered as well, making cost recovery even more challenging. The take-away is to carefully analyze any ongoing casino marketing offer, as the amount of play needed to ensure acceptable profit margins is usually greater than most would expect. Keep this in mind when reading the following descriptions of monetary offers aimed at premium players.

Airfare Reimbursements

This practice began as a travel subsidy for premium guests. Their play was valuable enough to warrant reimbursement of travel expenses. Typically, the magnitude of the airfare award is a function of the player's credit line. In most cases, those that qualify for an airfare award are not required to produce an airfare receipt of any kind. Competition among casinos has created increasingly liberal policies regarding airfare awards to premium players. In fact, it is not uncommon for a coveted player to receive multiple airfare awards (from competing casinos) on a single trip to Las Vegas.

Let's consider the effect of a $3,000 airfare reimbursement for a baccarat player who only bets the banker-side of the game. This wager carries a house advantage of 1.06%, assuming a 5% commission on winning banker-side wagers. Now, let's compute the amount of wagers needed to break even, assuming a gaming tax of 7.5% on gross win. Here is the equation we will use.

$$X = \$3,000 \div ((1 - 0.075)(0.0106))$$

The *(1 – 0.075)* represents the after-tax portion of the wager that is retained by the casino and *X* represents the amount of wagers needed to cover the after-tax cost of the airfare award.

In this example, X is equal to $305,966. Let's assume the player's average bet is constant, at $3,000 per hand. On average, the casino would need the player to make about 102 wagers of $3,000, before the after-tax cost of the airfare award would be covered. Assuming a baccarat game produces 70 hands per hour, just short of 90 minutes of play would be needed to offset the award.

Before moving on, let's assume the casino is operating in a jurisdiction outside of Nevada, where the gaming tax rate is equal to 30%. How would this change our calculations? All else held constant, X equals $404,313, when a 30% tax rate is plugged into the previous equation. Assuming an average bet of $3,000, this casino would need just less than two hours to recoup the after-tax cost of the same $3,000 reward.

As the number of gaming hours per trip is limited, it is important to understand how much play is absorbed by these offers. It is also important to note that players routinely receive several different forms of play incentives, each of which requires some number of hands to offset its cost. Remember, revenue is easy to buy, but it does not equal profit. Profit or loss represents the difference between revenues and expenses.

Cash Deposits

Often referred to as front money, this incentive entails a cash-award that is immediately transferable to players who deposit an eligible amount of cash, in the cage, prior to play. This award is usually equal to 2% to 3% of the amount of cash deposited. For example, if a player deposited $100,000 in the cage, he would receive a $2,000 to $3,000 cash award. Players receive the award regardless of the outcome of their wagering activity. That is, the award is theirs to keep, whether they win or lose. The basis of such an offer is the elimination of credit risk. Front money eliminates the risk of issuing an uncollectible marker. This incentive can be offered in conjunction with all other play incentives listed here, with the exception of the Quick Pay incentive.

Comps: Room, Food, & Beverage (RFB)

This is a policy-driven incentive, which is considerably influenced by competitive pressures. The RFB awards are valued at retail or near-retail prices. For example, if a player were awarded a complimentary hotel room, it would be charged against his t-win at or near a retail rate. In general, a Nevada casino will allow a player to receive complimentary RFB awards up to an amount equal to either 45% of his t-win or 15% of his actual loss.[2] These generally accepted limits are arbitrary, evolving out of competition for players, as much as anything. As a result of the market process, there is little variation in the comp policies across Las Vegas properties. Finally, RFB awards could be considered as trip facilitators, similar to airfare awards. That is, casinos will cover basic trip and travel costs, if players are willing to provide sufficient wagering activity. Player losses are not required to obtain RFB awards.

Discounting Losses

Rebating or discounting the actual losses of players has grown increasingly common since the early 1990's. There are two forms of this practice. First, *a priori* discounts are an agreement between casino marketers and the player to refund a stated percentage of the player's losses, should he lose. Second, post-play discounts are negotiated by players who incur substantial losses. Post-play discounts are negotiated after a player loss occurs, whereas *a priori* discounts are agreed upon prior to any wagering activity. Hence, the former could be considered a payment incentive, while the latter could be thought of as a play incentive. Quick-loss programs (described subsequently) are a subset of the discounting practice. All forms of discounting can be very deceiving. In effect, the practice changes the expected value formula of the games. Most discounting offers cost the casino far more than the face value of the rebate.

---

[2] While popular, basing comp awards on actual player losses is a very dangerous practice, which should be limited to special cases. Casinos should not have an established operating policy of basing comp awards on actual player losses. The default basis of player reinvestment should be t-win, with all exceptions justified.

Promotional Chips

Non-negotiable chips are given to premium table game players as a patronage incentive. These chips have no cash value and must be wagered on casino games. The player's winning wagers are paid in negotiable casino cheques (i.e., regular cheques). The betting value is equal to the face value of the chips, so they carry a considerable cost to casino. For example, on a table game with a 1% house advantage, 98 additional wagers would need to be placed, to offset the cost of only one promotional chip. This assumes the magnitude of each of these 98 wagers is equal to the face value of the promotional chip. These chips are usually offered to premium players along with other play incentives.

Dead Chip Programs

These programs also employ non-negotiable chips, hence the name dead chips. For example, table game players might receive an award equal to 1% of the dollar-amount of dead chips lost. The dead chips must be lost for the players to realize the award (a.k.a. the premium). However, all winning dead chip wagers are paid in negotiable casino cheques. Therefore, in the extended process of losing $100,000 in dead chips, it is possible for the player to win an amount such as $110,000 in negotiable cheques. Of course, this would result in a net gain of $10,000, plus the dead chip premium (e.g., 1% of $100,000, or $1,000). If the player were to stop at this point, he would be up a total of $11,000. In effect, dead chip programs work like slot clubs for table game players.

Typically, these programs also provide participants with predetermined airfare awards and RFB comp status. Program costs also include player representative fees, as the dead chip players are usually provided by external and independent agents. As a result of this arrangement, casino hosts employed by the host casino are not permitted to talk to the dead chip players supplied by the independent agents. Dead chip programs, also known as rolling programs, are very popular in Asia.

Quick Loss Benefits

Occasionally, players (usually table game players) lose a substantial portion of their credit line before satisfying the play requirements for airfare reimbursement or a desired RFB award. Quick loss policy addresses those players who generate considerable actual losses before producing sufficient t-win to qualify for comp awards under the standard policy. Quick loss offers are a subset of discounting offers and should be used with extreme caution. In fact, quick loss awards exceed t-win, by design. Because casinos do not retain the full amounts lost by losing players, casino executives cannot profitably refund actual losses or award benefits in excess of the t-win value. To do so creates two losers - the player and the casino. There are cases when casino marketers must consider an unusual loss produced by a valued customer; but, to have a predetermined refund policy in place for such matters is a mistake. These matters should be carefully considered as exceptions and dealt with on a case-by-case basis.

Quick Pay

When credit players repay markers within a specified number of days, the amount of their debt is discounted. Most properties require players to pay markers within 14 days to receive this incentive. The amount of the discount varies by property, but is usually equal to 3%. Quick-pay terms are typically standing offers. In fact, even players who negotiate discounts on losses are eligible for the quick-pay discount. That is, if the negotiated discount is equal to 15%, the player can increase that discount to 18% by paying within 14 days. The quick-pay terms are offered in conjunction with most other play incentives, with the exception of cash deposits (i.e., front money).

Walk-in Money

This incentive is typically offered to top-tier players, and consists of a cash payment for agreeing to play at the casino. Although walk-in awards are usually negotiated, there are seldom constraints related to length of play or outcome. In fact, the players receive the award prior to any play, and are not required to play for a minimum duration. Further, the walk-in money is not refunded, should the player win. This type of award is also known as show-up money.

Miscellaneous Incentives

This section describes an abridged list of some of the more common play incentives and events aimed at the premium player market. It would be very difficult, if not impossible, to produce a complete list of play incentives. For example, incentives not mentioned include the following: Private jet service, limousine service, and discounts for international players who are willing to retire their debts in U.S. dollars. Additionally, it is not unusual for players to demand suite amenity packages valued at $25,000 or more. This room set-up can include exotic chocolates, monogrammed bath robes, expensive cases of wine, and more.

Property Amenities

Although amenities do not fit the definition of a play incentive or a special event, a property will not be able to attract premium players without a competitive amenities offering. With regard to amenities, competition for premium players has increased the list of compulsory features. For example, premium players now expect the following amenities: World class retail shopping and gourmet dining, extravagant private pool and spa facilities, private gaming salons, enormous hotel suites with butler service, and more. Several Las Vegas Strip resorts cannot compete for the most valued premium players, as the rising cost of the compulsory amenities package has excluded them from this market. In fact, resort amenities often play a critical role in determining a property's target markets.

Promotional Activities Targeting Unassigned Players

For the most part, the promotional activities described in this section are designed for and aimed at unassigned players. However, premium players would certainly not be prohibited from participation in any of these activities. In fact, it is very likely that some premium players would participate in several of the promotions described in this section. While there are casino marketing activities reserved for premium players, there are few if any that exclude them.

Lottery Promotions

These promotions are designed for use in casinos that rely on a repeater clientele. Lottery or drawing-based promotions usually last for one month. Typically, the majority of the promotion is comprised of qualification days, with drawings or lotteries conducted twice weekly. That is, there are usually only 8 drawing days over the course of these promotions. During the qualification days, any slot player that wins a top-award jackpot earns tickets for drawings to be held on the designated days. Some casinos offer table game players a chance to qualify for the drawings as well, by designating certain hands as ticket eligible. For example, a blackjack hand comprised of three sevens would earn the player a certain number of tickets for the drawings.

A ticket earned on the first qualifying day of a promotion could be selected as the winning ticket on the final drawing day of the event. For this reason, the structure of the promotion favors a repeater market, as participants must usually be present to win. For example, such a promotion would not appeal to a Las Vegas Strip casino's clientele, as the typical stay spans only a few days. It is possible that no drawing would occur over the course of such a brief visit.

The more a customer plays, the more tickets/entries he wins, thus increasing his chances of winning a cash prize. Cash prizes are the most common form of award; however, new cars are also popular top-awards. It is not uncommon for a Las Vegas locals' market casino to award in excess of $250,000 in cash prizes over the course of a single promotion.

Lottery promotions are popular worldwide, as no slot system is required to facilitate this type of promotion. Players can simply notify a promotional attendant to verify the qualifying event and award the tickets. However, despite their popularity, the only published research related to lottery promotions found them to produce negative cash flows.[3] In fact, the findings suggested that the promotions failed to produce enough incremental revenue to offset the cash prizes, let alone the considerable advertising and promotional costs. Although this was only one study, the authors of this text have replicated that study using data from other casinos and produced very similar results. Casino executives must be cautious when executing lottery promotions, as rigorous measurement of the effects requires the use of advanced statistical modeling.

Merchandise Offers

These offers can take many forms, but in general, they embody the same tactical approach. Common forms of this offer include jacket give-aways for top-award jackpot

---

[3] Lucas, A.F. & Bowen, J.T. (2002). Measuring the effectiveness of casino promotions. *International Journal of Hospitality Management, 21*(2), 189-202.

winners. Typically, the jackets are of respectable quality and bear the casino's logo. T-shirts, caps, and coffee mugs are also given away along similar lines. Another popular form of the merchandise offer features a 12-pack of beer or soda for all top-award jackpot winners. The 12-packs are stacked throughout the casino to promote this event.

Players' Club Birthday Parties

This is a monthly event that celebrates the birthdays of all players' club members born in that month. This is an attempt to build a bond with the customer by acknowledging a personally significant event. The extravagance of these events varies considerably by property. Casino marketers would need to determine either their level of commitment to such an activity, or its success, before deciding on an event budget. The players' club is further defined in a subsequent section of this chapter.

Paycheck Promotions

In a paycheck promotion, the casino operator assumes the role and risks of a bank. Patrons who cash their payroll check at the casino cage are awarded one spin of the prize wheel. The top awards on the paycheck prize wheel are usually attractive cash prizes (e.g., $1,000). Awards consisting of free spins on actual slot machines are also popular prizes (i.e., free-play awards). Free-play awards will be further described in a subsequent section of this chapter.

The casino marketers are willing to endure the risks associated with cashing checks in order to put cash in the hands of their customers, while these customers are in the casino. In fact, casino marketers are willing to offer prizes to those who are willing to cash their payroll checks at the casino. Additionally, for some customers, cashing their payroll check at the casino is actually more convenient than cashing it at the bank. As you may have guessed, paycheck promotions were designed for casino operators who cater to a frequently visiting clientele. That is, Caesar's Palace in Las Vegas is not likely to run a paycheck cashing promotion.

At some properties, the prize wheel is a physical device located in front of or near the main cage. Such a wheel is similar in design to that of the Big Six wheels located on the casino floor. Customers spin the paycheck wheel, to determine their prize. In most cases, at a minimum, every customer comes away with a nominal prize. Some casino operators have replaced the physical wheel with an electronic prize wheel, which appears on a monitor much like the display screen on a video slot machine. Most electronic prize wheels also guarantee that every participant wins at least a nominal prize.

Given the popularity of these promotions, casino marketers must believe that the gains in business volume are greater than the costs of the paycheck promotion. However, as of the writing of this text, there is no published empirical research to support such a conclusion. Empirical studies of the incremental benefits of paycheck promotions are likely to suggest changes to the associated prize structures. That is, it is likely that many paycheck promotions are giving away too much or too little, in terms of prizes. This is important research, as paycheck promotions are usually long-running affairs. In fact, some run for durations that suggest they are a cost of doing business, rather than a promotion.

Vacation Events

Ocean-going cruises and vacation promotions are examples of qualification events. Invitation to these events results by qualification, according to stated promotional rules. For example, players that earn a minimum amount of club points during the qualification period become eligible for a cruise vacation. The number of customers able to qualify for the cruise can be capped or unlimited. For example, the promotional rules might state that the first 50 players to reach the point threshold will be awarded the trip. Additionally, the promotional offer might include incentives such as the top-five point earners will have their cabin upgraded to a suite. Typically, club points can be earned via table game or slot play. This type of award would also include travel costs as well, such as airfare and ground transportation. Generally, these trips are awarded to players without reducing their players' club point balance. That is, the trip costs are incremental to the casino's point liability, in spite of the fact that players must accumulate players' club points to qualify for the trip.

These events are structured with the hope that the baseline level of profit is increased during the lengthy qualification periods, by offering a desirable incentive. The qualification period of a cruise event could last six months or more. However, the measurement task of estimating the incremental play resulting from such a promotion remains a challenge and usually requires sophisticated measurement techniques.

Shopping Events

There are multiple forms of shopping events, but the customers are usually invited. The number of attendees is often capped for these events. A required minimum gaming value (ADT or ATT) is used to determine eligibility for such an event. Gift cards are awarded to the invitees based upon their historical value to the casino. The gift cards are usually redeemable in a store or stores that management believes would be desirable to the invitees. In destination markets such as Las Vegas, invitees would also be likely to receive accommodations for a three-night stay. In fact, participants are sometimes required to stay a minimum of three nights. Over the course of their stay, participants might also be given the opportunity to earn additional gift cards for play on their current trip. Gift card values do not expire once the event ends. That is, the balance is usually redeemable at any time in the future. The purpose of the event is to provide a desirable visitation incentive for valued players. The event also serves as a vehicle for reinvestment in players commensurate with their historical value.

Other forms of shopping promotions include annual events, usually on a much grander scale. For example, some casinos contract with companies that provide an assortment of merchandise. These casinos host the shopping event at the property, using convention space to house the merchandise. Invitees are permitted to buy the merchandise using their club points as currency. In some cases luxury cars have been purchased via shopping events. However, when casino marketers contract with external companies to provide the merchandise, they are often required to pay a fee related to the decrease in the market value of unsold merchandise. This is a fee that is not incurred under the gift-card format. However, the variety of goods is often greater when they are provided by an external procurement company. The purpose of these events is to reinvest in valued players, increase the baseline operating profit during the qualifying periods, and create an event that brings these valued players to the property.

Monetary Offers Targeting Unassigned Players

While the intent of this section is to describe the monetary offers used by casino marketers to reach unassigned players, several of these offers would be extended to premium players as well. Again, premium players are not likely to be excluded from any form of casino marketing activity.

Players' Club Overview

The players' club is the primary delivery mechanism for monetary offers to unassigned players. Of course, the players' club is an electronic system that tracks, records, and rewards individual players for their patronage.[4] However, to receive credit for their patronage, the players must present/use their club card when gambling. For example, slot players must insert their card in the machine for their wagering activity to be tracked and recorded. Similarly, table game players must present their club card prior to play to receive credit for their gambling activity. Figure 16.1 illustrates the front side of a players' club card. The actual size is equal to that of a credit card. Of course, an actual card would colorfully bare the logo and/or name of the casino or gaming company.

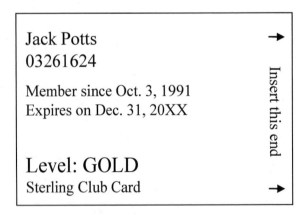

Figure 16.1. Players' Club Card.

From Figure 16.1, this card belongs to Jack Potts.[5] Mr. Potts has been assigned a club identification or customer number of 03261624. He is a gold level member, which suggests that this is a tiered players' club. Tiered clubs usually offer increased benefits

---

[4] For more on players' clubs see Lucas, A.F. & Kilby, J. (2008). *Principles of Casino Marketing*. San Diego: Gamma Press. See also: principlesofcasinomarketing.com

[5] None of the information displayed in Figure 16.1 is intended to describe any actual person. It is solely intended to illustrate the type of information/content found on the face of a players' club card.

and rewards as players ascend the levels of the club. Of course, management will only graduate a club member to a loftier tier, once her gaming value reaches a predetermined level. The name of this casino's players' club is the Sterling Club. Notice the text on the far right side of the card, instructing slot players to insert that end of the card into the card reader located on the slot machine. In most cases, the other end of the card would be inserted, to obscure the player's name from public view. This same card could also be used to identify Jack Potts on any table game.

While most players' club members do not have hosts assigned to them, management is able to meaningfully gauge their value by way of each player's recorded gaming activity. This allows casino marketers to put forth measured offers that are commensurate with each player's historical gaming value. Some marketers even attempt to structure offers based on a player's estimated future gaming value, rather than solely on past performance. Use of the players' club card allows all of this to happen.

Point Offers

Players' club members often earn points to be used toward comps or other forms of benefits. Point offers are usually specific to certain days and entail substantial bonuses for play that occurs on the designated days. Usually, the bonus is awarded by way of a multiplier. That is, if a given amount of play is worth 500 points under the normal point accumulation scheme, the player would be awarded 1,500 points on a 3X promotion day. In this example, we assumed the point multiplier was equal to three (i.e., 3X).

Figure 16.2 is an actual point multiplier offer from a Las Vegas resort. It was a shotgun offer sent to prospective slot club members, as part of a direct mail prospecting campaign. Figure 16.3 is the back side of the same coupon. Depending on the technology and the casino marketing system available to management, there are multiple ways to alert existing and prospective club members to such offers.

3X Points

Expires Dec. 14, 20XX

Present this coupon at the Awards Center and receive 3X your points for play during one 24-hour period, 12 am – 12pm.

Not valid in conjunction with any coupon or point multiplier offer. Management reserves all rights.

Figure 16.2. Front Side of a Point Multiplier coupon from a Direct Mail Piece.

3X Points

Players' Club Card # _____

For one day only, 12:01am – 11:59pm. Holidays
excluded. Valid only at Property X. Must present slot
club card with coupon. Redeem coupon at Awards
Center. One coupon per person. Not valid with any offer
or promotion. Maximum point adjustment of 70,000 in
one 24-hour period. Must 21 years of age or older.
Management reserves all rights.

Figure 16.3. Back Side of a Point Multiplier Coupon from a Direct Mail Piece.

Some properties have technology that allows players' club members to simply swipe their cards in a kiosk[6] to activate the point multiplier offer. The casino's player tracking system is set to multiply the points accumulated during the duration of the offer by the stated multiplier. Figure 16.4 illustrates the terms of such an offer. The offer shown in Figure 16.4 was adapted from an actual direct piece sent to Las Vegas residents.

Earn 10X Points on All Three Days...

10X PTS. Friday, October 3!
10X PTS. Saturday, October 4!
10X PTS. Sunday, October 5!

Just swipe your Awards Club Card at any
redemption kiosk to activate your 10X point
multiplier offer.

Figure 16.4. Kiosk-activated Point Multiplier Offer.

Cash Mail & Free-play Offers

These offers challenge the classic definition of promotion, as they are not temporary. In fact, many believe that they have become entitlements in mature markets such as Las Vegas. Although many think of Las Vegas as a destination market, it also features a robust repeater market comprised of local residents, many of whom are employees of the

---

[6] A kiosk is an unmanned device similar to an automated teller machine (ATM). Kiosks are able to handle many different types of casino transactions, one of which is activating point multiplier offers.

casinos. Both cash mail and free-play offers are direct marketing activities and represent the greatest marketing expense to most repeater-market casinos.

Cash mail offers are based on the historical t-win of tracked slot players. To be tracked, a player must insert his club card when playing slots. The dollar-value of an individual's cash mail offer is a function of his t-win. Typically, the player will receive a buy-in bonus. For example, if the player buys-in for $100, he would receive another $20 from the casino. One problem with cash mail offers is that the player is not required to place a wager on the day he redeems the offer. In fact, many players just cash-in the offer and walk out of the casino.

Free-play offers are a technological patch for the walk-out phenomenon. That is, free-play offers require the players to buy-in, and wager any buy-in bonus at least one time. For example, if a player were awarded a $20 buy-in bonus, he would need to place at least $20 in wagers before he could claim the buy-in bonus. Let's assume he made 20, one-dollar wagers on a slot machine with a 5% house advantage. He could expect to leave with $19, after satisfying the promotional requirement of the free-play offer. In effect, the play requirement decreases the cost of the incentive by an amount equal to the average house advantage of the games. That is, the house advantage would represent the minimum long-run percentage cost reduction. However, the free-play technology also forces the customer to play a slot machine to redeem the award. Casino executives are hoping to further reduce free-play offer costs by enticing players to place wagers beyond the minimum requirement. The first step in this process is requiring those who redeem the offer to play a slot machine.

Match-play Offers

These are table game offers that assume one of two forms. The most popular form is the single-decision offer, whereby the match-play coupon is valid for one decision only (i.e., win or lose). That is, if the player wins or loses the hand, the coupon is retired. In blackjack, only a push (i.e., tie) would allow a single-decision offer to be in play for an additional hand. The second form is the multiple-decision offer, which is valid until the player loses a hand. The multiple-decision offer could stay in play for multiple hands, should the player continue to win. As a result, the multiple-decision offer is the more costly of the two forms. Typically, match-play coupons are offered in the following denominations: $5, $10, and $25.

The rationale behind the offers is that they serve as game starters. That is, the financial incentive offered to prospective players is intended to stimulate table game trial. However, the only published research addressing the plausibility of the game starter theory found no evidence of increased play associated with a single-decision offer.[7] Figures 16.5 and 16.6 illustrate an actual match-play offer taken from a direct mail piece sent to residents living near a hotel-casino located in suburban Las Vegas.

---

[7] Lucas, A.F. (2004). Estimating the impact of match-play promotional offers on the blackjack business volume of a Las Vegas hotel casino. *Journal of Travel & Tourism Marketing, 17*(4), 23-33.

> # $5 Match Play
>
> Expires Dec. 14, 20XX
>
> Present this coupon at any table game and we'll match your $5 bet for 1 hand, win or lose.
>
> Even-money bets only. Management reserves all rights.

Figure 16.5. Front Side of a Match-play Coupon from a Direct Mail Piece.

> # $5 Match Play
>
> Players' Club Card # _____
>
> Good for one bet up to $5, win or lose. Valid only at Property X. Must present players' club card with coupon. Present this coupon to the dealer before play. One coupon per person. Not valid with any offer. Coupon has no cash value. Must 21 years of age or older. Management reserves all rights.

Figure 16.6. Back Side of a Match-play Coupon from a Direct Mail Piece.

First Card Ace Coupons

In blackjack, each player is dealt two cards to begin the hand. Casino marketers offer a coupon that is used in place of the first card dealt to the player. Specifically, this coupon represents an ace (a.k.a. a free ace coupon). A player redeeming this coupon would be dealt only one additional card, as the coupon itself would represent the other card in the player's original two-card hand. Players are permitted to request additional cards when redeeming the free ace coupon. For example, if a player were dealt a 2 to accompany her free ace coupon, she would be permitted to draw additional cards in an attempt to improve her hand total.

When the player's first card is an ace, the probability of the casino winning the hand plummets. Depending on the rules of the game, the player can usually expect to win an amount just over 50% of his wager. For example, let's assume the player has a 51% advantage with a free ace coupon. If he were to wager $100, he would expect to win $51, on average. Because of the considerable advantage afforded the player, free ace coupons often limit the maximum bet. For example, a player who wishes to redeem such a coupon may be limited to a maximum wager of $25.

These coupons are often mailed to customers as part of a multiple coupon offer. They also frequently appear in coupon booklets, which contain additional play incentives such as match-play and free-play offers, as well as dining coupons. These booklets are most often offered to players who are provided by domestic wholesalers. These wholesale travel and tour companies often negotiate with casinos regarding the value of the offers contained in the coupon booklets. Coupon booklets containing free ace coupons are also mailed to all households within targeted local zip codes, in an attempt to stimulate business and/or gain new customers.

Hotel Room Discounting

Many casino marketers discount hotel rooms as part of their direct marketing campaign. For example, a free-play offer will be accompanied by a discounted room rate. Additionally, discounted room rates are often bundled with other gaming offers to form an incentive package aimed at wholesalers. The other gaming offers might include match-play coupons, a free ace, or buy-in premiums for slot players. The wholesalers are often relied upon to fill the rooms of Las Vegas resorts during low occupancy periods, such as midweek days. Wholesalers are discount travel companies that specialize in affordable group packages to destinations such as Las Vegas.

Game Rules & Betting Limits

Modification of game rules or house advantage is employed as a marketing tactic in all target markets. For example, most players believe that single-deck blackjack games carry a lower house advantage. As a result, casino executives may choose to offer and promote the availability of these single-deck games. All else constant, single-deck blackjack games do have less of a house advantage than multiple-deck games. However, what if management were to offer a single-deck game that paid blackjacks at a rate of six to five, instead of three to two? Such a revision would substantially increase the casino's advantage. In this case, management would be hoping to benefit from the general perception of single-deck value, while considerably reducing this value by way of rule modification.

There is a long list of possible blackjack rule modifications such as surrender options, doubling options, and the dealer hits soft 17. Regardless of the game, rule modifications are nothing more than price promotion, where the house advantage represents the price of the casino's product. That is why it is important to remember that a 50%-decrease in price requires a 100%-increase in the amount wagered, just to maintain the original amount of win. Casino marketers should ask themselves if they truly believe that reducing the house advantage will be an effective tactic. At a minimum, will the price reduction produce the required increase in wagering volume needed to maintain the pre-existing win level?

The rules of slot machines are not so easily changed, as they are coded into the game chips. However, casino marketers often attempt to offer promotions whereby a certain four-of-a-kind pays something greater than that offered in the pay table. For example, let's assume a video poker game pays 250 coins for a four-of-a-kind, per the original pay table. Casino marketers might decide to offer a 400-coin payoff for a four-of-a-kind, in four's, over the July 4th holiday. By increasing this payout from 250 to 400 coins, the price or house advantage would be reduced. This reduction in the house edge would require an increase in wagering volume to maintain the preexisting win level. Casino marketers would need to know exactly how much additional wagering volume would be required to cover the reduction in the house advantage. Without this information, management would not be able to determine whether the promotion was effective.

With regard to betting limits in table games, lower minimum bets are attractive to a broader group of gamblers, as less bankroll is necessary to stay on the game. Management will increase the minimum bet to push the average bet upward, when sufficient demand is present (e.g., on a Saturday night). The maximum betting limits are an accommodation for premium players who wish to increase their wagers. However, not every casino will or should accept unusually great wagers from one or two players, as inventories of players with similar average bets are needed to manage earnings volatility. Allowing greater wagering limits is an attempt to pull the average bet upward by facilitating an atmosphere of hopefully contagious excitement. In review, management uses the minimum bet requirement to *push* the average bet upward and the maximum betting limit to *pull* the average bet upward.

Slot machines address betting limits differently. The minimum wagering unit on a slot floor could range from a half-penny to $1,000. The availability of lower denomination games appeals to a certain clientele, just as the availability of $100 games appeals to another clientele. While the availability of greater denomination games allows for greater wagers to be placed, the penny games are always there as well. In other words, the minimum and maximum betting limits of slot machines are not nearly as flexible and cannot be managed according to daily demand.[8]

Casino Marketing Activity by Target Market

Table 16.1 classifies the marketing activities covered in this chapter with regard to target market applications. That is, an X is placed in each of the target market columns in which the listed activity is likely to be employed. For example, discounts on loss might occasionally be offered by casino marketers catering to a low-end or mid-market clientele, but this activity is common in casinos targeting the premium player market. Therefore, regarding the practice of discounting, an X would be placed in the premium column, but not in the low-end or mid-market columns.

From Table 16.1, although no X appears in the corresponding cells, there are casino marketers who send premium players slot club point offers and match-play coupons. That is, Table 16.1 attempts to summarize the activities that are common and critical to the pursuit of each market segment. As with any attempt to generalize to this extent, there will surely be exceptions.

---

[8] This assumes that technology such as server-based gaming is not in place.

Table 16.1
Casino Marketing Activities by Target Market

Activity	Target Market		
	Premium	Mid-market	Low-end
Special Events:[9]			
Golf Tournaments	X	X	
Blackjack Tournaments		X	X
Slot Tournaments		X	X
Title Fight Events	X		
New Year's Eve Event	X		
Concerts	X	X	
Airfare Awards	X		
Cash Deposit Awards	X		
Room, Food & Beverage Comps	X	X	X
Discounting Gaming Losses	X		
Promotional Chips	X		
Dead Chip Programs	X		
Quick Loss Offers	X		
Quick Pay Discounts	X		
Walk-in Money	X		
Lottery Promotions		X	X
Merchandise Offers		X	X
Monthly Birthday Events		X	X
Paycheck Promotions		X	X
Shopping Events	X	X	
Vacation Events	X	X	
Slot Club Point Offers		X	X
Cash Mail/Free-play	X	X	X
Match-play Offers		X	X
First Card Ace Coupons		X	X
Restaurant Discount Coupons		X	X
Game Rule Changes	X	X	X
Betting Limits	X	X	X
Amenities:			
Restaurants	X	X	X
Entertainment:			
Lounge Acts			X
Cabarets		X	X
Showrooms	X	X	
Pool & Spa	X	X	
Hotel Suites	X		
Night Clubs	X	X	

---

[9] Most blackjack and slot tournaments are invitational, aimed at customers who have established themselves in the casino database. The events feature a gambling competition that is tracked by casino personnel such that a winner can be determined. Those who finish in the top spots receive cash prizes.

When to Promote

Thus far, this chapter has described many different forms of casino marketing activities, but the issue of activity timing has not been addressed. That is, should casino marketers promote during slow periods or during peak periods? The answer may appear obvious to the reader, but there are two competing theories regarding this issue. First, there are those who believe promotions should drive business in slow periods, as promoting during peak periods would be a waste of marketing dollars. Second, there are those who believe casino marketers should promote during peak-demand periods. This school of thought holds that the consumption of leisure services such as gaming is directly related to the availability of leisure time. It is for this reason that weekend days consistently produce greater gaming volumes than midweek days, in U.S. casinos. That is, most people don't work on weekends and holidays. As a result, these are the periods in which casino marketers should offer promotions and events. This theory contends that most customers are making casino patronage decisions on weekends and holidays, so this is when promotions can sway players toward a particular property. The goal of peak-demand promotion is to make the periods of the greatest gaming volume even greater, by offering promotional incentives during these high-demand periods.

While the advantages and disadvantages of both theories can be argued indefinitely, the verdict lies in the ability of casino executives to measure the effects of their promotional activities. Unfortunately, this is often difficult to accomplish due to the complex marketing and operational environments of many hotel-casino resorts. It is possible that both theories are valid, given specific circumstances. Once again, the ability to measure the effectiveness of promotions seems to be the key to advances in casino marketing theory.

Questions/Exercises:

1. Assume the following: A player has received an airfare award of $2,500. That same player wagers only on the player-side of a baccarat game. The player wagers $2,000 on each hand. The house advantage on the banker-side wager is equal to 1.06%, while the house advantage on the player-side wager is equal to 1.24%. On average, the baccarat game produces 67 hands per hour. The gaming tax rate is equal to 25% of gross gaming win.

   Estimate the amount of gaming time (in hours) that will be required to cover the after-tax cost of the airfare award. Round your answer to the nearest tenth of an hour.

2. Notwithstanding the lack of play constraints and detailed information, what is wrong with the following deal?

   Player X will receive a 10% discount on loss, a 3% discount for playing against $150,000 of front money, an airfare award, RFB comps (per the casino policy), and a quick-pay discount of 2%.

3. Is the match-play coupon shown in Figures 16.5 and 16.6 a single-decision or multiple-decision offer? How do you know?

4. While some of the following casino marketing activities could certainly be offered across multiple market segments, name the primary target market for the following casino marketing activities:
    a. Special events such as golf tournaments, title fights, and New Year's Eve parties;
    b. Discounting player losses resulting from gambling activity;
    c. Lottery promotions;
    d. Paycheck promotions;
    e. Quick loss incentives;
    f. Match-play offers; and
    g. Point multiplier offers.
5. What is the central issue regarding the separation of duties between those who propose and plan the special events and those who analyze the results of the events?
6. How is manipulation of game rules similar to price promotion?
7. What is meant by push and pull, with respect to betting limits?
8. Describe the differences between the competing theories related to the timing of promotional activities.
9. How do a property's non-gaming amenities affect the ability of its casino marketers to pursue particular market segments?
10. In comparison to table games, what is one disadvantage related to slot machines with regard to betting limits?
11. What is the primary concern of casino marketers when their players attend an event at another property? How can this concern be addressed?
12. Once the invitations are mailed, how can casino marketers improve event attendance and improve their chances of creating an incremental visit?

Index

C

D

E

F

G

T

U

V

W